JEWISH AMERICANS

ETHNIC GROUPS IN AMERICAN LIFE SERIES

Milton M. Gordon, *editor*

JEWISH

SIDNEY GOLDSTEIN
Brown University

CALVIN GOLDSCHEIDER
University of California, Berkeley

AMERICANS

Three Generations in a Jewish Community

PRENTICE-HALL, INC., ENGLEWOOD CLIFFS, NEW JERSEY

JEWISH AMERICANS

Three Generations in a Jewish Community

GOLDSTEIN/GOLDSCHEIDER

Library of Congress Catalog Card No.: 68-24185

Current printing (last digit):

10 9 8 7 6 5 4 3 2 1

Printed in the United States of America

PRENTICE-HALL INTERNATIONAL, INC., *London*
PRENTICE-HALL OF AUSTRALIA, PTY. LTD., *Sydney*
PRENTICE-HALL OF CANADA, LTD., *Toronto*
PRENTICE-HALL OF INDIA PRIVATE LTD., *New Delhi*
PRENTICE-HALL OF JAPAN, INC., *Tokyo*

*To Beth, David,
and Brenda
and to Judah
and Avigaiyil*

Foreword

The problem of how people of diverse racial, religious, and nationality backgrounds can live together peaceably and creatively within the same national society is one of the most crucial issues facing mankind, second in importance only to the overriding problem of international war itself. Indeed, these two problem areas, while not identical, are, from the viewpoint of recurring social processes of group interaction, interrelated at many points. The United States of America, as the classic example of a highly industrialized nation made up of people of diverse ethnic origins, constitutes, both in its history and its current situation, a huge living laboratory for the serious study of various underlying patterns of ethnic interaction—patterns which produced in this country both corroding failure (particularly with respect to the treatment of racial minorities), and certain modified successes which, however, have by no means been free of a residue of unfulfilled personal hopes, psychological scars, and unjustified hardships for those who were not born with the majority sociological characteristics of being white, Protestant, and of Anglo-Saxon cultural origins.

The explosion in the 1960's of the Negro's or black American's anger and growing revolt against centuries of white prejudice and discrimination has shocked the nation out of an attitude of mass complacency with regard to ethnic group relations. Now, not only social scientists, academic liberals, and well-meaning humanitarians, many of whom had waged valiant battles against racism before, but at last millions of other Americans in all walks of life are becoming aware that to devalue another human being simply on the grounds of his race, religion, or national origins, and to act accordingly, is to strike at the very core of his personality and to create a living legacy of personal hatred and social disorganization. All the great religious and ethical traditions had spoken out prophetically against ethnic prejudice (however weak their followers have been in implementation). Now it has become increasingly clear that sheer self-interest and the desire to preserve a viable nation sternly countenance the conclusion that prejudice and discrimination are dubious luxuries which Americans can no longer afford.

We have spoken of the social scientific knowledge to be derived (and, hopefully, to be creatively used) from intensive study of American ethnic groups. There is another reason to commend such focused scientific attention. The history and the decisive contributions of the various racial, religious, and national origins groups to the warp and woof of American life is not a story that, to say the least, has been overly told in American publication or pedagogy. The important pioneer studies on the Negro of E. Franklin Frazier, John Hope Franklin, and Gunnar Myrdal, and on the white immigrant of Marcus Hansen, Oscar Handlin, and John Higham, all stem from either the present generation or the one immediately preceding it. In the main, American minority ethnic groups have been, by patronizing omission, long deprived of their past in America and of a rightful pride in the nature of their role in the making and shaping of the American nation. It is time for a systematic overview, group by group, of this long neglected portion of the American experience, one that on the one hand avoids filio-pietistic banalities, and on the other, does justice to the real and complex nature of the American multi-ethnic experience.

A final and equally compelling reason for instituting a series of studies of America's ethnic groups at this time is that more adequate theoretical tools for carrying out the respective analyses are currently at hand. In my book, *Assimilation in American Life,* published in 1964, I presented a multidimensional approach to the conceptualization of that omnibus term "assimilation" and endeavored to factor it into its various component processes, at the same time offering certain hypotheses concerning the ways in which these processes were related to each other. Such an approach appears to facilitate dealing with the considerable complexity inherent in the functioning of a pluralistic society. Furthermore, studies of social stratification or social class which have burgeoned to become such an important part of American sociology in the past few decades have made it abundantly clear that the dynamics of ethnic group life, both internally and externally, constantly involve the interplay of class and ethnic considerations. And, lastly, the passage of time, producing a third generation of native-born children of native-born parents even among those ethnic groups who appeared in large numbers in the last great peak of emigration to America in the early part of the twentieth century, has emphasized the need for considering generational change and the sociological and social psychological processes peculiar to each successive generation of ethnic Americans.

For all these reasons, I am proud to function in the capacity of General Editor of a series of books which will attempt to provide the American public with a descriptive and analytic overview of its ethnic heritage in the third quarter of the twentieth century from the viewpoint of relevant social science. Each book on a particular ethnic group (and we include the white Protestants as such a sociologically definable entity) is written by an expert in the field of intergroup relations and the social life of the group about which he writes, and in many cases the author derives ethnically himself from that group. It is my hope that the publication of this series will aid substantially in the process of enabling Americans to understand more fully what it means to live in a multi-ethnic society, and concomitantly, what we must do in the future to eliminate the corrosive and devastating phenomena of prejudice and discrimination, and to ensure that a pluralistic society can at the same time fulfill its promised destiny of being truly "one nation indivisible."

MILTON M. GORDON

Preface

Rather than being a general review of what has been discovered or said about the Jews in America, this volume in the Prentice-Hall series on ethnic groups is largely, and by intent, a report on the findings of a specific community study. A considerable literature has been developed about the Jews, but many of the conclusions are based on speculation, on personal experiences and observations, or on research of uneven quality. Another such essay could do little more than either repeat what other studies have already reported or speculate on the basis of equally fragmentary evidence. The opportunity to draw upon a comprehensive body of research data therefore provided a welcome alternative. Although the conclusions may be limited in character because of their origin in a single community study, the fact that they are based on a representative sample of almost 1,500 Jewish families argues strongly in their favor. The findings, it is hoped, may provide a new benchmark in the development of a more objective approach to the evaluation of generation changes in the Jewish population of the United States.

This study of generation change in a Jewish community is very largely a report on the Jewish population of the metropolitan area of Providence, Rhode Island. During the winter of 1962 the leaders of the Jewish community of Greater Providence recognized the need for a census of the Jewish population of the area as the basis for solid planning for the future. In Providence, as elsewhere in the United States, such locally sponsored surveys were necessary in the absence of any official information on religion. Beyond the purely local value of such a census for planning purposes, we regarded the collection of these data as a unique opportunity to gain important insights into the social and demographic structure of an American Jewish community; as sociologists and demographers, we were particularly aware that the absence of a question on religion in the United States decennial census greatly inhibited evaluation of the role of religious identification in affecting both the social structure and the vital processes of the American population. More seriously, less was known about the demography of the American Jewish community than about other religious groups, since even those surveys that incorporated a religious dimension failed generally to obtain sufficient numbers of Jews in their sample because of the small proportion of Jews in the total population. Intensive analysis of the demographic structure and the behavior of the Jewish segment of the population was thereby precluded. Thus, both as members of the Jewish community of Greater Providence and in our professional roles as sociologists and demographers, we welcomed the opportunity to participate in the census. Sidney Goldstein, as research director of the study, authored the summary volume, *The Greater Providence Jewish Community, A Population Survey.* Calvin Goldscheider served as research associate with particular responsibility for preparing the report on fertility, "Trends and Differentials in Jewish Fertility; A Study of the Providence Metropolitan Area." The investigation of generation change in the Jewish community, and the writing of this volume, is a joint undertaking for which each of us shares equal responsibility.

Since the census was sponsored primarily for local fact gathering, the number of additional questions we could incorporate in the questionnaire was restricted. At a minimum, we tried to insure sufficient coverage of the basic social and demographic characteristics to permit comparisons with the general population, and of those specifically Jewish items which would serve as indicators of the extent and character of Jewish identification. The coverage can, however, by no criteria be regarded as comprehensive. Nor can Providence be regarded as a typical American Jewish community. Yet, as the data were collected and initially analyzed for the report to the community, we were impressed by the wealth of information that had become available and by the opportunities afforded for further use of the materials to evaluate patterns of generation change. Moreover, careful evaluation of existing literature indicated a virtual vacuum with respect to research findings on such patterns of change.

It was particularly gratifying, therefore, that both the National Foundation for Jewish Culture and Hadassah (the Women's Zionist Organization of America) agreed to the desirability of exploiting the Providence data fully for studying generation change. The support given for such purposes in the form of the first Alexander Dushkin Fellowship, awarded by Hadassah to the senior author, is gratefully acknowledged, as is the personal interest and cooperation of Mrs. Frieda Lewis, Educational Director of Hadassah, and Dr. Judah Shapiro and Mr. Harry Baron, successive Executive Directors of the National Foundation for Jewish Culture.

Of course, primary gratitude is due to the officers and staff of the General Jewish Committee of Greater Providence. Their foresight led to initiation of the study; their leadership insured its success; and their full support encouraged us in the field work, in the preparation of the initial report, and in the decision to go back to the data for purposes of this special investigation. Special appreciation is due to Joseph W. Ress and Merrill L. Hassenfeld, Presidents of the General Jewish Committee, to Joseph Galkin, Executive Director, to Arthur J. Levy, Chairman of the Community Planning Committee, and to Judge Frank Licht, Chairman of the Population Study Committee. Leadership requires followers; the small army of voluntary field workers who solicited the responses from the sample households, headed by Mrs. Joseph Adelson, as well as the respondents themselves deserve our particular recognition.

We also wish to extend our appreciation to Leon Bouvier, William Feinberg, Edward T. Pryor, Jr., Andrew Twaddle, Owen Thornberry, Martin Broomfield, and Diana Schaffer, all students at Brown University during some period of the study, for their assistance in coding and statistical processing of the survey materials.

To Dr. Milton M. Gordon, editor of this series, we are most indebted for the care with which he read the manuscript and for the valuable criticisms. We, of course, accept full responsibility for any factual or interpretive errors.

Finally, these acknowledgments would not be complete without particular expression of thanks to our wives, Alice and Barbara, for the many hours they have devoted to preparation of statistical tables and charts and to editing and criticism of the manuscript drafts. But above all, their encouragement, interest, and understanding have been mainstays in the early and successful completion of this study.

During the very period in which we were engaged in this study, both our fathers passed away. Their lives and their commitments to Judaism are reflected in this work. In dedicating this book to our children, we have every confidence that the memory of our fathers will serve as inspiration to our children of the newer generation.

SIDNEY GOLDSTEIN
CALVIN GOLDSCHEIDER

Acknowledgments

Portions of this book have previously been published elsewhere. The authors wish to thank the publishers for permission to use this material:

The Greater Providence Jewish Community: A Population Survey. Providence, R.I.: The General Jewish Committee of Providence, 1964.

"Ideological Factors in Jewish Fertility Differentials," *The Jewish Journal of Sociology,* VII, No. 1 (1965), 92-109.

"Socio-Economic Status and Jewish Fertility," *The Jewish Journal of Sociology,* VII, No. 2 (1965), 221-37.

"Trends in Jewish Fertility," *Sociology and Social Research,* L, No. 2 (1966), 173-86.

"Jewish Mortality and Survival Patterns: Providence, Rhode Island, 1962-1964," *Eugenics Quarterly,* XIII, No. 1 (1966), 48-61.

"The Providence Jewish Community After 125 Years of Development," *Rhode Island History,* XXV, No. 2 (1966), 51-58.

"Social and Demographic Aspects of Jewish Intermarriages," *Social Problems,* XIII, No. 4 (1966), 386-99.

"The Changing Socio-Demographic Structure of an American Jewish Community," *The Jewish Journal of Sociology,* VIII, No. 1 (1966), 11-30; also in *Papers Read at the Fourth World Congress of Jewish Studies, Jerusalem, 1965; Papers in Jewish Demography,* Part III. Jerusalem: The Hebrew University, 1967, 11-30.

"Fertility of the Jews," *Demography,* IV, No. 1 (1967), 196-209.

"Generational Changes in Jewish Family Structure," *Journal of Marriage and the Family,* XXIX, No. 2 (1967), 267-76.

Contents

CHAPTER ONE
Separation or Integration 1

Dimensions of Assimilation, 3
Overview of the Three Generations, 6
Maintenance of Jewish Identification, 9
The Research Gap, 14

CHAPTER TWO
"Take Ye the Sum . . ." 18

The Survey Community, 21
The Jewish Community, 24
The Nature of the Survey, 28

CHAPTER THREE
The Changing Demographic Profile 36

Emergence of the Third Generation, 38
Age and Sex Composition, 41
Residential Clustering and Dispersal, 46
Leaving the Old Ghetto, 49
Stability and Mobility, 52

CHAPTER FOUR
The Changing Social-Class Profile 62

Veneration for Learning, 64
The Division of Labor, 71
Occupational Patterns, 77
Owning a Home, 91
Status Consistency, 95

CHAPTER FIVE
Marriage and the Family 101
Are Jewish Families Different?, 102
The Family in Transition, 106
Social Differentials, 111
Stability Despite Change, 113

CHAPTER SIX
"Be Fruitful and Multiply" 115
Religion and Fertility, 116
Fertility Trends, 121
Social and Ideological Differentials, 125
Jewish Fertility Reexamined, 133

CHAPTER SEVEN
Mortality and Life Expectancy 137
The Search for Evidence, 138
Mortality Patterns, 142
Length of Life, 144
Cause of Death, 148
Religion and Mortality, 150

CHAPTER EIGHT
Intermarriage and Conversion 152
Conflicting Evidence, 152
Losses and Gains, 155
Residential and Social Factors, 161
Fertility of the Intermarried, 166
Implications, 169

CHAPTER NINE
Religiosity: Ideological and Ritualistic Dimensions 171
Facets of Religiosity, 171
The Ideological Dimension, 175
Variations in Identification and Membership, 181
Attendance at Religious Services, 186
Observances in the Home, 195

CHAPTER TEN

Religiosity: Organizational and Cultural Dimensions 206

Structural Assimilation, 206
Transmitting the Heritage, 211
Scope of Religious Education, 215
Yiddish, A Disappearing Language, 225
Religion and the Three-Generation Hypothesis, 228

CHAPTER ELEVEN

Being Jewish and Being American 232

Generation Changes, 234
Jewish Exceptionalism, 239
Jewish Heterogeneity, 240

APPENDIX A

Number of Sample Cases 244

APPENDIX B

Sampling Error 251

APPENDIX C

Interview Schedule 257

Selected Bibliography 263

Author Index 265

Subject Index 267

CHAPTER ONE

Separation or Integration

Social and cultural change constitute the outstanding features of modern societies. The degree of change varies among societies, fluctuates in time, and differentially affects social structures, social institutions, and social groupings within societies. When distinct groups come into contact, interact, and exchange ideas, values, and life styles, social and cultural changes accelerate. Although these contacts may affect each group, a minority population experiences more rapid and visible changes, particularly when integration into the majority is valued: American Jews in some ways exemplify this process. The transition from immigrant status to "being American" reshaped the nature and character of the American Jewish community. The confrontation of Jewish and American society and culture was circumscribed by internal and external pressures which at times encouraged greater Jewish identification and at times greater assimilation.

In order to understand the dynamics of change characterizing Jews in the United States, a brief sketch of the demographic and socio-historical setting is essential. Two interrelated factors set into motion social forces which determined the pattern of Jewish life in the United States. First, from the end of the nineteenth century to the mid-1960's, the size of the Jewish population increased rapidly. In 1880 American Jews numbered less than a quarter of a million and represented less than one-half of one per cent of the total population; in 1965 the Jewish population in the United States was estimated at about six million, or 3 per cent of the total.[1] The American Jewish population therefore experienced a twenty-five fold increase in 85 years, compared to less than a four-fold increase for the total United States population during the same period. This population increase converted the Jewish community in America from an insignificant minority, too small to establish anything more complex than localized Jewish communal life, to a substantial and vibrant national American subsociety. The United

[1] Population estimates for the early period of American Jewish history are contained in Cyrus Adler, ed., *American Jewish Yearbook* (Philadelphia: Jewish Publication Society of America, 1901), II, 157; see also *The Jewish Encyclopedia* (New York: Funk and Wagnalls Company, 1905, 1909), XII, 370-71; Nathan Goldberg, "The Jewish Population of the United States," in *The Jewish People, Past and Present* (New York: Central Yiddish Culture Organization, 1948), II, 25-34. Recent population estimates were taken from *American Jewish Yearbook* (1966), LXVII, 81-91.

States in the 1960's has the largest concentration of Jews in the world, more than two and a half times the size of the Jewish State of Israel, and accounts for nearly half of world Jewry.[2]

The second factor transforming the American Jewish community lies in the source of this population growth. The tremendous increase in the number of Jews living in the United States was not the result of natural growth—the excess of births over deaths—nor were population increases evenly spread over the time period. Rather, the increase was primarily the consequence of the immigration of a large number of Eastern European Jews between 1870 and 1924. During this period, approximately two and a half million Jews arrived, along with other ethnic populations, to share in American society and, eventually, to recast and reshape its character.[3] Before the 1870's the majority of Jews in the United States were first- and second-generation German Jews who immigrated between 1820 and 1870; some American Jews were of Sephardic origin, descendants of the original Spanish-Portuguese settlers of the Colonial period, and others were from Central Europe, descendants of a pre-nineteenth-century migration.

For a short period, only until the second decade of the twentieth century, the German and East European Jews maintained two distinct communities. But by the 1920's the German and Sephardic Jews no longer constituted the dominant Jewish subcommunity in America. By that time, some had assimilated and lost their Jewish identity and the rest were intermingled with the overwhelming numbers of East European immigrants. Until the 1940's, however, German Jews continued to dominate the organizational structure, reflecting social-class factors associated with community leadership.[4] The immigration quota laws of the 1920's ended the mass movement of Jews from Eastern Europe to the United States, and the growth of the American Jewish population has since been remarkably slow. Consequently, the conditions that define the character of the American Jewish community in the 1960's evolved out of the Jewish immigration at the turn of the century.

The immigration, which led to rapid Jewish population growth and the shift from a predominantly German and Sephardic to an East European heritage, set the stage for significant social and cultural changes within the Jewish population. The transition from a foreign-born, ethnic-immigrant subsociety to an Americanized second- and third-generation

[2] See statistics presented in *American Jewish Yearbook* (1966), LXVII, 471-77.

[3] Will Herberg, *Protestant-Catholic-Jew* (Garden City, N.Y.: Doubleday & Company, Inc., Anchor Books, 1955, 1960), p. 178.

[4] *Ibid.*, pp. 179 ff.; also, E. Digby Baltzell, *Philadelphia Gentlemen* (Glencoe, Ill.: The Free Press, 1958), pp. 276-91; and Baltzell, *The Protestant Establishment* (New York: Vintage Books, 1966), pp. 59-62.

community has had major consequences for the structure of the Jewish community and for the lives of American Jews. Thus, the focus on the immigrants and their descendants provides the vehicle by which the socio-demographic structure of the American Jewish community may be studied. The assimilation-integration process characterizing American Jews illustrates the more general pattern of Americanization of immigrant groups. According to Will Herberg,

> . . . in its own history [Jews in the United States have] exemplified with exceptional clarity the fundamental restructuring of American society which transformed the "land of immigrants" into the "triple melting pot." Nothing is more characteristically American than the historical evolution of American Jewry, revealing, as it does, the inner patterns of American social development.[5]

The accelerated pace of social and cultural changes which typifies Jews in the United States may foreshadow future trends among other minority populations.

DIMENSIONS OF ASSIMILATION

American Jews express and reflect two social realities, which at first glance appear contradictory. On the one hand, Jews have become a thoroughly Americanized group, acculturated to the American middle-class way of life, and they are viewed by others as participants in the mainstream of American society. Yet, at the same time, there appears to be an increasing emphasis among Jews on "being Jewish," including association with Jewish culture, religion, and organizational life. American Jews, while being American, are most conscious of their identity as Jews, and this feeling is encouraged, reinforced, and legitimated by American society. The dual nature of the social identity of Jews has been posed by a number of observers of American and Jewish society; most prominent among these is Will Herberg. His analysis and interpretation focus on the religious system, which reflects religious revival and religiosity co-existing with pervasive secularism and secularization.[6] However, the sociological analysis of religion cannot be understood in isolation from the rest of society. Religion is part of the larger social system, affected by and affecting the social, economic, and political processes of society, fam-

[5] Herberg, *Protestant-Catholic-Jew,* p. 172.

[6] *Protestant-Catholic-Jew,* Chapter I. Sherman identifies the two conflicting tendencies as isolation and assimilation; C. Bezalel Sherman, *The Jew Within American Society* (Detroit: Wayne State University Press, 1965), Chapter II; Nathan Glazer and Daniel P. Moynihan, *Beyond the Melting Pot* (Cambridge, Mass.: The M.I.T. Press, 1963), pp. 137-80.

ily patterns, technology, and community structure.[7] The paradox of being Jewish and being American must be examined as it impinges on all aspects of the Jewish community—demographic, social, religious, and cultural.

In attempting to deal with the duality of American Jewish life and the changes in the American Jewish community, it is necessary to analyze the complexity of the assimilation process in general. Such a framework provides theoretical guidance and orientation within which the transformation of American Jewry may be viewed. The paradox of Jewish identification and Americanization may be resolved or understood in terms of the relationship between generational changes and the dimensions of assimilation.

Social scientists have defined the concepts of assimilation and acculturation in many ways. Some have argued that acculturation is a continuum with total assimilation at one end and total nonassimilation at the other.[8] However, assimilation cannot be only a matter of degree, since Jews appear to have assimilated in some ways and not in others. Rather, it must be viewed multidimensionally, and a clearer delineation of the major variables or factors involved must be outlined. Milton Gordon has isolated and specified the variety of elements involved in the assimilation process. His paradigm of assimilation stresses the importance of a multidimensional view of assimilation and the complex factors involved.[9]

The first dimension of assimilation which may be identified is "structural," defined as the entrance of one group into primary relations with another group. This type of assimilation assumes the desire of the "out" group to join on the primary level the cliques, institutions, and organizations of the "in" group, as well as the desire on the part of the core society to accept the newcomers. Another area of assimilation is "identificational," or the exclusive sharing of the core group's sense of peoplehood and, in turn, the loss of the unique "out" group identification. Third, "cultural" assimilation or acculturation involves the change of the newcomers' cultural patterns to those of the host society. Cultural changes may occur in intrinsic traits (language, sense of common past,

[7] J. Milton Yinger, *Sociology Looks at Religion* (New York: The Macmillan Company, 1961), pp. 17-38.

[8] William Petersen, *Population* (New York: The Macmillan Company, 1961), p. 128; Ralph Beals, "Acculturation," in *Anthropology Today*, ed. A. L. Kroeber (Chicago: University of Chicago Press, 1953), pp. 627-28; Leonard Broom and John Kitsuse, "The Validation of Acculturation: A Condition of Ethnic Assimilation," *American Anthropologist*, LVII (February, 1955), 48.

[9] *Assimilation in American Life* (New York: Oxford University Press, Inc., 1964), pp. 60-83.

ethics, religion) or extrinsic traits (dress, mannerisms, emotional expression). Fourth, "marital" assimilation represents the large-scale intermarriage between members of the newcomer group and the core society.

Cutting across these four types of assimilation are the degree of prejudice and discrimination toward the newcomers, identified as "attitude and behavior receptional assimilation," and the degree of conflict in values and power, termed "civic assimilation." Prejudice, discrimination, and civic assimilation are conditioning elements in the assimilation process and serve as limits to the boundaries of the system. This typology of assimilation seems interrelated with the broader distinction between cultural change (changes in norms, values, traits) and social change (changes in interaction, social structure, organizational participation on the primary group basis). Both identificational and marital assimilation depend on the degree of social and cultural changes. Unless interaction between the groups occurs, unless members of both groups accept one another as social equals, and unless cultural values of the two groups are congruent, it is unlikely that large-scale intergroup marriages will occur, nor will the groups share a common sense of peoplehood. Structural and cultural assimilation are dependent on the degree of acceptance, willingness to integrate, and congruency of social structure and cultural values characterizing the host and newcomer populations.

A number of propositions or generalizations are derived by Gordon through the examination of the interrelationships of the various dimensions of assimilation. First, cultural assimilation is likely to be the first type of assimilation that occurs when an immigrant minority group arrives in a new country. Secondly, cultural assimilation or acculturation may take place independent of and to the exclusion of other types of assimilation. Thus, acculturation often characterizes minority populations that have not structurally assimilated or that maintain a separate group identity. Finally, structural assimilation assumes the pivotal position among all the assimilation processes. Once structural assimilation occurs, either simultaneous with or subsequent to cultural changes, all the other types of assimilation naturally follow.[10]

Evolving out of the analysis of the dimensions of assimilation and their interrelationships are two ideal typical models. The first is the pattern of total assimilation. This involves the loss of unique cultural patterns, integration into the social structure of the core population, shedding of any subgroup identification, and large-scale exogamy, all of which assumes the absence of prejudice, discrimination, and value-power conflict. At the other end of the continuum are those subpopulations that

[10] *Assimilation in American Life,* pp. 77, 81.

retain their cultural distinctiveness, primarily interact with members of their own group, identify themselves as a unique population, and marry among themselves. This pattern may reflect the core society's expression of prejudice and discrimination and desire not to absorb the subpopulation, or the desire on the part of the newcomers to remain separate and isolated, or some combination of these factors.

As with all ideal types, these extremes of assimilation or nonassimilation rarely reflect reality. Rather, minority populations usually assimilate in some ways and not in others and there are degrees of change within each type, conditioned by internal and external situations. Furthermore, subgroups are rarely homogeneous in their rate of integration. Within any minority group there are some persons who are more receptive to change and others who are more resistant. Thus, in order to examine the assimilation patterns of a minority population, three issues must be considered: (1) the multidimensionality of the assimilation process; (2) internal and external social forces which condition change or stability for each type of assimilation; and (3) heterogeneity in the rates of assimilation within the minority population.

OVERVIEW OF THE THREE GENERATIONS

The assimilation of Jews in American society is intertwined with distance from the immigrant generation. To provide the socio-historical context within which social and cultural changes of the Jewish population occurred, a brief description of the nature and character of the Eastern European immigrants and their descendants is necessary. This description is limited to the information and characterizations that emerge from the social scientific literature.

First-generation Jews migrating to the United States around the turn of the century had little formal education, were occupationally unskilled, and were imbued with the traditional values of Eastern European ghetto life. Their goal in America was to survive economically in the voluntary ghettos in which they resided. Preoccupied with economic survival and disoriented through migration and resettlement, they sought the comfort of their own communal institutions.[11] The immigrants

[11] Herberg, *Protestant-Catholic-Jew,* p. 10; Gordon, *Assimilation in American Life,* pp. 110-11. According to Eisenstadt there is a general feeling of inadequacy and insecurity in most immigrants, based on two interdependent factors: (1) the adjustment to a strange and new environment and (2) the shrinking of their social life and participation through their confinement to smaller groups for social participation and identification; S. N. Eisenstadt, "The Process of Absorption of New Immigrants in Israel," *Human Relations,* V (1952), 225.

needed self-contained segregation and a tightly knit community life as a kind of decompression chamber in which they could begin the adjustment process to the new forces of a society vastly different from the "old country." [12] The newly arrived immigrants attempted to transplant and reestablish the Eastern European life style in their new country. In the American ghettos, as in their European counterparts, religion played a vital role. Indeed, religion and religious institutions functioned to ease the problems of adjustment; oftentimes they helped to pave the way for acculturation.[13]

Nevertheless, Jews arrived in America with middle-class values internalized, even though most had to start at the lower end of the socio-economic scale. Their ambition, veneration for education, willingness to defer immediate gratification, urban mentality, and other middle-class value traits, coupled with the burgeoning economic and educational opportunities in the United States, guided the social forces which were changing the Jewish community in America and American society generally.[14] The congruence of Jewish and American values represented the potential for future integration. The large number of immigrants provided opportunities for sufficient in-group interaction and protection, and their "foreignness" and low socio-economic status were not conducive to generating the desire for structural assimilation. Neither was there any sign of welcome for the first generation to join the mainstream of American society.[15]

The children of the immigrants, second-generation Jews, were on the whole remarkably receptive to Americanization. The acculturation process was overwhelmingly successful, primarily through public school education and the media of mass communication. In extrinsic cultural traits (language, dress), second-generation Jews were quite similar to native-born non-Jews. Yet, they also lived with their immigrant parents and relatives. The second generation was torn between two worlds—the world of the ghetto, foreign to America, limiting social and economic expression and advancement, and the new world of America with unlimited economic opportunity and the apparent welcome sign to become American. The adjustment to the conflict of these two worlds charac-

[12] Gordon, *Assimilation in American Life,* p. 106. An analysis of the daily life of Eastern European Jews in the "shtetl" is presented by Mark Zborowski and Elizabeth Herzog, *Life Is With People* (New York: Schocken Books, 1962).

[13] Herberg, *Protestant-Catholic-Jew,* pp. 8, 11. For the classic description of the way of life of immigrant Jews in the United States, see Louis Wirth, *The Ghetto* (Chicago: University of Chicago Press, 1928).

[14] Nathan Glazer, "Social Characteristics of American Jews," in *The Jews* (3rd rev. ed.), ed. Louis Finkelstein (Philadelphia: Jewish Publication Society of America, 1960), II, 1705-11.

[15] Gordon, *Assimilation in American Life,* pp. 110-11.

terized the second generation. The plight of the immigrant's children accentuated the problem of being Jewish and being American.[16]

The second generation prospered economically and rapidly moved upward in the social structure. As they advanced, acculturation speeded up, which in turn quickened their upward social mobility. The relationship was interdependent in the classical sense—a small change in upward mobility led to an increment in cultural assimilation, which enhanced a further change in social mobility, and so on.[17]

But the acculturation and upward mobility patterns of the second generation merely brought to a climax the conflicts, tensions, and problems of their two worlds. The reaction of the second generation was one of escape—a rejection of the foreignness of their parents, of the stifling and limiting ghetto environment, and of the focal values of the social world of the first generation, Judaism. However, their rejection of ghetto life and its implications left the second generation in search of an identity. Some believed that they would be welcome in the cliques, social clubs, and institutions of white Protestant America. But the invitation was never really there and, rejected, they turned to their Jewishness as a source of comfort and a means of identification.[18]

The alienation and marginality of the second generation and the different social situations they faced led them to develop parallel social structures to harmonize with their newly found success and status. Rejecting the Orthodoxy of their parents, they searched for new modes of religious expression more in congruence with their Americanized way of life. Thus, the social organizations and religious institutions that were developed became parallel to but separate from those of the majority Protestant American society, yet distinguishable from those of the immigrant generation. It appears that acculturation took place much more rapidly than structural assimilation and intrinsic cultural change more slowly than extrinsic change.[19]

If survival and uprootedness characterized the immigrant generation, and the tensions of success and marginality epitomized their children, the third generation may be described as the generation of security. For the third generation had no urgency to escape the world of

[16] *Ibid.,* pp. 190-94; Herberg, *Protestant-Catholic-Jew,* p. 16; Marcus Lee Hansen, "The Third Generation in America," *Commentary,* XIV (November, 1952), 492-500; Oscar Handlin, *The Uprooted* (Boston: Little, Brown and Company, 1951); Oscar Handlin, *Children of the Uprooted* (New York: George Braziller, Inc., 1966).

[17] Herberg, *Protestant-Catholic-Jew,* p. 29.

[18] *Ibid.,* p. 18; Gordon, *Assimilation in American Life,* p. 111; Judith R. Kramer and Seymour Leventman, *Children of the Gilded Ghetto* (New Haven: Yale University Press, 1961), pp. 9-14.

[19] Herbert Gans, "American Jewry: Present and Future," *Commentary,* XXI (May, 1956), 422-30.

the second generation nor were they eager to reject the middle-class status attained by their fathers. Their search was for security, for continued and greater conformity to American middle-class cultural patterns, and for greater integration. At the same time, they searched for continuity in their Jewish identification and perpetuated the parallel social structures erected by their forebears. Secure in their middle-class backgrounds, the third generation did not face the conflict of two worlds. The problem of a focal point of identification had been resolved by their parents and legitimated by American society in the concepts of cultural pluralism and triple melting pot.[20]

The third generation were Americanized much more than had been possible for their parents. The emergence of the native-born Jew of native-born parents again changed the entire picture of American Jewry. Each of the previous waves of immigration—the Sephardic and the German—had their third generation, but each had been overwhelmed by the huge number of new immigrants who in turn defined the American Jewish pattern. With the end of mass Jewish immigration in the 1920's, the third-generation American Jew was able eventually to define the character of Jewish life in mid-twentieth-century America.[21]

Third-generation Jews realize that integration into American life does not necessarily require or imply total structural or identificational assimilation. The members of this generation think of themselves as Jews, are identified by others as Jews, and are linked to other members of their group by attributes that serve to enforce their separation.[22] On the other hand, some cultural assimilation is inevitable and desired, given the quest for integration.

MAINTENANCE OF JEWISH IDENTIFICATION

Second- and third-generation Jews did not lose their Jewish identity, and, perhaps, the sense of Jewish identification among third-generation Jews has increased.[23] What are the underlying factors that support this Jewish identification? In American society why do Jews turn to their religion and socio-cultural heritage? According to some, Nazism and the establishment of the State of Israel have led to greater in-group cohesion. Nazism may have had two possible consequences for American

[20] Kramer and Leventman, *Children of the Gilded Ghetto;* Hansen, "The Third Generation in America"; Herberg, *Protestant-Catholic-Jew,* pp. 22-30, 188-91.

[21] Herberg, *Protestant-Catholic-Jew,* pp. 186-88.

[22] Glazer and Moynihan, *Beyond the Melting Pot,* pp. 14-15.

[23] The question of generation changes in Jewish identity is discussed in greater detail in Chapter 9; see especially pp. 175-80.

Jews. It may have led to greater Jewish identification because of the realization that the Jewish people can become a scapegoat in America as other Jews have become throughout history, and it may have indicated to American Jews that assimilation does not inevitably lead to a loss of Jewish identity in the eyes of others. The lesson of the assimilated Jew in Germany who died in a gas chamber as a Jew along with his coreligionists is still a powerful one.[24] The establishment of Israel may have played a positive role in making the Jew proud of his people, boosting his ego and self-image. Even those alien to any manifestation of religion, those long acculturated, have begun to express an interest in the fate of the Jewish people.[25]

These two external factors are indirect influences on Jewish identification and may be overemphasized.[26] A more direct influence is the rejection of Jews by non-Jews in the United States. Jews have not been fully admitted to the American social structure or the social world of the Protestant majority.[27] A number of community studies have repeatedly pointed to the caste-like line between the non-Jewish and Jewish communities in terms of primary group interaction.[28] Even if the social exclusion of the Jew is declining, the fear of discrimination, and con-

[24] L. Kahn, "Another Decade: The American Jew in the Sixties," *Judaism,* X (Spring, 1961), 110; Will Herberg, "Religious Trends in American Jewry," *Judaism,* III (Summer, 1954), 230; Nelson R. Burr, *A Critical Bibliography of Religion in America* (Princeton: Princeton University Press, 1961), p. 503.

[25] See Marshall Sklare and Benjamin Ringer, "A Study of Jewish Attitudes Toward the State of Israel," in *The Jews,* ed. Marshall Sklare (Glencoe, Ill.: The Free Press, 1958), p. 450; Kahn, "Another Decade: The American Jew in the Sixties," p. 110; Solomon Grayzel, *A History of Contemporary Jews* (Philadelphia: Jewish Publication Society of America, 1960), p. 158.

[26] Nathan Glazer, *American Judaism* (Chicago: University of Chicago Press, 1957), p. 115. Perhaps these factors should be viewed as shaping rather than creating or maintaining Jewish identity and consciousness. See Glazer and Moynihan, *Beyond the Melting Pot,* pp. 291-94.

[27] See Isidore Chein, "The Problem of Jewish Identification," *Jewish Social Studies,* XVII (July, 1955), 221; Samuel Koenig, "The Socio-Economic Structure of the American Jewish Community," in *Jews in a Gentile World,* eds. I. Graeber and S. Britt (New York: The Macmillan Company, 1942), pp. 216-17. Vance Packard calls this rejection "the 5 o'clock shadow," wherein the Jew cannot socially participate with non-Jews after work; *The Status Seekers* (New York: David McKay Co., Inc., 1959), p. 234.

[28] See Robert and Helen Lynd, *Middletown in Transition* (New York: Harcourt, Brace & Company, 1937), p. 408; W. Lloyd Warner and Leo Srole, *The Social System of American Ethnic Groups* (New Haven: Yale University Press, 1945); Gerhard Lenski, *The Religious Factor* (Garden City, N.Y.: Doubleday & Company, Inc., 1961), p. 356; Albert Gordon, *Jews in Transition* (Minneapolis: University of Minnesota Press, 1949), p. 44; Lucy C. Dawidowicz, "Middle-Class Judaism: A Case Study," *Commentary,* XXIX (June, 1960), 502-3; Forrest E. La-Violette, "The Negro in New Orleans," in *Studies in Housing and Minority Groups,* eds. Nathan Glazer and Davis McEntire (Berkeley: University of California Press, 1960), p. 112. A number of Jewish community studies contained in *The Jews,* ed. Marshall Sklare, report similar findings: see John P. Dean (p. 310), Solomon Sutker (p. 262), and E. Digby Baltzell (p. 286).

comitant insecurity, may be a powerful factor in the identification of Jews with their own group. Moreover, the decline in discrimination, prejudice, and anti-Semitism has been more prominent in the formal sphere of society where legal pressures are more effective (occupations, education, housing) than in the informal social structure (country clubs, recreation, personal interaction).

One of the ramifications of the rejection (or feeling of rejection) of the Jew from the majority social structure is that his search for security is focused inwardly toward his own group. Since the Jew knows that his quest for status within the general community has predefined limits, he turns to the Jewish social structure for a sense of identification.[29] Thc need for identification is most pronounced in a society characterized by anonymity and alienation. "American" is not a sufficient label for identification, and members of subsocieties in the United States seek more narrowly circumscribed identities. The American Jew, unlike most other Americans, does not identify himself ethnically, as a Russian or Pole or German. Consequently, he has no alternative but identification as a Jew.[30] The continuing residential self-segregation of Jews is part of the fulfillment of the social need for belonging. The modern gilded ghetto is the result of a long tradition of ghetto life, group consciousness, family values, and cohesion not easily discarded in a mass society distinguished by anonymity.[31]

Middle-class Americans identify with one of the three religions—Protestantism, Catholicism, or Judaism—for in American society it is a fundamental way of adjusting or belonging. Like members of other religions, the Jew is expected by others to belong to the Jewish community and is actively made aware of his Jewish identification in his contacts with non-Jews.[32] Although third-generation Jews realize that integrating into American life implies cultural changes, there is no expectation of identificational or structural assimilation. Moreover, the relationships and organizations developed by the second generation have formalized and institutionalized Jewish group solidarity. Patterns of life orientations which have been legitimated by the society and subsociety are not easily disregarded. The similarity of background, experience, and cultural heritage further enhances group identification.

[29] Kahn, "Another Decade: The American Jew in the Sixties," pp. 104-5. See other community studies referred to in footnote 28.

[30] See Herberg, *Protestant-Catholic-Jew,* pp. 22-30; Glazer and Moynihan, *Beyond the Melting Pot,* pp. 14-15.

[31] Glazer, *American Judaism,* p. 121.

[32] Herberg, *Protestant-Catholic-Jew,* pp. 260-361. See also Julius Gould, "American Jewry: Some Social Trends," *The Jewish Journal of Sociology,* III (June, 1961), 63.

In describing American society as a mosaic of ethnic groups based on race, religion, and, to a declining extent, national origins, Gordon has suggested that some persons remain marginal to the resulting social units and tend to form a subsociety of their own. He hypothesizes that intellectuals form one such subsociety and the only one in which persons of different ethnic backgrounds interact with considerable frequency, closeness, and comfort. Members of this subsociety wear their ethnicity lightly and their intellectual interests strongly. Although conclusive research is virtually lacking, some evidence suggests the possible existence of such a subsociety consisting partially of Jews who express an overwhelming estrangement from the ideologies, issues, and concerns of Jewish life in America. Although the number of such "marginally ethnic Jewish intellectuals" must remain speculative, the concentration of Jews among the college educated may result in a disproportionate number of Jews identifying with an intellectual subsociety.

If anything, the data of this study suggest that the educated, professional Jews (no effort was made to identify intellectuals *per se*) do not en masse become alienated from the Jewish community in favor of an intellectual subsociety; rather, they focus their Jewish identification on selected aspects of the religio-cultural complex. However, since this study is based on the current residents of a single metropolitan area of medium size, the selective out-migration from the area of persons with higher education in pursuit of professional careers elsewhere would result in geographic dispersal of potential members of a local intellectual subcommunity and would lead to their exclusion from a study such as this.[33]

Thus, the distinctive character of the three generations of American Jews primarily reflects the differential adjustment of a minority group to American society. It is important to bear in mind, however, that the changes in the American Jewish community occurred in the context of changes in the larger American society. The generational conflicts between the immigrants and their children were perhaps intensified by the accelerating social, economic, and political changes in the United States in the first three decades of the twentieth century. During periods of rapid social change, the potential discrepancy which exists in all modern societies between the family structure and the society as a whole is maximized, giving rise to intensified conflict between generations. This conflict may give impetus in the younger generation to various forms of alienation and estrangement from values shared by the older generation.[34]

[33] Gordon, *Assimilation in American Life,* pp. 224-32.

[34] S. N. Eisenstadt, *From Generation to Generation* (Glencoe, Ill.: The Free Press, 1956), p. 310; Kingsley Davis, "Adolescence and the Social Structure," *The Annals of the American Academy of Political and Social Science,* CCXXVI (1944), 3-17; Rudolf Heberle, *Social Movements* (New York: Appleton-Century-Crofts, 1951), p. 125.

Immigrant families undergo the most rapid social change of any family type in a given society.[35] Four complex factors determine the degree of conflict between parents and their children: the rate of social change, the extent of social structure complexity, the degree of cultural integration, and the velocity of vertical mobility.[36] Considering these structural determinants in the context of American society, concomitant with the clash of the socio-cultural milieu of immigrants and their native-born children, it may be hypothesized that the conflict, and hence the difference, between first- and second-generation Jews will be greater than between the second and third generation.

It should be clear that a delineation of the assimilation patterns of American Jews must take into primary consideration the differential generational responses. The acculturation process has dramatically modified American Jewish life in the direction of greater conformity to the middle-class American style of life. However, examining other types of assimilation—particularly the structural and identificational—it appears that Jewish community organization and Jewish identification have flourished despite the increasing acculturation of the Jewish population. Thus, the paradox of Jewish life in America exists only if assimilation is viewed as a unidimensional process. When the complex nature of assimilation is examined and the various types of assimilation are unraveled it becomes clear that subgroups within society can assimilate in some ways and not in others. Furthermore, changes in each type of assimilation are matters of degree. Jews are neither totally acculturated nor immune from some structural assimilation but may have experienced more dramatic changes of an acculturative rather than of a structural nature.

The description of each of the three generations as a homogeneous unit is an oversimplification. Certainly, some members of each generation were more successful than others in their economic activities; some acculturated more rapidly and were more upwardly mobile; some intermarried and totally lost their Jewish identity while others retained their traditional religious convictions and never left the comforts and security of the ghetto. Thus, a systematic sociological analysis of the American Jewish community must attempt to discover the extent of heterogeneity within generations.[37] The rationale for the examination of

[35] Kingsley Davis, "The Sociology of Parent-Youth Conflict," *American Sociological Review,* V (August, 1940), 524.

[36] *Ibid.,* p. 535.

[37] The distinction between generations as homogeneous and the social units within generations is discussed by Karl Mannheim, "The Problem of Generations," in *Essays on the Sociology of Knowledge* (London: Routledge & Kegan Paul, Ltd., 1952), pp. 304-7. For the application of Mannheim's theoretical discussion to the study of the Jews, see Kramer and Leventman, *Children of the Gilded Ghetto,* pp. 3-20.

differentials within generations extends beyond the desire for systematic analyses. The examination of subgroups which have been in the forefront of social and cultural changes may provide some insight into the determinants of change. The susceptibility to change may also shed light on the potential diffusion of change to other subgroups, particularly if the subgroup represents the direction in which the total population is moving. Furthermore, information on the proportional representation of subgroups within a population may reveal the changing influence of subgroups on the character of the total population. For these reasons, a socio-demographic analysis of the Jewish population should have as one major theme the examination of differential response of subgroups to the assimilation-integration process.

THE RESEARCH GAP

The characterization of assimilation among three generations of Jews and the discussion of factors conditioning Jewish identification are preludes to a brief evaluation of data sources upon which social scientists base their analyses of the American Jewish community, what type of research on the assimilation of Jews in the United States is necessary, and how the data to be presented in ensuing chapters lend themselves to such an analysis.

Although the Jewish group is often portrayed as having a veneration for study and learning, ironically, systematic and comprehensive self-knowledge of this group is limited. The literature on the American Jewish community is uneven in quality and coverage. The foregoing brief description and discussion was based on the available information, and, in general, remains more hypothesis than established generalization. Sources of information on the Jews vary in scientific quality and fall into four major categories: (1) official data, (2) by-product data, (3) local community studies, and (4) personal observations, speculations, and interpretations.

The federal censuses and annual national vital statistics information in the United States do not include questions on religious affiliation. Statisticians, demographers, social scientists, and other professional groups and organizations have repeatedly attempted to get a question on religion included in the decennial census because of the important impact that religious identification has on the demographic characteristics and behavior of the population. It has been argued that such information would permit more meaningful scientific analysis of the census materials and would also provide valuable planning information to groups whose programs cater to specific religious segments of the population. The only general population survey conducted by the U.S. Bureau of the Census containing information on Jews was the Current Population Survey (CPS) of 1957. The CPS is a monthly survey based on a national sample of about 35,000 households, and in 1957 approximately 1,000 Jewish households were contacted.[38] However, only limited information from this survey was published, mainly crude data on population structure, intermarriage, and fertility of major religious groups.[39] The inclusion of a question on religion in this survey evoked minimal objections from the respondents. Yet the inquiry on religion was omitted from the 1960 census largely because of the opposition of some groups, as a matter of principle, to its inclusion in a decennial census for which replies are mandatory. The same objections have led to its exclusion from the 1970 census.

The federal government has also sponsored "Censuses of Religious Bodies," but these have been limited to reports from organizations and community institutions rather than individuals. The last such census was conducted in 1936 and, owing to its limited usefulness for government or community planning, has been discontinued.[40] Some researchers have explored indirect data available from the decennial census, particularly the analysis of those reporting Yiddish as their mother tongue or Russia as their place of birth.[41] As an indirect estimate of the Jewish population, such information is of limited value, and with the Americanization of

[38] U.S. Bureau of the Census, "Religion Reported by the Civilian Population of the United States: March, 1957," *Current Population Reports,* Series P-20, No. 79 (February 2, 1958). For guides to the literature on religious statistics in general see Dorothy Good, "Questions of Religion in the United States Census," *Population Index,* XXV, No. 1 (1959), 3-16; Benson Y. Landis, "A Guide to the Literature on Statistics of Religious Affiliation with References to Related Social Studies," *Journal of the American Statistical Association,* LIV (June, 1959), 335-57.

[39] In addition to the basic tabulations in U.S. Bureau of the Census, "Religion Reported by the Civilian Population of the United States: March, 1957," for information on intermarriage and fertility data by religious groupings see Paul Glick, "Intermarriage and Fertility Patterns Among Persons in Major Religious Groups," *Eugenics Quarterly,* VII (March, 1960), 31-38. While this book was in press, previously unavailable data from the March, 1957, Current Population Survey were released by the Bureau of the Census. These include information on education, marital status, labor force, occupation, and income by religion. See U.S. Bureau of the Census, "Tabulations of Data on the Social and Economic Characteristics of Major Religious Groups, March, 1957" (Unpublished).

[40] Uriah Z. Engelman, "Jewish Statistics in the United States Census of Religious Bodies (1850-1936)," *Jewish Social Studies,* IX (1947), 127-74.

[41] See particularly the work of Nathan Goldberg, "Occupational Patterns of American Jews," *Jewish Review,* III (October–December, 1945, and January–March, 1946); "Jewish Population in America," *Jewish Review,* V (January–December, 1948), 36-48; "Demographic Characteristics of American Jews," in *Jews in the Modern World,* ed. Jacob Fried (New York: Twayne Publishers, 1962), Vol. II.

the Jewish population these data are becoming even less meaningful. No national studies directed specifically at the Jews have been undertaken.

The second group of studies containing information on American Jews—by-product data collected for other purposes—is represented by some secondary analysis of surveys that use religious affiliation as a variable. Some public opinion polls have included questions on religion, demographic studies of fertility have included measures of religion and religiosity, and Lenski's study of Detroit concentrated on "the religious factor." [42] However, all of these studies have been plagued by the small number of Jewish persons included in the sample, reflecting their small percentage of the total United States population. No study, national or local, where information on Jews is a by-product of a larger or different research focus, has had a sufficient number of Jewish persons for any detailed analysis. Since the number of Jews included in most of these studies is less than 100, two additional complications arise: (1) the question of the representativeness of the sampling and (2) the inability to examine heterogeneity within the Jewish population.

Studies of local Jewish communities are potentially fruitful sources of information. Although their number is increasing, community studies vary widely in coverage, quality, and comparability, and most are descriptive rather than analytic.[43] The majority are reports to the Jewish community; a few notable exceptions focus on special topics such as stratification and anti-Semitism.[44] In the past these studies have generally been characterized by a lack of rigorous scientific methodology, inadequate sampling procedures, incomplete data analysis, unanswered basic questions, and lack of focus on major variables or control for intervening variables. Since the majority of these studies have not met minimum standards of scientific inquiry, their potential contribution has not been realized.

Basing judgments and interpretations on such evidence may be dangerous and misleading. However, a number of social scientists have utilized such data in combination with their own skills as observers, and often as participants, to describe and analyze social and cultural changes in the American Jewish community. Prominent observers of the Jewish scene such as Nathan Glazer, Milton Gordon, Will Herberg, and Marshall Sklare are thought-provoking and show insight. The validity of many of

[42] See studies cited in Chapter 6.

[43] See studies cited in Chapter 2.

[44] On stratification, see Kramer and Leventman, *Children of the Gilded Ghetto;* on studies related to anti-Semitism, see the review by Melvin Tumin, *An Inventory and Appraisal of Research on American Anti-Semitism* (New York: Freedom Books, 1961).

the hypotheses and insights they provide, however, are still to be fully tested.[45] The two-volume Lakeville study by Sklare, Greenblum, and Ringer, which appeared as this book was going to press, will undoubtedly make an important contribution toward our understanding of changing patterns of Jewish identification in the United States as increasing numbers of Jews participate in the suburban movement.[46]

Taken together, the information on social and cultural changes among American Jews is limited in coverage and uneven in quality. The major objective of this book is to analyze data based on one community, the Providence metropolitan area, which shed light on the changes in the sociological and demographic parameters of the Jewish community. The focus is on the transformation of Jews in the process of integration into American society. Theoretically, we seek to explore changes in the structure of an American Jewish community which reflect the emerging balance between separation and loss of Jewish identity, between Jewishness and Americanism, and, in turn, between Jewish survival and total absorption.

Three major interrelated themes provide the guidelines for the analysis. The first theme relates to the question of Jewish exceptionalism: To what extent does the Jewish population differ from the total population in reference to socio-demographic characteristics and behavior? Second, what changes have occurred in the structure of the Jewish community and in the lives of Jews as a consequence of assimilation, and in what way is assimilation interrelated with generation status? The third theme centers on Jewish heterogeneity: Are there variations in the degree of assimilation within generations, and which social groupings within each generation are more receptive or more resistant to changes?

These three themes will be applied to the analysis of Jewish life and Jewish community structure; this entails an examination of demographic as well as sociological changes. The general areas of inquiry include population structure and distribution, socio-economic status, family structure, fertility, mortality, intermarriage, and the religio-cultural system. Throughout, the goal is to identify the manner in which generation changes have affected the demographic and social structure of the Jewish community.

[45] For studies of this type see Glazer, *American Judaism;* Herberg, *Protestant-Catholic-Jew;* Gordon, *Assimilation in American Life;* Sherman, *The Jew Within American Society;* Stuart Rosenberg, *The Search for Jewish Identity in America* (Garden City, N.Y.: Doubleday & Company, Inc., 1965).

[46] Marshall Sklare and Joseph Greenblum, *Jewish Identity on the Suburban Frontier,* I (New York: Basic Books, Inc., Publishers, 1967); Benjamin Ringer, *The Edge of Friendliness: A Study of Jewish-Gentile Relations,* II (New York: Basic Books, Inc., Publishers, 1967).

CHAPTER TWO

"Take Ye The Sum..."

History records many experiments in the counting and surveying of people. Among the earliest reports of these was God's command to Moses in the wilderness of Sinai, "Take ye the sum of all the congregation of the children of Israel, by their families, by their fathers' houses, according to the number of names." (Numbers 1:2.) The reasons for taking censuses have varied historically. In earliest times they were used most frequently for assessing the number of men available for war or for counting the number of persons on whom taxes could be levied. The history of the United States Census reflects the way in which the purposes of the census have been extended well beyond the mere enumeration of persons.[1] Whereas the first several decennial censuses, beginning in 1790, were limited largely to the numbers of population by age, sex, color, and whether free man or slave, succeeding censuses have included an increasing array of population characteristics, reflecting the changing needs of American society for information touching on a wide range of problems. The U.S. Census of 1960 includes data on such widely different subjects as education, income, occupation, migration status, fertility, housing, and number of radios and television sets.[2] Notable because of its omission from the U.S. Census is any question on religion.

In the absence of official and comprehensive information on religion, social scientists concerned with problems in which religion is a key variable have had to turn to privately sponsored surveys for information.[3] Similarly, both local and national agencies concerned with the welfare of members belonging to particular religious groups have been frustrated in their efforts by the absence of reliable information on the size, location, and composition of the population they were attempting to serve. To obtain the factual basis that is essential to services and planning, an increasing number of such agencies—Catholic, Protestant, and Jewish—have been forced to undertake their own surveys. Thus, since

[1] Ralph Thomlinson, *Population Dynamics* (New York: Random House, Inc., 1965), pp. 26-46.

[2] U.S. Bureau of the Census, *U.S. Census of Population: 1960,* Vol. I, *Characteristics of the Population,* Part 1, United States Summary (Washington, D.C.: Government Printing Office, 1964).

[3] See, for example, Council of Jewish Federations and Welfare Funds, "Jewish Population Studies by Community Federations," *Council Reports* (May 21, 1963).

1955 over a dozen Jewish communities have undertaken population censuses, and plans are in progress for a nationwide study of the Jewish population under the sponsorship of the Council of Jewish Federations and Welfare Funds.[4]

Considerations similar to these lay behind a study of the Jewish population of Greater Providence undertaken by the General Jewish Committee, the central coordinating body of that Jewish community.[5] Recognizing the limited sociological information that was available on the structure of the Jewish community, on the demographic characteristics of the American Jewish population, and on the effects of changing generation status on the demographic characteristics and processes of the population, the survey included questions designed to obtain data on these variables. In doing so, the survey went beyond the immediate planning needs of the local community. The generally small number of Jews included in most general surveys and the intention to study intensively about 1,500 Jewish households in this survey argued strongly in favor of such an expanded focus. The initial report based on the population survey was directed toward meeting the needs of the local community for information that would allow realistic planning for the future. A second report focused on the fertility behavior of the Jewish population.[6] This third report, focusing on generational change, represents the completion of the final phase of the over-all study.

In any study based on a single community, the question can legitimately be raised whether that particular community is representative of the country as a whole. No single community is *the* typical one; it differs in size, in composition, in age from others. By its very size, the Providence Jewish community is obviously atypical of the great centers of Jewish settlement in the United States such as New York, Chicago, and Los Angeles. The sheer number of Jews living in these places affects all aspects of Jewish communal life as well as individual behavior. Yet, any observer will note that Jewish life in even two such large Jewish communities as New York and Los Angeles differs markedly, being affected by relative numbers, by settlement pattern, by the age of the community, and by the character of the Jewish population attracted to it. Only a nationwide survey encompassing representative communities of all sizes,

[4] The Council of Jewish Federations and Welfare Funds is a national organization devoted to assisting and coordinating the welfare and research activities of Jewish community organizations.

[5] Sidney Goldstein, *A Population Survey: The Greater Providence Jewish Community* (Providence, R.I.: General Jewish Committee of Providence, Inc., 1964).

[6] Calvin Goldscheider, "Trends and Differentials in Jewish Fertility" (Unpublished Ph.D. dissertation, Brown University, 1964).

locations, and composition can aspire to portray correctly the Jewish population of the United States.

Findings based on any single community must obviously be hedged with qualifications based on the unique features of that community. Yet, such studies have value from two perspectives: First, to the extent that other local investigations are made, they will provide comparable information by which the typicality of the findings can be judged. Second, cross-sectional comparisons made among the various segments of the socio-demographic structure of the community will provide insights into the processes of change which may be occurring longitudinally as the population of the specific community and of the country as a whole changes in its composition. For, although absolute numbers or percentages with respect to any single variable may change from one community to another, the trends over time as measured by cross-sectional comparisons across generation lines are likely to be similar for different communities and to be indicative of the general direction of change in the American Jewish community as a whole. It is these trends that will receive key focus in this investigation. The value of this study must therefore be judged by these criteria. Unfortunately, the number of Jewish community studies is limited; moreover, few have focused on generation as a key explanatory variable. As a result, only limited opportunities exist for a comparative approach. From this perspective, therefore, the value of the present analysis must rest on the benchmark it provides against which the results from later studies of other Jewish communities can be compared. The more immediate function served by this investigation is the insights to be gained into future trends in the socio-demographic structure of the American Jewish community through the cross-sectional evaluation of the demographic characteristics and religious and social behavior of the various generations of Jews in 1963.

If there is any validity in the assumption that the future of the American Jewish community will be at least partially patterned by the current characteristics of the third-generation group, then comparison of this group with those Jews who are the American-born children of immigrants, and, in turn, with the immigrant group itself should point to the direction of change on the American scene. Reliance upon cross-sectional data referring to a particular point in time has limitations for inferring the direction of change over time. Differences between the first and third generations in the 1960's do not necessarily reflect either the changes that have already taken place as the Jewish population moved from being largely immigrant to increasingly American born, or the exact patterns to be expected as this trend continues. Yet, in the absence of longitudinal data in which the same cohort of persons is followed through time, cross-sectional comparisons should suggest the direction of changes to be expected of third- and fourth-generation American Jewry. Indeed, it may well be that cross-sectional comparisons based on a community such as Providence can go far in explaining the over-all differentials that have been noted among various communities. For if generation status is a useful explanatory variable, the nature of Jewish life may vary significantly among communities according to the differential generational composition of their populations.

THE SURVEY COMMUNITY

Rhode Island has the distinction of being the smallest state in the Union, covering an area of only 1,214 square miles. In this small territory, the city of Providence, with a population of about 200,000 in 1963, dominates the area.[7] The rise of Providence can be traced back to the American Revolution, when Newport was devastated by the British occupation. Providence, never occupied by the British, weathered the war more successfully; its ships had retained access to the sea, and, with the return of peace, the city experienced a boom in shipbuilding and became a center of maritime trade. Early in the nineteenth century Providence emerged as one of the country's leading manufacturing centers, noted for a variety of products, especially textiles and metals.

The rapid growth of manufacturing in the nineteenth century was reflected in a sharply increasing population. In 1800 the city numbered 7,614 persons, but by 1850 its population had risen to 41,513. This rapid growth continued through the second half of the century, with the population reaching 176,000 persons in 1900. Whereas the city had accounted for only 11 per cent of the state's total population at the beginning of the century, by 1900 41 per cent of the people were living in Providence. Through the first four decades of the twentieth century, the city continued to grow, reaching a peak of 253,500 persons in 1940. Yet, after 1910 the city's rate of population growth fell off sharply while the balance of the state grew much more rapidly. As a result, the proportion of the state's population living in Providence began to decline in 1910. By 1940-1950 Providence had actually begun to lose population, and this decrease accelerated, so that by 1960 the number of people living in the city itself was 207,500; by 1965 the city's 187,000 people accounted for only 21 per cent of the state's population.[8]

[7] Sidney Goldstein and Kurt B. Mayer, *Metropolitanization and Population Change in Rhode Island,* State Planning Section Publication No. 3 (Providence, R.I.: Rhode Island Development Council, 1962).

[8] U.S. Bureau of the Census, "Special Census of Rhode Island, October 1, 1965," *Current Population Reports,* Series P-28, No. 1393 (January 24, 1966).

Several factors account for the stabilization and subsequent decline in the population of Providence. Like the state as a whole, the city was adversely affected by the decline of the textile industry which was severe enough to arrest further growth of the manufacturing sector of the city's economy. In addition to the decline in job opportunities, the residential development of the city also contributed to the changing pattern of population. By 1930 residential growth had approached the far limits of the city. Space limitations were made even more stringent by the highway building and urban renewal activities begun during the 1950's and accelerated in the 1960's. These changes contributed heavily to the increased tempo of suburban development which began in the late nineteenth century. Between 1950 and 1960 there was a net outflow from the city of 61,000 people, much of this to the suburban areas. (An even sharper loss was avoided because of the 20,000 excess of births over deaths.) Thus, a growing proportion of the area's population has come to reside in the suburban sector of the metropolitan area rather than in the central city. In 1900 almost half of the metropolitan area's population lived in the central city; by 1965 only one fourth lived there.

The experience of Providence is not unique; rather it has presaged that of other areas. For the United States as a whole, an intrinsic part of the increased metropolitanization has been a major shift of population to the suburbs. Between 1950 and 1960 the population of the central cities of the 212 metropolitan areas increased by only 11 per cent, compared to a growth rate of 49 per cent for those parts of the metropolitan areas outside the central cities. In fact, as evidenced by the 1960 census, more than one-quarter of the central cities of the United States actually experienced population losses between 1950 and 1960, at the very time that metropolitan populations were increasing more rapidly than were other segments of the nation.[9]

In addition to the redistribution of population between city and suburbs, the nativity composition of the population has undergone significant change. The original colonists in Rhode Island were English, and initially other population stocks were not welcome.[10] Yet the eighteenth century witnessed the influx of a limited number of Huguenots, Portuguese, Jews, and Scots, as well as the introduction of Negroes. Together with the remnants of the vanquished Indians, their presence marked the beginning of an increasing heterogeneity among the Rhode

[9] U.S. Bureau of the Census, "Population of Standard Metropolitan Statistical Areas: 1960 and 1950," *Supplementary Reports,* PC(S1)-1 (April 10, 1961).

[10] Sidney Goldstein and Kurt B. Mayer, *The People of Rhode Island, 1960,* State Planning Section Publication No. 8 (Providence, R.I.: Rhode Island Development Council, 1963), pp. 5-9.

Island population, an experience again typical of the United States as a whole. The census of 1850 provides the first reliable evidence of a phenomenon which was beginning to effect major changes in the ethnic composition of the area's population: the massive influx of the foreign born. The census showed that 16 per cent of all the residents of the state were born abroad. Almost 70 per cent of these came from Ireland and another 23 per cent came from the other British Isles. The arrival of the Irish represented the first of a series of waves of immigrants that would change the original homogeneous Anglo-Saxon Protestant population. After the Civil War there was a great influx of French Canadians, which reached its peak around 1890, when it was superseded by a massive migration from Italy and, to a lesser extent, from Eastern Europe and Portugal. The state census of 1905 showed that for the first time Catholicism was the faith of the majority of the population. By 1910 the foreign born constituted 33 per cent of Rhode Island's total population, and almost seven out of every ten inhabitants were either foreign born or the children of foreign born.

The interruption of immigration during World War I, followed in the next decade by the imposition of quotas, produced a continuous decline in both the number and the proportion of foreign born. Since few new immigrants arrived and the old ones began to die, the number of those born abroad decreased from 178,000 in 1910 to 86,000 in 1960, exactly 10 per cent of the state's population. Four out of ten inhabitants were either foreign born or of foreign or mixed parentage in 1960. Among the foreign stock, those of Italian and of Canadian origin each constituted 23 per cent, 14 per cent were from the United Kingdom, and 8 per cent each were Irish and Portuguese. Poland and Russia each furnished about 4 per cent, most of the latter being Jewish.

The foreign born were not distributed randomly throughout the state but were concentrated in the larger cities and in selected smaller towns, most of which offered unique employment opportunities, particularly in the textile industry. On the whole, suburban communities as well as rural towns have had relatively few foreign-born residents. In the suburbs, this is due to the younger age structure of the resident population. The rural part of the state, which constitutes a small proportion of the total population, has never attracted many foreigners. Although Negroes constituted as high as 10 per cent of colonial Rhode Island's population, in 1965 the nonwhite population of 25,444 persons represented less than 3 per cent of the total, with almost 60 per cent of it concentrated in Providence. The state has never been as attractive to Southern Negro migrants as other industrial centers of the North because of the presence of a relatively large working-class immigrant population.

THE JEWISH COMMUNITY

The American Jewish community traces its beginnings to the Colonial period. From the arrival of the first group of Jews in New Amsterdam in 1654 until the Revolution, a number of small Jewish communities were established, primarily in the cities along the eastern seaboard. The Jews came from the countries of Western Europe or the West Indies and were generally prosperous merchants or artisans. By the end of the eighteenth century approximately 2,500 Jews lived in the United States.[11]

It was not until the middle of the nineteenth century that any sizeable number of Jewish immigrants arrived; then they came predominantly from Germany and the countries under German domination. During the period of German Jewish immigration—1840 to 1880—the number of Jews in the United States increased from about 15,000 to 250,000.[12] The new immigrants, unlike their predecessors, did not concentrate in a few large cities, but participated in the great westward movement and in the settlement of the country as a whole. The Jewish peddler became a familiar figure to the pioneers in the western frontier towns as well as to the residents of the smaller towns in the East. Although not wealthy merchants as the colonial Jews had been, the newer arrivals soon progressed from itinerant peddlers to owners of sizable stores or tailor shops. Because of their residential dispersal and their still small numbers, it became relatively easy for them to fit into the larger community, so that until 1880 Jews were characterized by a relatively high degree of integration into American life.[13]

The character and size of American Jewry was radically transformed in the four decades after 1880 as immigrants from Eastern Europe poured into the country. During these 40 years the more than two million immigrants increased the Jewish proportion of the total population from 0.6 per cent to 3.5 per cent.[14] Moreover, the majority of them settled in the urban centers, especially in the northeast, where employment opportunities were most readily available. The new arrivals rapidly changed the occupational composition of the American Jewish population. Whereas only a small proportion of the Jews until 1890 were blue-collar

[11] Nathan Glazer, "Social Characteristics of American Jews, 1654-1954," in *American Jewish Yearbook* (Philadelphia: Jewish Publication Society of America, 1955), LVI, 3-8.

[12] Ruth Gay, *Jews in America* (New York: Basic Books, Inc., Publishers, 1965), pp. 45-46.

[13] Glazer, "Social Characteristics of American Jews," pp. 8-9.

[14] *Ibid.*, p. 11.

workers, the majority of the new immigrants entered industries as workers, and many were concentrated in a single industry, clothing manufacture. Although the immigrants were able to do little more than earn a living wage, they gave high priority to learning English and to assuming the obligations and rights of citizenship in their adopted country.[15] Even more important, they saw to it that their children received a good education. Thus, although the Eastern European immigrants were unable to advance as rapidly economically as had the German Jews, the second generation was able to make great strides in terms of both economic and social mobility. By the middle of the twentieth century, when the third generation began to dominate the American Jewish community, economic security was no longer a problem for most.

In general, the development of the Providence Jewish community followed a pattern similar to that of the United States as a whole. Jews settled in Newport as early as the middle of the seventeenth century (thereby becoming one of the earliest Jewish communities in Colonial America), although they did not arrive in Providence until almost two centuries later.[16] In 1838 Solomon Pareira, a native of Holland, moved to Providence with his wife. Here he opened a succession of clothing stores and raised his family. Within the next decade, the nucleus of a Jewish community had formed. By 1850 nine families with Jewish names were listed in the city directory, and, like Solomon Pareira, all but one of the new arrivals were engaged in the clothing trade, either as merchants or tailors.

The commercial climate of Providence must have been kind to these settlers. Indicative of their vigor and prosperity, as well as their generosity, was the rivalry that sprang up between two of them—Louis Lewisson and John Nathan, both proprietors of clothing stores. Through advertisements in the *Providence Journal* they invited the poor of the city to come to their stores on Thanksgiving Day, 1853, Lewisson promising "a good substantial Thanksgiving Dinner in front of my prosperous bazaar," and Nathan offering "a good substantial bargain in ready made clothing at my far famed clothing store." [17]

From 1850 until after the Civil War, Providence attracted few additional Jewish families. Nevertheless, the Jewish community began to have formal organization. In 1849 land was purchased for use as a cemetery. In 1855 the first congregation in the city was established, with Solomon Pareira its first president. After 1870 the number of Jews in

[15] *Ibid.*, p. 15.

[16] The history of the Providence Jewish community is based on material found in *Rhode Island Jewish Historical Notes,* I-III (June, 1954, to May, 1962).

[17] *R.I. Jewish Historical Notes,* I, No. 2, pp. 121-124.

the area increased considerably, so that by the following decade about 150 Jewish families lived in the Providence-Pawtucket area. Most of these were still merchants of various kinds—from peddlers to owners of substantial dry goods emporia—but they also included a physician, an optician, and a librarian. The bulk of these early arrivals came from Western Europe. In fact, it was not until 1875 that a sufficient number of Eastern European families lived in the community to organize their own congregation.

The significant growth of the Jewish community began after 1880, as immigrants from Eastern Europe poured into the city. By 1885 the city directory listed about 250 Jewish names. Their number grew to almost 450 in the next five years and swelled to almost 1,000 by 1895—a four-fold increase in ten years. Such growth was especially impressive when compared to the growth of the city as a whole. From 1890 to 1895 the Providence population increased 23 per cent while the number of Jewish families increased 131 per cent. By 1900, 1,607 Jewish names were listed in the city directory.

As early as 1851 there are records of naturalization for Jews in Providence County. By 1906, 1,721 Jews had become American citizens. Of these, only 161 had come to the United States before 1880—the earliest in 1845. The years 1885 through 1890 accounted for 43 per cent of all arrivals. Data on place of birth in the naturalization records reveal that by 1906 the Jewish community of Providence was overwhelmingly of Eastern European origin. Of 1,718 persons naturalized from 1851 to 1906, almost three-quarters were born in Russia or Poland; Austria-Hungary contributed 15 per cent; and all of Western Europe supplied less than 5 per cent, mostly from Germany.

With greater numbers came greater occupational diversity. By 1900 merchants, tailors, and peddlers were still numerous, as were shoemakers and jewelry workers, but there were also two lawyers, five physicians, seven rabbis, fourteen teachers, four musicians, and a bartender. Jews could, in fact, be found throughout the occupational structure. As the community's size grew, so did its formal organizations and institutions. The first synagogue building in Providence was erected in 1891. By that time four other congregations had appeared and were meeting in homes or rented halls. Some of these catered to particular ethnic segments of the community, such as the Romanian or Polish groups. During the next 55 years no less than 23 separate synagogues received charters. Not all of these existed for the entire period, and several merged during the ensuing decades; but many were the antecedents of congregations in existence in the 1960's. Like the original Jewish settlers, the early synagogues located near the center of the city. As the population spread out, so did the synagogues, first to the peripheral areas of the city, then to the suburbs. The first suburban temple received its charter in 1948.

As the religious institutions of the city grew, so did the assistance and benevolence societies traditionally associated with Jewish life. As early as 1870 a lodge of B'nai Brith was organized for "mutual benefit and for benevolent and charitable purposes." [18] From then until World War I, scores of mutual aid associations sprang up to attend to the various needs of the community. Some were open to all; others were restricted to specific occupations, such as the Rhode Island Shoe Makers Aid Association. Many of the associations were organized by women, beginning with the Ladies Hebrew Benevolent Association of 1880; others had strong fraternal appeal.

Not all of these organizations concerned themselves with their members' religious or physical welfare. The large number of Jews who were naturalized during this period indicates both the huge inflow of immigrants and their desire to become citizens of their adopted country. Organizations helped them to do so. In 1890 the Wendell Phillips Educational Club stated as its purpose not only beneficial aid to its members but also the goal of "educat[ing] the members in the English language." [19] Fifteen years later the United Hebrew Citizens Association of Rhode Island organized "to qualify men of the Hebrew faith in the highest duties of citizenship, and to inspire them with such a proper regard for American institutions and ideals as will tend to make them a valued factor in society." [20] Having attained citizenship, the newly Americanized minority struggled to achieve the rights as well as duties conferred upon them. The North End Political Club, begun in 1906, hoped "to secure to Hebrew residents of the State of Rhode Island equal rights and protection in their enjoyment of citizenship." [21]

By the end of World War I the tremendous growth of new organizations ceased. The institutional structure of the Jewish community of Providence was well established, and few new organizations were chartered during the following decades. Although some of the more important present-day institutions received their charters in more recent decades, all have their roots in the early period.

The history of the Jewish community of Providence may well be divided into three phases. From 1840 to 1880 the basis of the community was established. The first congregations and associations were founded, and Providence was seen to be a city where Jews could settle and establish

[18] *R.I. Jewish Historical Notes,* II, No. 2, p. 22.
[19] *Ibid.,* p. 24.
[20] *Ibid.,* p. 39.
[21] *Ibid.,* p. 43.

roots, and where they could use their skills and knowledge. The next three to four decades, 1880 to World War I, were years of enormous growth and change. The fact of the already existing Jewish community as well as the possibilities for employment offered by Providence's industries drew hundreds of immigrants to the area. These were the years of the Eastern European migration, the years that left their greatest mark on the structure and character of the community. After World War I began a period of consolidation and maturation, as the immigrants and their offspring built upon and molded the earlier structure to meet their changing needs and gradually spread throughout the city and into the suburbs.

By 1950 the Jewish community of Providence, as well as of the United States, had entered the fourth stage of its history. The Americanization process had been at work for several decades and the role of the immigrant was greatly reduced. Although the immigrant past has left its strong stamp, the future is increasingly in the hands of the American-born Jews. Evaluation of the future course of American Jewry therefore requires more intensive examination of the ways in which the younger generations differ from the older ones with respect to both their socio-demographic characteristics and their identification with Judaism.

THE NATURE OF THE SURVEY

Plans for a study of the Jewish community were initiated in late 1962. At the very onset, because of the recognition that the Jewish population had participated very strongly in the suburban movement, it was agreed that the survey should encompass not just the city of Providence, but rather the Greater Providence area, which is approximately equivalent to the built-up area included by the Bureau of the Census in the urbanized sector of the Providence metropolitan area. This includes both the central cities of Providence and adjoining Pawtucket and their immediate environs, as well as the suburban communities to the southwest, east, and southeast of Providence.[22] During the two-month period in which the study design was being organized, the questionnaire developed and tested, and the sample chosen, a public relations campaign was initiated within the Jewish community. In addition to soliciting the cooperation of the organized sectors of the community and its leaders, it also strove to inform the general public of the needs and purposes of the survey.

Because of the anticipated comprehensiveness of the questionnaire,

[22] The suburban towns include Cranston, Warwick, East Providence, Barrington, Bristol, Warren, East Greenwich, and West Warwick.

the most feasible method for collecting information was through personal interviews, rather than by telephone or mail. For this field operation, volunteer interviewers were organized into small interview teams headed by 22 captains. In all, 225 persons volunteered their services as interviewers, but a variety of screening devices reduced their number to about 150 by the time the field operations began in May, 1963.

In undertaking a field study of the Jewish population of Greater Providence, two alternatives for identifying Jewish households were possible. Ideally, a cross section of the total population of the area should have been screened for religious identity; those households reporting one or more Jewish members would then have been interviewed intensively. Yet, the relatively small percentage of Jews in the total population would have made such an operation highly inefficient, since many households would have had to be approached to yield the desired number of Jewish households for interviews. The second alternative—reliance on a master list of all Jewish households in Greater Providence—provided sufficient promise for yielding comprehensive coverage to warrant serious attention as the best method for selecting the sample.

The central Jewish committees of Greater Providence and Pawtucket maintain files which, to the best of their knowledge, list almost every Jewish family living in the area. Through constant checking with organization membership rosters, real estate purchases, obituary columns, marriage announcements, birth announcements, and other news items, as well as through information obtained from personal contacts, these lists are constantly updated. They therefore give a substantial basis for identifying the universe of Jewish households in the area.

When first examined for purposes of this study, the combined lists of the Providence and Pawtucket files contained 5,783 Jewish household units. As a double check, membership rosters were solicited from every Jewish organization—religious, social, and secular—in Greater Providence. These lists often included names of persons who were not affiliated with any particular group, but who were regarded as potential members. Information was thereby obtained on both those actively involved in Jewish organizations and those who were known to be Jewish but were not actively affiliated. Only a few small organizations failed to provide such lists. Every name on the organization rosters was then checked against the master lists of the General Jewish Committee. In all, over 20,000 names—many of them duplicates—were double checked. Indicating the completeness of the original master files, only 213 new household units had to be added to the original 5,783 units, and many of these were new residents of the community.

Judged by this fact, the master file gave well over 90 per cent coverage. Although the addition of the 213 names raised the level of coverage, some households in which no member was affiliated with any group and which were not known as Jewish households were probably missed. Such omissions represent the most serious limitation of use of a master list as the basis for sample selection, particularly since the characteristics of the unaffiliated individuals are undoubtedly quite different from those listed. Additional checks to ascertain the extent of such omissions were therefore employed. Data available from several independent social surveys conducted in the area provided one such check. In these surveys, cross sections of the general population of different areas of Greater Providence had been interviewed, and religious identification had been obtained. Names of all households containing one or more Jews were abstracted from these samples, and these names were then cross checked in the revised master file of the General Jewish Committee. It was found that 97.5 per cent of the Jewish households included in the independent samples also appeared in the master file, lending strong support to the evidence that the files gave excellent coverage to the Jewish population of Greater Providence. It was therefore decided to use these files, to which the new names found in the general samples had been added, as the basis for selecting the sample of Jewish households to be interviewed.

At the same time, several additional checks were built into the questionnaire itself to provide still further basis for later evaluation of the completeness of the coverage. A question in the interview asked the respondent to list any Jewish families who had moved into the Providence area within the last year. This question elicited 260 names, all of which were cross checked in the files. Forty-four new names were found, almost all of them recent in-migrants to the community, and these were included in the sample to be interviewed. Information was also collected concerning membership in organizations and enrollment in Sunday Schools and Hebrew Schools. These data made possible comparison of the number actually on the membership lists and the number reporting themselves as members. For example, the Jewish Community Center reported a membership of 4,265 persons; in the survey, 4,240 persons identified themselves as Community Center members. The Bureau of Jewish Education reported for the fall of 1963 a total enrollment in all schools of 2,766 children; in the survey a total of 2,778 children were reported as enrolled in Hebrew Schools. The close correspondence of these and other figures gives added confidence to the completeness of the coverage provided by the master lists. These latter comparisons do not necessarily prove that the coverage of the unaffiliated population was equally complete, but the other checks discussed earlier point strongly in this direction.

In its final form, the master list included all households in which one or more adult members were known to be Jewish. In the survey, a household was defined as all members of a unit living together, and information was obtained concerning the entire unit regardless of whether all of the members of the household were Jewish. In all, 5,996 households constituted the universe from which the sample was chosen.

On the basis of the kinds of information that were desired and the kinds of tabulations of the data which would be made, a sample of 1,500 household units was regarded as necessary to provide a sufficient number of cases for statistical analysis. Since the total universe approximated 6,000 households, a sample of one in every four households was required. At the same time, since separate analyses were desirable for individual sections of Greater Providence, seven areas were originally delineated for such local use.[23] For this report, these seven areas have been combined into three categories: (1) the older urban area, (2) the newer urban area, and (3) the suburbs (Figure 2-1). Since several of the original seven areas contained too few Jewish households to yield a sufficient number of cases if a one-in-four sample were applied to them, the sampling ratio was increased in these areas.[24] In the later tabulation of the results of the survey, appropriate weights were applied to the data from each area to insure their proper representation in the combined results for Greater Providence. Applying these sampling ratios resulted in a total sample of 1,559 household units to be interviewed. Selection of the desired number of sample units within each area was then made through the use of Tippett's Table of Random Numbers,[25] thereby insuring that every household unit within the area had an equal chance of being included in the sample.

Name and address of every household selected for the sample was then copied onto the questionnaires. The interviewer thus had the entire sample selection process predetermined and was simply required to go to the address listed on the questionnaire and request an interview with any adult member of the household. In addition to the 1,559 household units selected in this way, the 44 units eventually identified as having been recent in-movers to the community were added to the basic sample in

[23] The seven areas are (1) Barrington, Bristol, East Providence, and Warren; (2) Cranston; (3) Warwick, East Greenwich, and West Warwick; (4) Pawtucket and its environs; (5) the South Side of Providence; (6) the North End of Providence; and (7) the East Side of Providence.

[24] In the Barrington area a sampling ratio of one out of every two Jewish households was used; for the North End of Providence the sampling ratio was one out of every three households. For each of the other five areas one out of every four households was sampled.

[25] *Tracts for Computers,* No. 15, Random Sampling Numbers, arranged by L.H.C. Tippett (London: Cambridge University Press, 1927).

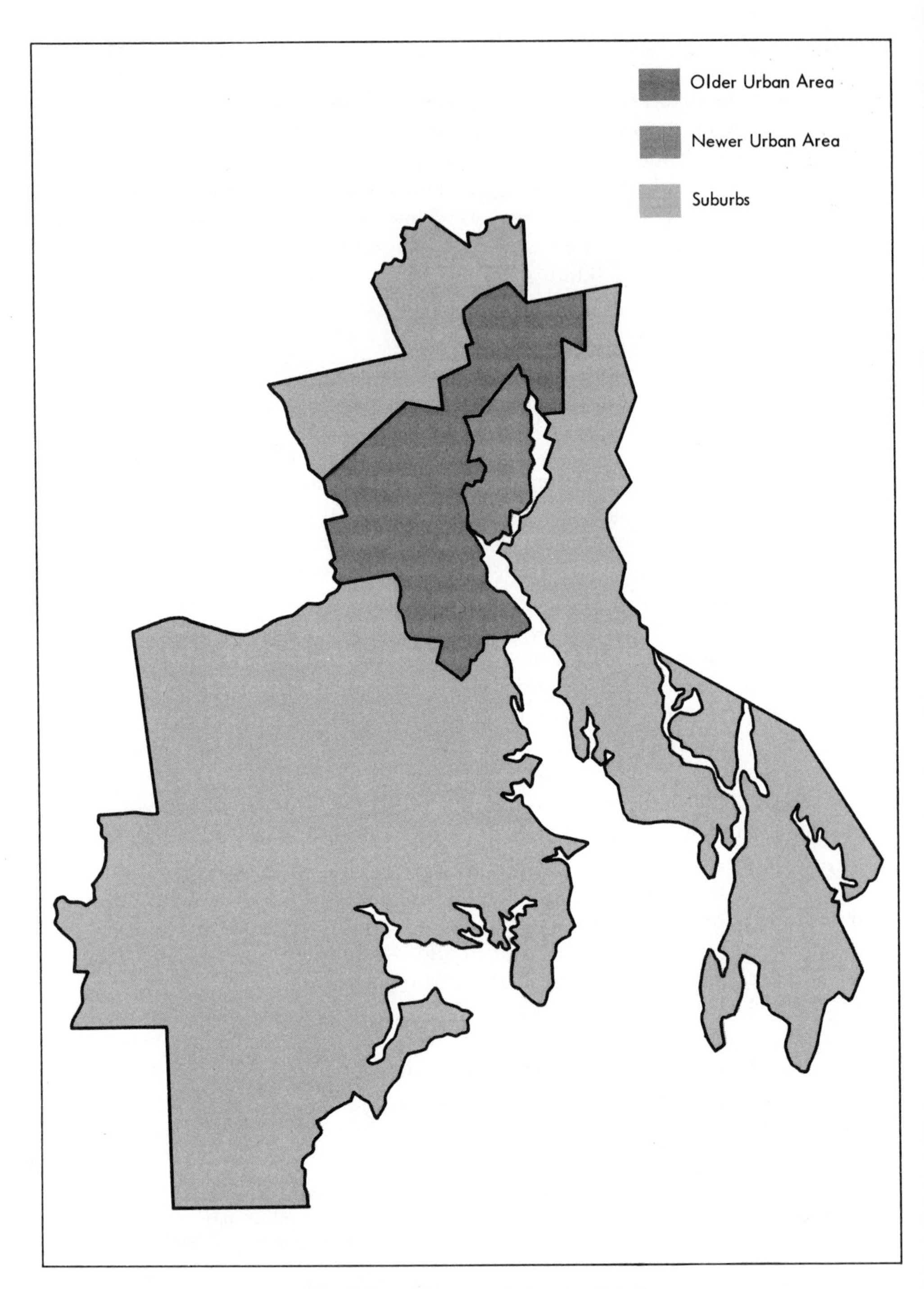

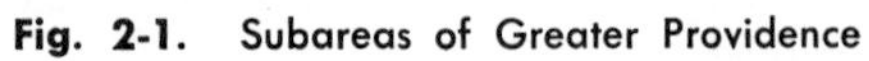

Fig. 2-1. Subareas of Greater Providence

order to give representation to new units not included in the master file. In all, therefore, 1,603 units constituted the basic sample.

In addition to containing questions covering the basic social, economic, and demographic characteristics of the population, the interview was designed to obtain information on a variety of factors indexing the extent of Jewish identification and religiosity of the individual households and their members. These included congregational affiliation, extent and type of Jewish education, synagogue attendance, membership in Jewish and non-Jewish organizations, intermarriage, and ritual practices. The survey was designed as a sample of households rather than of individuals; any adult member qualified as respondent on behalf of the entire household, if he considered himself able to furnish the factual data called for by the questions. Both because of this design, and because of the original goal of the study as a fact-finder for planning purposes, no attitude questions were included in the interview schedule. As a result, all of the measures of Jewish identification are restricted to behavioral factors and exclude subjective evaluations by the respondents.

Interviewing began on May 15, 1963, following an extensive publicity campaign which familiarized the community as a whole with the purposes of the survey and encouraged the fullest possible cooperation. Of the 1,603 households in the original sample, 47 proved to be ineligible for several reasons. The respondents in seven units maintained that no member of the household was Jewish; 28 of the households had moved out of the survey area; six had ceased to exist due to the death of the single person in the unit; and six more had been disbanded because the sole household member had moved to the Jewish Home for the Aged. In all, therefore, 1,556 units remained in the sample. Among these units, complete interviews were obtained from 1,420, giving an over-all response rate of 91.3 per cent. Only 79 units refused to cooperate with the interviewers, a refusal rate of only 5 per cent. It was impossible to contact 57 units, or 3.7 per cent of the total eligible sample units. Since the names and the addresses of the units which either refused to cooperate or which could not be contacted were known, a limited amount of information was obtained on these units from secondary sources, such as city directories, in order to ascertain whether they differed markedly from the units that cooperated with the interviewers. Comparison of the residential and occupational characteristics of the cooperating units and those from which no interviews were obtained did not point to any significant difference.

To account for those 136 family units from whom no interview had been obtained either because of refusal or no contact, 136 cases were chosen randomly from among the 1,420 cases for whom schedules were completed. The IBM cards of these cases were then duplicated and added to the 1,420, giving an inflated total of 1,556 records, or a number equal to the number of eligible households in the original sample. This procedure was carried out for each area individually so that the replacements came from within the same area as the refusals and the no-contacts.[26] Since earlier research had shown that the refusals and no-contacts did not differ significantly from those who cooperated, the inflated group of 1,556 households should be very similar to the original universe of eligible units with respect to the various social, demographic, and religious characteristics analyzed in this investigation.

In collecting information on household members, the interviewers were instructed to include all persons living in the household regardless of whether or not they were related to the family. This included live-in servants, boarders, and roomers. In line with Bureau of the Census procedure, children who were away at school or in the armed forces at the time of the survey were not included as members of the household. A separate series of questions, however, obtained limited information on them. Finally, the survey itself did not collect information on the institutionalized population, but data on the sex and age composition of the residents of the Jewish Home for the Aged were provided by its staff.

In the analysis of the survey results, these different segments of the population are handled as follows: (1) All non-Jewish domestic servants, boarders, and roomers are excluded from all enumerations. (2) The tabulations on the total size of the population include students living at school or college, persons in the armed forces, and residents of the Jewish Home for the Aged. Since information was not collected on the detailed socio-economic and Jewish characteristics of these persons, they are not included in any other analyses. The students, the military, and the institutionalized population totaled 647 persons. In all, the population survey identified 19,600 Jews living in Greater Providence.

The wealth of data available to this analysis made the selection of material to be included as tables particularly difficult. Of necessity, the number of tables and the amount of detail in particular tables had to be limited. Saliency of the information was the key criterion. At times, the reader will find that the text, in order to clarify given relations and to provide insights into the effect of other variables, makes use of data not presented in tabular form. Also, where the text analysis requires greater documentation, certain tables present more detail than others. Readers

[26] For a similar use of this procedure, see P.K. Whelpton and Clyde V. Kiser, "Social and Psychological Factors Affecting Fertility," *The Milbank Memorial Fund Quarterly*, XXIV, No. 1 (1946), 49-93.

who are interested in particular data which are not presented in tables are invited to request these of the authors.

To simplify the tabular presentations accompanying the text and to avoid repetition, the number of cases upon which the text tables are based are not given in those tables, but are presented in Appendix A. Since the survey was based on a sample of the Jewish population, the resulting statistics are subject to sampling variability. Appendix B discusses the sampling errors involved in using the data contained in the text tables.

CHAPTER THREE

The Changing Demographic Profile

Until recent decades, the character of the American Jewish community has generally been determined by the nature of Jewish immigration and the characteristics of the immigrants. At no time has this been more overwhelmingly true than during the first half of the twentieth century as a result of the huge influx of persons between 1880 and 1924. In 1880 the American Jewish population was estimated at a modest 250,000.[1] During the ensuing four and a half decades, approximately 2,300,000 immigrants swelled the ranks and completely altered the characteristics and distribution of the American Jewish population.

Immigrants in general are motivated to leave their native country by a desire to escape from poverty or persecution and by the opportunities available to them in their country of destination. Very often, they remain in the host country a number of years until they have been able to amass some money; then they return to their native land. Unlike other immigrants, however, Jews operated under a much greater compulsion to come to the United States. The Eastern European Jew fled pogroms, economic deprivation, political oppression, and generally restrictive government policies. These expulsive forces led him to break almost all of his ties with his native country and for the most part to immigrate with his immediate family. For him, return was almost unthinkable.

As a result, Jewish immigration to the United States was one of families to a much larger extent than was true of other immigrant groups. This difference is clearly reflected in both the age and sex composition of the total and Jewish immigration. In general, immigration is heavily selective of males in the 14-44 age group. Yet the Jewish immigrants had only a slightly larger proportion of males than females, and included a large number of children as well as persons above age 45.[2] For example, during the first decade of the twentieth century, when immigration was at a peak, at least two-thirds of the total immigrant group was male and

[1] Ruth Gay, *Jews in America* (New York: Basic Books, Inc., Publishers, 1965), p. 46.

[2] Samuel Joseph, *Jewish Immigration to the United States from 1881-1910* (New York: Columbia University Press, 1914), p. 178.

at times this proportion exceeded 70 per cent. In contrast, the proportion of males among Jews fluctuated between 50 and 60 per cent, going above 60 per cent in only two years, when the pogroms in Russia were unusually severe. During this same period children under 14 constituted almost one-quarter of the Jewish immigration, and persons 45 and over accounted for another 5 to 6 per cent.[3] Among the total immigrants, well over 80 per cent were 14 to 44 years of age. These differences persisted during the next two decades, until the legislation of the 1920's put an end to large-scale immigration. During the 1930's the age distributions of the Jewish and total immigrant groups were similar, with about two-thirds in the 14-44 age group.[4]

Another indication of the permanence with which Jews settled in the United States is the proportion of immigrants leaving the country. For Jews this was exceptionally low, ranging between only 0.7 and 17.0 per cent, annually, of the Jewish arrivals here between 1899 and 1943, and averaging only 4.6 per cent annually.[5] By comparison, the proportion for the total immigration ranged between 10 and 350 per cent from 1908 to 1943 and averaged 35 per cent annually. Such differences in intent to settle permanently assume great significance in terms of the immigrant groups' adjustment to their new environment.

Between 1899 and 1914 Jewish immigration averaged over 90,000 persons annually.[6] This huge inflow was virtually stopped during World War I, so that in the five years between 1915 and 1920 slightly less than 80,000 Jews are estimated to have entered the United States. With the cessation of hostilities, the pace accelerated sharply; and 1921 was a peak year with 119,036 Jewish immigrants constituting almost 15 per cent of the total immigration. Thereafter, the volume declined, dropping sharply after the restrictive legislation of 1924. Although an average of 10,000 to 11,000 Jews entered the United States annually between 1925 and 1930, this number decreased to only 4,000 per year in the next six years. The advent of Hitler and the anti-Semitic legislation of his regime led to a subsequent rise in Jewish immigration, so that between 1937 and 1943 an average of 21,000 Jews arrived in the United States annually, with a peak of 43,450 persons in 1939. By that time, close to four and a half million Jews were estimated to be living in the United States.

After World War II, under emergency legislation designed to facilitate the resettlement of displaced persons, several thousand displaced

[3] *Ibid.*, p. 177.

[4] C. Bezalel Sherman, *The Jew Within American Society* (Detroit: Wayne State University Press, 1965), p. 60.

[5] *American Jewish Yearbook* (Philadelphia: Jewish Publication Society of America, 1950), LI, 75.

[6] *American Jewish Yearbook* (1949), L, 753.

persons were admitted to the United States, including about 60,000 Jews. But in effect, immigration no longer played a significant role in the growth of either the Jewish community or the larger American community.

EMERGENCE OF THE THIRD GENERATION

In 1930 in the United States the 40 million white persons who were either foreign born or the children of foreign born or mixed parentage constituted 36 per cent of the total white population.[7] By 1960 the number decreased to 33 million, a 15 per cent reduction. At the same time the number of persons of native parentage rose 44 per cent. As a result, in 1960 the foreign born and their children constituted only 21 per cent of the total white population. Moreover, the foreign born were heavily concentrated among the older age groups: In 1960 almost three-fourths of the white foreign born were over 45 years of age, and one-third were 65 and over. In contrast, only one-quarter of the second generation and less than one-fourth of the third generation were over 45 years old, and only 8 per cent were aged 65 and over.

Because the growth of the Jewish population in the United States has been largely the result of immigration, generation status and the degree of assimilation have played crucial roles in the shaping of its communal life and in its position in the larger community. The cessation of large-scale Jewish immigration and the consequent decline in the proportion of foreign born are likely to alter significantly the nature of the Jewish community in America. Changing generation status, therefore, becomes a major variable in any evaluation of the structure of the American Jewish community. For purposes of the major part of this study four generation groups are used: (1) "First generation," which includes all foreign-born persons; (2) "Second generation," which includes all United States born persons of foreign-born parents; (3) "Mixed parentage," which includes all United States born persons of one foreign-born and one United States born parent; (4) "Third generation," which includes all United States born persons of United States born parents. Third generation thus encompasses third-, fourth-, and higher-generation persons.

As the later analysis will show, a high proportion of the foreign-born migrated to the United States as children and therefore spent most of

[7] U.S. Bureau of the Census, *U.S. Census of Population: 1960,* Vol. I, *Characteristics of the Population,* Part 1, United States Summary (Washington, D.C.: Government Printing Office, 1964), Table 66.

their formative years in America. One might question the validity of classifying these persons as first generation together with those who came at later ages. Ideally, one would want to distinguish, as did Warner, between the P_1 and P_2 generations. Immigrants who arrived as children might more properly be regarded as a group in themselves or even as second generation. Yet, without exact data on these individuals' family situations and social environment, no sound basis exists for assigning them to a different generation status. A separate category might still represent a fairly heterogeneous grouping. It would have the added disadvantage of creating smaller numbers for analytic purposes in both the original first-generation group and the newly established category. The assignment of these persons to the second generation would have similar limitations, since their home and social environments would not necessarily be similar to those of American-born children of foreign-born parents. In the absence of a sound basis for further delineation of generation, these youthful immigrants were classified in the immigrant, first-generation group.

Recognizing both the problem created by this classification scheme and the fact that age groupings in themselves might validly be used as the basis of delineating the different generations of the Jewish population, this investigation of generational changes in the demographic, social, economic, and religious characteristics of the Jewish population relies heavily on data cross-tabulated by both generation status and age. In this way, the effects of both nativity and age can be evaluated in order to gain insights into past and future changes on the community's structure.

An exception to this approach is employed in the analysis of fertility patterns, where only age is used as the index of generation. Similar results are obtained if nativity is employed. However, the desirability of examining the effect of other variables on fertility and the need to make more refined age breaks because age is such a crucial factor in fertility analysis argues in favor of relying upon age alone as an index of generation status for that segment of the analysis.

Throughout this analysis, generation status thus provides the key variable through which changes in the characteristics of the Jewish population and community are evaluated.[8]

In a number of Jewish communities studied before World War II, the foreign born constituted at least one-third of the population; some-

[8] W. Lloyd Warner and Leo Srole, *The Social System of American Ethnic Groups* (New Haven: Yale University Press, 1947), Chap. II. See also Bernard Lazerwitz and Louis Rowitz, "The Three-Generations Hypothesis," *American Journal of Sociology*, LXIX, No. 1 (1964), 529-38; Karl Mannheim, "The Problem of Generations," in *Essays on the Sociology of Knowledge* (London: Oxford University Press, 1952), p. 291.

times half of the community were first-generation persons.[9] This proportion has changed rapidly as the flow of new immigrants stopped and as the older immigrants died. By the 1950's about three-fourths of the Jewish population were native born. This trend has continued so that the proportion of foreign born constitutes a progressively smaller segment of the community.

Our data show that by the mid-1960's only 17 per cent of the Providence Jewish population were foreign born, and somewhat over 40 per cent were the children of foreign born or mixed parents; most striking and perhaps most significant, 40 per cent were native-born Jews of native-born parents. In short, an overwhelming majority of the Jews are American born, and a large proportion are actually third-generation Americans. In addition, over half of the third-generation group have at least one grandparent also born in the United States.

Further insight into the generation status of the population is gained by examination of the date of arrival in the United States of the foreign-born group (Table 3-1). Despite their foreign birth, the majority of these individuals have spent the greatest proportion of their lives in the United States. Over one-third have been in this country for over a half century and an additional third have been here for at least 25 years.

TABLE 3-1

FOREIGN BORN POPULATION, BY CURRENT AGE AND DATE OF ARRIVAL IN THE UNITED STATES*

	Current Age					
Date of Arrival	Under 15	15-24	25-44	45-64	65 and Over	Total
Before 1900	–	–	–	0.3	13.5	5.7
1900-1909	–	–	–	24.6	44.0	28.7
1910-1919	–	–	–	26.9	30.2	24.0
1920-1929	–	–	15.7	26.0	5.4	15.1
1930-1939	–	–	19.3	6.3	1.2	5.2
1940-1949	8.7	22.7	30.1	4.3	1.5	6.3
1950-1959	21.7	45.5	21.7	4.4	0.6	6.2
1960-1963	69.6	31.8	13.2	1.4	0.6	5.1
No Information	–	–	–	5.8	3.0	3.7
Total Per Cent	100.0	100.0	100.0	100.0	100.0	100.0

*The number of cases upon which this and succeeding tables are based may be found in Appendix A. Unless otherwise specified, the data in this and succeeding tables refer to the Providence, R.I., Jewish population in 1963.

[9] C. Bezalel Sherman, "Demographic and Social Aspects," in *The American Jew*, ed. Oscar I. Janowsky (Philadelphia: Jewish Publication Society of America, 1964), pp. 34-35.

Of all the foreign born, three out of every four entered the United States before 1930, and the great majority did so before 1920. The number who arrived in any particular decade after 1930 never exceeded 7 per cent of the total current foreign-born population, reflecting the relatively small flow of Jewish immigrants into the United States in recent decades and testifying to the dependence of the larger Jewish community on natural increase rather than on immigration for continued growth. As expected, date of entry into the United States is closely correlated with current age, over 80 per cent of the aged migrants having immigrated before 1920. The fact that 84 per cent of all the foreign born are over 45 years old and that most of these came to the United States as children and have lived here for three decades or more lends further weight to the evidence suggested by the over-all analysis of changing generation status of the population: The Jewish population is an increasingly American-bred and -raised population.

AGE AND SEX COMPOSITION

According to the Bureau of the Census sample survey in 1957, the Jewish population is on the average older than the total population in the United States. Of persons 14 years old and over, the median age of the Jewish respondents was 44.5 years compared to 40.4 years for the total population.[10] This same pattern of differentials characterizes Greater Providence. The 1960 federal census found the median age of the total population, including the under 14 group, to be 33.2 years; the median age of the Jewish population is 36.2. This difference does not stem from a large proportion of Jews in the very oldest age groups, but rather from a higher concentration in the age groups between 45 and 64. At both extremes of the age pyramid the proportion of Jews is less than the proportion of the total population, but this is particularly true of the under-5 age group. At the other end of the age hierarchy the difference is minimal, with 11 per cent of the total population and 10 per cent of the Jewish population being over 65. Such an age structure is not surprising in view of both the heavy immigration of the Jews at the beginning of the century (all of these immigrants would have been at least 40 years old by 1963) and the lower fertility rate characterizing the Jewish community.

The effects of immigration become quite clear when age is related

[10] U.S. Bureau of the Census, "Religion Reported by the Civilian Population of the United States, March, 1957," *Current Population Reports,* Series P-20, No. 79 (February 2, 1958).

TABLE 3-2

GENERATION STATUS* BY AGE

Age	First Generation	Second Generation	Mixed Parentage	Third Generation	Total Per Cent
		Distribution by Age			
Under 15	2.8	1.9	22.0	56.6	26.0
15-24	2.2	2.1	17.3	24.0	12.5
25-44	10.5	32.9	43.0	16.5	23.7
45-64	42.7	55.7	16.5	2.6	28.1
65 and Over	41.8	7.4	1.2	0.3	9.7
Total Per Cent	100.0	100.0	100.0	100.0	100.0
		Distribution by Generation			
Under 15	1.7	2.4	9.3	86.6	100.0
15-24	3.1	5.3	15.2	76.4	100.0
25-44	7.6	44.8	19.9	27.7	100.0
45-64	25.9	63.9	6.5	3.7	100.0
65 and Over	72.9	24.5	1.3	1.3	100.0
Total Per Cent	17.0	32.2	11.0	39.8	100.0

*In this and succeeding tables, "First Generation" refers to the foreign born; "Second Generation," to U.S.-born persons of foreign-born parents; "Mixed Parentage," to U.S.-born persons of one foreign-born and one U.S.-born parent; "Third Generation," to U.S.-born persons of U.S.-born parents. Third Generation thus refers to third, fourth, or higher-generation persons.

to generation status (Table 3-2). Of the foreign born, almost 85 per cent are 45 years of age or older; and of this group, half are 65 or over. The proportion of older persons diminishes steadily with distance from the immigrant generation: The second generation has three times as many persons in the 25-44 year group as does the first generation; and for those born in the United States of mixed parentage, the proportion in the younger age cohorts is even higher. Finally, over half of the third generation are under 15 years of age and, by contrast, less than 5 per cent are 45 or over (Figure 3-1).

As a result, the older segments of the population are, to a large extent, foreign born. Of the 65 and over age group, almost three-fourths are foreign born, and of those 45 to 64 years of age, one-quarter are first-generation Americans. These proportions change radically with decreasing age, so that a sizeable majority of middle-aged Jews are second generation and increasing proportions are third generation. Of the youngest age cohort, the overwhelming proportion (86.6 per cent) are third generation, and only a small fraction are foreign born.

Since the character and leadership of a community are generally determined by persons in the middle-aged segments of the population,

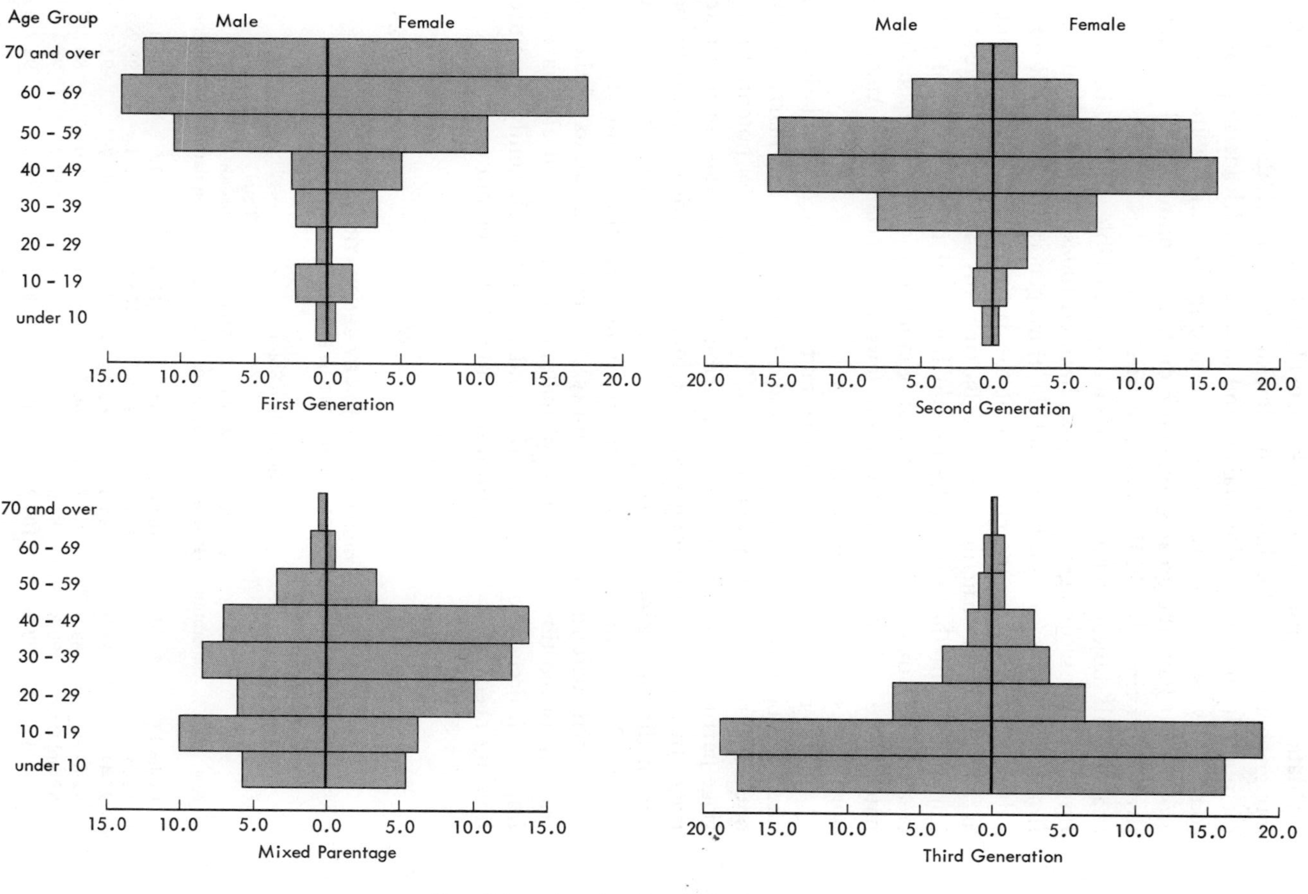

Fig. 3-1. **Age-Sex Pyramids, by Generation**

the data on age distribution make it evident that until recent years the foreign born have dominated the Jewish community; they have been the majority of the decision-makers and have supplied leadership for the community. Second-generation Jews are now in the majority in those age groups that have the greatest influence on the community, and in a relatively short time the third generation will be in the ascendency. As later analysis will show, generation status is a major variable affecting behavior. Insofar as the second-generation Jews have attitudes and values different from those of the foreign born, and the third generation have still other values, we can expect the character of the Jewish community to change as its generation structure changes. Barring any unforeseen large-scale immigration in the future, the foreign born will play a constantly decreasing role in the American Jewish community, which will be dominated more and more by native-born Jews and especially by American-born Jews of native-born parents.

The relative number of males and females in a population can affect its social structure in several ways. Opportunities to marry within one's own religious group depend on sufficient numbers of potential marriage partners. An imbalance may contribute to higher rates of intermarriage. In addition, assuming that most marriages involve persons living within the same general geographic area, any reduction in the marriage rate for lack of marriageable partners could affect the fertility rate and the growth patterns of the community. At the higher points of the age scale, disproportionate numbers of males or females could also have an impact on occupational composition and income level, family structure, housing needs, and the organizational life of the community.

TABLE 3-3

SEX RATIO* OF JEWISH POPULATION BY GENERATION AND AGE, AND OF TOTAL POPULATION BY AGE

	Generation Status					
Age	First Generation	Second Generation	Mixed Parentage	Third Generation	Total Jewish Population	Total Area Population
Under 15	–†	163.6	105.5	110.6	111.6	103.0
15-24	–	106.7	111.9	103.6	106.3	93.7
25-44	68.0	98.8	62.5	76.0	81.7	92.5
45-64	89.0	107.1	66.7	44.1	96.0	88.2
65 and Over	90.8	83.6	–	–	87.7	74.4
TOTAL	89.6	103.2	79.1	99.6	96.5	92.2

*Number of males per 100 females.
†In this and succeeding tables, use of – denotes less than 10 cases.

The number of males and females in the total Jewish population is quite similar, with a sex ratio of 96.5, indicating that for every 100 males in the population there are 97 females (Table 3-3). This contrasts with a ratio of only 92 for the total population. The ratio of Jewish males to females differs considerably, however, among the various age segments of the population. Following a pattern that is typical of the population at large, the youngest groups of the Jewish population contain more males than females, but the ratio tends to decline thereafter as sex selective mortality affects the males more than the females. This is seen in the data by age for the total Jewish population. The sex ratio drops from 111.6 for the age group under 15 to 87.7 for the oldest segment of the population, although the decline is irregular. The proportionately smaller number of males, as reflected in the low sex ratio, of the 25-44 age group and the larger number in the 45-64 age group reflects the disturbing effects of both internal and international migration on sex composition.

The somewhat low ratio of the 25-44 age group, 82 compared to 93 in the general population, probably stems from sex selective migration from the community to places of greater economic opportunity. The tendency of males to return from college to the community in which they were brought up is weakened in the face of the economic attractiveness of other places. As later discussion will suggest, younger Jews are increasingly taking up occupational careers that encourage, if not actually require them to be residentially mobile if they are to be economically successful. It is to be expected, therefore, that older, middle-sized communities may exercise population losses to areas that offer greater economic challenges and opportunity.

The higher sex ratios of the older groups in part represent the fact that persons now 45 and over did not tend to move away from the community when they were younger. In larger part, the higher sex ratios reflect the higher proportion of immigrants in these age categories. Although Jewish migration was heavily composed of families, it was still sufficiently sex selective to create a surplus of males over females. The sex selective nature of mortality served to diminish these sex imbalances so that among the foreign born 65 and over there are only 90 males per 100 females; but even such a ratio is comparatively high, and because the foreign born constitute almost three-fourths of the aged group, their characteristics largely determine the characteristics of the aged in general. With several exceptions, the sex ratios characterizing each of the native-born generation groups follow the general pattern of declining magnitude with increasing age. At specific age levels, however, considerable variation exists among generations, probably reflecting the differential cumulative effects of selective in- and out-migration.

RESIDENTIAL CLUSTERING AND DISPERSAL

The 19,500 Jews living in Greater Providence constitute 4 per cent of the area's total population, a percentage somewhat above that of the country as a whole; the 5.7 million Jews in the United States constitute 3 per cent of the total population.[11] This difference reflects the greater concentration of the Jewish population in the densely settled urbanized areas of the United States. Whereas 64 per cent of the total American population 14 years old and over live in urban areas, virtually the entire Jewish population (96.1 per cent) is urban.[12] The differential is even more extreme; only 37 per cent of the nation's population live in urbanized areas of 250,000 or more, compared to 87 per cent of the Jewish population.

The concentration of Jews within the Providence metropolitan area was not uniform, however (Table 3-4). Reflecting the historical tendency of Jews to concentrate in cities, just under 70 per cent of the Jews were living in the urban part of the metropolitan area. Such concentration in the urban centers exceeded the proportion of the total population living there—54 per cent. Moreover, within the urban center itself, the distribution of the Jewish population was concentrated in particular areas, with over one-half living in the newer settlement area—an area of comparatively high socio-economic status. In fact, to the consternation of the Jewish community, the sector is often referred to as the "gilded ghetto." Only 23 per cent of the total population live in the same area. The heavy concentration of Jews is reflected most clearly in the fact that in the four census tracts [13] in the heart of this area, Jews constitute from 35 to 50 per cent of the total of the respective tracts; of the remaining 102 census tracts encompassed by the study, Jews accounted for as much as 10 per cent of the total population in only 6 and were below 2 per cent in 83 tracts.

Some indication of the changes that have taken place in the size and distribution of the Jewish population is available through comparison of the results of the 1963 survey with an enumeration undertaken in 1951.[14]

11 Alvin Chenkin, "Jewish Population in the United States," *American Jewish Yearbook* (1965), LXVI, 148.

12 U.S. Bureau of the Census, "Religion Reported by the Civilian Population," p. 104.

13 Census tracts are small, homogeneous geographic units into which the Bureau of the Census has subdivided the metropolitan area.

14 *Group Work and Leisure Time Needs in the Jewish Community of Providence* (Providence, R.I.: General Jewish Committee of Providence, Inc., 1951), pp. 7-11.

TABLE 3-4

RESIDENTIAL DISTRIBUTION OF JEWISH AND TOTAL POPULATION OF GREATER PROVIDENCE, 1951* AND 1963†, AND COMPARATIVE RATES OF CHANGE

	Distribution by Area				Percentage Change 1951-63†		Jewish Population as Per Cent of Total Population	
	1951†		1963†					
Place of Residence	Jewish	Total	Jewish	Total	Jewish	Total	1951†	1963†
Total Urban	88.2	63.8	69.1	54.4	– 22.7	–12.6	5.3	4.7
Older Urban	45.0	39.2	18.5	31.6	– 59.5	–17.2	4.4	2.1
Newer Urban	43.2	24.6	50.6	22.8	+ 15.6	– 5.3	6.7	8.2
Suburban	11.8	36.2	30.9	45.6	+160.7	+29.3	1.2	2.5
Total Per Cent	100.0	100.0	100.0	100.0				
Total Number	19,698	517,167	19,457‡	530,484	– 1.2	+ 2.6	3.8	3.7

*1951 data for the Jewish population is based on *Group Work and Leisure Time Needs in the Jewish Community of Providence* (Providence: General Jewish Committee of Providence, Inc., 1951), pp. 7-11.
†1950 and 1960 for Total Population
‡Excludes 138 individuals resident in Jewish Home for the Aged

Although results of the earlier survey are much less exact, they do provide a useful benchmark for evaluating changes in size and distribution. According to that enumeration, the area had about 19,700 Jews, living in about 6,000 family units. This points to a very high degree of stability in the size of the Jewish population, with only a one per cent change during the twelve-year interval. During the ten years between 1950 and 1960, the total population of the same area grew by 2.6 per cent, also a relatively low rate of change. The experience of both the Jewish population and the total population has, therefore, been very similar, with a high degree of stability in total number. This close similarity, in contrast to the generally faster rate of growth of the non-Jewish population in the United States as a whole, probably stems from both the somewhat poorer economic conditions, making the area less attractive to in-migrants, and the highly urban character of the area.

Although the over-all size of both the Jewish and the total populations have not changed markedly, very sharp alterations have occurred in the distribution of the population within the metropolitan area. In 1951, 88 per cent of the Jewish population lived in the urban center; in contrast, only 69 per cent resided there in 1963. This compares to a decline in the proportion of the total population living within the central cities, from 64 per cent in 1950 to 54 per cent in 1960. The changes for the older urban area are even more striking, with the number of Jews living in this location declining by almost two-thirds between 1951 and 1963. As a result, only 18 per cent of the total Jewish population lived in the older sections by 1963 in contrast to 45 per cent in 1951. Within the central cities only the newer area grew in numbers and increased its proportion of Jewish residents, from 43 per cent in 1951 to 51 per cent in 1963. The old ghetto all but disappeared, although vestiges of it remained in the form of various Jewish institutions located in the older areas; the newer urban area now contained over half of the entire Jewish population and had located within its boundaries an increasing number and variety of Jewish religious, educational, and social institutions.

The changes for the suburban areas were even more dramatic. While still containing only a minority of the Jewish population, the suburbs had increased their proportion of the Jewish population from 12 per cent in 1951 to 31 per cent in 1963. Quite clearly, the Jews participated in the very strong suburban movement which characterized the metropolitan area during this period. In fact, they did so to a much greater extent than did the total population. Whereas the total central city population declined 13 per cent between 1950 and 1960, the Jewish population in the cities declined 23 per cent. At the same time, whereas the total population living in the suburbs increased only 29 per cent, the Jewish population more than doubled. Moreover, the suburban sector of the metropolitan area was characterized by quite different degrees of dispersal of the Jewish population than was the urban area. In the latter, 90 per cent of all Jews were concentrated within one-fourth of the census tracts; in the suburbs, the population of at least 40 per cent of the census tracts must be added together before encompassing 90 per cent of all suburban Jews, and these tracts tend to be more scattered over a larger geographic area. Further indicating the greater dispersal of the suburban Jewish population, in only one tract in the suburbs did Jews constitute as much as one-fourth of the total population and in none did they exceed 30 per cent. By contrast, Jews numbered more than one-fourth of the residents in four of the urban tracts (all in the newer urban area) and in fact exceeded 40 per cent in two. Over all, therefore, these data point to a general dispersal of the Jewish population over the metropolitan area, but also to a persistent concentration of a significant portion of this population within the newer area of urban settlement. Of the two forces, however, the much faster rate at which the suburbs have developed and the deconcentration of the Jewish population within the suburbs suggest the general tendency for the old ghetto areas to disappear, in part to be replaced by a new and higher status area, but in even larger measure to be replaced by a more general residential integration of the Jewish community into the larger population of the metropolitan area. Residential clustering of the Jewish population has been an important variable in helping to perpetuate traits, values, and institutions which might otherwise disappear. The greater residential dispersal of the Jews may therefore become a critical factor in explaining the changing extent and character of their ties to Judaism.

LEAVING THE OLD GHETTO

Wide differences in age distribution characterize the older urban, the newer urban, and the suburban segments of the metropolitan area, reflecting the history of settlement patterns within these areas and the corresponding differences in their family structures. The suburban movement has, to a very great extent, been selective of persons in the early stages of family formation; three-fourths of the persons living in the suburbs are under 45 years of age. By contrast, over half of those living in the older urban sections are 45 or over. The differences in age structure are perhaps illustrated best by the continuous and sharp decline in the median ages of the population living in the three areas, going from 46.1 years in the older urban area to 35.7 for the newer urban area to only 28.4 for the suburbs.

Because the foreign born are concentrated very heavily among the aged and the third-generation group consists disproportionately of younger individuals, and because of the corresponding relationship between place of residence and age, the various generations are characterized by different patterns of settlement (Table 3-5). These differences again reflect the history of settlement. In the older urban area, which was the first to be settled by Jews, the foreign born still constitute over one-third of the population. Yet surprisingly almost one-fourth of the residents of this section are third-generation Americans. These are the young children of second-generation families who have remained loyal to the older residential areas. In the newer urban areas, only 15 per cent are foreign born, but 40 per cent are third generation. The suburbs are the most recently settled areas, and here almost half of the population are third generation, with only 10 per cent foreign born. Quite clearly then, as one moves from the older urban areas to the outlying suburbs, the proportion of foreign born in the population decreases considerably and the proportion of

TABLE 3-5

RESIDENTIAL DISTRIBUTION, BY GENERATION AND AGE

Residence and Age	First Generation	Second Generation	Mixed Parentage	Third Generation	Total Per Cent
All Ages					
Older Urban	34.6	31.8	9.0	24.6	100.0
Newer Urban	15.1	34.8	10.1	40.0	100.0
Suburban	10.0	28.8	13.4	47.8	100.0
Under 15 Age Group					
Older Urban	4.5	3.0	12.7	79.8	100.0
Newer Urban	2.6	2.6	5.2	89.6	100.0
Suburban	0.3	2.0	12.5	85.2	100.0
15-24 Age Group					
Older Urban	6.1	7.0	14.9	72.0	100.0
Newer Urban	3.5	4.5	13.8	78.2	100.0
Suburban	0.0	5.7	18.4	75.9	100.0
25-44 Age Group					
Older Urban	10.4	56.0	19.2	14.4	100.0
Newer Urban	7.1	44.1	20.0	28.8	100.0
Suburban	7.4	42.4	20.0	30.2	100.0
45-64 Age Group					
Older Urban	38.8	53.1	6.2	1.9	100.0
Newer Urban	21.1	68.3	7.3	3.3	100.0
Suburban	23.9	64.7	4.9	6.5	100.0
65 and Over Age Group					
Older Urban	83.7	15.8	0.5	0.0	100.0
Newer Urban	63.1	32.5	2.2	2.2	100.0
Suburban	77.5	20.4	0.0	2.1	100.0

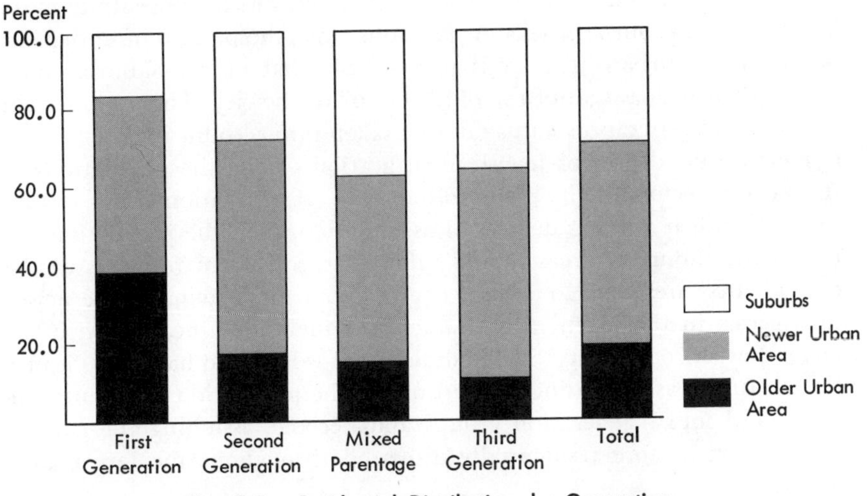

Fig. 3-2. Residential Distribution, by Generation

third-generation Americans undergoes a sharp rise. As a result of this pattern, over one-third of all foreign born live in the older urban section compared to only 11 per cent of all third-generation persons; only 18 per cent of the foreign born live in the suburbs compared to relatively twice as many third-generation individuals (Figure 3-2).

The attractiveness of the suburbs to third-generation persons is not entirely a function of their concentration in the younger age cohorts. Differentials by generation persist within both younger and older categories of the population. For example, in the 25-44 age range 7 per cent of the persons living in the suburbs are foreign born, compared to 10 per cent of those in the older sections of the city; the differences are much sharper for third-generation Americans: 30 per cent of the suburban residents are third generation, compared to only 14 per cent of those who still live in the older section of the city. Although the magnitude of the differences varies, the same pattern holds for the 45 to 64 year group. Among those in this age category living in the older section of the city, 39 per cent are foreign born and only 2 per cent are third generation; in contrast, of those in the suburbs only 24 per cent are foreign born, but 7 per cent are third-generation Americans.

These data suggest that no section is completely homogeneous with respect to either age or generation status. They do indicate that the selective movement of younger persons to the suburbs helps to account for the higher proportion of third-generation Americans living there. Yet, regardless of age, the foreign born tend to be residents of the older sections of the city and the third-generation Americans to concentrate more heavily in the suburban areas. At the same time, the pattern of settlement of the newer urban area tends to resemble that of the suburbs more closely than it does that of the old "ghetto" of the city. These residential variations in generation status must be taken into account in any attempt to measure the degree of Jewish identification among the populations in the various sectors of the metropolitan area. If generation status has associated with it varying degrees of assimilation, then the population living in the suburban areas should differ markedly from residents of the old "ghetto" area and, to a lesser degree, from those living in the newer urban area in the extent and character of their identification with the larger Jewish community. Such a differential would also have significance for the future as increasing proportions of the population move into the third- and fourth-generation groups and become, assuming the current trends persist, more residentially dispersed throughout the larger community.

STABILITY AND MOBILITY

Several questions focusing on the mobility experience and intentions of the respondents elicited indications of the relative stability of the various residential areas. Mobility information was obtained through a question on the place of residence prior to the current residence and the year of movement into the present residence; also included were questions on whether the household had any intentions of moving within the next five years, and, if so, to what destination.

Date of arrival at current address is useful as an index of the residential stability of the population. At the same time, it indirectly suggests the relative period of settlement in a particular area. The recency of the suburbanization movement among the Jews is illustrated by the fact that almost two-thirds of the Jewish population living in the suburbs moved into their present place of residence within the last ten years (Table 3-6). An additional 12 per cent, almost all children, were born in the suburbs. Only one in four persons can therefore claim stability of residence in the suburbs as measured by residence in the same house for at least ten years.

The data for the older area of the central city present quite a contrasting picture. Only 40 per cent of this population had moved into their present residence within the last ten years, and exactly half of the population reported living within the same house for ten years or more. Further reflecting the older age of this population, only 9 per cent reported having been born in the house in which they were living, and most of these were the children of second-generation persons. The residential

TABLE 3-6

YEAR OF MOVEMENT TO CURRENT ADDRESS, BY PLACE OF RESIDENCE AND GENERATION

Generation and Current Residence	Born Here	Before 1945	Year of Movement 1945-1954	1955-1959	1960-1963	No Information	Total Per Cent
All Areas							
First Generation	0.0	23.1	30.9	18.3	27.1	0.6	100.0
Second Generation	1.5	13.6	34.9	27.8	21.6	0.7	100.0
Mixed Parentage	9.9	4.5	27.2	26.8	31.5	0.0	100.0
Third Generation	21.6	1.1	19.6	26.8	30.8	0.2	100.0
TOTAL	10.1	9.2	27.3	25.6	27.3	0.5	100.0
Older Urban							
First Generation	0.0	30.3	30.3	17.0	21.3	1.0	100.0
Second Generation	2.5	24.7	34.5	20.0	17.1	1.1	100.0
Mixed Parentage	15.4	6.4	30.8	17.9	29.5	0.0	100.0
Third Generation	28.8	1.9	24.7	19.5	25.1	0.0	100.0
TOTAL	9.2	19.5	30.3	18.6	21.7	0.7	100.0
Newer Urban							
First Generation	0.0	22.9	30.2	16.9	29.4	0.6	100.0
Second Generation	1.3	14.7	35.5	26.9	21.2	0.4	100.0
Mixed Parentage	4.2	6.8	32.2	23.3	33.5	0.0	100.0
Third Generation	20.6	1.5	20.9	27.8	29.3	0.0	100.0
TOTAL	9.1	9.7	28.6	25.4	26.9	0.3	100.0
Suburban							
First Generation	0.0	8.9	33.6	24.0	33.6	0.0	100.0
Second Generation	1.0	4.3	33.8	34.5	25.2	1.2	100.0
Mixed Parentage	14.5	1.0	20.0	34.5	30.0	0.0	100.0
Third Generation	20.7	0.3	16.3	27.6	34.7	0.4	100.0
TOTAL	12.1	2.4	23.5	30.0	31.4	0.6	100.0

stability of the newer urban area falls in between the older urban and the suburban, with 52 per cent of its population having moved into their current residence within the last ten years and almost 40 per cent reporting stability for as long as ten years.

Because of their greater concentration in the older age groups, the foreign born display generally greater stability than do the second and third generation. Whereas only 45 per cent of the former have moved within the last ten years, this is true of 57 per cent of the third-generation group. The greater stability of the foreign born also characterizes specific age levels, although the differences are considerably narrower. For example, within the 45-64 age group, 49 per cent of the foreign born and 53 per cent of the third-generation persons moved within the last ten years.

Further insight into the relation between generation status and residence can be obtained by comparison of the current place of residence with the previous place (Table 3-7). Such a comparison must recognize

TABLE 3-7

PREVIOUS RESIDENCE, BY CURRENT RESIDENCE AND GENERATION

	Previous Residence							
Generation and Current Residence	Older Urban	Newer Urban	Suburbs	Balance of State	Other U.S. and Foreign	Resident Since Birth	No Information	Total Per Cent
All Areas								
First Generation	50.4	31.1	5.3	0.9	9.3	0.0	3.0	100.0
Second Generation	39.2	40.3	9.8	0.9	7.4	1.2	1.2	100.0
Mixed Parentage	30.4	34.7	12.5	1.6	11.7	9.2	0.0	100.0
Third Generation	24.1	32.4	12.2	1.6	8.6	20.8	0.3	100.0
TOTAL	34.3	34.8	10.3	1.3	8.7	9.6	1.1	100.0
Older Urban								
First Generation	78.9	7.0	0.3	0.0	9.1	0.0	4.7	100.0
Second Generation	79.9	6.6	3.3	0.0	6.2	1.8	2.2	100.0
Mixed Parentage	71.8	3.8	3.8	1.3	3.8	15.4	0.0	100.0
Third Generation	61.7	2.3	3.7	0.5	7.0	24.8	0.0	100.0
TOTAL	74.7	5.4	2.5	0.2	7.1	8.0	2.3	100.0
Newer Urban								
First Generation	26.6	59.5	0.0	1.7	9.6	0.0	2.5	100.0
Second Generation	21.3	64.5	3.8	1.5	6.6	1.1	1.2	100.0
Mixed Parentage	11.9	63.6	5.1	2.1	13.1	4.2	0.0	100.0
Third Generation	9.8	52.9	5.4	2.6	8.4	20.7	0.2	100.0
TOTAL	16.6	58.8	4.1	2.0	8.6	9.0	1.0	100.0
Suburbs								
First Generation	50.0	11.6	28.1	0.7	8.9	0.0	0.7	100.0
Second Generation	47.6	15.0	25.7	0.5	9.8	1.0	0.5	100.0
Mixed Parentage	36.2	12.6	24.6	1.0	13.1	12.6	0.0	100.0
Third Generation	31.7	14.1	24.0	0.7	9.3	19.8	0.4	100.0
TOTAL	38.9	13.8	24.9	0.7	9.9	11.4	0.5	100.0

that a significant proportion of the population moves within the same general area. Thus, among those currently living in the older urban section, three out of four reported their previous residence as also having been within this same area of the central city. Similarly, of those in the newer urban sector, almost 60 per cent had moved into their current place of residence from another house within the newer area. It was only in the suburbs that a minority of the population, one out of four persons, reported their previous residence as also being in the same area.

The statistics point clearly to the direction of population flow: only a very small minority—8 per cent—of the persons in the older urban sections made their most recent move there from either the newer section of the central cities or from the suburbs. By contrast, 17 per cent of the persons moving to the newer section of the central city had their previous residence in the older urban section, and a small number, 4 per cent, in the suburbs. Since the newer urban sector represents the higher prestige residence for the metropolitan area, it is an avowed goal of a number of families currently living in the suburbs, as soon as they become sufficiently mobile, socially and economically, to warrant such a move. Yet, as later analysis will show, only a small proportion have any definite plans to move there in the near future. Of the suburban population, 39 per cent had moved to the suburbs directly from the older urban section and an additional 14 per cent from the newer sector of the city. As in all mobility, there are counter flows. Part of the movement from the newer section of the city to the suburbs stems from the tenements and older housing on the fringe of the new section; some stems from persons who, wishing to own their own home or to have more area around their house, are able to do so more economically in the suburbs.

Reflecting the heavy concentration of foreign born in the older urban section, a higher proportion of the foreign born currently living in the newer urban and suburban sections trace their previous residence to the older urban section than do the second- and third-generation persons. In fact, the proportion of individuals currently living in the newer urban section and the suburbs whose previous residence was in the older urban section varies directly with generation status, declining from 27 per cent of the foreign born to only 10 per cent of the third generation in the newer urban section and from 50 per cent of the foreign born to 32 per cent of the third generation in the suburbs. However, these differentials are largely accounted for by the much higher proportion of the third generation compared to the second generation who are actually born in their current place of residence. Over all, therefore, these data suggest that the old ghetto area persists mainly because a sufficient number of its current residents remain there; it draws very little reinforce-

TABLE 3-8

NET POPULATION MOVEMENT WITHIN THE METROPOLITAN AREA, BASED ON COMPARISON OF CURRENT AND PREVIOUS ADDRESS OF RESIDENCE

	Current Address			
Previous Residence	Older Urban	Newer Urban	Suburban	Total
Older Urban	–	+1,375	+2,198	+3,573
Newer Urban	–1,375	–	+ 464	- 911
Suburban	–2,198	- 464	–	–2,662
TOTAL	–3,573	+ 911	+2,662	–

ment from persons moving in from outside the area. On the other hand, the newer urban section and particularly the suburbs have drawn quite heavily upon the original areas of settlement for their residents, so that the older urban section has contributed both to the development of the newer area of concentration within the central city and to the dispersal of population among the suburban communities.

The net effect of this population redistribution within the metropolitan area is probably best indicated by the statistics on net movement (Table 3-8). A comparison of current place of residence with previous place of residence indicates that the older urban section lost 3,573 persons. In this general exchange, the older urban sections lost 1,375 persons to the newer part of the city but almost 2,200 to the suburbs. Whereas the newer section gained in its exchange with the older section of the central city, it lost 464 persons to the suburbs. Finally, the suburbs themselves gained in their exchange with both other sectors of the metropolitan area. Quite clearly, then, the older area of residence has undergone a very sharp decline, and the suburbs have benefitted most.

Fifteen per cent of the individuals studied were members of households that had definite plans to move within a five-year period (Table 3-9). Two factors reflect the trend toward increasing depopulation of the older areas of settlement. Somewhat more of those living in the older sections expressed an intent to move compared to those in the newer urban area and in the suburbs. The differences, however, extended beyond these general figures to the proposed destination of the moves. It must be emphasized here that although a relatively large number of persons expressed an intent to move, a majority actually did not know their exact destination. Among those living in the older urban areas, the largest number designating a specific destination indicated the newer urban area as their goal. These individuals accounted for 17 per cent of the total, compared to only 9 per cent who intended to move to the suburbs and even fewer, 5 per cent, who intended to seek a home within the older area of the city. For those in the newer section, the strong attractiveness of this section led 33 per cent of the total to plan a move within the area itself and only 3 per cent to seek a home in the suburbs. Well below one per cent of those living in the newer urban section indicated the older area of the city as the destination of their proposed move. Evidently, the suburbs also hold a very strong attractiveness for the persons already living within them; almost one-quarter of the suburban units expressing an intent to move planned to seek another home within the suburbs. Only 3 per cent expressed an intent to move to the newer section of the central city, and again less than one per cent indicated their intent to move to the older area of settlement.

Within each of the three subareas, there tended to be minimal

TABLE 3-9

PER CENT OF PERSONS PLANNING TO MOVE WITHIN FIVE YEARS AND PER CENT REPORTING PROPOSED DESTINATION, BY CURRENT RESIDENCE AND GENERATION

Generation and Current Residence	Per Cent of Persons Having Definite Plans to Move Within 5 Years	Per Cent Reporting Destination of Planned Move As:				
		Older Urban	Newer Urban	Suburbs	Balance of State	Other U.S. and Foreign
All Areas						
First Generation	14.5	2.8	25.2	4.2	0.0	7.0
Second Generation	11.3	1.7	17.1	10.4	0.6	5.1
Mixed Parentage	15.8	1.3	17.9	12.8	1.9	16.7
Third Generation	17.5	1.2	21.4	12.4	2.1	4.5
TOTAL	14.8	1.6	20.3	10.3	1.3	6.5
Older Urban						
First Generation	16.0	5.7	19.9	2.1	0.0	7.8
Second Generation	13.4	5.9	16.3	10.4	0.0	4.4
Mixed Parentage	16.6	2.9	11.4	5.7	0.0	25.7
Third Generation	24.1	3.3	16.4	15.6	0.8	4.9
TOTAL	17.2	4.8	16.9	8.7	0.2	7.3
Newer Urban						
First Generation	15.0	0.0	41.0	1.9	0.0	4.8
Second Generation	10.4	0.0	25.8	3.3	1.4	3.3
Mixed Parentage	19.9	1.4	33.3	4.2	4.2	12.5
Third Generation	18.3	0.3	35.9	3.2	3.2	3.8
TOTAL	15.3	0.3	33.1	3.1	2.3	5.1
Suburbs						
First Generation	10.3	0.0	2.5	17.5	0.0	10.0
Second Generation	11.7	0.0	3.2	22.4	0.0	8.8
Mixed Parentage	10.5	0.0	0.0	30.6	0.0	16.3
Third Generation	14.4	1.3	4.0	23.5	1.3	5.3
TOTAL	12.6	0.7	3.2	23.3	0.7	7.9

variation by generation status in the planned destination of those units intending to move. In the older section, slightly more of the foreign born expressed an intent to move within the area, but also more indicated their intention to move to the newer section of the city; considerably fewer pointed to the suburbs as their desired goal. This is largely a function of the age composition of the foreign born. The same pattern, particularly the desire to remain within the newer area of settlement, characterized the foreign born already living in the newer urban area. Within their limitations, these data suggest the continued depopulation of the older area of the city and the increased growth of the newer urban section and the suburbs as areas of residence for the Jewish population of the metropolitan area. In this sense, both processes of concentration in the newer area and decentralization in the suburban area seem likely to continue.

To evaluate whether the pattern of population mobility has changed, those who moved into their current place of residence since 1955 (the recent movers) have been compared with those who did so before 1955 (the early movers). Individuals who were born in the place where they are now living have been omitted. Some interesting changes emerge. Among the early movers living in the older section of the city, 82 per cent also had their previous residence in that section, whereas among those living in the newer urban area, only 27 per cent had moved there from the older urban section; among the early movers living in the suburbs, 56 per cent had come directly from the older area of the city. Among the more recent movers, in the older urban area a high proportion continued to be persons whose previous residence had also been in the older urban section, 80 per cent; but for the newer urban areas and for the suburbs, the proportion reporting their previous residence as the older area declined markedly, to 11 per cent and 39 per cent respectively. The decline in the suburbs is at least partly attributable to the fact that as the areas built up and the number of persons living there increased, more persons were moving about within the suburbs themselves; almost 32 per cent of the new movers within the suburbs had had their previous residence within the suburban part of the metropolitan area. Part of the decline, however, also stems from a higher proportion of persons moving to both the newer urban areas and to the suburbs from outside the metropolitan area. This was also true of movement to the older section of the city, so that the older section was actually attracting more persons from outside than from within the metropolitan area. The older section may thus serve for some as a kind of funnel through which they eventually move into the newer urban or suburban places of residence.

Minimal differences characterize the different generation groups of the older urban population, regardless of whether they are early or recent migrants. The only noteworthy variation is that among early movers a higher proportion of foreign-born than third-generation persons had moved to the older area of settlement from the newer area. Reflecting the higher concentration of foreign born in the older urban sections, among both the early and the recent movers to the newer urban sections a considerably higher proportion of the foreign born reported previous residence in the old ghetto areas. In fact, among the recent migrants this ratio was two to one, comparing the foreign born and the third-generation group. No such differential characterized the early movers to the suburbs. This possibly reflects the relatively insignificant flow of foreign born to the suburbs during the early development of these areas. Among the more recent movers, proportionately more foreign born in the suburbs had their previous residence in the older section of the city compared to the third-generation group, more of whom came either from the newer section, from other places in the suburbs, or from outside the metropolitan area.

These data therefore point to increased mobility within the suburban areas and a lower proportion of individuals moving from the older urban sections. Since the older areas of settlement are already heavily depopulated, they have relatively fewer individuals available as a source of migrants to either the suburbs or the newer areas of settlement. As the general exodus from the old areas of settlement declines, the rate of change in both the newer area and the suburbs may stabilize. A considerable amount of movement may still occur within the respective areas. No significant exchange between them seems likely within the foreseeable future. If, however, the experience of other metropolitan areas is at all typical, it may very well be that within a generation or two the area now labeled as "newer" will provide a major source of mobility to either a third area of still newer settlement or to the suburbs, or even to redeveloped sections of what now constitute deteriorated areas of the central cities.

In sum, evaluation of both past and future mobility patterns as indicated by expressed intent to move points to two simultaneous developments with respect to the distribution of the Jewish population: A significant proportion of Jews will continue to be concentrated in the newer urban section of the central cities. At the same time, greater decentralization of the total Jewish population within the metropolitan area will take place, as evidenced by the growth of the suburban sector. Decentralization through suburbanization is accentuated by the relatively greater dispersal of Jews within the suburbs. Jewish migrants to the suburbs have taken up residence in a number of different towns; and within the towns there are no single points of concentration, but rather several such points coupled with more general dispersion.

Residential clustering in either old or new ghetto areas has been a factor in the continued vitality of the Jewish community. The continued maintenance of a significant geographic concentration of Jewish population and institutions in the central cities, and to lesser degrees in the various suburban communities, may therefore be indicative of the positive value placed on Jewish identity by considerable portions of the Jewish population. At the same time, the dispersal of a relatively large number of Jews among the suburban sectors of the metropolitan area must have an impact on the future commitment of these individuals to the Jewish community. To some degree they have created their own institutions; to some degree they remain dependent on those of the central cities. Yet, as later analysis will show, the suburban Jews are generally characterized by weaker ties to Judaism. Their exodus from the Jewish residential centers of the city to more integrated areas may reflect an attempt to escape a Jewish environment; or, conversely, movement to places of lower Jewish density (both residential and institutional) may in itself result in lowered levels of practice and identity regardless of the motive for movement. Such cause-and-effect evaluations would require longitudinal information. Within the limits of a cross-sectional study such as this, one can only emphasize the crucial role that residence *per se,* in addition to generation status, may play in the future vitality of the American Jewish community.

One other aspect of the redistribution process merits brief discussion. The analysis has shown that with the general exodus from the older, original areas of residence about finished, the greater part of the mobility will be the continual shift of population within the newer urban area and within the suburbs. Such repeated mobility, even though of restricted distance, could have the effect of weakening ties to the institutional structure of the community. To the extent that such ties are expressed through membership in temples, enrollment of children in educational programs, and participation in local organizations, repeated movement may either disrupt such patterns of participation or weaken the loyalties they generate. More seriously, they may result in the failure of individual families to identify themselves with any organized life in the local community. The chances that persons who move frequently will be fully integrated into the social life of a community are greatly restricted; as a result, they probably remain marginal persons. Studies have demonstrated that when migrants first enter a new community, they are much less active in the formal structure than are long-time residents. With time, their participation rate increases. The adjustment has been shown, however, to take at least five years; and in some types of behavior the migrants never attain the same level of participation as persons who grew up in the community.[15]

This evaluation of mobility patterns has not focused extensively on movement into and out of the metropolitan area from other parts of the country. Since the data on which this analysis is based were obtained through a survey of the people resident in the area, those households that have moved away have necessarily been excluded. Yet, the very low rate of growth of the Jewish population and the heavy out-migration which has characterized the general population [16] both suggest that the Jewish community has experienced considerable out-migration. Our knowledge of mobility patterns in the United States would also lead us to expect that a considerable proportion of out-migrants are persons who had only recently moved into the community.[17] Particularly as the proportion of Jews holding positions as executives and professionals increases, the rate of population mobility is likely to increase. Higher than average mobility rates have always characterized professionals because of the more limited demand for their talents in particular localities. Moreover, in recent years many national firms have adopted as company policy the repeated relocation of their executives and professionals among different branches of their firms. The participation of such "national" migrants in local organizations and social life can be expected to be even more marginal than that of those whose mobility is more local in character. To the extent that such national mobility will characterize the Jewish population to an ever greater degree, it will contribute an important new dimension to the problem of Jewish identification and participation in Jewish communal life.

[15] Basil G. Zimmer, "Participation of Migrants in Urban Structures," *American Sociological Review,* XX, No. 2 (1955), 218-24.

[16] Sidney Goldstein and Kurt B. Mayer, *Metropolitanization and Population Change in Rhode Island,* State Planning Section Publication No. 3 (Providence, R.I.: Rhode Island Development Council, 1962).

[17] Sidney Goldstein, *Patterns of Mobility, 1910-1950* (Philadelphia: University of Pennsylvania Press, 1958), pp. 196-214.

CHAPTER FOUR

The Changing Social-Class Profile

Ethnicity and religious identification are not the sole, or necessarily the major, dimensions in terms of which American society is structured. Differences in educational achievement, occupation, and income also provide a basis for categorizing the population. The resulting social-class strata are each composed of individuals having approximately equal economic interests and opportunities, and similar socio-cultural values which are of primary importance in shaping life styles.[1] Thus, as Milton Gordon has pointed out,[2] American society is "criss-crossed" by at least two sets of stratification structures—one based on social status, economic power, and political power differences regardless of ethnic background, and the other on a set of status and power relationships based precisely on race, national origin, and religion. Vertical population divisions along racial, ethnic, and religious lines are differentiated horizontally by a series of strata or classes based upon the social values attached to occupation, education, place of residence, and association membership. The over-all status system therefore emerges from the complex interplay of a host of factors revolving about the ethnic and socio-economic characteristics of the population. In fact, Gordon has proposed that the subsociety created by the intersection of the vertical stratification of ethnicity with the horizontal stratification of social class be referred to as the "ethclass."

The relevance of this emphasis on the interplay of ethnic and class factors lies in the recognition that the two sets of factors may operate differently in affecting group identity, social participation, and cultural behavior. Gordon hypothesizes, for example, that social class is more decisive than ethnic group membership in regard to cultural behavior, but that the ethclass largely determines social participation in primary groups; that is, individuals tend to restrict their primary relationships to other persons belonging to their own social class segment of their own ethnic group. In general, the ethnic group is the locus of a sense of his-

[1]Kurt B. Mayer, *Class and Society* (Garden City, N.Y.: Doubleday & Company, Inc., 1955).

[2]*Assimilation in American Life* (New York: Oxford University Press, 1964), pp. 47-54.

torical identification, but the ethclass is the locus of a sense of participational identification.[3]

Since this study of the Jewish population obtained information on both generation status and such class variables as occupation, education, and home ownership, some of the relationships suggested by Gordon can be explored. For example, what is the interplay of generation and class in affecting cultural behavior with respect to religious practice, or with respect to such a "purely" demographic process as fertility? How do class and generation status interact to affect synagogue membership and participation in Jewish and non-Jewish organizations? Before turning to such considerations, attention must focus on the class structure of the Jewish population and the way in which it is related to generation status.

A number of Jewish community studies as well as various national public-opinion surveys which included information on the Jewish population [4] have clearly documented that Jews are disproportionately concentrated in the upper ranks of the class structure, especially in the strata represented by the managers and proprietors of retail, wholesale, and manufacturing establishments. The extent of such concentration varies, however, by type of community, tending to be greater in medium-sized and small communities compared to the very large metropolitan centers such as New York, where a considerable number of Jews are located in the manual-labor sector of the economy.[5]

Strong incentives to take advantage of the supposed equal opportunities available in America characterized the value system of the great majority of Jews migrating to the United States. Yet, many lacked either the secular education, language facility, or technical skills necessary to move far up the occupational scale; others encountered barriers to either educational or occupational achievement or both because of the very fact that they were immigrants and too "foreign" seeming, or simply because they were Jewish. For many, the efforts to move ahead socially and economically had to be transferred to children as a result of the insurmountable barriers the immigrants themselves faced. In particular, Jews came to recognize that the amount of formal secular education an individual receives is a major determinant of the occupations open to him, the income he will eventually receive, and the opportunities he will have to realize desired values and to enhance life chances. Yet, because of in-

[3] *Assimilation in American Life,* p. 53.

[4] See, for example, Charles F. Westoff, *A Population Survey* (Cherry Hill, N.J.: Jewish Federation of Camden County, 1964), pp. 43-53; also, Alvin Chenkin, "Jewish Population in the United States, 1962," in *American Jewish Yearbook* (Philadelphia: Jewish Publication Society of America, 1963), LXIV, 65-68.

[5] Nathan Glazer and Daniel P. Moynihan, *Beyond the Melting Pot* (Cambridge, Mass.: The M.I.T. Press, 1963), p. 144.

herent differences in individual abilities, inequality in access to opportunities for mobility, and variations in the amount of religious bias encountered, the educational, occupational, and other achievements of Jews have by no means been homogeneous. To the extent that these variables provide an important basis of differentiation in the American social structure, it becomes crucial to evaluate how the socio-economic position of Jews compares to that of the general population and how it differs among various segments of the Jewish population itself. For such purposes, the three variables of education, occupation, and home tenure will be explored.

VENERATION FOR LEARNING

An important feature of the changing American scene in the second half of the twentieth century has been the sharp rise in the educational level of the population. More and more persons are receiving a college education; and of those completing four years of college, an increasing proportion go on to graduate and professional schools.[6] Throughout their history Jews have placed a high value on education. Although study traditionally implied Talmudic learning, the Enlightenment provided Jews with an opportunity for secular learning, which many eagerly accepted. In Germany especially, a class of Jewish intellectuals and professionals developed. Because of the restrictive policies of the German government after 1848 many of this group fled to America, thereby adding a corps of highly educated persons with a strong tradition for secular learning to the already prospering, though numerically small, Jewish communities in the United States.

The Eastern European immigration, beginning in the 1880's, also added a sizeable group of secularists to the growing American Jewish community. The majority of the immigrants were Orthodox Jews, but, they too placed great stress on education, and in the American setting transferred this from Talmudic to secular learning. Moreover, they quickly perceived that education was the key to social and economic advancement. Poverty limited the goals many immigrants could set for themselves; but if the immigrant himself had to be content to remain a peddler or laborer, he was determined that his offspring should do better. With specialization demanding even greater skills and even more training, the incentives for ever-increasing education have reinforced the traditional value placed by Jews on education.

[6] U.S. Bureau of the Census, *U.S. Census of Population: 1960,* Vol. I, *Characteristics of the Population,* Part 1, United States Summary (Washington, D.C.: Government Printing Office, 1964), Table 76.

TABLE 4-1

YEARS OF SCHOOL COMPLETED, PERSONS 25 YEARS OLD AND OVER, JEWISH AND TOTAL POPULATION, BY SEX

Years of School Completed		Males Jewish	Males Total	Females Jewish	Females Total	Both Sexes Jewish	Both Sexes Total
No School Years Completed		4.3	3.0	5.1	3.2	4.8	3.1
Elementary:	1-4 Years	1.1	4.5	1.4	4.1	1.2	4.3
	5-7 Years	2.7	15.9	2.7	15.3	2.7	15.6
	8 Years	5.6	18.3	5.9	19.1	5.7	18.8
High School:	1-3 Years	8.5	23.5	7.1	22.2	7.8	22.8
	4 Years	27.5	19.3	40.0	24.8	34.2	22.2
College:	1-3 Years	14.2	6.9	17.9	6.6	16.2	6.7
	4 Years	14.1 } 33.8	8.6	9.9 } 17.6	4.7	11.9 } 25.3	6.5
	5 or More	19.7 }		7.7 }		13.4 }	
No Information		2.2	0.0	2.3	0.0	2.2	0.0
Total Per Cent		100.0	100.0	100.0	100.0	100.0	100.0
Median Education		13.0	10.1	12.7	10.1	12.8	10.1

This emphasis on education is reflected in the strikingly higher than average educational level of the Jewish population compared to the total population (Table 4-1). In the total Providence metropolitan area, the Jewish population 25 years old and over had completed an average of 12.8 years of school—or the equivalent of almost one year of college; the total population averaged only 10.1 years—or the equivalent of two years of high school. A three-year difference in average education is great in itself; yet there are even more significant variations in the proportions of those completing given levels of education. Forty-one per cent of the Jews 25 years old and over attended college, compared to only 13 per cent of the general population. Moreover, 25 of every 100 Jews graduated from college, compared to only 6.5 per cent for the total. In fact, proportionally more Jews continued on to graduate education, 13.4 per cent, than had had any college education in the total population. Yet, at the other end of the scale, Jews had a slightly higher proportion with no schooling than did the total population. This differential is due to the older, foreign-born members of the Jewish community, as can be clearly seen when age and generation are controlled. These differentials characterize both males and females (Figure 4-1).

The patterns of educational differentials for the Providence area closely parallel those shown by two nationwide sample surveys conducted in 1953 and 1955.[7] The results showed that Jewish respondents, together with Episcopalians, were better educated than all other religious groups.

[7] Donald J. Bogue, *The Population of the United States* (Glencoe, Ill.: The Free Press, 1959), pp. 700-702.

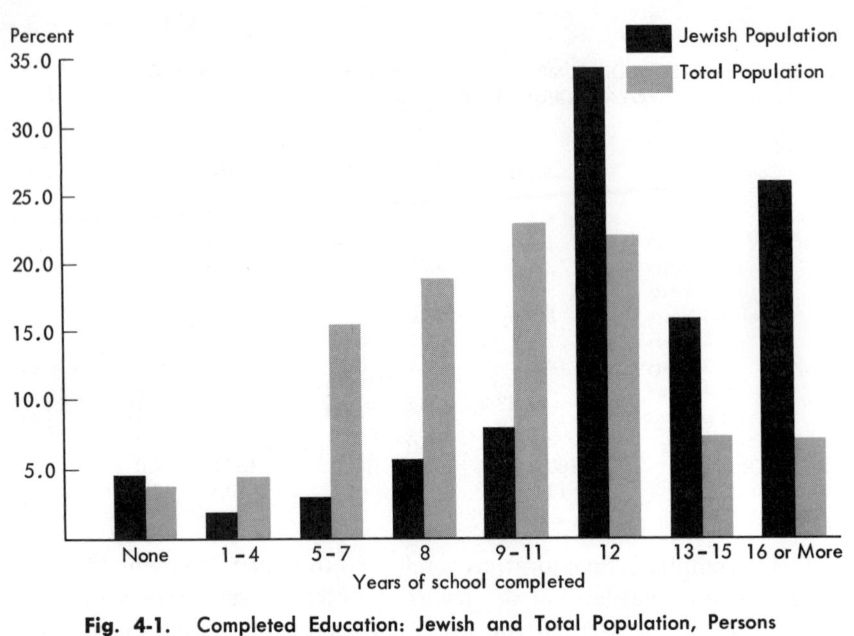

Fig. 4-1. Completed Education: Jewish and Total Population, Persons 25 Years Old and Older

Whereas 19.4 per cent of all white household heads in the two samples had some college education, one-third of all Jewish household heads did so. Consistent with the Providence findings, the surveys also showed that Jewish respondents had more than the average number with very low education. Just over 8 per cent of the Jewish household heads had completed less than five years of school compared to a national average of not quite 7 per cent.

A more recent national study of 14- to 19-year-old whites also attests to the higher educational achievement and aspirations of the Jewish population.[8] Collected as part of the Bureau of the Census *Current Population Survey* in October, 1965, this set of data showed that 99 per cent of all Jewish children aged 14 to 19 who had not yet graduated from high school were still enrolled in school. This contrasted with 88 per cent for the total white group. Restriction of the comparison to children of white-collar workers reduced the differential considerably, with all of the Jewish children and 95 per cent of the total group of children still in school. The differential extends to aspirations for further education. Almost 90 per

[8] Charles B. Nam, A. Lewis Rhodes, and Robert E. Herriott, *Study of Inequalities in Educational Opportunities* (Tallahassee: Florida State University, 1965-67), Tables 21 and 30.

cent of the Jewish children, in contrast to only 58 per cent of the total group, planned to attend college. For the children of white-collar workers the differential persisted, but not as strongly—94 per cent compared to 75 per cent. For children of non-white-collar workers it was sharper—72 per cent for the Jewish children compared to 49 per cent for the non-Jewish. These differences, although varying in level, characterized both boys and girls. Although the specific values and the nature of the data differ, the basic similarity between these national patterns and the Providence data attests to the generality of the Providence findings. The value of the Providence data lies in the opportunities they afford for probing the relation of other variables to education, particularly generation status.

The level of educational achievement rises steadily with changing generation status, from an average of 9.4 years for the foreign born to 15.0 years for the third generation (Table 4-2). Among the foreign born, over 17 per cent had no formal schooling, only 60 per cent achieved as much as an elementary education, and less than 19 per cent attended college. Almost all of the second- and third-generation persons had at least an elementary education, and the proportion attending college increased from 43 per cent of the second generation to 67 per cent of the third generation.

These differentials by generation persist when age is controlled, although the educational level of the youngest cohorts within each generation was considerably higher than that of those aged 65 and over. Among the foreign born over 65 years of age, a group composed largely of survivors of the earlier Eastern European immigration, almost one-third had no schooling; only 11 per cent were high school graduates and still fewer had attended college. Yet in the same generation group the proportion reporting no education declined to 7 per cent among those 45 to 64 years of age; 31 per cent of this group were high school graduates, and an additional 23 per cent attended college. Among the youngest cohort of foreign born, those 25 to 44, 40 per cent were high school graduates and almost half had some college training. The same pattern holds for the other generations, yet generational differences persist: among the 25-44 year age cohort of the third generation, the median level of education was 15.7 years, compared to 12.9 for the equivalent age group of foreign-born persons. Moreover, among the younger third generation, almost three-fourths attended college and most of the others were high school graduates. Clearly, the education that the immigrant could not afford for himself was available to his children. In fact, the evidence suggests that Jews have been in the forefront in the trend toward practically universal college education.

TABLE 4-2

EDUCATION COMPLETED, BY GENERATION AND AGE

Generation and Age	None	Elementary School 1-4	5-7	8	High School 9-11	12	College 1-3	4	5 or More	No Information	Total Per Cent	Median Yrs. of School
All Ages												
First Generation	17.6	4.3	9.2	11.3	9.6	23.0	7.6	5.1	5.8	6.3	100.0	9.4
Second Generation	0.2	0.2	0.7	5.0	8.4	42.4	16.5	12.1	13.9	0.7	100.0	12.8
Mixed Parentage	0.3	0.0	0.0	0.6	3.2	31.4	26.6	18.3	19.2	0.3	100.0	14.6
Third Generation	0.0	0.0	0.0	1.1	5.2	26.2	24.2	19.6	22.9	0.8	100.0	15.0
TOTAL	4.8	1.2	2.7	5.7	7.8	34.2	16.2	11.9	13.4	2.2	100.0	12.8
25-44 Age Group												
First Generation	2.4	0.0	4.8	1.2	4.8	39.3	15.5	11.9	20.2	0.0	100.0	12.9
Second Generation	0.0	0.0	0.2	0.4	2.2	41.9	21.3	16.1	17.7	0.2	100.0	13.7
Mixed Parentage	0.0	0.0	0.0	0.0	1.4	31.7	26.2	19.5	20.8	0.5	100.0	14.9
Third Generation	0.0	0.0	0.0	0.0	4.2	23.1	25.3	22.4	24.7	0.3	100.0	15.7
TOTAL	0.2	0.0	0.4	0.3	2.8	34.4	22.9	18.4	20.3	0.4	100.0	14.5
45-64 Age Group												
First Generation	7.0	2.3	7.9	11.7	13.2	31.0	11.4	5.3	6.4	3.8	100.0	12.1
Second Generation	0.2	0.2	0.7	5.7	10.8	44.0	14.7	10.9	12.1	0.5	100.0	12.7
Mixed Parentage	1.2	0.0	0.0	1.2	5.9	31.8	28.2	16.5	15.3	0.0	100.0	14.1
Third Generation	0.0	0.0	0.0	2.0	12.2	42.9	20.4	4.1	14.3	4.1	100.0	12.7
TOTAL	2.1	0.8	2.5	6.9	11.1	40.0	14.8	9.5	10.8	1.7	100.0	12.6
65 and Over Age Group*												
First Generation	32.3	7.5	11.7	13.5	7.2	10.8	1.8	3.3	1.5	10.5	100.0	4.8
Second Generation	0.9	0.9	2.7	19.6	17.9	32.1	8.9	2.7	10.7	3.6	100.0	12.1
TOTAL	23.7	5.7	9.1	15.7	10.2	16.5	3.7	3.0	3.9	8.5	100.0	8.2

*In this and succeeding tables, no data are presented for the mixed parentage and third generation categories of the 65 and over age group because of the small number of cases.

TABLE 4-3

MEDIAN YEARS OF SCHOOL COMPLETED, BY GENERATION, AGE, AND SEX

Generation and Age	Males	Females	Total
All Ages			
First Generation	9.2	9.5	9.4
Second Generation	13.1	12.7	12.8
Mixed Parentage	16.0	13.9	14.6
Third Generation	16.2	14.3	15.0
TOTAL	13.0	12.7	12.8
25-44 Age Group			
First Generation	15.6	12.7	12.9
Second Generation	15.1	12.9	13.7
Mixed Parentage	16.2	14.1	14.9
Third Generation	16.2	15.0	15.7
TOTAL	15.9	13.6	14.5
45-64 Age Group			
First Generation	12.1	12.1	12.1
Second Generation	12.9	12.6	12.7
Mixed Parentage	15.0	13.5	14.1
Third Generation	12.8	12.7	12.7
TOTAL	12.7	12.5	12.6
65 and Over Age Group			
First Generation	5.6	4.0	4.8
Second Generation	12.4	11.6	12.1
TOTAL	8.3	8.1	8.2

Within the Jewish population the educational achievements of males and females differ markedly (Table 4-3). Traditionally, men have received more education than women, since women were released from the obligation to study in order to take care of their homes. This tradition has probably been replaced now by the greater importance of education for career preparation. The 13.0 median years of education of the Jewish male exceeds that of the female by only 0.3 years, but this relatively small difference is somewhat misleading. Considerably more females received only a high school education than did males; and conversely, more men than women received college education at all levels. Nevertheless, a much higher proportion of Jewish females received higher education than did females in the general population.

For both Jewish males and females, the level of education is highly correlated with generation status. For males it increased from an average of 9.2 years for the foreign born to 16.2 for the third generation. The level of education of females, though lower than that of males, shows the same pattern in relation to generation, increasing from 9.5 years on the average among the foreign born to an average of 14.3 years among the third generation. The education differences largely reflect variations in age composition among the generation groups. Within particular age categories there is much greater similarity in the educational level among generations. In fact, for the youngest group of males the differences are very slight. For females in this age group, the difference in the educational level between the foreign born and the third generation is only 2.3 years, in contrast to the 4.8-year difference for females when age is not controlled. Generation status has apparently ceased to be a major variable affecting the educational achievement of younger Jewish males, but persists in influencing how much education a girl will receive. We hasten to add, however, that for both males and females in all generation groups, the younger individuals display higher educational achievements than do the older ones. The rate of adjustment has, however, been faster for the young foreign-born male than for the female.

Since both the age composition and generation status of the population living in various segments of the metropolitan area vary, residential differences in educational level may be expected as well. Based on both the younger age and the higher proportion of third-generation persons in the suburbs and, to a lesser extent, in the newer urban areas, the educational level of these areas should be higher than that of the older urban section, which consists disproportionately of older, foreign-born persons. Superimposed on the age and generation differences is the difference in socio-economic level. The newer urban section contains the highest status residential areas of the metropolitan area, reflecting both high property values and the high income, occupational, and educational level of its total population.

The combined effect of these several factors is evidenced in the median educational level of the Jewish population living in the areas, which increases from 12.1 years in the older urban section to 12.9 years in the newer urban and suburban areas (Table 4-4). In part, however, these over-all differentials mask some interesting variations by generation status. The older urban section shows the greatest range in the median educational level, from a low of 6.4 for the foreign born to a high of 14 years for the third generation. Both the newer urban and the suburban sections show the same direction of change with respect to generation status, but the differentials between the foreign born and the third generation are lower, ranging from 10.9 to 15.8 in the newer urban section and from 12.3 to 14.6 in the suburbs. Judged by the median, therefore, the suburbs represent a much more homogeneous population with respect to educational level. This reflects the selective character of the movement to the suburban communities and the younger age of even the foreign born living there compared to those in the older and the newer urban sections. The particularly low educational level of the first generation in

TABLE 4-4

MEDIAN YEARS OF SCHOOL COMPLETED, BY RESIDENCE, GENERATION, AND AGE

Generation and Age	Place of Residence		
	Older Urban	Newer Urban	Suburban
Generation			
First Generation	6.4	10.9	12.3
Second Generation	12.4	13.0	12.8
Mixed Parentage	12.9	15.2	14.3
Third Generation	14.0	15.8	14.6
Age Group			
25-44	12.8	15.3	14.1
45-64	12.3	12.6	12.6
65 and Over	2.7	8.9	8.7
TOTAL	12.1	12.9	12.9

the older urban section reflects the lack of any secular education of approximately half of the foreign born 65 years old and over living there. This situation also accounts for the very low median level of education, only 8.2 years, for the total Jewish population aged 65 and over living in the entire metropolitan area. Over all, these data, like those on sex differentials, point to increasing homogeneity of the Jewish population with respect to education, particularly among those living in the suburbs and, to a somewhat lesser degree among those living in the newer urban area. Most of the variations stem from age differentials rather than from differences in generation status; thus, as the population ages and as the foreign born form a continuously smaller segment of the total, educational homogeneity will probably increase.

THE DIVISION OF LABOR

The position of the Jew in the occupational structure of the American community reflects the skills, values, and intellectual orientation which the immigrants brought with them to America. As a comparative evaluation of Jewish and Italian mobility in a Connecticut community has pointed out, "There is some evidence that Jews came to America with occupational skills better suited to urban living. . . . The cultural tradition of veneration of rational control and learning in the Jewish religion has no parallel [for example] in the Catholic belief of Southern Italians; and, insofar as this tradition had been transformed into a greater respect and desire for higher education in America, it has probably contributed

TABLE 4-5

PER CENT OF JEWISH AND TOTAL POPULATION
15 YEARS OLD AND OVER IN LABOR FORCE,
BY AGE AND SEX

	Males		Females	
Age	Jewish	Total	Jewish	Total
15-24	21.8	60.8	19.2	43.7
25-44	98.3	96.0	22.5	43.7
45-64	98.0	90.2	33.3	47.8
65 and Over	47.1	27.8	5.7	9.7
TOTAL	78.1	78.6	23.7	39.3

strongly to Jewish upward mobility." [9] In combination, these traits maximize the incentive for movement up the occupational ladder either by the immigrant himself or by his children.

Before considering the occupational composition of the Jewish population and the ways in which it is affected by generation, we will examine the extent to which Jews participate in the labor force (Table 4-5). Of the Jewish male population 15 years old and over, just over three-fourths were active participants in the labor force, almost identical to the rate for the total population. This over-all similarity, however, masks significant differences among selected age segments of the two populations. The proportion of Jewish males in the labor force increases from 21.8 per cent for those under 25 years of age to virtually 100 per cent for those between 25 and 64. After age 65, the proportion declines to 47 per cent. Two points in particular are noteworthy about this pattern. For the cohort under age 25, the percentage of Jewish males in the labor force is considerably below the comparable proportions for the total population. The difference is attributable very largely to the much higher proportion of Jewish males who remain in school until the late teens and mid-twenties. Almost 80 per cent of the Jewish males between 15 and 24 were still in school, reflecting the greater value placed by Jews on education and the need for more extensive training for those occupations in which Jews are concentrated. For the middle age range, 25 to 44, the proportions in the labor force are quite similar—with practically universal labor force participation by both groups. In the older age groups, Jews show a much greater tendency to remain active members of the labor force than does the total male population. For the 45-64 age group, the level of participation by Jewish males remained very high, 98 per

[9] Fred L. Strodtbeck, Margaret R. McDonald, and Bernard C. Rosen, "Evaluation of Occupations: A Reflection of Jewish and Italian Mobility Differences," *American Sociological Review*, XXII, No. 5 (1957), 547.

cent, whereas that of the total population dropped to 90 per cent. Among those 65 and over, the differential was much greater, with almost twice as many Jewish males remaining economically active. This pattern stems directly from the greater concentration of Jews in trade and in the professions; that is, a high percentage are self-employed and therefore not subject to involuntary retirement at age 65. The tendency to remain economically active is also typical of professionals and businessmen in the total population, but they constitute a much smaller proportion of the total labor force.

Among Jewish women, participation in the labor force was considerably below that of women in the total population, of whom 39 per cent were economically active. As with men, labor force participation of Jewish women rises between the late teens and the 25-44 age group. The low level of the youngest group reflects the high proportion of girls still in school (66 per cent). The relatively low level of the 25-44 age group masks an initial rise as women enter the labor force following school, followed by a sharp decline as females withdraw from the labor force to take on the responsibilities of marriage and motherhood. As their children grow older, Jewish women, like those in the total population, return to work, and their percentage in the labor force increases, reaching the one-third level for the 45-64 age group. Subsequently, the participation rate of aged Jewish women declines sharply to less than 6 per cent.

In contrast to those of the males, the labor force participation rates of Jewish females are considerably lower than those of the total female population at all ages. In the youngest groups, this may stem largely from the noted tendency of Jewish girls to remain in school. In the older ages, this results from two factors: (1) The high degree of family orientation among Jews may result in more women remaining home to care for their families; this is particularly true of the foreign born, who contribute a larger proportion of the older groups. (2) The generally high socio-economic status of the Jewish population may require fewer Jewish women to enter the labor force in order to supplement the family income.

Participation in the labor force varies by generation status, but to a very great extent these differentials are attributable to the different age structures of the various generation groups (Table 4-6). Reflecting the younger age composition and the high proportion of those under 25 who are still in school, the labor force participation rate of the third-generation American males is the lowest of all groups, just under 50 per cent. Next lowest is that of the foreign-born males; but in this case, the percentage reflects the considerably higher proportion of persons aged 65 and over, over half of whom are retired. During the middle years, when most males participate in the labor force, the differences among genera-

TABLE 4-6

MALE LABOR FORCE STATUS, BY GENERATION AND AGE

Generation and Age	Labor Force Status: In Labor Force: Employed	Unemployed	In School	Retired	No Information	Total Per Cent
All Ages						
First Generation	69.6	0.8	3.0	26.6	0.0	100.0
Second Generation	93.7	1.2	1.6	2.9	0.6	100.0
Mixed Parentage	75.2	2.9	20.7	0.0	1.2	100.0
Third Generation	48.8	2.1	48.3	0.5	0.3	100.0
TOTAL	76.6	1.5	14.2	7.1	0.6	100.0
15-24 Age Group						
First Generation	0.0	0.0	100.0	0.0	0.0	100.0
Second Generation	25.0	0.0	75.0	0.0	0.0	100.0
Mixed Parentage	21.3	4.3	72.3	0.0	2.1	100.0
Third Generation	19.2	2.7	78.1	0.0	0.0	100.0
TOTAL	19.1	2.7	77.9	0.0	0.3	100.0
25-44 Age Group						
First Generation	94.1	0.0	0.0	5.9	0.0	100.0
Second Generation	98.8	1.2	0.0	0.0	0.0	100.0
Mixed Parentage	98.8	0.0	1.2	0.0	0.0	100.0
Third Generation	94.0	1.5	3.7	0.0	0.8	100.0
TOTAL	97.3	1.0	1.1	0.4	0.2	100.0
45-64 Age Group						
First Generation	97.5	0.6	0.0	1.9	0.0	100.0
Second Generation	97.0	1.4	0.0	0.7	0.9	100.0
Mixed Parentage	88.2	8.8	0.0	0.0	3.0	100.0
Third Generation	93.4	0.0	0.0	6.6	0.0	100.0
TOTAL	96.5	1.5	0.0	1.1	0.9	100.0
65 and Over Age Group						
First Generation	40.9	1.3	0.0	57.8	0.0	100.0
Second Generation	60.7	0.0	0.0	37.4	1.9	100.0
TOTAL	46.3	0.8	0.0	52.4	0.5	100.0

tions are minimal, ranging, with only one exception, between 93 and 98 per cent for persons aged 25 to 64. Among the aged, the participation rates of the foreign born are below those of the second-generation group, 41 per cent compared to 61 per cent. This probably stems from the larger proportion of foreign born who worked for others, probably in manual-labor jobs, and who had to retire at age 65, whereas more in the second-generation group were self-employed and could remain active members of the labor force.

In general, the females follow the same pattern of generation differences as do the males (Table 4-7). Within generation groups, however, there are some interesting variations by age. Like males, and probably for the same reasons, the proportion of older women in the labor force is lower for the foreign born than for the second-generation group, 4.5

compared to 8.2 per cent. The differences extend beyond this age group, however. Among the foreign born those in the 25-44 year age group have a higher labor force participation rate than do those aged 45 to 64, whereas for both the second and third generation the reverse pattern holds. Moreover, the participation rates of the foreign born in the younger group are considerably higher than those in the second- and third-generation categories; in contrast, the labor force participation of foreign-born women in the 45-64 year group is below that of second- and third-generation women of comparable age. The latter differential may reflect several phenomena: (1) Older foreign-born women may place a higher value on housekeeping and raising a family as the responsibility of the Jewish woman. (2) The proportion of foreign-born women in this age group who are either professionals or members of families in business

TABLE 4-7

FEMALE LABOR FORCE STATUS, BY GENERATION AND AGE

Generation and Age	Labor Force Status: In Labor Force: Employed	Unemployed	Keeps House	In School	Retired	No Information	Total Per Cent
All Ages							
First Generation	17.4	0.5	72.3	2.0	5.8	2.0	100.0
Second Generation	29.4	0.4	68.0	0.7	0.4	1.1	100.0
Mixed Parentage	25.0	0.4	64.2	9.1	0.4	0.9	100.0
Third Generation	16.9	1.1	43.5	36.8	0.7	1.0	100.0
TOTAL	23.1	0.6	62.4	10.8	1.7	1.4	100.0
15-24 Age Group							
First Generation	–	–	–	–	–	–	–
Second Generation	46.7	0.0	20.0	33.3	0.0	0.0	100.0
Mixed Parentage	31.0	2.4	19.0	45.2	0.0	2.4	100.0
Third Generation	13.3	2.3	13.3	71.1	0.0	0.0	100.0
TOTAL	17.1	2.1	14.0	66.4	0.0	0.4	100.0
25-44 Age Group							
First Generation	34.0	4.0	60.0	0.0	0.0	2.0	100.0
Second Generation	23.7	0.0	75.1	0.0	0.0	1.2	100.0
Mixed Parentage	19.9	0.0	77.9	1.5	0.0	0.7	100.0
Third Generation	17.7	0.0	80.0	2.3	0.0	0.0	100.0
TOTAL	22.2	0.3	75.5	1.0	0.0	1.0	100.0
45-64 Age Group							
First Generation	26.0	0.0	70.2	0.4	1.7	1.7	100.0
Second Generation	35.5	0.5	63.3	0.0	0.0	0.7	100.0
Mixed Parentage	35.3	0.0	64.7	0.0	0.0	0.0	100.0
Third Generation	38.3	0.0	49.9	0.0	3.0	8.8	100.0
TOTAL	33.0	0.3	64.5	0.1	0.6	1.5	100.0
65 and Over Age Group							
First Generation	4.5	0.0	80.6	0.0	12.0	2.9	100.0
Second Generation	8.2	1.6	82.1	0.0	4.9	3.2	100.0
TOTAL	5.3	0.4	80.1	0.0	11.0	3.2	100.0

TABLE 4-8

PER CENT OF LABOR FORCE MEMBERS WHO ARE SELF-EMPLOYED,* BY SEX, GENERATION, AND AGE

Generation and Age	Males	Females	Total
All Ages			
First Generation	59.0	22.1	50.5
Second Generation	55.8	25.2	47.0
Mixed Parentage	50.4	8.1	36.9
Third Generation	39.4	26.1	33.2
TOTAL	53.2	21.2	45.0
15-24 Age Group			
First Generation	–	–	–
Second Generation	–	–	–
Mixed Parentage	–	–	–
Third Generation	20.0	3.3	13.8
TOTAL	16.7	2.0	10.4
25-44 Age Group			
First Generation	34.4	17.6	28.6
Second Generation	50.0	17.3	42.7
Mixed Parentage	50.0	9.9	39.5
Third Generation	44.4	27.8	40.7
TOTAL	47.1	18.7	40.4
45-64 Age Group			
First Generation	57.9	19.2	48.3
Second Generation	57.7	29.7	50.4
Mixed Parentage	67.7	11.1	46.9
Third Generation	64.3	7.7	40.7
TOTAL	58.2	25.8	49.2
65 and Over Age Group			
First Generation	73.8	–	71.2
Second Generation	81.3	–	71.8
TOTAL	76.0	40.0	71.3

***Includes not more than 1.5 per cent for any generation group who reported working for family.**

for themselves is relatively low. (3) Older women may receive economic help from their children, reflecting strong family ties. In the absence of strong economic pressures to work, such women would therefore remain out of the labor force. The greater tendency of foreign-born women in the 25-44 year group to be in the labor force may reflect the greater economic pressures under which they are operating because of the relative recency of their move to the United States. A number of persons in this age group arrived within the last decade or two. This interpretation receives support from the much higher proportion of women in this age-generation category employed as manual workers, almost 30 per cent; for no other age-generation group of women does this proportion exceed 12.5

per cent. At the same time, the considerable proportion of professionals within this group also contributes to their higher labor force participation rate.

The data also permit determination of how many in the labor force are self-employed and how many make their living by working for others (Table 4-8). Since many persons who earn their living in a family business consider themselves self-employed, these two categories are considered jointly. Just over one-half of the employed Jewish males were self-employed, compared to only 11 per cent of the total population. Among Jewish females, the level of self-employment is much lower, only one out of five, but also considerably in excess of the proportion of females in total population who were self-employed, only 3 per cent.

For both males and females, the percentage of self-employed varies significantly by age, increasing from 16.7 per cent of males in the under-25 age group to over three-fourths of those in the oldest group; and for females from only 2 per cent of the youngest cohort to four out of every ten employed females 65 and over. In part, these age differences reflect the time it takes to establish a career or to obtain financial resources to own a business. At the same time, two other factors may be operating. Since the self-employed person can exercise greater control over the time of his retirement, a higher proportion remain economically active longer, thereby accounting for the increased proportion of self-employed among the oldest group. Yet, since a higher proportion of young Jewish men are now entering occupations other than trade, more of them will be working for others rather than for themselves. If this assumption is valid, the percentage of Jews who are self-employed should decrease as those now in the older age groups withdraw from the labor force.

OCCUPATIONAL PATTERNS

C. Bezalel Sherman in *The Jew Within American Society* suggests that "Mass immigration from Eastern Europe may be divided into two periods. In the first period, which extended from 1870 to 1900, the immigrants were mostly artisans, unskilled laborers, and economically déclassé elements. The second period witnessed the arrival of large numbers of skilled workers. Seventy per cent of all bread winners among the Jewish immigrants during the first quarter of the twentieth century were skilled workers, whereas the proportion of such workers in the general immigration of the period was only 20 per cent. Nevertheless, it is only up to the time of World War I that one may speak of increasing Jewish proletarianization in terms of growing numbers of industrial workers.

TABLE 4-9

OCCUPATION OF EMPLOYED PERSONS, JEWISH AND TOTAL POPULATION, BY SEX

	Males		Females	
Occupation	Jewish Population	Total Population	Jewish Population	Total Population
Professionals	20.7	9.2	17.9	10.5
Managers and Proprietors	40.7	10.5	12.7	2.4
Clerical Workers	4.5	8.1	41.5	27.2
Sales Workers	20.9	7.4	18.3	6.2
Skilled Laborers	6.8	21.9	0.4	2.4
Semiskilled Laborers	4.2	23.9	5.2	31.6
Service Workers	0.8	7.0	1.5	11.6
Unskilled Laborers	0.3	5.1	0.0	0.7
Not Reported	1.1	6.9	2.4	7.4
Total Per Cent	100.0	100.0	100.0	100.0

Thereafter, a drift away from the shops began, leading at first to a relative decrease in the number of Jewish industrial workers, and later to an absolute decrease, in relation to the Jewish population as a whole."[10] According to estimates prepared by Nathan Goldberg, 59.6 per cent of the Jewish gainfully employed were industrial workers in 1900, compared to only 13.7 per cent by 1930. Conversely, the number of Jews employed in the professions increased from only 3 per cent in 1900 to 13 per cent in the 1930's.[11] Sherman compared ten Jewish communities surveyed during 1935-1945 with 14 surveyed during 1948-1953 and found that the proportion of professionals rose from 11 to 15 per cent within this interval.[12]

What little data are available concerning historical changes in the occupational structure of the Providence Jewish community suggest that it underwent the same transition that Sherman has described for the total Jewish community of the United States. Although merchants continued to dominate the occupational structure, by 1900 the number of professionals had increased, and a sizeable number of Jews had also entered the blue-collar segment of the labor force. The heavy concentration of Jews in business and in the professions, a pattern that typifies Jewish communities throughout the United States, also characterizes the Providence area. Almost nine out of every ten employed Jewish males are in white-

[10] *The Jew Within American Society* (Detroit: Wayne State University Press, 1965), p. 98.

[11] "Occupational Patterns of American Jews," *Jewish Review*, III, No. 4 (1946), 275.

[12] *The Jew Within American Society*, p. 101.

collar occupations, compared to only 35 per cent of the total male population of the area. Similarly, nine out of every ten employed Jewish females are white-collar workers, compared to only five out of every ten in the total population.

Sharp differences characterize each of the detailed categories into which the occupational structure has been subdivided (Table 4-9). The single largest occupational category for Jewish males is that of managers and proprietors, which accounts for 41 per cent of all employed Jewish males, compared to only 11 per cent of those in the total population. Professionals and sales workers each account for 21 per cent of the Jewish employed males but less than 10 per cent of the total population. Only 12 per cent of the Jewish males are employed in blue-collar work, and almost all of these are concentrated in the skilled and semiskilled categories. By contrast, blue-collar work accounts for 58 per cent of the jobs held by employed persons in the total population in the area, with the large majority of these also included in the craftsmen and operative groups (Figure 4-2).

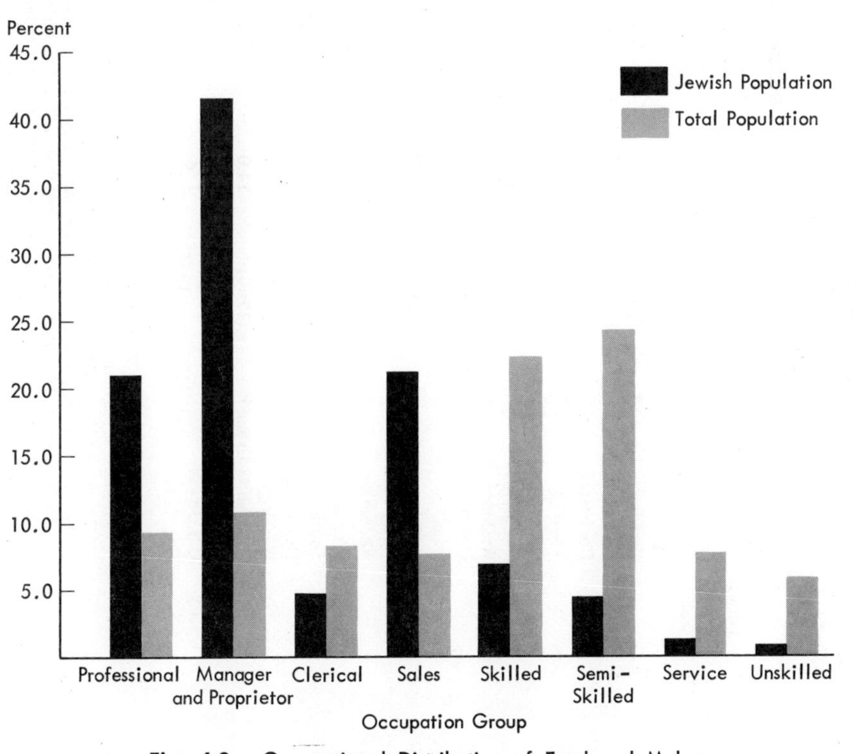

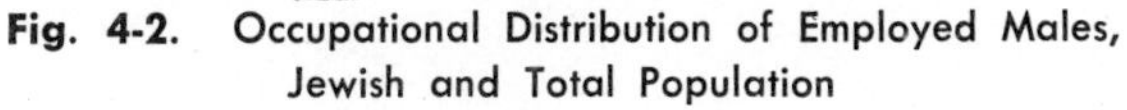

Fig. 4-2. Occupational Distribution of Employed Males, Jewish and Total Population

TABLE 4-10

OCCUPATIONAL DISTRIBUTION OF THE JEWISH POPULATION, BY SEX, FOR SELECTED COMMUNITIES

			Occupation				
			Professionals	Managers and Proprietors	Clerical and Sales Workers	Skilled and Semiskilled Laborers	Service and Unskilled Laborers
Males							
Camden	*	(1965)	34.0	31.0	22.0	11.0	2.0
PROVIDENCE		(1963)	20.7	40.7	25.4	11.0	1.1
Rochester	*	(1961)	26.7	29.5	24.2	16.6	2.9
Trenton	*	(1961)	27.4	54.0	13.4	——— 5.2 ———	
South Bend	*	(1961)	17.6	56.5	15.3	8.0	2.6
Des Moines	*	(1956)	13.7	52.8	23.6	5.1	2.3
Washington	†	(1956)	37.8	24.5	20.8	——— 9.7 ———	
U.S. White Urban	‡	(1960)	12.9	13.3	17.2	40.4	11.8
Females							
Camden	*	(1965)	25.0	18.0	47.0	4.0	6.0
PROVIDENCE		(1963)	17.9	12.7	59.8	5.6	1.5
Rochester	*	(1961)	17.8	7.1	55.5	16.6	3.0
Trenton	*	(1961)	17.0	29.3	46.3	——— 7.4 ———	
South Bend	*	(1961)	17.2	24.1	51.1	4.7	3.0
Des Moines	*	(1956)	9.7	23.6	55.6	1.4	2.8
Washington	†	(1956)	15.1	7.8	59.9	——— 8.6 ———	
U.S. White Urban	‡	(1960)	14.0	4.1	44.6	15.9	16.0
Heads of Household§							
U.S. Jewish		(1953 and 1955)	17.6	37.3	24.6	19.2	1.3
U.S. Total		(1953 and 1955)	10.0	23.4‖	11.2	39.2	15.7

**American Jewish Yearbook* (1963), LXIV, p. 68.
†Stanley K. Bigman, *The Jewish Population of Greater Washington* (Washington, D.C.: The Jewish Community Council of Greater Washington, 1957), p. 30.
‡U.S. Bureau of the Census, *U.S. Census of Population: 1960,* Vol. I, *Characteristics of the Population,* Part 1, U.S. Summary (Washington, D.C.: Government Printing Office, 1964), Table 88.
§Donald J. Bogue, *The Population of the United States* (Glencoe, Ill.: The Free Press, 1959), Table 23-12.
‖Includes 10.8 per cent farm operators and managers, in contrast to 1.3 per cent for Jews.

In general, the pattern of differentials between the Jewish population and the total population is quite similar for females, with more Jewish females concentrated in the professional, managerial, and sales worker categories, and fewer in each of the categories of manual work. The one notable exception is the much higher proportion of Jewish females in clerical work than is true of females in the total population, 42 per cent compared to only 27 per cent.

The heavy concentration of both males and females in the general population in manual work reflects the industrial character of the area. In this respect, the local area differs from the national pattern. However, only a small minority of the Jewish population holds manual employment. That this pattern of differences between the total and the Jewish population is not unique to this local area is clearly evidenced by comparable statistics for Jewish communities in other cities (Table 4-10). Although the specific values differ, depending on the kinds of employment opportunities available in each of these communities, a greater than average concentration of Jews was found in professional and managerial work and a lower than average proportion in the blue-collar occupations.

The close similarity of the Providence distribution for Jewish males to the national distribution for Jewish heads of household is particularly noteworthy. Except for a higher concentration among skilled and semiskilled workers in the national sample, the percentage in any particular category varies minimally between the local and national data. Thus, the same parallels between the local and the national statistics which characterized education extend to occupation as well.[13]

Some indication of the changes that may be taking place in the occupational composition of the Jewish population is shown by statistics on occupation by age (Table 4-11). These point in the direction of a reduced percentage of Jews in the managerial and proprietor group and an increasing proportion in both the professions and sales work. For example, among males the proportion of professionals increases from 17 per cent of those 65 and over to 25 per cent of those 25 to 44; and conversely, the proportion employed as managers declines from over half of the oldest group to just above one-third of the 25-44 year group. At the same time, the proportion of sales personnel increases from 11 per cent of the oldest to almost one-quarter of the 25-44 year group.[14] The concen-

[13] *Cf.* Liston Pope, "Religion and the Class Structure," in *Class, Status and Power,* eds. Reinhard Bendix and Seymour M. Lipset (Glencoe, Ill.: The Free Press, 1953), pp. 316-23.

[14] Although data for the 15-24 year age group are included in Tables 4-11 and 4-12, inclusion of this group in any age comparison is somewhat risky since a large proportion of them are still in school; and the occupational affiliation of those who are currently employed is not necessarily indicative of what the occupational com-

TABLE 4-11

OCCUPATION STATUS OF MALES, BY GENERATION AND AGE

Generation and Age	Professionals	Managers	Clerical Workers	Sales Workers	Skilled Laborers	Other Laborers	Total Per Cent*
			Occupation				
All Ages							
First Generation	15.7	44.1	3.2	16.1	12.6	8.3	100.0
Second Generation	23.7	42.0	4.1	19.5	5.6	4.2	100.0
Mixed Parentage	25.8	32.0	6.3	26.6	6.3	2.3	100.0
Third Generation	15.2	40.0	6.8	26.8	4.2	5.8	100.0
TOTAL	20.7	41.0	4.5	20.9	6.9	5.2	100.0
15-24 Age Group							
First Generation	–	–	–	–	–	–	–
Second Generation	–	–	–	–	–	–	–
Mixed Parentage	–	–	–	–	–	–	–
Third Generation	10.0	28.0	14.0	24.0	10.0	12.0	100.0
TOTAL	12.3	24.6	13.9	24.6	12.3	9.2	100.0
25-44 Age Group							
First Generation	37.5	25.0	0.0	18.8	12.5	6.2	100.0
Second Generation	26.4	39.3	5.0	20.7	4.1	4.5	100.0
Mixed Parentage	28.6	33.3	5.9	26.2	4.8	1.2	100.0
Third Generation	17.4	41.2	4.8	31.0	2.4	2.4	100.0
TOTAL	24.6	37.9	4.8	24.3	4.6	3.6	100.0
45-64 Age Group							
First Generation	15.9	42.0	2.5	17.2	13.4	9.0	100.0
Second Generation	21.0	44.1	3.8	19.6	6.4	3.7	100.0
Mixed Parentage	16.1	38.7	6.5	29.0	3.2	6.5	100.0
Third Generation	14.3	71.5	0.0	0.0	0.0	14.1	100.0
TOTAL	19.0	43.6	3.5	19.5	7.7	5.7	100.0
65 and Over Age Group							
First Generation	4.6	58.5	6.2	12.3	10.7	7.7	100.0
Second Generation	38.7	35.5	0.0	9.7	6.4	9.7	100.0
TOTAL	17.2	50.5	4.0	11.1	9.1	8.1	100.0

*Includes small percentage of unknown occupation.

tration of older males in managerial positions must again be interpreted within the context of the high percentage of such persons who are self-employed and therefore have a tendency to remain in the labor force while those in the lower white-collar and manual-labor groups are forced to retire. Yet, as many as 17 per cent of the aged segment of the employed population hold manual jobs, compared to only 13 per cent of those in the 45-64 year group and only 8 per cent of those in the 25-44 year group.

In general, the same pattern by age characterizes the employed females although the differentials are not always as sharp (Table 4-12). The trend among professionals is clear-cut and reflects a pattern characteristic of the total population: an increased proportion of younger females is in professional work. Whereas none of the employed women 65 years old and over and only 9 per cent of those in the 45-64 year age group are professionals, almost one-third of those between the ages of 25 and 44 are so employed. By contrast, the proportion of women in the managerial and proprietor group declines from almost one-third of the oldest group to only 10 per cent of those in the 25-44 year group. The very high proportion of older women in this occupational category is due to the higher mortality rate of males, with the result that a number of widows continue to operate the family business after the husband has died. Few older women are employed as clerical workers. On the other hand, the proportion of women employed in sales work increases from 16 per cent of those in the 25-44 year group to one-fourth of those in the oldest age category. As was true of males, the younger segments of the population are decreasingly employed in manual jobs. Whereas almost one out of every five older Jewish females held a manual job, only one out of every 16 women under 45 did so.

Over all, the occupational differentials by generation conform to what one would expect on the basis of the variations by age (Table 4-11). The foreign born have proportionally fewer persons who are professionals, somewhat more in managerial positions, fewer clerical and sales workers, and considerably more manual workers. Yet, several differences in occupational composition are noteworthy. Within the foreign-born group the proportion of professionals increases from only 5 per cent of the oldest segment to over one-third of those in the 25-44 age group. Conversely, the proportion of managers and proprietors declines from almost 60 per cent of the oldest group to only one-quarter of those 25 to 44. Among the

---

position will be once those who are in school enter the labor force. In fact, the chances are great that the occupation of the latter will be quite different as a result of their education. This is already suggested by the fact that the relatively high proportion of males aged 15 to 24 who are now employed hold jobs as manual workers or clerical and sales workers, with a correspondingly low proportion in top white-collar positions.

TABLE 4-12

OCCUPATION STATUS OF FEMALES, BY GENERATION AND AGE

Generation and Age	Professionals	Managers	Occupation Clerical Workers	Sales Workers	Skilled Laborers	Other Laborers	Total Per Cent*
All Ages							
First Generation	11.7	14.3	31.1	20.8	2.6	16.9	100.0
Second Generation	13.2	14.5	41.7	23.4	0.0	5.5	100.0
Mixed Parentage	32.8	9.8	42.6	13.1	0.0	1.7	100.0
Third Generation	26.6	8.8	51.9	6.3	0.0	5.1	100.0
TOTAL	17.9	12.9	41.6	18.4	0.4	6.8	100.0
15-24 Age Group							
First Generation	–	–	–	–	–	–	–
Second Generation	–	–	–	–	–	–	–
Mixed Parentage	30.8	0.0	61.5	7.7	0.0	0.0	100.0
Third Generation	20.0	3.4	70.0	0.0	0.0	3.3	100.0
TOTAL	22.0	4.0	64.0	2.0	0.0	6.0	100.0
25-44 Age Group							
First Generation	41.2	11.8	11.7	5.9	0.0	29.4	100.0
Second Generation	24.6	5.8	44.9	23.2	0.0	1.5	100.0
Mixed Parentage	40.0	13.3	26.7	16.7	0.0	3.3	100.0
Third Generation	36.1	13.9	36.1	8.3	0.0	5.6	100.0
TOTAL	32.3	10.3	34.8	16.1	0.0	5.8	100.0
45-64 Age Group							
First Generation	3.9	11.5	40.4	26.9	1.9	11.5	100.0
Second Generation	8.6	17.9	41.1	23.8	0.0	6.6	100.0
Mixed Parentage	22.2	11.1	55.5	11.1	0.0	0.0	100.0
Third Generation	15.4	7.7	53.8	15.4	0.0	7.7	100.0
TOTAL	8.9	15.3	42.8	22.9	0.4	7.2	100.0

*Includes small percentage of unknown occupation.

second- and third-generation groups, comparison of the 25-44 with the 45-64 year group suggests that more younger persons go into professional work, but the differences are by no means as great as those characterizing the foreign born. Similarly, fewer young second- and third-generation person tend to become managers and proprietors. Despite this age differential within generation groups, compared to the 25-44 year group of foreign born, fewer young second- and third-generation individuals are professionals and more are managers. The latter group is not restricted to self-employed, but includes persons holding salaried positions as managers and officials.

Particularly interesting is the considerable proportion of third-generation persons in the 25-44 year age range who are engaged in sales work. With the gradual disappearance of small businesses an increasing proportion of Jewish men may turn to sales work or to executive positions instead of operating their own firms, as did many of their parents and grandparents.

Kramer and Leventman reported in their study of North City that almost all of the members of the third generation who are in business are in their fathers' businesses. Only a few were operating their own small businesses. Moreover, they found that continuation in business or as independent professionals was dependent on the economic success of the father in this type of career. More of those sons whose fathers were less successful in business or in the independent professions entered new and traditionally non-Jewish careers, such as the salaried professions.[15]

The generally low proportion of third-generation males in the professions in Providence is more difficult to explain. Two possibilities exist: (1) The nature of the economic opportunities available in the Providence metropolitan area may force individuals who are trained as professionals to migrate elsewhere in order to find positions commensurate with their training. (Persons with graduate degrees in social science, the humanities, physics, or chemistry, for example, may have only limited chances for employment in Greater Providence.) (2) Since the 25-44 year group of the third generation is heavily weighted toward the younger end of this age category, a number of persons may still have been receiving their training and therefore would not have returned to the community to practice their careers.

For women, too, the foreign born have a lower proportion of professionals and clerical workers and a somewhat higher proportion, together with the second-generation group, of managers and of sales workers (Table 4-12). The sharpest differential is the considerably higher

[15] Judith R. Kramer and Seymour Leventman, *Children of the Gilded Ghetto*, pp. 130-34.

proportion of foreign-born women, 20 per cent, who are manual workers, compared to only 5 per cent of the third-generation group. Yet, as in the case of males, the patterns are by no means uniform by age. For example, although the proportion of professionals among foreign-born women aged 45 to 64 is the lowest of all generation groups, the proportion in the 25-44 age group is the highest of all generation groups. In general, the detailed data by generation for women do not point to any clear-cut trends in occupational affiliation when age is controlled. In part, this stems from the relatively small proportion of the total female sample who are employed, so that *no* patterns emerge for the specific subdivisions. The data by age therefore probably provide the best indication of the general direction of change; these point to more women entering the professions, fewer in managerial positions and sales work, and, to a lesser extent, fewer in clerical work. Most outstanding, however, was the significant shift into professional work and the decline in the proportion of women engaged in manual work.

The three residential areas into which the metropolitan area has been subdivided differ from each other in several major respects. As one moves from the older urban centers to the suburbs, the population becomes younger, proportionally more third generation than foreign born, and generally more educated. All three of these factors should affect the occupational composition of the population; on the basis of the relationships already demonstrated among age, generation status, and education, one would expect to find persons living in the suburbs more heavily concentrated in the upper white-collar occupations than are those living in the older urban sections. At the same time, because of the generally high socio-economic status of the newer urban area of settlement, one would expect to find minimal differences between it and the suburbs. In fact, this area may have even higher concentrations of persons in the upper white-collar occupations.

In general, the findings support these expectations (Table 4-13). The proportion of professionals increases from only 10 per cent of the employed labor force in the older area of settlement to over 20 per cent of those living in the newer urban area and in the suburbs, with the former somewhat higher than the latter. Similarly, the proportion of managers and proprietors increases from one out of every four persons in the older area to approximately one out of every three persons in the newer urban area and in the suburbs; again, the concentration in managerial positions is somewhat higher for the newer area of the central city than for the suburbs. Such sharp differentials by residence do not characterize the lower white-collar positions, but do hold with respect to manual workers; one out of every four employed persons in the older

TABLE 4-13

OCCUPATION, BY GENERATION AND RESIDENCE

Generation and Residence	Occupation						
	Professionals	Managers	Clerical Workers	Sales Workers	Skilled Laborers	Other Laborers	Total Per Cent*
Older Urban							
First Generation	9.1	25.3	11.1	14.1	20.2	18.2	100.0
Second Generation	10.5	26.5	19.8	21.0	10.5	11.1	100.0
Mixed Parentage	21.2	33.3	9.1	18.2	12.1	6.1	100.0
Third Generation	5.9	11.8	38.2	26.5	0.0	17.6	100.0
TOTAL	10.4	25.1	17.9	19.7	12.5	13.4	100.0
Newer Urban							
First Generation	16.6	40.8	12.1	17.2	6.4	7.0	100.0
Second Generation	23.9	39.4	12.0	19.0	1.6	3.1	100.0
Mixed Parentage	32.6	21.1	22.1	22.1	1.1	1.1	100.0
Third Generation	21.6	39.2	15.2	20.0	0.8	3.2	100.0
TOTAL	23.0	37.8	13.3	19.2	2.3	3.8	100.0
Suburban							
First Generation	18.7	45.3	2.7	21.3	5.3	6.6	100.0
Second Generation	21.9	31.9	12.7	23.1	5.4	3.5	100.0
Mixed Parentage	24.6	26.2	16.4	24.6	4.9	1.6	100.0
Third Generation	19.1	27.3	20.0	20.0	6.4	4.5	100.0
TOTAL	20.9	32.0	13.3	22.6	5.5	3.9	100.0

*Includes small percentage of unknown occupation.

urban area earns his living as a manual worker. In the newer urban area only 6 per cent of all employed persons hold manual jobs, and in the suburbs this proportion amounts to just under 10 per cent. On the whole, therefore, these data point to a close interplay between place of residence and type of work. Persons with high-status occupations are most concentrated in the newer urban area and next most concentrated in the suburbs; those living in the older urban area are considerably lower on the occupational scale.

Interestingly, these differences generally extend to most age categories as well as to most of the generation groups, suggesting that the residential concentration of occupations is not strictly a function of age nor of generation status. For example, in the 25-44 age group the proportion of professionals increases from 14 per cent in the older urban centers to 29 per cent in the newer urban area and to 27 per cent in the suburbs. Similarly, for the same age group the proportion of managers rises from 22 per cent in the older area to over 30 per cent in the newer urban and the suburban areas. The same pattern characterizes the 45-64 year age group. At the other extreme of the occupational scale, the proportion of manual laborers decreases from 27 per cent of the employed members of the 45-64 year group living in the older urban centers to 6 per cent of those in the newer urban area and 10 per cent of those in the suburbs.

Turning to generation status, the same pattern of residential differences emerges (Table 4-13). The proportion of professionals among the foreign born increases from 9 per cent of those living in the older urban center to 17 to 19 per cent for those in the other areas; and the proportion of managers rises from 25 per cent in the former to over 40 per cent in the latter areas. Conversely, almost 40 per cent of the employed foreign born in the older urban section hold manual jobs, compared to under 15 per cent in the two other areas. The same general pattern characterizes the occupational distribution of the third generation. Proportionally over three times as many of the third generation in the suburbs and newer urban area are professionals compared to those in the older urban section, and twice as many are managers. At the other extreme of the occupational scale, 18 per cent of the third generation living in the older urban section are manual laborers, compared to only 4 per cent in the newer urban section and 11 per cent in the suburbs. Even when more detailed data are examined by age within generation, the underlying pattern of residential differentials persists, although the differences narrow at times.

That the composition of the population living in the various sectors of the metropolitan area is differentially affected by the selective in- and out-movement of persons is evident from the information on the occupational identification of persons in the various streams of movement (Table 4-14). The older urban section has gained very little from in-movement. Yet, even among these small numbers there is a significant difference depending on place of origin of the movers. Over one-third of those coming from the newer urban section are manual laborers, compared to only 10 per cent of those moving from the suburbs and one-fourth of those moving from outside the state. Only 30 per cent of the movers from the newer urban and suburban areas are professionals or managers, compared to half of those moving in from out of state. For the latter persons, residence in the older area is probably temporary, used as a stepping stone before taking up residence in the other sectors of the metropolitan area. The selective character of the out-movement is indicated by the fact that approximately half of the persons moving from the older urban area to either the suburbs or the newer urban area are professionals or managers, and less than 15 per cent are manual workers.

By contrast, the movement into the newer urban area, regardless of origin, consists of a majority of persons (at least two-thirds) in high white-collar positions—that is, professionals and managers—with the movement from outside the metropolitan area having a slightly higher concentration of these persons than the movement from the suburbs. The greater attractiveness of the newer urban area to professionals and managers accounts for the higher proportion of such persons among the residents there. With the exception of the movement from the older urban area, the suburbs also attract a majority of persons from the upper rungs of the occupational hierarchy, but again, this is somewhat more characteristic of the movers from outside the metropolitan area. For both the suburbs and the newer urban area, there is a relatively heavy concentration of upper white-collar persons among the migrants, especially among those moving in from outside the metropolitan area, compared to the resident population. This differential attests to the higher than average mobility rates of these occupational groups. In addition, since this differential is more characteristic of the suburbs than of the newer urban sector, it may help to account for the weaker Jewish identification of the suburban Jews.

The conclusion seems warranted, therefore, that particular areas not only attract individuals on the basis of their age and generation, but also on the basis of their general social and economic status. The ability to own a home, and even more than this, to own a home of a certain quality, has resulted in the quite unequal distribution of the Jewish population with respect to such status indicators as education and occupation. More persons holding jobs lower on the occupational scale

TABLE 4-14

CURRENT RESIDENCE BY PREVIOUS RESIDENCE, BY OCCUPATION

	Occupation							
Previous Residence	Professionals	Managers	Clerical Workers	Sales Workers	Skilled Laborers	Other Laborers	Occupation Not Reported	Total Per Cent
Older Urban								
Older Urban	9.0	25.7	17.5	21.3	14.2	12.3	0.0	100.0
Newer Urban	10.0	20.0	20.0	15.0	10.0	25.0	0.0	100.0
Suburban	0.0	30.0	10.0	40.0	0.0	10.0	10.0	100.0
Other R.I.	–	–	–	–	–	–	–	–
Other U.S. & Foreign	30.0	20.0	20.0	5.0	10.0	15.0	0.0	100.0
Newer Urban								
Older Urban	12.9	41.8	14.7	19.4	3.5	5.9	1.8	100.0
Newer Urban	25.2	35.6	12.7	20.6	2.1	3.5	0.3	100.0
Suburban	12.8	56.4	17.9	7.7	2.6	2.6	0.0	100.0
Other R.I.	41.2	29.4	11.8	17.6	0.0	0.0	0.0	100.0
Other U.S. & Foreign	31.7	37.8	12.2	15.8	0.0	2.4	0.0	100.0
Suburban								
Older Urban	16.8	30.2	14.7	24.1	6.9	6.0	1.3	100.0
Newer Urban	18.5	37.0	19.8	22.2	0.0	1.2	1.2	100.0
Suburban	25.5	34.5	7.6	23.4	6.9	2.1	0.0	100.0
Other R.I.	–	–	–	–	–	–	–	–
Other U.S. & Foreign	36.6	26.8	7.3	14.6	2.4	4.9	7.3	100.0

are concentrated in the older urban sections of the city, where property value is considerably below that of the other two sectors. The differences between the newer urban area and the suburbs tend to be much narrower, but favor the newer area, which is recognized as the higher-status section of the metropolitan area. The major current differences are, therefore, between the older urban area on the one hand and the suburban and the newer urban areas on the other. With the further decline in the older area due to the death of the aged foreign born and the exodus of the younger second- and third-generation persons, and with increasing proportions of persons in all areas being third generation, these occupational differences among areas are likely to diminish further.

Yet, despite the increasing homogeneity of the population with respect to generation status and the narrowing of educational and occupational differentials, the newer urban and the suburban areas of the community nevertheless display variations in educational and occupational composition which go beyond age and generation differences. It might be emphasized that the considerable spatial distance between the newer urban area and the suburbs reinforces the status differences. Unless complete leveling in education and occupation occurs, this situation has inherent in it the possibility that a new basis for division of the community may replace the role previously played by generation status. If the suburbs, in contrast to the newer urban area, continue to select a somewhat different kind of Jew—different with respect to socio-economic status as well as identification with Judaism—then place of residence may remain a crucial variable in the evaluation of the Jewish community. The previous distinctions were drawn between the old ghetto area, with its high concentration of foreign born, and the newer urban and suburban centers with their disproportionate number of second- and third-generation Jews; the new distinctions may be between the newer urban and the suburban areas, but drawn not on the basis of generation status and its associated characteristics, but rather on the basis of socio-economic status and strength of ties with Jewish institutions and practices. The residential choice of the future may be between living in areas of Jewish concentration—the modern gilded ghetto as represented by the newer urban area—and integrating more fully into the larger community by movement to the suburbs.

OWNING A HOME

Home ownership represents still a third factor in terms of which the class position of the Jewish population can be examined. Since information on income was not collected as part of the population survey,

TABLE 4-15

HOME OWNERSHIP, BY GENERATION AND AGE OF HEAD OF HOUSEHOLD

Generation and Age	Home Ownership Owner	Renter	Other	Total Per Cent
All Ages				
First Generation	67.1	32.2	0.7	100.0
Second Generation	76.7	22.9	0.5	100.0
Mixed Parentage	68.9	31.1	0.0	100.0
Third Generation	72.5	26.8	0.7	100.0
TOTAL	72.5	27.0	0.5	100.0
25-44 Age Group				
First Generation	74.2	25.8	0.0	100.0
Second Generation	84.6	14.2	1.1	100.0
Mixed Parentage	67.7	32.3	0.0	100.0
Third Generation	72.0	27.3	0.7	100.0
45-64 Age Group				
First Generation	70.3	28.6	1.1	100.0
Second Generation	74.3	25.5	0.2	100.0
Mixed Parentage	69.2	30.8	0.0	100.0
Third Generation	82.4	17.6	0.0	100.0
65 and Over Age Group				
First Generation	62.9	36.6	0.5	100.0
Second Generation	64.5	35.5	0.0	100.0

the information on home ownership, as a very approximate index of wealth, becomes important. In contrast to the material on education and occupation, both of which were collected for individuals, the data on home ownership refer to household units; the analysis by specific characteristics such as generation status, age, sex, and education refers to the head of the household.

The great majority of Jews in the metropolitan area own the homes in which they live; three out of every four households reported home ownership (Table 4-15). This compares to only two out of every four in the general population of the area,[16] suggesting that the rate of home ownership is considerably higher among Jews and is consistent with the higher than average levels of education and the greater concentration in the upper echelons of the occupational hierarchy. Home ownership is not, however, uniform for all segments of the population. Fewer units headed by an older person own their home, 63 per cent among those aged 65 and over compared to 79 and 73 per cent among the two age groups under 65. The oldest age group generally has a heavier concentration of

[16] U.S. Bureau of the Census, *U.S. Census of Housing: 1960,* Vol. 1, *States and Small Areas, Rhode Island,* Final Report HC(1)-41 (Washington, D.C.: Government Printing Office, 1961), Table 2.

foreign born and of persons in the lower educational levels, and it has proportionally more persons in the manual-labor groups. Judged by these indicators of social class, one would therefore expect the aged Jews also to include proportionally fewer home owners. Yet, despite this variation by age, a high proportion of Jews in all age groups owned their dwelling.

In general, the pattern of home ownership does not show a particularly sharp variation by generation status. Among all four generation groups the proportion of home owners ranges within the relatively narrow limits of 67 to 77 per cent, with the lowest proportion characterizing the foreign born and the highest the second generation. The aged foreign born had the lowest proportion of home ownership of any generation-age group, only 63 per cent; although this proportion is lower than for most other segments of the Jewish population, it is relatively high when judged against the criterion of the total population.

Only the foreign born and the second generation have a sufficient number of cases in all three age groups to warrant comparisons by age within generation. For both, the proportion of home owners declined from the youngest to the oldest age group, and the differences were quite substantial. Within the third generation, comparison of the two age groups under 65 shows that the older group had a higher rate of ownership than the younger one. This conforms to the pattern that characterizes the population as a whole, for whom age tends to be positively correlated with home ownership. The reverse trend among the foreign born and the children of foreign born may stem from the sharper age differentials in education and occupation which characterize these generation groups.

Home ownership also varies by the sex of the head of the household (Table 4-16). Whereas three-fourths of all units headed by a male owned their homes, this was true of less than half of the units headed by a woman. This pattern of sex differentials characterizes both generation groups in which there are a sufficient number of female heads of household to warrant comparisons. Although fewer units headed by a foreign-born male owned their home compared to the second-generation group, the foreign-born females had a higher ownership rate than did the second-generation units. One can only speculate about the reasons for this reversal. It may reflect the greater importance that is attached to the family *per se,* being regarded as the basis for greater family stability in the absence of a male head. It may also have the economic advantage of reducing housing costs.

For the general population of the metropolitan area the rate of home ownership is considerably higher in the suburban sectors (65.4 per cent) than in the central cities (38.6 per cent). The Jewish population is

TABLE 4-16

PERCENTAGE OF UNITS REPORTING HOME OWNERSHIP BY GENERATION AND SEX, BY RESIDENCE, AND BY EDUCATION OF HEAD OF HOUSEHOLD

Characteristic of Head of Household	First Generation	Second Generation	Mixed Parentage	Third Generation	Total
Sex					
Male	70.3	80.8	–	–	75.9
Female	53.8	46.8	–	–	46.8
Residence					
Older Urban	55.2	51.3	–	–	52.4
Newer Urban	68.0	76.5	63.0	59.7	71.3
Suburban	89.3	93.3	83.3	90.3	91.1
Education					
Elementary	66.1	64.2	–	–	65.8
High School	61.7	72.1	–	87.2	70.7
College	68.0	78.0	61.9	74.2	73.3
Postgraduate	87.9	89.0	64.7	62.5	80.7

also characterized by considerable residential variation in home ownership. Just over half of the units living in the older urban area owned their own homes compared to almost three-quarters of those in the newer urban area and over nine out of ten of the units living in the suburbs. Quite clearly, residence affects the pattern of home ownership among Jews in the same direction as it does for the total population, but in all sectors the Jewish rate of home ownership is considerably above the level characterizing the population as a whole.

The relation between rate of home ownership and residence holds for all generations, suggesting again that both residence and socio-economic status may operate more decisively in many instances to affect the behavior of the Jewish population than does generation status itself. Differences within particular residential categories exist for units in the different generation groups, but the variations do not conform to any fixed pattern. For purposes of relating place of residence to generation status, it may well be that more detailed geographic units are required. For example, the third-generation group living in the newer urban areas probably reside disproportionally on the fringe of these areas, where property values are lower and where rental opportunities are greater because of the larger number of multiple-family dwellings. As these persons, many of whom are concentrated in the younger age groups and in the younger half of the age cohorts, move up the occupational ladder and establish themselves more favorably economically and more permanently in the community, they can be expected to display higher rates of home ownership in the newer urban areas. In the meantime, they are characterized by very high rates of ownership in the suburban communities, where property values on the average are below those in the newer areas of the central city. This pattern suggests that residential concentration is based on socio-economic considerations within the Jewish community; and these considerations are likely to provide an important basis for structuring the community as generation status itself becomes increasingly less important.

The important role of education in affecting socio-economic status is evidenced in the positive relation between educational achievement and home ownership. For the Jewish population, the rate of home ownership increased from two-thirds of those with only an elementary education or less to over 80 per cent of those who had received a post-graduate education. Yet, this positive relation between education and home ownership characterized only the first- and the second-generation groups. For the third generation, the rate of home ownership declined from almost nine out of ten of those with a high school education only to under two-thirds of those with post-graduate training. This reversal is related to the differentials in home ownership by place of residence for the third-generation group. A disproportional number of college educated persons, many of whom are professionals, live in the newer urban section where the rates of home ownership are considerably below those of the suburbs, particularly for the younger members of the third-generation group.

In general, therefore, these data on home ownership support the conclusions reached with respect to occupation and education. The exception in the third-generation group can be interpreted within the context of the particular stage of their occupational and family career. As proportionally more persons move into the older age segments of this particular generation category, the pattern for the third generation will probably conform more closely to that of the Jewish population as a whole.

STATUS CONSISTENCY

In evaluating the socio-economic status of the population, occupation and education, either individually or jointly, are often used as indices of social class, as they have been here. In this evaluation of the Jewish population, both their occupational composition and their educational achievement point to the very favorable status position they occupy in the community compared to the general population. Yet, the question of status consistency has increasingly become a matter of concern—that is, the degree to which a given group of individuals who are rated on several different status dimensions occupy statuses that are consistent with each other.[17] In view of the unique occupational and educational characteristics of the Jewish population, it seems appropriate to ascertain to what degree the different generations of the Jewish population are characterized by status consistency.

Age affects the distribution of socio-economic status because shifts in status patterns occur as persons pass through the life cycle.[18] Moreover, the peak level of the various components of status occurs at different times in the life span of the average individual. For example, educational achievement is generally fixed relatively early in the adult life cycle, but peak occupational achievement and income generally come considerably later. With respect to generation, it can be hypothesized that because the opportunities for higher education were more limited among the first and, to some extent, the second generation, there is greater likelihood of status inconsistency with occupation for these generation groups than for the third generation, for whom high-level education can be expected to be associated more closely with high-status occupation. For this evaluation, the occupation categories have been reduced to three: (1) professionals and managers, classified as high-status occupations; (2) clerical and sales workers classified as medium-status occupations; and (3) manual and service workers, classified as low-status occupations. Four educational levels have been designated: elementary school (or less), high school, college, and postgraduate work. The evaluation is restricted to those for whom information on current occupation was available. Since the analysis refers only to those 25 years of age and over, the major omissions encompass older persons who have already withdrawn from the labor force.

For all age groups, the relation between educational achievement and occupational level is clear-cut (Table 4-17). Considerably higher proportions of persons with only an elementary education are concentrated in low-status occupations and larger proportions of college-educated persons hold high-status positions. Although the patterns are consistent, the

[17] In recognition of this increased concern with status consistency, the Bureau of the Census itself has examined the population data collected in the 1960 Census in terms of the status consistency among the three components—occupation, education, and family income—of the socio-economic status scores which it has prepared. U.S. Bureau of the Census, *Methodology and Scores of Socioeconomic Status,* Working Paper No. 15 (Washington, D.C.: Government Printing Office, 1963).

[18] Charles B. Nam and Mary G. Powers, "Variations in Socio-economic Structure by Race, Residence, and the Life Cycle," *American Sociological Review,* XXX, No. 1 (1965), 97-103. See also, A. Dennis Kelly and William J. Chambliss, "Status Consistency and Political Attitudes," *American Sociological Review,* XXXI, No. 3 (1966), 375-82.

specific levels of consistency are not, particularly for those with only high school or elementary school education. Comparisons of educational achievement and occupational level for the various age segments confirm the status inconsistencies expected on the basis of career patterns.

Among those with a postgraduate education, there is minimal variation by age. For those with some college education, the aged group has achieved higher occupational status than members of the two younger groups. This may reflect the retirement of salaried persons and wage earners and the continued employment of self-employed professionals and manager-proprietors. It may also stem partially from the fact that younger persons have not yet reached their peak occupational achievement and status. The same factors may also account for the differentials at lower educational levels. The percentage of high school educated persons in high occupational positions increases from only one-third of the 25-44 year group to 55 per cent of the aged group; and the percentage of those with only an elementary education goes from one-third of the 45-64 year group to 59 per cent of the aged. On the other hand, both these situations may reflect the high occupational achievement of the aged, attained despite their limited education. Younger persons with comparably low education are unlikely to achieve as high an occupational level; for these persons, occupational achievement is currently and will probably remain more consistent with education.

TABLE 4-17

STATUS CONSISTENCY: OCCUPATIONAL DISTRIBUTION BY EDUCATIONAL LEVEL, BY AGE

	Occupational Level			Total
Education and Age	Low	Medium	High	Per Cent*
25-44 Year Age Group				
Elementary	–	–	–	–
High School	15.8	47.7	36.6	100.0
College	3.4	37.0	59.5	100.0
Postgraduate	0.0	13.3	86.6	100.0
45-64 Year Age Group				
Elementary	30.9	34.0	34.0	100.0
High School	14.4	40.5	43.9	100.0
College	5.3	39.0	55.1	100.0
Postgraduate	0.0	10.4	88.8	100.0
65 and Over Age Group				
Elementary	24.4	16.3	59.2	100.0
High School	16.2	25.9	54.8	100.0
College	0.0	21.4	78.6	100.0
Postgraduate	0.0	14.2	85.7	100.0

*Total includes a small percentage of unknown.

Comparisons of educational achievement with occupational level according to generation point to some inconsistencies, but these do not always follow a clear pattern (Table 4-18). For example, over one-third of the foreign born with less than a high school education occupy high occupation positions; among the second-generation group the comparable proportion is even higher, amounting to almost half of all persons with an elementary education or no education. Quite clearly, for this segment of the population high educational achievement was not a prerequisite for occupational achievement. In both of these instances, however, almost all of the individuals involved held managerial positions, which may cover a considerable range of achievement and includes the proprietors of small retail shops. In the other two generation categories the very small number of persons with just an elementary education makes comparisons impossible.

TABLE 4-18

STATUS CONSISTENCY: OCCUPATIONAL DISTRIBUTION BY EDUCATIONAL LEVEL, BY GENERATION

Generation and Education	Occupational Level			Total
	Low	Medium	High	Per Cent*
Elementary				
First Generation	38.0	24.0	38.0	100.0
Second Generation	21.2	29.8	46.9	100.0
Mixed Parentage	–	–	–	–
Third Generation	–	–	–	–
TOTAL	31.8	27.1	40.4	100.0
High School				
First Generation	15.5	37.1	47.4	100.0
Second Generation	14.1	41.8	42.7	100.0
Mixed Parentage	16.0	48.0	36.0	100.0
Third Generation	15.3	53.8	30.8	100.0
TOTAL	15.0	42.1	42.1	100.0
College				
First Generation	11.1	31.7	57.1	100.0
Second Generation	3.3	35.8	60.7	100.0
Mixed Parentage	1.5	47.8	50.8	100.0
Third Generation	3.6	39.3	57.2	100.0
TOTAL	4.2	37.4	58.1	100.0
Graduate School				
First Generation	0.0	2.7	97.3	100.0
Second Generation	0.0	12.6	86.9	100.0
Mixed Parentage	0.0	10.9	89.2	100.0
Third Generation	0.0	17.3	82.7	100.0
TOTAL	0.0	12.2	87.5	100.0

*Total includes a small percentage of unknown.

On the other hand, for the high school educated a different pattern emerges. Whereas the proportion of persons with a high school education who held low-status occupations remains constant among the various generation groups (14 to 16 per cent), the proportion occupying high-status positions declines from almost half of the first generation to less than one-third of the third generation. This is consistent with the hypothesis that despite the more limited education available to first-generation persons, they were able to move higher in the occupational hierarchy. For this particular educational level, there is more status inconsistency for the foreign born than for the third generation.

Reflecting the general tendency for occupational achievement to be consistent with educational level, the proportion of individuals occupying low-status jobs decreases in all generation groups as educational level rises; conversely the proportion occupying high-status occupations increases sharply from those with an elementary education or less to those with postgraduate training. Among the latter, the proportion in high occupation groups ranges from 83 per cent among the third generation to as high as 97 per cent among the first generation; in no generation group are any persons with such high educational achievement in low-status occupations. Yet the proportion of persons with high educational achievement (postgraduate) occupying medium occupation categories rises from only 3 per cent of the foreign born to 17 per cent of the third-generation group. Postgraduate studies may therefore not always lead to a professional or managerial career; evidently, a number of persons, particularly in the third generation, undertake graduate studies, although their initial positions following completion of their education are as sales or clerical workers. The data do not permit determination of the income these positions may command; this may still be quite high. Moreover, many of these persons, a number of whom are in the 25-44 age group, are likely to move up the occupational scale as they are promoted into positions on the managerial level.

Such a pattern is even more characteristic of college educated persons, but in no fixed relation to generation; the proportion of college educated persons occupying medium level occupations ranges between 32 and 48 per cent. Only small proportions of the second- and third-generation college educated persons became manual workers, but as many as 11 per cent of the foreign born with a college education did so. At the same time, for all generations, a majority of those with a college education and high occupational achievement held managerial positions; but among those with a graduate education the professionals far outnumber the managers and the proprietors.

In general, those with lower education were more heavily concentrated in occupations of low status; and, conversely, a significantly higher proportion of those with high-level education were in the high-status groups, especially the professional category. Yet, as many as two out of every five persons with an elementary education held high-status occupations. Since this is largely a function of the classification system, inclusion of a more refined occupational classification and of income data might affect the relationship. Nonetheless, to the extent that affiliation with the managerial and proprietor category does represent high status, such an achievement has provided an important channel for the social mobility of that segment of the Jewish community that has had only limited opportunities to obtain a good secular education.

CHAPTER FIVE

Marriage and the Family

The family may be viewed as one of the primary human institutions and it is formally developed in most societies. As a social subsystem, the family not only functions to reproduce and maintain the species but is the instrumental foundation of the larger social structure. All other institutions of society depend on the family to act as one of the major agents of socialization in the transmission of values, attitudes, goals, and aspirations.[1] In this sense, the structure and functions of the family reflect the society or subsociety within which it is located. Important changes in American society since the mid-nineteenth century have led to modifications in the composition, structure, and nature of the American family. In general, there has been a tendency toward increases in divorce and remarriage, larger proportions of the population who marry at some time in their life cycle, and a reduction in the ages at which people first marry.[2]

Inasmuch as the structure of the family is sensitive to alterations in other institutions of society, some changes in Jewish family patterns should be expected. Moreover, the family is an instrument of cultural continuity; as such, the degree to which Jewish family structure varies with generation is an indicator of the strength of cultural continuity and, in turn, a measure of cultural assimilation. Nevertheless, changes which may result from acculturation must be balanced by the values of family life and family cohesion characteristic of the Jewish population, as well as by the concentration of Jews in social and economic categories associated with greater family cohesion.[3] However, no systematic research has focused on the consequences

[1] William J. Goode, *The Family,* Foundations of Modern Sociology Series (Englewood Cliffs, N.J.: Prentice-Hall, Inc., 1966), pp. 1-7.

[2] John Hajnal, "The Marriage Boom," in *Demographic Analysis,* eds. Joseph J. Spengler and Otis D. Duncan (Glencoe, Ill.: The Free Press, 1956), pp. 220-42; Kingsley Davis, "Statistical Perspective on Marriage and Divorce," in *Demographic Analysis,* eds. Spengler and Duncan, pp. 243-55; Paul C. Glick, *American Families* (New York: John Wiley & Sons, Inc., 1957); Paul C. Glick and Robert Parke, "New Approaches in Studying the Life Cycle of the Family," *Demography,* II (1965), 187-202; Hugh Carter and Alexander Plateris, "Trends in Divorce and Family Disruption," *Health, Education and Welfare Indicators* (Washington, D.C.: National Vital Statistics Division, Public Health Service, August, 1963). For a general discussion of the family, see Ernest Burgess, Harvey Locke, and M. Margaret Thomes, *The American Family* (3rd ed.), (New York: American Book Company, 1965).

of acculturation and assimilation for the Jewish family. This chapter investigates a number of basic questions concerning the nature of Jewish families. First, in what ways do the families of Jews and non-Jews differ? Second, what changes in the Jewish family result from generational acculturation and assimilation? Third, what variation in Jewish family patterns may be observed by area of residence, level of education, and type of religious identification?

Four aspects of the Jewish family will be examined: (1) marital status, categorized into single, married, separated, divorced, and widowed; (2) number of times married for all ever-married persons, dichotomized into those who have been married once only and those who have been married more than once; (3) household type defined in terms of nuclear, extended, and one-person units; and (4) age at first marriage.

ARE JEWISH FAMILIES DIFFERENT?

To place the analysis of generation changes in Jewish family structure in perspective, it is important to examine some general differences between Jewish and non-Jewish families. Some argue that the Jewish population is characterized by stronger family ties, tightly knit kinship relationships, and greater family stability than Protestants and Catholics.[3] Several community studies have found that divorce rates and to some extent remarriage rates among the Jewish population are lower than those for the total population.[4] In order to provide additional insight into the differences between the family structure of Jews and that of the total population, data on marital status, remarriage patterns, and age at first marriage obtained from our survey of the Jewish population are compared to 1960 census data.[5]

These sets of data indicate that for both males and females a higher proportion of the Jewish population is married and a lower proportion is divorced or separated (Table 5-1). Almost three-quarters of

3 Fred Strodtbeck, "Family Interaction, Values, and Achievement," in *The Jews*, ed. Marshall Sklare (Glencoe, Ill.: The Free Press, 1958), pp. 147-65; Gerhard Lenski, *The Religious Factor* (Garden City, N.Y.: Doubleday & Company, Inc., Anchor Books, 1963), pp. 212-59.

4 Lenski, *The Religious Factor*, pp. 218-19; Ben B. Seligman and Aaron Antonovsky, "Some Aspects of Jewish Demography," in *The Jews*, ed. Sklare, pp. 60-62.

5 Comparisons are limited to the published census data. Marital status data are available for total whites in the Providence-Pawtucket urbanized area, which is the area most comparable to that covered by our survey (see Chapter 2). Remarriage data are available only for the total population in the Providence-Pawtucket SMSA. For sources see Table 5-1. Since the Jewish population is concentrated in high educational and occupational categories, comparisons between the Jewish sample and the total population should be done with socio-economic status controlled. Unfortunately, such data are not available and the analysis must be viewed as suggestive.

TABLE 5-1

MARITAL STATUS AND REMARRIAGE PATTERNS OF THE JEWISH AND TOTAL POPULATION 14 YEARS OLD AND OVER, BY SEX

	Males		Females	
Marital Status and Times Married	Jewish Population	Total* Population	Jewish Population	Total* Population
Marital Status				
Single	23.2	25.2	19.5	22.7
Married	74.0	67.8	68.7	60.3
Separated	0.2	1.0	0.2	1.5
Divorced	0.3	1.6	1.5	2.5
Widowed	2.2	4.4	10.1	13.0
Total Per Cent	100.0	100.0	100.0	100.0
Times Married				
Once only	92.8	91.2	93.2	91.9
More than once	6.3	8.7	5.6	8.2
No information	0.9	0.0	1.1	0.0
Total Per Cent	100.0	100.0	100.0	100.0

*Marital status for the total white population was obtained for the Providence-Pawtucket urbanized area and remarriage patterns were obtained for the total population of the Providence-Pawtucket Standard Metropolitan area. Adapted from U.S. Bureau of the Census, *U.S. Census of Population: 1960,* Vol. 1, *Characteristics of the Population,* Part 41, Rhode Island (Washington, D.C.: Government Printing Office, 1963), Table 21, p. 41-33 and Table 105, p. 41-139.

all Jewish males over age 14 were married, compared to two-thirds of the total white male population; and 2.6 per cent of all white males were divorced or separated, compared to 0.5 per cent of the Jewish male population. Similar patterns characterize females. However, these data represent a cross section of current marital status. Consequently, they may not represent differences in actual divorce rates in either the general or the Jewish populations. The observed current differences in the proportion divorced are affected by the extent of remarriage and also by the different age structures of the two populations. A further examination of this problem, however, suggests that the lower proportion of divorced and separated persons and the higher proportion married among the Jewish population do not result from such differences. Indeed, the data reveal that the proportion of Jews who marry more than once is slightly below that of the total population. Furthermore, information on marital status by age for the Jewish and total population indicates that, for each age group, Jews have a lower proportion separated or divorced and a higher proportion married (Table 5-2). The exception in the youngest age group, wherein a larger proportion of Jews are single, probably reflects the pattern of later age at marriage which characterizes the Jew-

TABLE 5-2

MARITAL STATUS OF JEWISH AND TOTAL POPULATION, BY AGE AND SEX

	Males				Females			
	15-24	25-44	45-64	65 and Over	15-24	25-44	45-64	65 and Over
Total Population*								
Single	81.1	14.1	9.2	8.0	66.2	10.8	12.7	14.5
Married	18.2	83.1	83.4	65.7	32.3	82.8	68.0	33.4
Separated	0.4	1.0	1.6	1.6	0.8	2.0	1.8	1.1
Divorced	0.2	1.5	2.5	1.5	0.7	2.8	3.5	1.6
Widowed	0.0	0.3	3.4	23.2	0.1	1.6	14.0	49.5
Total Per Cent	100.0	100.0	100.0	100.0	100.0	100.0	100.0	100.0
Jewish Population								
Single	92.7	8.6	4.0	1.9	80.9	5.0	7.0	3.3
Married	7.3	89.7	94.1	86.0	18.8	92.0	80.6	49.6
Separated	0.0	0.6	0.0	0.5	0.0	0.3	0.1	0.0
Divorced	0.0	1.0	0.2	0.0	0.3	1.5	2.5	0.4
Widowed	0.0	0.2	1.7	11.7	0.0	1.1	9.8	46.7
Total Per Cent	100.0	100.0	100.0	100.0	100.0	100.0	100.0	100.0

*For the source of data on the total population of the Providence-Pawtucket SMSA see note to Table 5-1.

ish population. Thus, it appears that the lower proportion divorced and separated, the higher proportion of those who are married, and the lower remarriage rate of the Jewish population primarily reflect the greater stability of Jewish marriages, the traditional Jewish value of family cohesion, and the emphasis on marriage and family life in the Jewish cultural heritage.

Within both the Jewish and total population, differences in the marital status of males and females are noteworthy. In both populations the proportion of females who are divorced and separated and, particularly, the proportion of women who are widowed exceed the comparable values for males. These differences, along with differences in the proportion of males and females who are married and single, are in large measure attributable to three factors: (1) the tendency among males to marry several years later than females, with the result that more males remain single for a longer period of time; (2) the slightly higher remarriage rate among males; and (3) sex differences in the mortality rate which favor the female.[6] The older ages at which men marry coupled with shorter life spans adds to the length of time the average woman may spend as a widow. This accounts for the fact that, among those 65 years of age and older, a disproportionate number of females of both populations were widowed when compared to males.

[6] See the discussion in Chapter 7 on sex mortality differentials in the Jewish population.

Several national studies have found that Jews marry at later ages than Protestants or Catholics.[7] Comparisons between the age at marriage of Jews in Providence and the total United States population lend support to this finding. The average age of Jewish males at first marriage was 26, compared to 23 for the total male population; Jewish women, on the average, marry at age 23 compared to age 20 for the total female population.[8] Trends in age at marriage among Jews and the total population may be obtained by categorizing women according to the date of their first marriage (Table 5-3).[9] An examination of ten such marriage cohorts reveals that later age at marriage has characterized Jewish women since the 1920-1924 cohort.[10] Patterns of earlier marriages in the post World War II cohorts appear for both populations. In addition, differences between the average age at marriage of women in the Jewish and total population have narrowed; the difference between the two populations in the last observation period (1950-1954) is the lowest since the 1910-1919 cohort. A final point regarding trends relates to the greater variation in age at marriage among Jews for the ten marriage cohorts observed. Among women in the total population, age at marriage varies only slightly, from a high of 21.2 to a low of 20.6, while among Jewish women the difference is as high as four years (from 23.3 to 19.3). The more striking fluctuation within the Jewish population partly reflects generation changes and rapid social mobility.

The later marriage age of Jews may be a concomitant of their concentration in social groupings that have traditionally been associated with deferred and delayed marriages—particularly in high education and occupation categories. But this explanation is incomplete since Jews marrying in the 1920's were also characterized by delayed marriages but were not concentrated in such social categories. Other factors that should be considered include aspirations for social mobility, the desire for integration into American society, and, perhaps, the minority status of the Jew and concomitant feelings of insecurity, all of which might lead to de-

[7] Ronald Freedman, Pascal K. Whelpton, and John W. Smit, "Socio-Economic Factors in Religious Differentials in Fertility," *American Sociological Review*, XXVI (August, 1961), Table 1, p. 610; Pascal K. Whelpton, Arthur A. Campbell, and John E. Patterson, *Fertility and Family Planning in the United States* (Princeton: Princeton University Press, 1966), Table 173, p. 321.

[8] Data on age at marriage for the total United States population are from *Current Population Reports* cited by William Petersen, *Population* (New York: The Macmillan Company, 1961), p. 233.

[9] Some of the limitations and biases of marriage cohort data obtained in sample surveys are discussed in Glick, *American Families*, pp. 55-56.

[10] For data on the later age at marriage of Jews at the turn of the century see John S. Billings, "Vital Statistics of the Jews in the United States," *Census Bulletin*, No. 19 (December 30, 1889), pp. 4-9.

TABLE 5-3

MEDIAN AGE AT FIRST MARRIAGE FOR JEWISH AND TOTAL U.S. POPULATION FOR ALL EVER-MARRIED WOMEN, BY MARRIAGE COHORTS

Period of First Marriage	Median Age at First Marriage: Jewish Population	Total Population*
Before 1910	19.3	–
1910-1919	20.4	20.6
1920-1924	22.4	20.7
1925-1929	22.8	20.7
1930-1934	22.7	20.8
1935-1939	23.1	21.2
1940-1944	23.3	21.1
1945-1949	23.2	21.0
1950-1954	21.6	20.6
1955-1963	21.4	–
TOTAL	22.6	20.8

*Data on total U.S. population adapted from Paul Glick, *American Families,* Table 34, p. 56. The data were collected in the *Current Population Survey* of 1954. For a slightly different set of data for the total population by marriage cohort see David Goldberg, "Fertility and Fertility Differentials: Some Observations on Recent Changes in the United States," in *Public Health and Population Change,* eds. Mindel C. Sheps and Jeanne Clare Ridley (Pittsburgh: University of Pittsburgh Press, 1965), p. 122.

layed marriage in favor of higher educational achievement and economic advancement.[11]

The distinctive characteristics that emerge from a comparison of Jewish with other families in the United States are the greater stability among Jewish families, the lower rates of divorce and separation, and their later age at marriage. These data lend support to the hypothesis that the Jewish value emphasizing greater family solidarity and cohesion is expressed and translated into behavior.

THE FAMILY IN TRANSITION

Because of the lack of previous research on generation changes in Jewish family structure, there are few guidelines for developing hypotheses. However, it appears that with the increased Americanization and acculturation of the Jewish population and with its concentration in the middle-class, some breakdown of traditional Jewish family values will occur, which in turn may have the following structural conse-

[11] See pp. 133-36.

quences: (1) increases in the frequency of marital dissolution among second- and third-generation Jews; (2) the proportion of remarriages increasing with distance from the immigrant generation; (3) increases by generation in the number of household units that contain only the nuclear family (husband and wife with or without children, or head only with children), and concomitant decreases in extended households (containing parents or other relatives of the head and/or spouse with or without children); and (4) reductions in the age at which Jews marry, following the general pattern observed for the American population as a whole. Although the focus here is on generation changes, the over-all stability of Jewish families must be emphasized.

These hypotheses are only partially confirmed. The stability of the Jewish family as well as the generation changes occurring in the acculturation process can be seen with data on marital status and remarriages (Tables 5-4 and 5-5). For the total Jewish population over age 25, 85 per cent were married and less than 1.5 per cent were divorced or separated.[12] Moreover, fully 94 per cent of the total Jewish population who were ever

TABLE 5-4

MARITAL STATUS, BY GENERATION AND AGE

Generation and Age	Single	Married	Widowed	Separated and Divorced	Total Per Cent
All Ages					
First Generation	1.2	79.6	18.2	0.8	100.0*
Second Generation	7.0	86.5	5.3	1.2	100.0*
Mixed Parentage	6.7	89.1	1.0	3.2	100.0
Third Generation	7.7	89.3	1.7	1.4	100.0
TOTAL	5.5	85.3	7.7	1.4	100.0
25-44 Age Group					
First Generation	2.4	95.2	1.2	1.2	100.0
Second Generation	6.4	91.3	0.8	1.4	100.0
Mixed Parentage	7.7	89.1	0.0	3.2	100.0
Third Generation	7.8	89.9	1.0	1.3	100.0
45-64 Age Group					
First Generation	0.6	88.6	9.1	1.2	100.0*
Second Generation	7.4	86.5	5.0	1.0	100.0*
Mixed Parentage	4.7	88.2	3.5	3.5	100.0
Third Generation	8.2	87.8	2.0	2.0	100.0
65 and Over Age Group					
First Generation	1.5	66.5	31.7	0.3	100.0
Second Generation	6.3	65.2	27.7	0.9	100.0

*Includes less than one per cent unknown marital status.

[12] In the ensuing analysis the divorced and separated were combined and the data are restricted to the Jewish population 25 years of age and over.

married were married only once. However, some breakdown of traditional Jewish family cohesion may be inferred from the slight increases, from first to later generations, in the proportion divorced and separated and in the proportion marrying more than once among third-generation Jews. The foreign born have the lowest proportion of divorced persons and those born in the United States of mixed parentage have the highest proportion. Although the increase in divorce is slight, it appears when age is controlled. Data not shown in the tables indicate that the pattern of slight increases in the proportion divorced among second- and third-generation Jews characterizes both sexes. However, what is most striking is the *lack* of clear-cut generation changes and the general stability of Jewish families in each generation.

Similar patterns of over-all stability and slight generation changes are reflected in the rate of remarriages. It was not possible to separate remarriages that followed divorce from those that were the result of widowhood; thus, these data are limited. As with increases in divorce and separation, there is a tendency among third-generation Jews toward higher rates of remarriage. Obviously, age differences between the generations are important. However, third-generation Jews, for the two age groupings where comparisons are possible, had a higher proportion of remarriages than earlier generations. The lack of smooth patterns of increasing remarriage rates may reflect the absence of change or the inability here to separate remarriages due to divorce from those due to

TABLE 5-5

NUMBER OF TIMES MARRIED, BY GENERATION AND AGE

Generation and Age	Once	More Than Once	Total Per Cent
All Ages			
First Generation	90.1	9.9	100.0
Second Generation	95.5	4.5	100.0
Mixed Parentage	98.3	1.7	100.0
Third Generation	92.7	7.3	100.0
TOTAL	94.0	6.0	100.0
25-44 Age Group			
First Generation	96.3	3.7	100.0
Second Generation	97.4	2.6	100.0
Mixed Parentage	99.0	1.0	100.0
Third Generation	94.0	6.0	100.0
45-64 Age Group			
First Generation	93.4	6.6	100.0
Second Generation	94.6	5.4	100.0
Mixed Parentage	96.3	3.7	100.0
Third Generation	88.4	11.6	100.0
65 and Over Age Group			
First Generation	84.8	15.2	100.0
Second Generation	93.3	6.7	100.0

widowhood. The higher rates of remarriages among native-born Jews of either mixed parentage or native parentage characterize both sexes when age is controlled. For example, more than one-and-a-half times as many third-generation males 45 to 64 years of age remarried compared to first-generation males, and more than twice as many third-generation females 25 to 44 and 45 to 64 years of age remarried when compared to first-generation females of the same ages.

An interrelated dimension of family structure is household composition—whether the Jewish household contains only the immediate family of husband-wife-children or other relatives such as grandparents. The importance of examining household composition lies in the implications any variations may have for social interaction and, particularly, strains and conflicts between family members of different generations. For analytical purposes, household type was trichotomized as (1) nuclear household units, (2) extended household units, and (3) one-person units.

Most of the evidence on families in the United States suggests the predominance of nuclear household units and the decrease in extended families sharing the same household.[13] This is clearly the pattern for

TABLE 5-6

TYPE OF HOUSEHOLD UNIT, BY GENERATION AND AGE

Generation and Age	Nuclear	Extended	One-Person Unit	Total Per Cent
All Ages				
First Generation	78.8	8.1	13.1	100.0
Second Generation	85.3	8.5	6.2	100.0
Mixed Parentage	77.7	9.0	13.3	100.0
Third Generation	96.7	3.3	0.0	100.0
TOTAL	84.8	7.6	7.6	100.0
25-44 Age Group				
First Generation	90.4	9.6	0.0	100.0
Second Generation	95.5	4.5	0.0	100.0
Mixed Parentage	86.2	6.9	6.9	100.0
Third Generation	97.8	2.2	0.0	100.0
45-64 Age Group				
First Generation	81.6	7.6	10.8	100.0
Second Generation	83.5	10.2	6.3	100.0
Mixed Parentage	64.3	14.3	21.4	100.0
Third Generation	87.5	12.5	0.0	100.0
65 and Over Age Group				
First Generation	74.4	8.2	17.4	100.0
Second Generation	63.6	9.1	27.3	100.0

[13] Burgess, Locke, and Thomes, *The American Family*. A recent analysis of 1875 and 1960 Rhode Island census data suggests that the nuclear small family pattern is not a new phenomenon. See Edward T. Pryor, Jr., "Family Structure and Change: Rhode Island, 1875 and 1960" (Unpublished Ph.D. dissertation, Brown University, June 1966).

TABLE 5-7

MEDIAN AGE AT FIRST MARRIAGE, BY GENERATION, AGE, AND SEX

Generation and Age	Male	Female	Total
All Ages			
First Generation	26.4	22.1	24.1
Second Generation	26.4	22.5	24.9
Mixed Parentage	25.6	22.6	23.7
Third Generation	24.5	21.4	22.6
TOTAL	26.0	22.6	24.2
25-44 Age Group			
First Generation	25.6	21.6	23.9
Second Generation	25.3	22.3	23.7
Mixed Parentage	24.8	21.9	23.0
Third Generation	24.1	21.2	22.3
45-64 Age Group			
First Generation	27.8	23.3	25.2
Second Generation	27.1	23.8	25.7
Mixed Parentage	28.4	24.1	25.4
Third Generation	–	22.9	24.4
65 and Over Age Group			
First Generation	25.3	21.1	23.1
Second Generation	27.7	23.5	25.6

Jewish households (Table 5-6).[14] Fully 85 per cent of all Jewish households were classified as nuclear, and the remainder were equally distributed between extended and one-person units. Generation changes toward an increase in nuclear households among third-generation Jews are evident. Classifying the household by the generation status of the head reveals that less than 80 per cent of the foreign-born households were nuclear; this increased to 85 per cent among the second generation; and fully 96.7 per cent of the third generation were living in nuclear household units. Part of these differences stem from the age concentrations of the generations. Nevertheless, when age is held constant, the increase in nuclear households among third-generation Jews remains. There are two exceptions to this pattern: those aged 65 and over and the native born of mixed parentage. The exception for the oldest age category results from an increase between the first and second generation in one-person units (17 to 27 per cent) rather than an increase in extended families. This may reflect the greater tendency on the part of the wid-

[14] The analysis of household type is based on data of the household unit and not on individuals. See the earlier discussion in Chapter 2. Generation status, age, and other characteristics discussed below were based on the characteristics of the head of the household. In almost 90 per cent of the households the male was the head.

owed and single of the second generation to live alone rather than move into their children's household. The deviation of the native born of mixed parentage is difficult to explain and may be a result of the small number of cases.[15]

Conforming to the marriage cohort trends in age at marriage are the patterns by generation status (Table 5-7). Early age at marriage characterizes first-generation Jews, followed by slightly later ages at marriage among the second generation, and consistently younger ages at marriage among the third generation. The tendency for third-generation Jews to marry at younger ages holds when age and sex are controlled. The later age at marriage among the second generation is only observed for females and is true of all age groups. Males are characterized by consistent reductions in age at marriage with distance from the first generation except in the oldest age group where the pattern follows females. Both Jewish men and women of the third generation are marrying at younger ages, and differences between the sexes have diminished; the more than four year difference between the average age at which first-generation males and females married decreased among the third generation to a three-year difference. This conforms to the pattern observed for the total American population.[16]

SOCIAL DIFFERENTIALS

Patterns of family structure are not uniform throughout American society. For example, divorce rates vary markedly among regions of the United States, among urban and rural areas, and among racial groups. Divorce seems to be related to occupation and education, although the evidence regarding the direction of relationship is not conclusive.[17] In this section attention is directed to differences in the family structure of Jews who live in various residential areas of the metropolitan area, who have different levels of educational attainment, and who identify with different religious denominations within Judaism. Earlier it was hy-

15 Inconsistencies in the pattern of native born of mixed parentage for other variables are reported by Bernard Lazerwitz and Louis Rowitz, "The Three-Generations Hypothesis," *American Journal of Sociology,* LXIX (March, 1964), 536, footnote 21; see also p. 180 of this book.

16 Glick, *American Families.*

17 See Carter and Plateris, "Trends in Divorce and Family Disruption," *Health, Education and Welfare Indicators,* especially sources cited on p. v; Paul Glick, "Marriage Instability: Variations by Size of Place and Region," *Milbank Memorial Fund Quarterly,* XLI (January, 1963), 43-55; Karen Hillman, "Marital Instability and Its Relation to Education, Income and Occupation: An Analysis Based on Census Data," in *Selected Studies in Marriage and the Family* (rev. ed.), eds. Robert F. Winch, *et al.* (New York: Holt, Rinehart & Winston, Inc., 1962), pp. 603-8.

pothesized that variation in Jewish family patterns is related to the degree of acculturation and Americanization. It would therefore follow that the more acculturated segments of the Jewish community, i.e., suburban residents, the more educated, and Reform Jews, have experienced greater family structural changes than the less acculturated segments. The empirical evidence to support this hypothesis is not clear-cut, and differences in family structure by residence, education, and religious identification were small. While this points to the over-all stability of Jewish families, some general differential patterns are noteworthy. These are discussed here without tabular presentation.

The younger suburban residents appear to have proportionally more divorced persons than comparable age groups in urban areas. Similarly, for most generation and age groupings, a larger proportion of suburbanites was married more than once when compared to Jews living in the older or newer sections of the city. Suburban families tend to be more nuclear than families in urban areas: almost 90 per cent of the Jewish households in the suburbs were classified as nuclear, compared to 85 per cent in the newer urban areas and 77 per cent in the older urban areas. These differences, while diminishing, remain when generation and age are controlled. No consistent pattern of residential differentials in age at marriage was observed.

Divorce and separation are somewhat more characteristic of Jews who have obtained higher levels of education. This pattern was observed only for the first generation and the native born of mixed parentage when age was controlled. This finding is in contrast to some studies which have concluded that the more educated of the general population have lower rates of divorce.[18] One possible explanation may lie in the consideration that among Jews, the more educated segments are generally more secular and acculturated and their divorce rates more closely approximate the non-Jewish rates; their higher rates of marital breakup are relative to the very low rates among the less acculturated groupings. Jews with the highest level of education have the highest concentration in nuclear household units and the latest age at marriage. Over 92 per cent of this group live in nuclear households, compared to 75 per cent of those with only an elementary school education. In general, Jews who had more than a four-year college education married three years later than Jews with only an elementary school education (age 26.4 vs. age 23.4) and two and a half years later than those with a high school or college education. Differences in age at marriage among various educational levels

[18] J. Richard Udry, "Marital Instability by Race, Sex, Education, and Occupation Using 1960 Census Data," *American Journal of Sociology,* LXXII (September, 1966), 203-9. Also see references cited in footnote 17.

have diminished over the generations and greater homogeneity characterizes third-generation Jews. This may be a function of the increasing homogeneity of Jewish social structure and the lack of wide class distinction among third-generation Jews.[19]

As expected, Jews identifying themselves with Reform Judaism are characterized by a higher proportion of divorce and separation and a larger proportion of remarriages compared to those who identify either as Conservative or Orthodox, when age and generation are controlled. Although Reform Jews are more concentrated in nuclear household units, this pattern stems from age and generation differences, i.e., the greater concentration of Orthodox Jews among the older foreign born and of Reform Jews among the younger native born.[20] Divorce rates, remarriage rates, and the concentration in nuclear household units have remained relatively stable and lower over the generations among the Orthodox segment. The slight generational increases in these family variables, noted earlier, appear to reflect primarily the changing family structure of Conservative and Reform Jews.

STABILITY DESPITE CHANGE

The data on marital status, number of times married, household type, and age at marriage of three generations of Jewish families point to several general conclusions.

First, Jewish families exhibit an over-all pattern of stability. Comparisons of the Jewish and the total population indicate that a smaller proportion of Jews were divorced or had married more than once. Furthermore, stability characterized each of the generations. Only a small proportion of first-, second-, and third-generation Jews were divorced or separated, few married more than once, and the nuclear family type predominated. Yet, slight increases in the proportion of divorced or separated, in the amount of remarriages, and in the proportion living in nuclear households were observed for more recent generations. In general, these patterns were not explainable in terms of age, sex, residence, religious identification, or educational differences between generations.

Second, females were more concentrated in widowed and divorced categories than were men. This pattern may be partially interpreted as a consequence of the greater longevity of women, the slightly higher rates of remarriage among males, and the older ages at which males marry.

19 Greater homogeneity among third-generation Jews characterizes other patterns also, including fertility, socio-economic status, and religiosity measures.

20 See pp. 177-80.

Third, the social groupings within the three generations who were more acculturated—i.e., suburbanites, the more educated, and Reform Jews—in general had higher rates of divorce, a larger proportion married more than once, and a higher proportion living in nuclear households. However, differences were small and the patterns were not clear-cut.

Finally, the trends of age at marriage among Jews followed the general downward trend characterizing the American population as a whole, although Jews continued to marry at later ages than non-Jews. Among Jews, reduction in age at marriage was sharper for males than for females. The decrease in age at first marriage was observed, when place of residence, religious identification, and education were controlled. Among the three differentials examined, education was the most significant differentiator of age at marriage, although the differences tended to diminish among third-generation Jews.

The two themes of over-all stability in Jewish family structure and slight generational increases in divorce, remarriages, and nuclear households fit well with the broader changes that have characterized three generations of American Jews. The value of family stability characterizing the Jewish population has slowly been changing, suggesting that cultural assimilation in terms of family structure has occurred for the Jewish group, although very slowly, and with the over-all retention of the value of family stability.

CHAPTER SIX

"Be Fruitful and Multiply"

Since the beginning of the twentieth century, research in the United States has pointed to the conclusion that Jews have lower fertility than members of other religious groups. The major fertility studies undertaken since the 1950's have consistently confirmed this finding for many aspects of fertility, including fertility behavior, attitudes toward family size and contraception, and family planning success. However, a careful review of the literature on fertility changes and variations within the Jewish population reveals contradictory findings and inconsistent explanations. This is partly so because conclusions have been based on the small numbers of Jewish couples included in the surveys. Moreover, demographers have not placed the analysis of fertility in a cogent and coherent sociological frame of reference which would integrate findings concerning Jewish fertility with other social behavior characterizing the Jewish population. Thus, the data that are available and the explanations that have been offered are too limited to allow for an analysis and understanding of Jewish fertility trends and differentials. In this chapter an attempt will be made to pinpoint and resolve a number of prevalent inconsistencies and misinterpretations by relating findings concerning Jewish fertility patterns to a sociological understanding of the Jews.

Before we turn to the analysis of Jewish fertility, a brief comment should be made concerning the sources of data available. Since decennial censuses of the United States have not included a question on religious preference, and religion is not obtained on birth records, the more detailed data available on American Jewish fertility have been limited to sample survey studies. Most of the information on the fertility behavior and attitudes of Jews is a by-product of the Growth of American Families Studies (GAF) and the Princeton Fertility Studies.[1] However,

[1] Ronald Freedman, Pascal K. Whelpton, and Arthur A. Campbell, *Family Planning, Sterility and Population Growth* (New York: McGraw-Hill Book Company, 1959); Pascal K. Whelpton, Arthur A. Campbell, and John E. Patterson, *Fertility and Family Planning in the United States* (Princeton: Princeton University Press, 1966); Charles F. Westoff, Robert G. Potter, Jr., Philip C. Sagi, and Elliot G. Mishler, *Family Growth in Metropolitan America* (Princeton: Princeton University Press, 1961); Charles

the GAF Study of 1955 included only 66 Jewish couples, and a little over 100 Jewish couples were interviewed in the 1960 GAF Study and in both phases of the Princeton Study. Detailed analysis using these data is impossible nor is there any assurance that the Jewish couples included in the samples are representative of any broader Jewish population.

To partially fill the gap in our knowledge concerning Jewish fertility trends and differentials, information on family size and birth spacing [2] was collected as an integral part of our larger study, thereby allowing for an analysis of the interrelationships between fertility and a broad range of sociological and demographic variables.

RELIGION AND FERTILITY

Research in American fertility patterns has emphasized religious differentials and, particularly, the lower fertility of Jewish couples. Smaller family size, delayed age at marriage, and extensive and efficient use of contraception have characterized the Jewish population in the United States since the latter part of the nineteenth century.

In 1889 a study of over ten thousand Jewish families revealed that the Jewish birth rate was lower than the non-Jewish birth rate.[3] In the only example of a state census that obtained information on religion and related this to family size, the Rhode Island Census of 1905 showed that the average family size of native-born Jewish women was 2.3, compared to an average family size of 3.2 for native-born Catholics and 2.5 for native-born Protestants.[4] Although smaller family size characterized both the native-born Jewish and Protestant women in Rhode Island, Jaffe in the late 1930's found that the net reproduction rates of foreign-born and native-born Jews were lower than the rate of economically comparable Protestants.[5] Related evidence on contraceptive practices during the 1930's indicates that a higher proportion of Jews used con-

---

F. Westoff, Robert G. Potter, Jr., and Philip C. Sagi, *The Third Child* (Princeton: Princeton University Press, 1963).

[2] Family size is measured by the total number of children ever born, excluding stillbirths; birth spacing was measured in three ways: (1) months between marriage and first birth, (2) months between marriage and second birth, and (3) months between first and second birth. See previous chapter for discussion of age at marriage.

[3] John S. Billings, "Vital Statistics of the Jews in the United States," *Census Bulletin*, No. 19 (December 30, 1889), pp. 4-9.

[4] Calculated from the *Rhode Island Census of 1905*, "Conjugal Conditions, Maternity Tables," Bulletin IV, part one of the annual report for 1907, Table VII, p. 551. The data are limited since they include number of children born to women 15 to 44 and not completed familites. *Cf.* J. J. Spengler, *The Fecundity of Native and Foreign Born Women in New England*, pamphlet series, Vol. II, No. 1 (Washington, D.C.: The Brookings Institution, June 30, 1930).

[5] A.J. Jaffe, "Religious Differentials in the Net Reproduction Rate," *Journal of the American Statistical Association*, XXIV (June, 1939), 335-42.

traceptives, planned their pregnancies, used more efficient methods of birth control, and began use of contraception earlier in marriage than Protestants or Catholics.[6]

Although the first major study of American fertility, the Indianapolis Fertility Study, was limited in its detailed analysis to Protestants, the general household survey, used to screen for eligible Protestant couples, obtained information on the fertility of various religious groups. Of the 41,498 native-born white, unbroken first marriages with wives 15 to 44 years of age in Indianapolis, 419 were Jewish. The fertility rates, standardized for age, were about 18 per cent higher for Catholics than for Protestants and about 25 per cent lower for Jews than for Protestants.[7] However, the small number of Jewish women included in the Indianapolis study prevented more detailed analysis.

The United States census in a 1957 sample population survey obtained for the first time information on religion as related to number of children ever born per 1,000 women of different age groups. Although only limited cross-tabulations were published, the results confirm the lower fertility of Jews. The cumulative fertility rate of Jewish women 45 years of age and older was 2,218 per 1,000 compared to 3,056 per 1,000 Catholic women and 2,753 per 1,000 Protestant women. Lower fertility also characterized Jewish women age 15 to 44. Even controlling for area of residence, the fertility rate for Jewish women was 14 per cent below the fertility rate for urban women of all religions combined.[8]

Comparisons between the fertility ratios of the Jewish and total population in over a dozen communities in the United States point to similar lower Jewish fertility.[9] For the Jewish population in the Provi-

[6] R. K. Stix and Frank Notestein, *Controlled Fertility* (Baltimore: The William & Wilkins Co., 1940), p. 29; Raymond Pearl, *The Natural History of Population* (New York: Oxford University Press, Inc., 1939), pp. 241-42. Pearl states, "The most striking and significant result that emerges from the data . . . is the much higher proportion of contraceptive effort among the Jews than among women of any other religious class" (p. 242). Both studies have serious methodological weaknesses and are reviewed here for their suggestive value and historical interest.

[7] Pascal K. Whelpton and Clyde V. Kiser, "Differential Fertility Among Native-White Couples in Indianapolis," *Social and Psychological Factors Affecting Fertility*, I, *Milbank Memorial Fund Quarterly*, XXI (July, 1943), 226-71.

[8] The main report is contained in U.S. Bureau of the Census, "Religion Reported by the Civilian Population of the United States: March, 1957," *Current Population Reports*, Series P-20, No. 79 (February 2, 1958). The fertility data were published only in U.S. Bureau of the Census, *Statistical Abstract of the United States* (Washington, D.C.: Government Printing Office, 1958), Table 40, p. 41. See also Paul Glick, "Intermarriage and Fertility Patterns Among Persons in Major Religious Groups," *Eugenics Quarterly*, VII (March, 1960), 31-38.

[9] See the review in Ben Seligman and Aaron Antonovsky, "Some Aspects of Jewish Demography," in *The Jews*, ed. Marshall Sklare (Glencoe, Ill.: The Free Press, 1958), Table 6, p. 67; Council of Jewish Federations and Welfare Funds, *Council Reports* (May 21, 1963), p. 3.

dence metropolitan area there were 450 children under 5 years of age for every thousand women aged 20 to 44. This fertility ratio is significantly lower than the fertility ratio of the total population in the metropolitan area (620) or the total white urban American population (635).

The results of the Growth of American Families Study indicate that in 1955 the average family size of Catholic and Protestant couples was 2.1 compared to an average family size of 1.7 for Jewish couples, and Jews expected significantly fewer children (2.4) than either Protestants (2.9) or Catholics (3.4). In summary, the study points out that Jews have the smallest families, marry later, expect and desire to have the smallest families, approve the use of contraception most strongly, are most likely to have used contraception, are most likely to plan the number and spacing of all their children, and are most likely to use effective methods of contraception.[10] The 1960 GAF Study reported similar patterns.[11]

Consistent with these findings are those reported by the Princeton Fertility Studies of 1957 and 1960. They found that Jews, when compared to Protestants and Catholics, desired fewer children and more successfully planned their pregnancies; fewer had a third child or an unplanned pregnancy. Fully 92 per cent of the Jewish couples used the most efficient contraceptive methods, compared to 66 per cent of the Protestants and 35 per cent of the Catholics. As a result, Jews had the lowest contraceptive failure rate of any religious grouping.[12] The authors state:

> The degree to which Jewish couples practice more effective contraception than either Protestants or Catholics both in the periods preceding, and following first pregnancy strains credulity. Not only do the Jewish couples of this sample rely more exclusively on the most effective methods, but they apparently manage these methods with unusual efficiency.[13]

The general relationship between religion and fertility, and the lower fertility of Jews in particular, was found by the Princeton Study even when metropolitan residence, social class, and other significant sociological variables were controlled. Evidence from our own study of the Jewish population further substantiates these conclusions. Compari-

[10] Freedman, Whelpton, and Campbell, *Family Planning, Sterility and Population Growth;* Ronald Freedman, Pascal K. Whelpton, and John W. Smit, "Socio-Economic Factors in Religious Differentials in Fertility," *American Sociological Review,* XXVI (August, 1961), 608-10.

[11] Whelpton, Campbell, and Patterson, *Fertility and Family Planning in the United States,* pp. 71-72, 247-52, and Tables 33 and 46.

[12] Westoff, Potter, and Sagi, *The Third Child,* Table 42, p. 89; Westoff *et al., Family Growth in Metropolitan America,* pp. 72-92.

[13] Westoff *et al., Family Growth in Metropolitan America,* p. 102.

TABLE 6-1

MEAN NUMBER OF BIRTHS, BY RELIGION AND EDUCATION, FOR WHITE MARRIED WOMEN 18 TO 39 YEARS OLD, 1962-1963, AND FOR THE JEWISH POPULATION, 1963

	Catholics*		Non-Catholics*		Jews*	
Education	18-29	30-39	18-29	30-39	18-29	30-39
Wife's Education						
Under 12 Years	2.7	3.3	2.2	3.0	–	–
12 Years	2.1	3.1	1.7	2.6	1.6	2.3
Over 12 Years	1.9	3.3	1.3	2.5	1.4	2.4
Husband's Education						
Under 12 Years	2.4	3.3	2.1	2.9	–	–
12 Years	2.1	3.1	1.8	2.5	1.8	2.2
Over 12 Years	2.0	3.1	1.5	2.5	1.4	2.4
TOTAL	2.2	3.2	1.8	2.7	1.4	2.3

*Data on Catholics and non-Catholics adapted from Ronald Freedman, David Goldberg and Larry Bumpass, "Current Expectations of Married Couples in the United States: 1963," *Population Index*, XXXI (January, 1965), Table 8, 14. Data for Jews refer to Providence.

son of the average family size of Jews in Providence with national data on Catholics and non-Catholics [14] (Table 6-1) suggests that, among those aged 18 to 29, Jews had 22 per cent fewer children than non-Catholics and 36 per cent fewer children than Catholics; among those aged 30 to 39, Jews had 15 per cent fewer children than non-Catholics and 28 per cent fewer than Catholics. The family size differences between the three religious groupings are not eliminated when education of wives and husbands is controlled. Catholics have higher fertility than non-Catholics for each educational level for both age groups, and non-Catholics have higher fertility than Jews in six of the eight comparisons. The two instances where Jews have the same (1.8) or slightly higher fertility (1.4 compared to 1.3) are in the younger ages, perhaps reflecting differential marriage and birth spacing patterns.

Much of the current research on religious differentials in fertility has focused on American couples. As a consequence, the illusion is created that lower Jewish fertility is confined to Jews living in the United States. However, the pattern is not unique to the American experience. Canadian census data, which include information on religion, show that as early as 1926 the Jewish birth rate was only 70 per cent of that of the

[14] For the limitations of this comparison see Calvin Goldscheider, "Socio-Economic Status and Jewish Fertility," *The Jewish Journal of Sociology*, VII (December, 1965), 233-34.

total population.[15] In 1941 the average size of Jewish families in Canada was 3.6; it had decreased to 3.2 by 1951. The family size of non-Jews for the same years was 3.9 and 3.7 respectively. Of the eight largest ethnic groups in Canada, Jews reported the smallest family size.[16] Although the Jewish population in Canada, as in the United States, is concentrated in urban areas, which are characterized by lower fertility, the Jewish fertility rate is still lower than the non-Jewish urban fertility rate.[17]

In Great Britain, an analysis of 3,281 hospital interviews (108 of them with Jews) suggested that a higher proportion of Jewish couples practiced birth control and used more efficient methods than women of other religious groupings.[18] It was estimated that the Jewish birth rate for 1945-1947 in Great Britain was 11.6 per 1,000, compared to 16.8 per 1,000 for the total population in the same period.[19] Although reliable data are not available, Jewish fertility in Great Britain seems to follow the prevalent middle-class pattern but there is a greater tendency toward the deliberate restriction of childbearing.[20]

Similar findings of lower Jewish fertility have been reported for ten Eastern European countries for the first thirty years of the twentieth century,[21] and for Italy, Switzerland, and the Netherlands,[22] and, controlling for urban residence, for Berlin (1851-1923), St. Petersburg (1910-1920), Budapest (1896-1934), Warsaw (1900-1936), and other Polish towns (1931-1932).[23] This evidence on the lower fertility of Jews in a

[15] Mortimer Spiegelman, "The Reproductivity of Jews in Canada, 1940-42," *Population Studies,* IV (December, 1950), 299-313.

[16] Louis Rosenberg, "The Demography of the Jewish Community in Canada," *The Jewish Journal of Sociology,* I (December, 1959), 217-33. See his discussion of Jewish and non-Jewish net reproduction rates, p. 227.

[17] Nathan Goldberg, "The Jewish Population in Canada," in *Jewish People, Past and Present,* II (New York: Central Yiddish Culture Organization, 1949), 35-39.

[18] E. Lewis-Fanning, *Report on an Enquiry into Family Limitation and Its Influence on Human Fertility During the Past Fifty Years,* Papers of the Royal Commission on Population, I (London: His Majesty's Stationery Office, 1949), 82.

[19] Hannah Neustatter, "Demographic and Other Statistical Aspects of Anglo-Jewry," in *A Minority in Britain,* ed. Maurice Freedman (London: Vallentine, Mitchell and Co., 1955), p. 82.

[20] Maurice Freedman, "The Jewish Population of Great Britain," *The Jewish Journal of Sociology,* IV (June, 1962), 95.

[21] Uriah Z. Engelman, "Sources of Jewish Statistics," in *The Jews: Their History, Culture and Religion* (3rd rev. ed.), II, ed. Louis Finkelstein (Philadelphia: Jewish Publication Society of America, 1960), Table 8, p. 1527.

[22] See Kurt B. Mayer, "Recent Demographic Developments in Switzerland," *Social Research,* XXIV (Summer, 1957), 350-51; Roberto Bachi, "The Demographic Development of Italian Jewry from the Seventeenth Century," *The Jewish Journal of Sociology,* IV (December, 1962), Table 13, 184; "Dutch Jewry: A Demographic Analysis," *The Jewish Journal of Sociology,* III (December, 1961), 195-243.

[23] Liebman Hersch, "Jewish Population Trends in Europe," in *Jewish People, Past and Present,* II, 11.

variety of countries for at least the last 75 years suggests that there may be a relationship between the fertility behavior of Jews and their position in Western societies. Certainly lower Jewish fertility is neither a recent phenomenon nor a uniquely American one.

FERTILITY TRENDS

Although various studies have consistently shown the lower fertility of Jews over time, in various countries, and controlling for key sociological variables, findings concerning fertility trends and differentials within the Jewish population are contradictory and based on inadequate and imprecise data. The ensuing discussion focuses on four major factors in Jewish fertility—generation, residence, socio-economic, and ideological differentials.

Little systematic data are available for the examination of trends in Jewish fertility. Indirectly, change may be measured by comparing the fertility of the native born and foreign born at one point in time. The assumption is that the fertility of the native born represents the changes that will occur as an immigrant group acculturates. Evidence available suggests that native-born Jews have lower fertility than foreign-born Jews, which implies a decline in fertility behavior. As early as 1905 in Rhode Island, native-born Jewish women had an average family size of 2.4 children, compared to an average of 4.0 children for foreign-born Jewish women.[24] In Buffalo, New York, at the end of the 1930's, the average completed family size of native-born Jewish couples was 2.4, compared to 3.6 for foreign-born Jewish couples.[25] Similarly, a study in 1948 of the Jewish population of Charleston showed that native-born Jewish couples had an average of 2.1 children, foreign-born couples had 3.7 children, and couples where only one partner was native born had an intermediate family size of 3.0 children.[26] These changes are similar to the general downward trend in family size during this period. Yet, some have argued that the decline was greater for Jews than for the total population. The sharper reduction in fertility occurred not only in average family size but also in the proportion of women with five or more children.[27]

Although the evidence on the decline in Jewish fertility can be

[24] *Rhode Island Census of 1905,* Tables VII and VIII, pp. 550-53.

[25] Uriah Z. Engelman, "A Study of Size of Families in the Jewish Population of Buffalo," *The University of Buffalo Series,* XVI (November, 1938), Chart III, 23.

[26] Uriah Z. Engelman, "The Jewish Population of Charleston," *Jewish Social Studies,* XIII (July, 1959), 195-210.

[27] Nathan Goldberg, "Jewish Population in America," *Jewish Review,* V (January-December, 1948), 36-48.

TABLE 6-2

FERTILITY BY DATE OF FIRST MARRIAGE

Marriage Cohorts	Average Number of Children Ever Born	Per Cent Childless	First Birth Interval (Average Months)	First Birth Interval (I)* (Average Months)	Second Birth Interval (II)* (Average Months)
Before 1910	3.5	0.0	12.8	76.0	48.5
1910-1919	2.8	3.4	18.3	68.5	37.5
1920-1924	2.2	6.6	24.3	63.5	44.5
1925-1929	1.9	9.8	27.0	85.0	51.0
1930-1934	2.0	11.4	27.1	82.5	55.0
1935-1939	2.0	7.8	30.8	70.4	41.8
1940-1944	2.0	7.7	30.0	72.2	44.6
1945-1949	2.2	5.7	23.8	62.5	37.4
1950-1954	2.3	7.3	22.4	55.5	30.8
1955-1963	†	†	19.2	44.8	28.5
TOTAL	2.1	8.9	24.4	65.1	36.2

* First Birth Interval (I) refers to months between marriage and second child; Second Birth Interval (II) refers to months between first and second child.

†Since this cohort is recently married, the families are in the early childbearing stage and the data on the number of children ever born are not meaningful.

indirectly obtained from the literature, no data are available to determine whether and to what extent Jews participated in the baby boom following World War II. Goldberg and Sharp, on the basis of the limited number of Jewish couples included in the Detroit area studies, suggest that "Jewish families seem to be relatively unaffected by the post World War II 'baby boom.' "[28]

The data from the Providence Jewish population survey shed light on both the downward trend in Jewish fertility and the post World War II recovery. Information on family size and birth spacing by date of first marriage indicates that Jewish family size declined steadily from the marriage cohort marrying before 1910 to those marrying between 1920 and 1924 (Table 6-2). Average family size among those marrying during the two decades between 1925 and 1944 stabilized at around two children. Although complete information is available for only two observation periods—1945-1949 and 1950-1954—the postwar marriage cohorts show a definite gradual increase in family size. These data clearly indicate that family size declined during the depression and pre-war years and that Jewish couples participated in the "baby boom" following World War II.

[28] David Goldberg and Harry Sharp, "Some Characteristics of Detroit Area Jews and Non-Jewish Adults," in *The Jews,* ed. Sklare, p. 110.

Patterns of birth spacing reveal the shorter birth intervals of the predepression cohorts, the longer birth intervals of the depression cohorts, and the earlier family formation patterns of the cohorts marrying after the end of World War II. These birth spacing patterns among Jewish couples conform to those observed for the general population. However, a comparison of the birth spacing data to similar data by marriage cohorts for total white women in the United States reveals that Jewish fertility was characterized by longer birth intervals.[29] Indirectly, these data point to the efficient use of contraception by Jewish couples for the planning of family size and the spacing of children.

Although the marriage cohort analysis reveals fertility trends which can be indirectly compared to similar changes in the general population, fertility changes may also be measured in the context of other social and economic changes that have taken place within the Jewish community. Generation status provides one such measure, which is especially important for a minority group whose acculturation patterns are intertwined with generation status.

In this analysis of fertility, age was used as an approximation of generation status. Although the over-all generation patterns are similar when nativity is used, it was not possible to cross-tabulate nativity with age controls by a number of other variables, owing to the attrition of cases. Age is a crucial factor in fertility analyses, especially because it permits separation of the complete from the incomplete families. Recent evidence suggests that by age 35 most women have their last child and end their childbearing cycle. For these reasons, as well as because of the high correlation between age and nativity, the use of age as an index of generation status seems warranted here.[30]

[29] See Whelpton, Campbell, and Patterson, *Fertility and Family Planning in the United States,* pp. 304 and 321, and Chapter 3; Pascal K. Whelpton, "Trends and Differentials in the Spacing of Births," *Demography,* I (1964), 83-93; Paul C. Glick and Robert Parke, Jr., "New Approaches in Studying the Life Cycle of the Family," *Demography,* II (1965), 190. See also David Goldberg, "Fertility and Fertility Differentials: Some Observations on Recent Changes in the United States," in *Public Health and Population Change,* eds. Mindell Sheps and Jeanne Clare Ridley (Pittsburgh: University of Pittsburgh Press, 1965), p. 122.

[30] Clyde V. Kiser, Wilson H. Grabill, and Joseph P. Schachter, "Plans for the APHA Monographs on Fertility in the 1960 Census Period," in *Emerging Techniques in Population Research* (New York: Milbank Memorial Fund, 1963), pp. 98, 99. Glick shows that the median age of the wife at the birth of her last child in 1890 was 31.9; in 1940, 27.1; in 1950, 26.1; Glick, *The American Family,* p. 54. See also references cited by Westoff, Potter, and Sagi, *The Third Child,* pp. 12, 13; and Pascal K. Whelpton, "Trends and Differentials in the Spacing of Births," *Demography,* I (1964), 83-93. For a discussion of age as a measure of generation, see, Karl Mannheim, "The Problem of Generations," in *Essays on the Sociology of Knowledge* (London: Oxford University Press, 1952), p. 291. Similar analysis is found in Ralph Linton, "Age and Sex Categories," *American Sociological Review,* VII (October, 1942), 589-603; Rudolf Heberle, *Social*

TABLE 6-3

FERTILITY BY GENERATION

Generation Status*	Average Number of Children Ever Born	Per Cent Childless	First Birth Interval (Average Months)	Second Birth Interval (I) (Average Months)	Second Birth Interval (II) (Average Months)
First Generation	2.8	6.4	16.6	63.0	38.0
Second Generation	1.9	11.5	26.2	74.5	46.2
Older Third Generation	2.3	4.3	26.7	65.3	38.0
Younger Third Generation	†	†	20.0	52.9	30.2
TOTAL	2.1	9.4	24.4	65.1	36.2

*Women aged 65 and over are labeled "first generation"; "second generation" are those 45 to 64 years of age; "older third generation," those 35 to 44 years of age; and "younger third generation," those below age 35.
†Incomplete families

First-generation Jews had larger families, married at younger ages, and had shorter first and second birth intervals than second-generation Jewish couples. On the other hand, the average family size of third-generation Jews was 22 per cent larger than that of the second generation, and third-generation Jews married earlier and had their first and second child sooner after marriage than Jews of the second generation (Table 6-3).

These findings are closely related to the social and demographic situation of the three generations. First-generation Jews had little formal education, were unskilled, and were imbued with the traditional values associated with Eastern European ghetto living, all of which are generally associated with relatively higher fertility. In contrast, most second-generation Jews were economically mobile, most had the benefits of a secular education, and most desired integration. Coupled with the economic depression of the 1930's, these factors led to reductions in family size, longer birth intervals, and delayed marriages. That the economic depression alone does not account for the fertility decline is indicated by the data on generation differentials within the same marriage cohort; second-generation Jews marrying before and during the depression had smaller families than first-generation Jews marrying at the same time.

Third-generation Jews, secure in their middle-class backgrounds, with college educations, and in white-collar occupations, participated, as did other middle-class couples, in the baby boom. The increases in fertility from the second to the third generation are partially the result of

Movements (New York: Appleton-Century-Crofts, 1951), p. 125. See also Calvin Goldscheider, "Nativity, Generation and Jewish Fertility," *Sociological Analysis,* XXVI (Fall, 1965), 137-47.

the greater stabilization of social and economic status among third-generation Jews and the concomitant socio-economic security.

SOCIAL AND IDEOLOGICAL DIFFERENTIALS

The Jewish population has participated in the suburban movement to a greater extent than the total population. Behavior patterns peculiar to suburbanites may have emerged not only because certain types of people are more prone to move to suburban areas but also as a result of social forces operating in the suburbs. Census and survey data have indicated that, in general, fertility tends to be higher among suburban residents than among those living in urban areas.[31] Yet, religion may be an important factor in analyzing urban-suburban fertility differences.[32] There are two reasons for expecting that Jewish suburban residents will have higher fertility than urban residents. First, suburban Jews are younger and thus may reflect the postwar fertility increases; conversely, urban residents are more concentrated in the depression cohorts, which are characterized by lower fertility. Second, as a result of the deconcentration and dispersion of the suburban Jewish population, assimilation may be higher and their fertility behavior may therefore more closely resemble the total population. Just as there tends to be a convergence of Protestant-Catholic fertility in the suburbs, there may also be a convergence of Jewish and non-Jewish fertility.[33]

The data on the fertility of the Jewish population in various residential areas in the Providence metropolitan area confirm these hypotheses.[34] Except for the second generation, Jews living in suburban areas had larger families than those in urban areas. The exception of second-generation Jews may be the result of the peculiarly high percentage childless among the suburban residents of that generation; in part, it may also

[31] Sidney Goldstein and Kurt B. Mayer, "Residence and Status Differences in Fertility," *Milbank Memorial Fund Quarterly*, XLIII (July, 1965), 291-310.

[32] Freedman, Whelpton, and Campbell, *Family Planning, Sterility and Population Growth*, pp. 309-13; Westoff *et al.*, *Family Growth in Metropolitan America*, pp. 263-81; Westoff, Potter, and Sagi, *The Third Child*, pp. 157-82, 241-42; Basil G. Zimmer and Calvin Goldscheider, "A Further Look at Catholic Fertility," *Demography*, III (Fall, 1966), 462-69.

[33] Zimmer and Goldscheider, "A Further Look at Catholic Fertility."

[34] The data on residential differentials are limited for the older groups since we obtained current residence rather than residence during the childbearing period. In addition to direct data on fertility, an indirect measure—the child-woman ratio (the ratio of children under 5 years of age divided by the number of women in the reproductive ages)—showed that suburban areas were characterized by substantially higher fertility ratios than urban areas. These differences are partly a function of differences in age distribution of suburban and urban areas and the proportion married within the reproductive age group. These data are discussed here without tabular presentation.

reflect the greater homogeneity in fertility which characterized childbearing during the depression. Although there were no differences in average family size among suburban and urban residents of the second generation, suburbanites of the second generation had a higher proportion of families with four or more children than urban residents. Similar higher parity concentrations characterize the third generation; 8 per cent of the Jewish younger third generation who live in suburban segments of the metropolitan area had four or more children, compared to less than 3 per cent of the Jewish urban residents. However, birth interval data, like age at marriage statistics, show no systematic pattern by residence.

The information on the larger families of suburban Jews is consistent with the earlier analysis pointing to the popularity of the suburbs for couples in the early stages of the family life cycle.[35] Moreover, over half the younger third generation and three-fourths of the older third generation who are currently living in the suburbs moved there after their first child was born. Taken together, these data imply that for a variety of reasons suburban areas are attractive to and selective of people with families. Residential differences in family size among the third generation may reflect the higher proportion childless among the urban residents and, more generally, differences between the suburban and urban population in the timing of family formation. Since the younger third generation is still in the early childbearing stages, it is too soon to evaluate their completed family size.

The available literature on the relationship between socio-economic status and Jewish fertility is not consistent. Some limited studies have found no relationship between occupation and Jewish fertility.[36] Nevertheless, a 1938 study of the Jewish community of Buffalo, New York, clearly showed an inverse relationship between occupation and fertility —the average completed family size of professional Jews was 2.9, in contrast to the family size of businessmen (3.2), artisans (3.5), and peddlers (3.7).[37] Based on a small number of Jewish couples, the Princeton Fertility Study found little association between occupation and Jewish fertility, although professionals tended to desire slightly larger families than managers or salesmen.[38]

When socio-economic status is measured by education, similar inconsistent findings have been reported. In a limited survey of fertility

[35] See Chapter 3, pp. 49-52.

[36] See Erwin S. Solomon, "Social Characteristics and Fertility," *Eugenics Quarterly,* III (June, 1956), 101; Myer Greenberg, "The Reproductive Rate of the Families of Jewish Students at the University of Maryland," *Jewish Social Studies,* X (July, 1948), 230.

[37] Engelman, "A Study of Size of Families in the Jewish Population of Buffalo," Table XVI, p. 29.

[38] Westoff *et al., Family Growth in Metropolitan America,* Table 41, p. 185.

of the mainly first-generation parents of Jewish college students an inverse relationship between education and Jewish fertility was obtained—college educated Jews had smaller families than those with only an elementary education.[39] The Princeton Study reported no association between education and family size preference for Protestants, but for Catholics and Jews (mainly third-generation Jewish couples) there was a definite positive correlation. Moreover, despite the exercise of effective control in family planning, better educated Jews desired larger families.[40] In the re-interview stage of the Princeton Fertility Study, the authors reported a higher positive correlation between number of children desired and education of wife among Jews than among the other religious groupings.[41]

One possible explanation for the discrepancies in these various studies may be that they have focused on different generations. Higher status groupings of the older generation were upwardly mobile, rejected the ghetto way of life, and broke with the traditional culture of their contemporaries. This acculturation pattern would lead to lower fertility. The lower status groupings of the earlier generations were less socially and economically mobile and were associated with Eastern European ghetto culture. These factors would probably result in their higher fertility. However, the inverse relationship of socio-economic status to Jewish fertility may not characterize the younger generations.[42] Considering the rationality with which Jewish couples plan their families, it is understandable that lower status socio-economic groupings in the younger generation will have smaller families than higher status socio-economic groupings.

Reliable data for the confirmation of generation changes in socio-economic differentials in Jewish fertility have been lacking. The Providence fertility data show a clear inverse relationship between socio-economic status and Jewish fertility of first-generation Jews. This pattern was found using three measures of socio-economic status—education of wife and education and occupation of husband (Table 6-4). However, patterns of socio-economic differentials in family size were unclear and differences were smaller for second- and third-generation couples. In order to assess the combined effects of occupation and education on fer-

[39] Greenberg, "The Reproductive Rate of the Families of Jewish Students at the University of Maryland," pp. 231-32.

[40] Westoff *et al., Family Growth in Metropolitan America,* pp. 215-16.

[41] Westoff, Potter, and Sagi, *The Third Child,* Table 60, p. 115.

[42] This conforms to patterns of socio-economic differentials in the fertility of couples who rationally plan their families and efficiently use contraceptive methods. See Westoff, Potter, and Sagi, "Some Selected Findings of the Princeton Fertility Study: 1961," p. 134; and Pascal K. Whelpton and Clyde V. Kiser, eds., *Social and Psychological Factors Affecting Fertility,* V (New York: Milbank Memorial Fund, 1958), 1,331-41.

TABLE 6-4

AVERAGE NUMBER OF CHILDREN EVER BORN BY EDUCATION OF COUPLE AND HUSBAND'S OCCUPATION, BY GENERATION

	Average Number of Children Ever Born			
Socio-Economic Measures	First Generation	Second Generation	Older Third Generation	Younger Third Generation
Education of Wife				
Graduate or Professional School	–	1.9	2.4	1.7
Completed College	–	2.1	2.5	1.8
Some College	–	1.9	2.2	1.8
Completed High School	2.3	1.8	2.2	2.1
Some High School	2.6*	1.9	2.3	–
Elementary School	3.6*	2.0	–	–
Education of Husband				
Graduate or Professional School	–	2.0	2.4	1.9
Completed College	–	2.2	2.4	1.9
Some College	–	1.7	2.1	1.7
Completed High School	2.3	1.9	2.2	2.0
Some High School	2.4*	1.8	2.6	–
Elementary School	3.3*	2.0	–	–
Occupation of Husband				
Professional	2.1	2.0	2.2	1.8
Manager	2.8	2.0	2.3	2.0
Clerical and Sales	2.5	1.8	2.2	1.9
Blue-Collar	3.0	1.8	2.3	1.4

***Since the number of older persons with some high school or elementary school education was small, "some high school" is considered as first to 11th grade, and "elementary school" is considered as no secular education in the case of the first generation only.**

tility, a single measure of social class, based on education of husband and wife and occupation of husband, was developed. In the resulting index, Social Class I represents professionals and managers who, with their wives, had high education; Social Class III represents low white-collar and blue-collar workers who, with their wives, had low education; Social Class II consists of two groups: (1) professionals and managers with low education, and (2) low white-collar and blue-collar workers with high education. Social Class II represents inconsistencies of the social class components. The degree of "high" and "low" education varies with generation, since generation changes have occurred in the degree to which Jews have received higher education.[43] This measure of social class indicates

[43] Since only those cases where the husband and wife were living together at the time of the study could be included, widows, predominantly in the first generation, were excluded. There is no known systematic bias in this approach. For a more detailed analysis of this measure, see Calvin Goldscheider, "Socio-Economic Status and Jewish Fertility," *The Jewish Journal of Sociology,* VII (December, 1965), 228-33.

that a reversal of the inverse relationship of social class and fertility characterizing first-generation Jews had occurred for second- and third-generation Jews. Higher status Jews of the second and third generations had larger families than lower status Jews within the same generations (Table 6-5).

These data lend support to the importance of generation changes in the relationship of social class to fertility. Moreover, the data clearly indicate the trend toward convergence and greater homogeneity in the fertility patterns of socio-economic groupings within the Jewish population, with distance from the first generation. The contraction of socio-economic differentials may be viewed as the result of the widespread rationality with which the majority of contemporary Jews plan their families, the absence of rapid upward mobility characteristic of earlier generations, and the greater homogeneity of contemporary Jewish social structure. Third-generation Jews are largely concentrated in the college trained group and in white-collar occupations. The lack of wide social-class distinctions for the third generation may account for the absence of striking fertility differences within this segment of Jewish population.[44]

TABLE 6-5

FERTILITY BY SOCIAL CLASS INDEX, BY GENERATION

Social-Class Index	Average Number of Children Ever Born	Per Cent Childless	First Birth Interval (Average Months)	Second Birth Interval (I) (Average Months)	Second Birth Interval (II) (Average Months)
First Generation					
Social Class I	2.4	8.3	31.5	72.0	52.5
Social Class II	2.7	5.7	26.0	73.0	40.0
Social Class III	2.9	4.8	12.9	63.0	36.5
Second Generation					
Social Class I	2.0	5.1	35.0	78.0	43.5
Social Class II	1.9	11.0	26.3	73.4	46.6
Social Class III	1.8	16.4	24.1	82.5	52.0
Older Third Generation					
Social Class I	2.4	1.4	31.3	64.8	34.8
Social Class II	2.2	5.9	25.5	64.2	38.0
Social Class III	2.2	4.6	24.8	66.2	41.5
Younger Third Generation					
Social Class I	1.9	15.7	19.8	51.0	27.5
Social Class II	1.9	8.9	21.9	52.6	30.3
Social Class III	1.7	18.8	17.8	53.3	33.0

[44] *Cf.* Ronald Freedman, "American Studies of Family Planning and Fertility: A Review of Major Trends and Issues," in *Research in Family Planning,* ed. Clyde V. Kiser (Princeton: Princeton University Press, 1962), pp. 220-21; Kurt B. Mayer, "Fer-

There are no reliable data available on the relationship between the religious commitment of Jews and their fertility. However, two available studies arrived at conflicting conclusions concerning the nature and role of religious ideological factors in Jewish fertility,[45] illustrating the prevailing confusion concerning the role of these factors in Jewish fertility differentials.

A study of the fertility of the parents of Jewish college students found that Orthodox, presumably more religious Jews, had slightly larger families than Conservative or Reform Jews.[46] In explanation of this finding, the author suggests that religious ideological factors are important in understanding Jewish fertility and that those who identify more strongly with Judaism have a deeper feeling of responsibility for the Jewish people, which influences them to have larger families.[47] The Princeton Study reached diametrically opposite conclusions. Their data showed that more religious-minded Jewish couples (measured by formal as well as informal religious orientation) had more success in planning their families than less religious-minded Jewish couples. After testing and rejecting the hypothesis that religious Jews were more educated, they concluded that non-Catholic religious ideology stresses "social responsibility in parenthood." [48]

Whatever the methodological merits of the two studies, their explanations in terms of ideology are conflicting, since religious ideology cannot at the same time encourage large families and rationally planned small families. Moreover, it is unwarranted to explain Jewish fertility in terms of ideological factors that are unknown and inoperative on the personal level or at best interrelated with generation, degrees of assimilation, and social class.[49] An alternative and more consistent explanation

---

tility Changes and Population Forecasts in the United States," *Social Research,* XXVI (Autumn, 1959), 347-66. For data on the class concentration of third-generation Jews, see Chapter 4 of this book.

[45] Greenberg, "The Reproductive Rate of the Families of Jewish Students at the University of Maryland," p. 233; Westoff *et al., Family Growth in Metropolitan America,* pp. 196-98.

[46] Greenberg, "The Reproductive Rate of the Families of Jewish Students at the University of Maryland," p. 233.

[47] *Ibid.,* p. 234.

[48] Westoff *et al., Family Growth in Metropolitan America,* pp. 196-98. The same reasoning is applied to Protestants. In the re-interview phase similar findings are reported. This time, however, caution was introduced in interpreting the findings of higher fertility among more "religious Jews" and the authors suggest that this relationship might be related to socio-economic security. Westoff, Potter, and Sagi, *The Third Child,* p. 87.

[49] For a more detailed discussion of ideological factors in Jewish fertility, see Calvin Goldscheider, "Ideological Factors in Jewish Fertility Differentials," *The Jewish Journal of Sociology,* VII (June, 1965), 92-105.

TABLE 6-6

FERTILITY BY WIFE'S RELIGIOUS IDENTIFICATION, BY GENERATION

Wife's Religious Identification	Average Number of Children Ever Born	Per Cent Childless	First Birth Interval (Average Months)	Second Birth Interval (I) (Average Months)	Second Birth Interval (II) (Average Months)
First Generation					
Orthodox	3.1	2.3	13.0	60.3	34.5
Conservative	2.7	6.7	23.0	73.5	39.0
Reform	2.5	12.5	14.5	79.0	51.5
Second Generation					
Orthodox	1.8	16.7	20.5	61.5	39.8
Conservative	2.0	8.6	27.9	74.8	49.6
Reform	2.0	9.8	28.0	76.5	42.5
Older Third Generation					
Orthodox	2.4	2.8	25.0	65.5	36.5
Conservative	2.2	4.3	25.7	64.9	40.8
Reform	2.4	3.6	30.0	65.0	36.3
Younger Third Generation					
Orthodox	1.5	33.3	42.0	–	–
Conservative	1.8	13.1	20.0	52.9	30.5
Reform	2.0	10.5	20.3	52.3	30.2

of the findings of these two studies, assuming the validity of their results, may lie in generational shifts. The pattern found among the parents of college students referred to first- and early second-generation Jews, whereas the Princeton Study was mostly concerned with third-generation Jews. Thus, the explanation of their findings may reside in the social-class concentrations of the three religious divisions of Judaism, and, more broadly, in the changing relationship of the social-class differential to Jewish fertility.

This hypothesis was tested and confirmed with our data. Generational shifts in the relationship of religious identification and Jewish fertility may be observed in Table 6-6. Orthodox Jews of the first generation had larger families, lower per cent childless, and had shorter birth intervals than first-generation Conservative or Reform Jews. On the other hand, Orthodox Jews of the second and younger third generation had lower fertility than Conservative or Reform Jews. This pattern reflects social-class differences; Orthodox Jews in each generation were concentrated in the lower social classes, Reform Jews in the higher social classes, and Conservative Jews in an intermediate position.[50] When social class was controlled, family size differences between those identifying with various religious divisions disappeared (Table 6-7). Thus, we may con-

[50] See Chapter 9.

TABLE 6-7

FERTILITY BY WIFE'S RELIGIOUS IDENTIFICATION AND SOCIAL CLASS, BY GENERATION

Social Class and Religious Identification	First Generation		Second Generation		Older Third Generation		Younger Third Generation	
	Average Number of Children Ever Born	Per Cent Childless	Average Number of Children Ever Born	Per Cent Childless	Average Number of Children Ever Born	Per Cent Childless	Average Number of Children Ever Born	Per Cent Childless
Orthodox								
Social Class I	–	–	–	–	–	–	–	–
Social Class II	3.2	0.0	1.9	6.8	2.2	0.0	–	–
Social Class III	2.9	4.3	1.8	22.4	2.5	4.8	–	–
Conservative								
Social Class I	2.5	7.7	2.3	0.0	2.5	2.7	1.8	16.0
Social Class II	1.9	8.3	2.0	9.7	2.1	5.2	1.8	9.6
Social Class III	3.0	7.7	1.8	9.4	2.2	4.4	1.7	15.6
Reform								
Social Class I	–	–	2.3	0.0	2.6	0.0	2.1	9.1
Social Class II	–	–	1.8	13.0	2.4	7.9	2.0	10.0
Social Class III	–	–	1.9	12.5	2.1	0.0	2.0	20.0

clude that religious ideology and religious identification have little relationship to Jewish fertility and that few differences appear that cannot be explained by social-class factors.

Moreover, frequency of synagogue attendance, kind and extent of Jewish education, and membership in Jewish and non-Jewish organizations showed little relationship to Jewish fertility. In most cases, what little relationship existed between these measures of religiosity and Jewish fertility was eliminated when social class was controlled. In general, the secular nature of religion for the modern Jew implies that Judaism as a religion plays a minor role in determining his fertility.

JEWISH FERTILITY REEXAMINED

The prevalent explanation of the patterns of Jewish fertility states that Jewish fertility is unique only insofar as the Jewish population is characterized by a peculiar combination of residential, social, and economic attributes. The authors of the Growth of American Families Studies suggest that the long urban experience of the Jews and their high educational and economic status would lead them to have lower fertility than Protestants or Catholics.[51] Similarly, Petersen argues that "the small family size of Jews derives from their concentration in cities, especially in those urban occupations that are always associated with low fertility." [52]

The data on the characteristics of the Jewish population in the United States suggest that these are the characteristics normally associated with lower fertility. According to the 1957 Current Population Survey, 96 per cent of the Jewish population were concentrated in urban areas, compared to 78.8 per cent of the Catholic population and 56.6 per cent of the Protestant population.[53] Moreover, the high educational and occupational achievements of Jews relative to other religious groupings have been well documented.[54] Thus, Freedman, Whelpton, and Smit state:

> The fertility norms and behavior of the Jews appear to be consistent with their distinctive social and economic characteristics. They have fertility characteristics we would expect to be associated with their high educational,

[51] Freedman, Whelpton, and Campbell, *Family Planning, Sterility and Population Growth,* p. 104; Whelpton, Campbell, and Patterson, *Fertility and Family Planning in the United States,* pp. 72-73.

[52] William Petersen, *Population* (New York: The Macmillan Company, 1961), p. 223; see also Ralph Thomlinson, *Population Dynamics* (New York: Random House, Inc., 1965), p. 179. For a similar approach see Erich Rosenthal, "Jewish Fertility in the United States," *Eugenics Quarterly,* VIII (December, 1961), 198-217.

[53] U.S. Bureau of the Census, "Religion Reported by the Civilian Population of the U.S.," Table 3, p. 7.

[54] See Chapter 4.

occupational and income status, their high concentration in metropolitan areas and small amount of farm background in their recent history. These social and economic characteristics have been associated generally in both theoretical discussions and in empirical work with low fertility, low fertility values and high rationality in family planning.[55]

To support this view, the authors of the GAF Study precision-matched on selected variables the 66 Jewish couples in their 1955 sample with Protestants and Catholics with similar characteristics. Comparisons between the matched groups indicated that the fertility complex for Protestants is very much like that for Jews when they have similar social and economic characteristics.[56] In addition, in the twelve largest cities of their national sample, Protestants and Jews expected to have the same number of children.[57] The authors of the GAF Study therefore speculate that the pattern of Jewish fertility may foreshadow what may come to characterize the Protestant population as social and economic differences between these groups diminish.

Empirically as well as theoretically, this approach to the understanding of Jewish fertility is incomplete. First, the findings of the Princeton Fertility Studies disprove the basic formulation. When metropolitan size, social class, and other variables were controlled, Jews varied significantly from Catholics and Protestants on a wide range of fertility variables. Similarly, comparisons of the Jewish population of Providence with national data on Catholics and non-Catholics, controlling for age and education, showed that Jews had smaller families.[58] Second, as pointed out earlier, Jews in a variety of European countries since the middle of the nineteenth century and in the United States since 1880 have had lower fertility than non-Jews. Thus, the "characteristics" explanation of Jewish fertility would have to assume Jews in other Western countries for at least the last century have had the same matrix of characteristics as Jews in the United States or that other factors unique to their circumstances contribute to their lower fertility. Moreover, a similar assumption would have to be made about Jews in the United States since 1880. Empirical evidence, however, shows the very opposite; i.e., contemporary Jews do not have the same matrix of social and economic characteristics that their fathers and grandfathers had. The "char-

[55] "Socio-Economic Factors in Religious Differentials in Fertility," p. 104.

[56] *Ibid.,* p. 612. Their findings may be explained by the different relationships between socio-economic status and fertility for Protestants, Catholics, and Jews. See Westoff, Potter, and Sagi, *The Third Child,* p. 227, Table 112, and footnote 5; Goldscheider, "Socio-Economic Status and Jewish Fertility," pp. 221-37.

[57] Freedman, Whelpton, and Campbell, *Family Planning, Sterility and Population Growth,* p. 287; similar findings are reported in their 1960 survey. Whelpton, Campbell, and Patterson, *Fertility and Family Planning in the United States,* p. 73.

[58] See Table 6-1.

acteristics" approach represents an *ad hoc* explanation which fails to account for existing evidence and generates little in the way of meaningful hypotheses.

An alternative explanation, which not only accounts for the existing data but also integrates the study of Jewish fertility with other social behavior characterizing the Jewish population, lies in the analysis of the relationship between Jewish fertility and the changing nature of Jewish social structure in the process of acculturation.[59] This approach treats the Jew as a member of a minority group, with perceptions of discriminations and feelings of insecurity, and without full acceptance in the non-Jewish world. The long history of low Jewish fertility in many countries may be explained by the minority position of Jews and cross-culturally shared Jewish values. Although the "characteristics" of Jews at the turn of the century were not the ones usually associated with low fertility, the aspirations of Jews for social mobility, as well as their desire for acceptance in American society and the insecurity of their minority status, tended to encourage small families.

This approach does not overlook the social and economic characteristics of Jews. However, it adds the structural and cultural dimensions to these characteristics. Furthermore, it posits a uniqueness based not only on a particular matrix of social and economic attributes but on the minority position of the Jew in the social structure. An examination of the combination of minority status, cultural values, and social characteristics of Jews provides a more fruitful direction for understanding Jewish fertility.

A parallel theme on the relationship between minority status and fertility may apply to recent studies of nonwhite fertility. In the past, the social and economic characteristics as well as the cultural values and family structure of nonwhites in the United States have led to patterns of high fertility. However, recent data have indicated that when the social and economic characteristics of nonwhites and whites are similar, nonwhite fertility tends to be *lower* than white fertility. The 1960 GAF Study found that college educated nonwhites expected 2.4 children on the average, 20 per cent fewer than college educated white women. Similarly, 1960 census data show that the number of children ever born per 1,000 college educated white women was higher than for college educated nonwhite women. Therefore, as equalization of social and economic characteristics of whites and nonwhites occurs and family stabilization among

[59] *Cf.* Nathan Goldberg, "The Jewish Population in the United States," in *The Jewish People, Past and Present,* pp. 28-29; Nathan Goldberg, "Jewish Population in America," pp. 30-55; Charles F. Westoff, "The Social-Psychological Structure of Fertility," *International Population Conference, Vienna, 1959* (Vienna: International Union for the Scientific Study of Population, 1959), pp. 361-62.

nonwhites increases, we should not necessarily expect a similarity of fertility patterns, but an accentuation of lower fertility among nonwhites. Likewise, although the pattern of Jewish fertility may foreshadow other groupings as successful family planning becomes more widespread, Jews may retain lower *levels* of fertility. The role of minority status may operate in a different way when the subgroup has a specific and clear-cut religious ideology, as, for example, Catholics.[60]

Research concerned with a meaningful analysis of the nature of Jewish fertility and, more broadly, with the meaning of religious differentials in fertility should not overlook the social structural and social psychological meaning of minority group status. Moreover, the minority status factor integrates the study of Jewish fertility with other social changes that have characterized the Jewish population in the process of acculturation and assimilation.

[60] See data cited and discussed in "New Patterns in U.S. Fertility," *Population Bulletin,* XX (September, 1964), 130; Whelpton, Campbell, and Patterson, *Fertility and Family Planning in the United States,* Chapter 8; U.S. Bureau of the Census, *1960 Census of the Population. Women by Number of Children Ever Born,* PC(2)-3A, Table 25; Anders S. Lunde, "White–Non-White Fertility Differentials in the United States," *Health, Education and Welfare Indicators* (September, 1965), p. 7.

CHAPTER SEVEN

Mortality and Life Expectancy

The general absence in the United States of any information on religion in the official census and in vital statistics has been a major barrier to the analysis of religious differentials in fertility and mortality. As noted in Chapter 6, a number of special surveys have been undertaken to fill this void for fertility, particularly as evidence suggests that religion has become an increasingly important factor in influencing the number of children born per family. Our knowledge of religious differentials in mortality remains much more limited.

This chapter explores the patterns of Jewish mortality and life expectancy and attempts to ascertain the ways, if any, in which they differ from those of the general population. In a discussion of population growth and of changes in fertility and mortality occurring to the general European population and to the Jewish population living in Europe in the mid-seventeenth century, Salo Baron observes that

> . . . the great destructive forces, contagious diseases and wars, seem to have claimed fewer victims among the Jews than among their Gentile neighbors. It is quite possible that Jewish religious life, through its prescriptions of continual washing, discrimination in food, a strict day of rest, and the like, helped build up greater resistance. The relatively longer experience of civilized and urban life may have endowed the Jewish race with a degree of immunity to certain bacilli, higher than that of their European neighbors.[1]

The value still placed on health measures and cleanliness in Jewish culture and religion, coupled with the higher than average socio-economic status of the Jewish population, would lead one to expect the Jewish group to continue to be characterized by lower mortality rates and longer survival. By comparing the mortality patterns of the Jewish and the total population, this analysis may suggest the extent to which the religious dimension remains a key variable in accounting for mortality differentials on the American scene. Yet, such an hypothesized difference may be weakened as a result of both the general improvement in health standards and the rise in the socio-economic status of the population at large.

[1] *A Social and Religious History of the Jews* (New York: Columbia University Press, 1937), II, 169.

THE SEARCH FOR EVIDENCE

Whereas the analysis of fertility lends itself to a survey approach, this is not equally true of the analysis of mortality, since the survey statistics may be biased in favor of those deceased persons who left behind them a family unit to be included in a sample; deceased persons who had lived alone would probably not be identified in such a survey.[2] As a result, any comprehensive analysis of mortality must necessarily begin with records that provide the maximum opportunity for identifying all deceased persons regardless of their household and family status at the time of death. Official death certificates provide the best means for achieving this goal. Yet, because vital statistics records do not contain information on religion, indirect clues to the religious identification of the deceased must be used.

Among the clues that have served this purpose in the several studies completed to date are the place of burial of the deceased and the particular funeral directors who handled the funeral. However, the value of such sources of information probably varies by religious group, largely reflecting the extent to which the deceased of a given religion are buried in a cemetery identified with their particular religious group or in a nonsectarian cemetery. A similar problem would extend to the question of whether funerals are largely handled by funeral directors of the same religious denomination as the deceased. Studies in New York City and in St. Louis indicate, for example, that a very high percentage of Jewish funerals are handled by a restricted number of funeral directors and that practically all Jewish burials occur in Jewish cemeteries.[3] The New York study, however, was restricted to identifying religious affiliation on the basis of cemetery of interment, and over 20 per cent of the total deaths had to be regarded as of unspecified religion because the bodies were either cremated, interred out of town, or buried in the city cemetery. These unspecified deaths were allocated to each religious group in the same proportion as the "specified" deaths based on known place of burial. This procedure weakens the value of this particular study for an analysis of the patterns of Jewish mortality. The St. Louis study, using informa-

[2] For an early attempt to analyze Jewish mortality through reliance upon survey data, see J. S. Billings, "Vital Statistics of the Jews," *North American Review,* CLII (1891), 70.

[3] H. Seidman, L. Garfinkel, and L. Craig, "Death Rates in New York City by Socio-economic Class and Religious Group and by Country of Birth, 1949-1951," *Jewish Journal of Sociology,* IV (December, 1962), 254-72; and K. Gorwitz, "Jewish Mortality in St. Louis and St. Louis County, 1955-1957," *Jewish Social Studies,* XXIV (October, 1962), 248-54.

tion on both the funeral director and the place of burial, probably better reflects the Jewish deaths.

In both the New York and the St. Louis studies another serious limitation was the absence of information on the Jewish population whose deaths were being analyzed. The New York study used correlation analysis to estimate the Jewish and non-Jewish white populations and death rates by age, sex, and socio-economic class. The St. Louis study made no attempt to estimate the Jewish population by age and used only over-all estimates of the Jewish population living in the St. Louis area as the basis for computing its crude death rates. In the absence of exact information on the population structure of the Jewish community, any analysis of the number of deaths and the age composition of the deceased has limited value for measuring differentials. Since age composition in particular is a major variable affecting the over-all level of mortality, information on age-specific mortality is essential to comparison of Jewish and non-Jewish mortality.

Within the limits imposed by its restricted information, the St. Louis study, based on 1,478 Jewish deaths and 25 Jewish stillbirths during 1955, 1956, and 1957, pointed to several major conclusions. Over all, it found that the Jewish mortality rate was approximately 14 per cent lower than that of the resident white population of the area. A much higher percentage of all deaths was concentrated between the ages of 45 and 85 for the Jewish population compared to the white population. This may, however, reflect nothing more than a comparable differential in the age concentration of the total population. Whether the risk of mortality in this age range is greater for the Jewish than for the non-Jewish population cannot be ascertained in the absence of the base population statistics. The St. Louis study also found that Jewish mortality rates were lower for most major causes of death. The differences were minor in the case of heart disease, cancer, and vascular lesions, but they were large in the case of accidents, pneumonia, diseases of early infancy, suicide, tuberculosis, syphilis, and alcoholism. Again, however, since the mortality rate from specific causes varies considerably by age group, such over-all comparisons cannot be used conclusively to ascertain differentials with respect to cause of death. Finally, the study found that, as in the case of the total death rate, the estimated Jewish infant mortality rate and stillbirth rate were substantially lower than the comparable rates in the total white population.

Although basing its findings on data of poorer quality with respect to the exactness of religious identification, the New York study represents an improvement over the St. Louis analysis in that an attempt was made to control for age differentials. Within the limits of the methods used, this study found that the male Jewish death rate was 14 per cent below the non-Jewish male death rate, holding age constant, whereas the Jewish female death rate was 4 per cent higher than that of the non-Jewish female population. The New York study considered socio-economic class as a major variable in addition to age and sex. It found that the Jewish death rates were much lower than non-Jewish death rates for persons of the same age, sex, and socio-economic class in the younger age groups; but this advantage was diminished and even reversed in certain of the older age groups. Within the Jewish group, it found the death rate 20 per cent lower in the high and middle socio-economic classes than in the low socio-economic class. Although direct comparison of the St. Louis and the New York findings is not possible, in general the conclusions point in the same direction—an over-all lower mortality for Jews.

Unlike the United States, Canada includes religion on its official census and vital statistics information. Utilizing materials from these sources, Mortimer Spiegelman analyzed the longevity of Jews in Canada for the period 1940-1942.[4] Comparative life tables for the Jewish population and the total population showed that life expectancy at birth for Jewish males was 4.6 years greater than that for males in the general population and that the difference for females of 3.6 years also favored the Jews. Like the more recent New York study, the Canadian analysis found that the differentials favoring the Jews decreased with advancing age and that the expectation of life for the Jews and for the total Canadian population was equal at age 25 for females and at age 35 for males. This pattern reflected the fact that Jewish infants in Canada started life with an infant mortality rate only 40 per cent as great as that of the general population and that this advantage, although decreasing in magnitude, persisted through childhood, adolescence, and early maturity. Beyond age 50 the Jews began to be characterized by higher mortality rates. As Spiegelman suggests, the reasons for these age variations between Jews and the general population require a detailed investigation of the causes of death in the two groups as well as controls for differences in place of residence, socio-economic status, nativity, and marital status.

A limitation of the Canadian analysis stems from the fact that deaths among Jews in Canada for the period of this study were distributed by sex, but not by age. The latter distribution had to be estimated on the basis of records available for the province of Ontario. There is no reason to believe, however, that this procedure seriously altered the findings. Spiegelman concluded his analysis by suggesting that

[4] "The Longevity of Jews in Canada, 1940-1942," *Population Studies,* II (December, 1948), 293-304.

the longevity and mortality characteristics of the relatively small Jewish population of Canada may be indicative of what might be found for the millions of Jews in the United States, for whom such information is not available. The later studies of the Jewish communities of St. Louis and New York, as well as this analysis, give support to his assumption.

The Jewish community of Greater Providence was so structured that almost all Jewish deaths were handled by a single funeral director. Moreover, practically all Jewish deceased were buried in the two Jewish cemeteries serving the area encompassed by this study. Finally, even the very small number of Jewish deceased who may have been cremated or buried in non-Jewish cemeteries were generally serviced through the one Jewish funeral director. All of the evidence available suggests, therefore, that reliance upon the records of the Jewish funeral director provides almost 100 per cent coverage for all Jewish deaths that occurred in Greater Providence or among Providence Jews who died elsewhere and were buried in Providence.

This analysis is based on deaths that occurred between August 1, 1962, and July 31, 1964, a period centered on the months during which the population survey was completed. First, the names of all deceased for this two-year period were obtained from the files of the Jewish funeral director. They were then checked through the files of the Rhode Island Division of Vital Statistics. From the original death certificates, information was abstracted on the sex, age, and birthplace of the deceased person and the cause of death. Ideally, all three of these variables should be used in the analysis—sex and age because they are known to be key variables affecting mortality, nativity as a means of evaluating the effect of generation status. Since the total number of deaths occurring in the two-year period was moderate (397) and a disproportional number was concentrated in the aged groups (72 per cent of the deceased were 65 and over), the opportunity to compare mortality differentials by generation status was limited. Since over three-fourths of the aged deceased were foreign born, statistically valid comparisons with the native population were precluded, particularly after subdivisions by sex and age within the older group. Conversely, the small total number of deaths under 65 and the high concentration of native born in this part of the age pyramid (88 per cent) precluded comparisons with the small minority of young foreign born deceased. For these reasons, the analysis of trends in mortality must be very largely restricted to cross-sectional comparison of age differentials. In so doing, insights into generational changes can be gained through recognition that the aged are basically the foreign-born group and those under 55 represent the native born.

The resulting mortality statistics by age and sex, encompassing all Jewish deaths in the two-year period under investigation, were related to the statistics from the population census in order to obtain both age- and sex-specific death rates for the Jewish population. These data in turn have been used to construct life tables for the Jewish population. To permit comparison with the mortality experience of the general population, both age- and sex-specific death rates were computed and life tables were constructed for the total white population of Rhode Island.

MORTALITY PATTERNS

In all, the 397 Jewish deaths that were identified for the two-year period under investigation gave a death rate of 10.1 per 1,000 Jewish persons. This was slightly below the crude death rates for the total white population, which for the period 1959-1961 was 10.3. The pattern of differentials was not uniform, however, for males and females (Table 7-1). The Jewish male death rate of 10.6 per 1,000 was below that of the total white male population, whereas the 9.7 death rate for Jewish females was slightly above that of the total white female population.

To ascertain whether these differentials stem from the differences in age structure of the Jewish and the total population, age-standardized

TABLE 7-1

DEATH RATES PER 1,000 POPULATION, BY AGE AND SEX, JEWISH AND TOTAL WHITE POPULATION*

	Males		Females	
Age	Jewish	Total White	Jewish	Total White
Under 1	10.9	25.7	14.3	20.0
1- 4	–	0.8	–	0.8
5-14	0.5	0.5	0.2	0.3
15-24	–	0.8	0.8	0.4
25-34	0.6	1.1	–	0.7
35-44	2.4	2.7	0.7	1.7
45-54	4.6	9.2	3.2	4.8
55-64	17.2	23.8	13.2	11.7
65-74	55.8	52.5	43.6	31.3
75-84	124.4	108.2	91.1	85.0
85 and over	380.9	232.8	328.1	202.9
TOTAL	10.6	11.3	9.7	9.4
Standardized for Age	11.0		11.2	

***In this and succeeding tables in this chapter, the Jewish population refers to Greater Providence, 1962-1964, and total white population refers to Rhode Island, 1959-1961.**

death rates were computed for the Jewish group. These rates show what the over-all Jewish rate would be if the Jewish population had the same age structure as the total population but retained its own age-specific death rates. For both males and females, standardizing the death rates for age raises the Jewish death rates, that of the males becoming 11.0 and that of the females, 11.2. For the males the standardized death rate differed little from that of the total male white population, thereby suggesting that the mortality experience of Jewish males varied only slightly from that of the total population. For the females, however, standardizing for age accentuated the differential between the Jewish and the total death rates, raising the former to 11.2 compared to a 9.4 rate for the total population.

Examination of the age-specific rates shows that at early ages for both males and females the mortality rates of the total population were higher than those of the Jewish group. This was particularly true of the infant mortality rate (deaths to children under one year of age) where the rate for Jewish males was less than half of that of the total white male population and the rate for Jewish females was only 60 per cent as high as that for female whites. Since infant mortality has generally been regarded as greatly affected by socio-economic and environmental factors, the considerably lower rates for the Jewish population may reflect the relatively better socio-economic status of the Jewish population in the larger community. For males, the lower rates favoring the Jewish group continued through the 55-64 age group; for females, except for minor exceptions, the lower rates persisted through the 45-54 age group. In all higher age groups the Jewish rates were higher than those of the total population, and the differential tended to become increasingly greater with older age. For the oldest group, for example, the Jewish rates were over 50 per cent greater than those of the total white population for both males and females.

One might, of course, ask whether the higher rate characterizing the aged group stems from the higher proportion of foreign born in this segment of the age structure. Unfortunately, data by nativity for the general population are not available. In the Jewish population, detailed evaluation of the influence of nativity does not seem justified. Some limited insights into the possible role of nativity can be gained by comparisons of the distribution of foreign born among the deceased and the general population for the age groups 45-64 and 65 and over. Since the patterns for males and females are identical, only the statistics for the combined sexes need be cited. The foreign born constituted 26 per cent of the Jewish population aged 45 to 64; among the deceased in this age group 29 per cent were foreign born. In the aged group, the foreign born constituted 73 per cent of the total population and 77 per cent of the deceased. In both age cohorts, therefore, there were proportionally more foreign born, but the differences were not great enough to account for the significantly higher age-specific mortality rates among the aged, particularly in view of the generally lower mortality of Jews in the 45-64 age range. At the same time, the fact that the deceased group consistently contained somewhat more foreign born, and this persists with even more detailed age breakdowns, suggests that nativity has played a small role in affecting life chances and that those older persons born in the United States have a somewhat better survival experience than those born abroad.

This changing pattern of age differentials conforms closely to those observed in other studies. Since proportionally more of the deaths occurring at early ages are due to infectious and communicable diseases, whereas more of those occurring in old age result from chronic illnesses, these differentials suggest that the rate of deaths due to communicable diseases is lower among Jews. As a result, more Jews survive to old age, when the chronic diseases assume increased importance as a cause of death. As Spiegelman suggests,[5] the higher Jewish death rates at older ages may arise from the effect, in later life, of their low mortality in early life. The better living conditions that may account for the lower rates of Jewish mortality in infancy, childhood, and through middle age may result in proportionally more physically impaired persons living until the upper ages, when the chronic diseases take a heavier toll. Later analysis of the data on cause of death will permit more detailed examination of this assumption. Before turning to these data, however, the life expectancy of Jews and of the total population will be compared.

LENGTH OF LIFE

Based on the mortality experience of the Jewish population in the period 1962 to 1964, the average life expectancy of Jews is 70.8 years for males and 73.4 years for females. Comparison of these life expectancies with those of the total white population (Table 7-2), based on mortality experience in the years 1959 to 1961, shows that Jewish males on the average could expect to live 3.3 years longer than males in the total white population. The life expectancy of Jewish females differed only minimally from that of the total white female population, being 0.2 years lower. The greater advantage that Jewish males held in life expectancy over the total white male population compared to the absence of such an advantage for the females corresponds to the pattern of differentials in over-all death rates by sex. For the Jewish population, as for

[5] Spiegelman, "The Longevity of Jews in Canada," pp. 300-301.

TABLE 7-2

EXPECTATION OF LIFE IN YEARS AT SPECIFIED AGES, JEWISH AND TOTAL WHITE POPULATION

	Males		Females	
Age	Jewish	Total White	Jewish	Total White
0	70.8	67.5	73.4	73.6
1	70.6	68.2	73.4	74.1
5	66.6	64.4	69.4	70.3
15	56.9	54.7	60.0	60.6
25	46.9	45.1	50.0	50.8
35	37.2	35.5	40.0	41.1
45	27.9	26.4	30.3	31.7
55	19.0	18.4	21.1	23.0
65	11.6	12.1	13.4	15.2
75	6.8	7.1	8.0	9.0
85	2.6	4.6	3.0	5.0

the total population, the life expectancy at birth of females exceeds that of males, but again because of the somewhat higher mortality of the females, this differential is not so great for the Jewish population as for the total population. For the latter, females can expect to live approximately 6 years longer than males, whereas for the Jewish population the differential amounts to only 2.6 years.

The more favorable life expectancy that characterizes the Jewish male population at birth persists up to age 65, although the balance in favor of the Jews diminishes with increasing age. Whereas Jewish male life expectancy at birth exceeds that of the total white population by 3.3 years, at age 15 the difference amounts to only 2.2 years; at age 45 it amounts to 1.5 years; and at age 65 the advantage turns in favor of the total white population. Thereafter the expectation of life among Jewish males continues to be lower, and the disadvantage becomes increasingly great. At age 85 Jewish males can expect to live on the average only 2.6 years longer, whereas the total white male population can expect 4.6 more years of life. The higher life expectancy of Jewish males at birth stems from the generally more favorable age-specific mortality patterns that characterize the younger age groups of the Jewish population; in turn, the higher age-specific mortality characterizing the older segments of the Jewish population accounts for the lower life expectancy that characterizes the older segments of the Jewish male group.

For females, the pattern is quite different. Jewish females begin life with a slightly lower life expectancy than the total white female population, and this disadvantage persists throughout the life cycle. The differential remains relatively small in the early years, never exceeding one year until age 35. At age 35 the life expectancy of Jewish females is 1.1 years below that of the total white population; this differential tends to increase, irregularly, with advancing age, reaching 2.0 years at age 85. Although the age-specific mortality rates of Jewish females at younger ages are lower than those of the total white female population, the differentials are generally not so great as those that characterize the males. At the same time, the age-specific mortality of older Jewish females exceeds that of the total white population, and the disadvantage begins at an earlier age than that of the Jewish males. Over all, this pattern of age-specific differentials results in lower levels of life expectancy for Jewish females both at birth and throughout the life cycle. Factors that operate to account for better survival experience on the part of Jewish males than of Jewish females in comparison with the respective segments of the total white population are not indicated by the data available in the current analysis.

Average life expectancy at birth reflects the mortality experience of the population throughout all later stages of the life cycle. Another perspective for evaluating the survival experience of the population is an examination of what proportion of the population will be alive by a given year of age (Table 7-3). Because these data also are based on the age-specific mortality rates. the survival experience of both Jewish males and Jewish females is more favorable than that of the total white population up to the very oldest age groups. If the mortality experience

TABLE 7-3

NUMBER SURVIVING TO SPECIFIED YEAR OF AGE, PER 1,000 BORN ALIVE, JEWISH AND TOTAL WHITE POPULATION

	Males		Females	
Age	Jewish	Total White	Jewish	Total White
0	1,000	1,000	1,000	1,000
1	989	975	986	981
5	989	972	986	978
15	984	968	984	975
25	984	961	976	971
35	978	950	976	964
45	955	924	969	948
55	912	843	938	904
65	768	664	822	804
75	433	388	528	587
85	101	182	197	237

of the population for the years 1962 to 1964 persists into the future, 95.5 per cent of all Jewish-born males will still be alive at age 45, compared to 92.5 per cent of the total white male population; at age 65, 76.8 per cent of the Jewish males will still be living, compared to only 66.4 per cent of the original cohorts of total white males. At this point in the age cycle, the differential between Jewish males and the total white male population is greatest. In the next category, age 75, proportionally more Jewish males are still alive, but the differential has diminished to 43.3 per cent compared to 38.8 per cent; and by age 85 the survival experience actually favors the total white population, with 18.2 per cent of the total white males surviving, compared to only 10.1 per cent of the original group of Jewish males.

Reflecting their lower age-specific mortality at earlier ages compared to the total white female population, proportionally more Jewish females survive to age 45, 96.9 per cent compared to 94.8 per cent, but the differential is not so great as that characterizing the males. At age 65, 82.2 per cent of the Jewish females are still alive, compared to 80.4 percent of the total white female population. Thereafter, the proportion surviving is greater for the total white females than for the Jewish females, with 23.7 per cent of the former still alive at age 85 compared to 19.7 per cent of Jewish females.

For both the Jewish and the total white population, the high proportion of individuals who survive to relatively late points in the life cycle is striking. That over 90 per cent of all Jewish-born persons will still be alive at age 55, if current mortality experience persists, and that 40 per cent of the males and over half of the females will survive to age 75 are indicative of this significant point. These data on survival also suggest that for the Jewish population, as for the total population, the sex differential in survival experience results in a considerably higher proportion of females surviving to old age. By age 85, only 10 per cent of the Jewish males will still be living, compared to twice as many Jewish females. It is this pattern of sex differentials in survival experience that already accounts for the unbalanced sex ratio among the older segment of the population. Among the Jewish population 65 and over, there are only 74 males for every 100 females.

In sum, the above-average mortality rates for Jews at older ages had the effect of reducing their expectation of life at somewhat younger ages for males and at all ages for females, below the average for the total white population as a whole. On the other hand, the low Jewish mortality in childhood, adolescence, and into the middle age results in the Jewish population having larger proportions surviving into middle age, and for males even into the early segments of older years.

CAUSE OF DEATH

Part of the differential between the mortality rates of the Jewish population and that of the white population as a whole may stem from variations in cause of death. Since cause of death generally varies significantly by age, comparison of the mortality statistics by cause of death for the total population is quite meaningless. Ideally, comparisons should be made in terms of both age- and sex-specific groups, but the rather limited number of cases upon which this analysis is based precludes such a complete analysis, particularly for the age groups under 45, among whom the number of Jewish deaths is very small.[6] In order to introduce some control, however, the cause-of-death analysis will be undertaken separately for persons aged 45 to 64 and for those 65 years old and over (Table 7-4).

For the 45-64 age group the Jewish mortality rate is well below that of the total white population, amounting to only 86 deaths per 10,000 persons compared to 116 deaths per 10,000 for the total white group.[7] Yet, the distribution of the Jewish deaths by cause generally

TABLE 7-4

PERCENTAGE DISTRIBUTION AND DEATH RATES PER 10,000 POPULATION, BY AGE AND MAJOR CAUSE OF DEATH, JEWISH AND TOTAL WHITE POPULATION

	45-64 Years				65 Years and Over			
	Percentage Distribution		Rate per 10,000 Population		Percentage Distribution		Rate per 10,000 Population	
Cause of Death	Jewish	Total White	Jewish	Total White	Jewish	Total White	Jewish	Total White
Accidents	1.1	2.4	0.9	2.8	2.1	2.1	15.2	13.5
Diabetes Mellitus	3.3	2.5	2.8	2.9	4.9	3.0	35.4	19.3
Heart Disease	52.2	43.6	45.0	50.6	47.4	51.4	341.1	329.8
Malignant Neoplasms	22.8	26.4	19.7	30.7	17.9	14.1	128.9	90.3
Respiratory Diseases	–	4.3	–	5.0	4.2	2.0	30.3	12.7
Suicide	4.3	1.0	3.7	1.2	0.7	0.2	5.1	1.1
Vascular Lesions	2.2	6.0	1.9	7.0	11.9	12.1	85.9	77.6
All Others	14.1	13.8	12.2	16.1	10.9	15.1	78.3	96.4
TOTAL	100.0	100.0	86.2	116.2	100.0	100.0	720.1	640.9

[6] The small number of Jewish deaths in the 15-44 age group were concentrated in two categories—cancer and accidents. The even smaller number of deaths in the 1-14 age group were equally distributed among three categories—accidents, respiratory diseases, and diseases of the digestive system.

[7] In contrast to age- and sex-specific death rates, which are expressed per 1,000 population, the cause-of-death–specific rates are expressed per 10,000 population because of the smaller number of cases in particular cells.

shows only minimal variation from the pattern of the population as a whole. For both Jews and total whites, heart disease represented the highest cause of death, accounting for 44 per cent of all deaths for the white population aged 45-64 and 52 per cent for Jews in this age group. For both groups, too, cancer contributed the second highest number of deaths, accounting for just over one-quarter of all deaths among the total whites and just under one-quarter of all deaths among Jews. Beyond these two major categories, no single cause of death accounted for as much as 10 per cent of all deaths, but there were small differences in order of importance; vascular lesions and respiratory diseases were the third and fourth most important factors among the total white population, whereas suicide and diabetes ranked third and fourth among the Jews. It must be emphasized, however, that all of these accounted for small proportions of total deaths and that particularly among the Jewish population the absolute number of cases involved in deaths from diabetes and suicide were less than five in each group.

Since the over-all level of Jewish mortality for the 45-65 age group is only 74 per cent as high as that of the total white population, the mortality from specific categories of disease is also generally lower for Jews. However, the level of difference is not uniform, and the extent of variation from the over-all differential of 74 per cent therefore provides some insight into whether certain diseases account for a higher than average mortality among Jews. It must be recognized, though, that, with the exception of suicide, the rates of mortality for specific diseases are in all instances below those of the general population. The question, therefore, is whether or not within this lower level there are meaningful differences. If 74 per cent is used as a standard, the data suggest that the cause-specific rates of mortality of Jews are well below those of the total white population for accidents and for vascular lesions and are somewhat below the average for cancer. On the other hand, the specific rates for Jews, compared to their over-all rates, are above average for heart disease, for diabetes, and particularly for suicide.

For the 65 and over age group, the over-all level of Jewish mortality exceeds that of the total white population by 12 per cent, being 720 per 10,000 population compared to 641 per 10,000 for the white population. Comparison of the percentage distribution of deaths by cause for the two groups shows some reversal in the relative importance of specific causal factors; for both groups heart disease remains the leading cause of death, but in this oldest age group it is somewhat higher for the total white population than for Jews. Cancer remains the second leading cause of death for both groups, but in contrast to the 45-64 age cohort, it accounts for proportionally more deaths among Jews than among the total white population, 18 per cent compared to 14 per cent. For both Jews and total whites, vascular lesions assume considerably more importance as a cause of death in the older population, accounting for 12 per cent of all deaths in both groups. With the exception of the miscellaneous category, none of the others accounts for more than 5 per cent of all deaths; in order of importance, they are diabetes, accidents, and chronic respiratory diseases for the total white population, and diabetes, respiratory diseases, and accidents for the Jewish population. For both groups the proportion of all deaths attributable to suicide declines considerably among the aged group, although the rate of death due to suicide is actually higher. On the whole, comparison of the percentage distribution of deaths by cause suggests minimal variation between Jews and total whites.

The over-all level of mortality for the 65 and over age group is about 12 per cent higher for Jews than for total whites. Comparison of the Jewish and total white rates for specific causes of death shows that with the exception of the miscellaneous category, the Jewish mortality rates are consistently higher than those of the total white population; however, the rates show considerable variation. For accidents and for vascular lesions, the relative difference in rates between Jews and total whites is about the same as the over-all difference; they are higher for cancer, diabetes, respiratory diseases, and suicide in that order; and they are lower for heart disease, although the difference is not particularly great.

RELIGION AND MORTALITY

For both males and females this research suggests that Jewish age-specific rates are below those of the white population at younger ages and are higher at older ages. The differences for males tend to be sharper than for females at all ages. The reversal in the pattern of age differentials at the older ages has been noted in other studies of Jewish mortality. The lower death rates at young ages may result from the better personal care associated with the high premium placed by Judaism on cleanliness and body care and the better environmental conditions resulting from the higher than average socio-economic status of Jews as judged by both education and occupation. They may also stem from long-continued genetic selection for resistance to the infectious diseases of urban living. The lower mortality in younger groups has led to speculation that proportionally more Jews with physically impaired lives may survive until later years, when the effects of chronic disease may take higher tolls, thereby raising the Jewish age-specific death rates of older persons above those of the general population. The statistics by cause of death lend support to such a contention; for Jews 65 and over, the death rates from all major chronic diseases are above those of the total white population.

Comparison of life tables constructed for both Jews and total whites suggests that average life expectancy at birth favors Jewish males but shows little difference for females. The advantage in life expectancy of Jewish males declines, however, with advancing age and actually becomes less than that of all whites beyond age 65. For females, life expectancy of Jews remains below that of total whites throughout the life cycle, and the differential tends to become increasingly higher from middle age onward. Because the proportion surviving to a particular age reflects the effects of mortality only up to that age, the lower Jewish mortality in childhood as well as in the early and middle adult stages of the life cycle accounts for higher proportions of Jews surviving into middle age and, in the case of males, even into the lower range of old age.

In sum, this research suggests that differences exist between the age-specific death rates, life expectancy, and survival patterns of Jews and of the total white population, generally more so for males than for females. Moreover, the patterns of differentials observed conform closely, where comparisons are feasible, to those noted in earlier studies of New York, St. Louis, and Canada. Since these various studies cover a 25-year range, it appears that identification as a Jew continues to affect the life chances of individuals.[8] Whether this is due to religious practices, to genetic selection, or to other factors associated with Jewish identification, such as higher socio-economic status, cannot be ascertained from these data; the New York analysis indicated that the differences persist even when socio-economic level is controlled. The specific reasons must remain speculative.

[8] In fact, differences in life expectancy favoring both Jewish males and females, but especially males, were noted for London Jews as early as 1905. See S. Rosenbaum, "A Contribution to the Study of Vital and Other Statistics of Jews in the United Kingdom," *Journal of the Royal Statistical Society*, XLVIII (September, 1905), 526.

CHAPTER EIGHT

Intermarriage and Conversion

A minority group may lose its identity in several ways. First, the group as a whole may not be reproducing itself; when the balance of the vital processes does not result in more births than deaths for a long period of time and no substantial immigration occurs, the minority group ultimately may commit "demographic suicide." More commonly, the survival of a minority group is threatened when losses to the majority through assimilation are heavy. As one aspect of the assimilation process, the nature and amount of intermarriage between members of a minority and members of the majority are of crucial importance to the social and demographic future of the minority. If marital assimilation takes place at a high rate, the minority group faces the threat of losing its ethnic identity in the larger society as the descendants of the original minority group become increasingly indistinguishable from the members of the majority.[1] Until recently, studies of intermarriage in the United States have shown that the Jewish group has been remarkably successful, compared to other groups, in maintaining religious endogamy.[2] Yet, the general paucity of good data and a suggestion that the rate of intermarriage may be changing rapidly make a reevaluation desirable.

CONFLICTING EVIDENCE

The only national data available on intermarriage are the results of the 1957 Current Population Survey conducted by the Bureau of the Census, which found that 7.2 per cent of existing marriages in which at least one spouse was Jewish had a non-Jewish partner. This compared to an intermarriage rate of 9 per cent for Protestants and 21 per cent for Catholics.[3] However, estimates of the rate of Jewish intermarriages based on local studies of varied quality range as high as 17.2 per cent for San Francisco, 18.4 per cent for New York City, and 53.6 per cent for Iowa.[4]

1 Milton Gordon, *Assimilation in American Life* (New York: Oxford University Press, Inc., 1964), pp. 80-81.

2 *Ibid.*, pp. 181-82.

3 U.S. Bureau of the Census, "Religion Reported by the Civilian Population of the United States: March, 1957," *Current Population Reports,* Series P-20, No. 79 (February 2, 1958), Table 6, p. 8.

4 Data for San Francisco are reported by Fred Massarik, *The Jewish Population of San Francisco, Marin County and the Peninsula, 1959* (San Francisco: Jewish Welfare

These estimates may reflect regional variation of the over-all national rate or may foreshadow the future national rate.

Although there is general agreement that the rate of Jewish intermarriage has increased, the extent of the increase has not been clearly determined. In New Haven, Jewish intermarriages increased in eighty years from no intermarriages in 1870 and 1.2 per cent in 1900 to 5.1 per cent in 1950.[5] More recent data on trends and differentials in Jewish intermarriage were analyzed for the Jewish population of Washington, D.C., in 1956. The rate of intermarriage was found to vary directly with distance from the immigrant generation. Jewish intermarriage among foreign-born husbands was 1.4 per cent; native-born husbands of foreign parentage, 10.2 per cent; and native-born husbands of native parentage, 17.9 per cent.[6] These data point to a sharp trend toward increased intermarriage between Jews and non-Jews and suggest that an over-all rate is lowered by the presence within a community of a high proportion of first- and second-generation persons. However, data for Washington, D.C., may not be typical of Jews in more stable communities because of the high mobility of its population and the high proportion of persons in government jobs. Thus, patterns of intermarriages among Jews in other communities cannot be generalized from these data. Furthermore, added to the paucity of data available on the extent and trends in Jewish intermarriage is the fact that several important areas of research concerning marriages between Jews and non-Jews have been neglected. For example, basic data have not generally been available concerning the pattern of conversions to Judaism, fertility and marriage patterns of intermarried couples, and religious identification of children of intermarried couples. Although speculations concerning these questions have been offered, no systematic research has been carried out to provide a basis for generaliza-

---

Federation, 1959), p. 44; New York data are taken from Jerold S. Heiss, "Premarital Characteristics of the Religiously Intermarried in an Urban Area," *American Sociological Review,* XXV, No. 1 (1960), 47-55; Iowa data were analyzed by Erich Rosenthal, "Studies of Jewish Intermarriage in the United States," *American Jewish Yearbook* (Philadelphia: Jewish Publication Society of America, 1963), LXIV, 34-51. See also Albert I. Gordon, *Intermarriage* (Boston: Beacon Press, 1963); and Marshall Sklare, "Intermarriage and the Jewish Future," *Commentary,* XXXVII, No. 2 (1964), 47.

5 Ruby Jo Reeves Kennedy, "What Has Social Science to Say About Intermarriage?" in *Intermarriage and Jewish Life,* ed. Werner J. Cahnman (New York: The Herzl Press, 1963), p. 29.

6 Rosenthal, "Studies of Jewish Intermarriage," p. 19, Table 3. Similar findings on the increasing rate of intermarriage for Canada are reported by Louis Rosenberg, "Intermarriage in Canada, 1921-1960," in *Intermarriage and Jewish Life,* ed. Cahnman, pp. 57-81. Rosenthal's study found these generational trends only for husbands, and no data are presented for native-born persons of mixed parentage.

tions.[7] Moreover, empirical evidence for examining trends for these dimensions of Jewish intermarriages has been lacking.

This chapter will utilize the material from the Providence survey to obtain insights into (1) trends and generation changes in the rate of Jewish intermarriages and conversions to Judaism; (2) residential differentials in Jewish intermarriages; (3) differentials in social characteristics and Jewish identification; (4) differences in the age at marriage and fertility patterns of intermarried couples; and (5) the question of the religious identification of the children of intermarried couples.

Several questions in the survey questionnaire provided the basis for the present analysis. Among the first questions asked in taking an inventory of all the members of the households was, "Which of these persons is Jewish?" Comparison of the identification of husband and wife on this question provides some indication of intermarriage. It is not a full measure, however, since persons who were converted to Judaism would not be identified as having been non-Jewish before marriage. The failure of the Bureau of the Census to go beyond such a question in its 1957 survey introduces a serious limitation in its intermarriage data. As a supplement, another question included in the Providence study ascertained whether any member of the household or any child of the head of the household was married to a person who was not born Jewish. Whenever a "yes" response was given, the non-Jewish-born person was identified, and a second question asked whether the non-Jewish individual had been converted to Judaism. These questions thus provided information on present intermarriages as well as conversions. The ability to cross-tabulate this information with a variety of other data on the social, religious, and demographic characteristics of the respondents enhances the value of the information on intermarriage. In addition, the questions about children not living at home provide the basis for extending the analysis beyond the immediate sample households. Finally, comparing the religious identification of the children of mixed marriages with the type of mixed marriage, that is, converted or nonconverted, permits determination of the extent to which mixed marriages affect the Jewish identification of children.

For the investigation of intermarriage, the sampling design has certain limitations. Studies have documented that the rate of intermarriage is higher if the data are based on a survey of both Jewish and non-Jewish households rather than on a study based primarily on files of Jew-

[7] For a review of neglected research in Jewish intermarriages, see Joseph Maier, "Intermarriage: A Survey of Unresearched Problems," in *Intermarriage and Jewish Life*, ed. Cahnman, pp. 92-110.

ish population.[8] The very nature of our sampling procedure may have resulted in failure to identify persons on the fringes of the Jewish community, that is, people who neither identify themselves as Jews nor are identified by others as Jews. For this reason, the results of the survey probably undercount the absolute rate of Jewish intermarriages, particularly among those Jews who converted to Christianity or have lost all identification with the Jewish community.

In an attempt at least partially to investigate this limitation, the survey inquired about the intermarriage of children of the sampled heads of households. This question applied to all children, whether or not they were living in the area. The resulting data may provide some insights into (1) whether, among at least the younger generation, a significant number of intermarriages are lost for the reasons cited earlier; and (2) whether a tendency exists for younger intermarried couples to seek greater anonymity by moving to communities away from those in which their parents live. Despite this limited attempt to correct for the methodological weakness of the sample for studying intermarriage, the data should be used with caution and the findings viewed as suggestive and exploratory in nature. Yet, the data collected contain unique information hitherto unavailable and shed new insights into the character of Jewish intermarriages.

LOSSES AND GAINS

Of the 5,140 married couples represented in the sample, 232 or 4.5 per cent were intermarriages, 4.4 per cent involving a Jewish male whose wife was not born Jewish and only 0.1 per cent representing a Jewish female whose husband was born non-Jewish. This higher intermarriage rate among Jewish males compared to females conforms to the pattern observed in almost all other communities.[9] The magnitude of the difference may, however, reflect a stronger tendency for those interfaith marriages with a Jewish-born wife and a non-Jewish husband to lose their identification with the Jewish community.

Judged by these statistics, the over-all rate of intermarriage among Jews in Greater Providence is considerably below that of many other communities in the United States. Yet, it is comparable to the findings of a 1950 survey of both Jewish and non-Jewish family units in New Haven, Connecticut, in which it was estimated that families with one

[8] Rosenthal, "Studies of Jewish Intermarriage," pp. 15-18.

[9] Rosenthal, "Studies of Jewish Intermarriage," p. 17; and Sklare, "Intermarriage and the Jewish Future," p. 47.

Jewish spouse constituted 5 per cent of all the Jewish families.[10] This relatively low level of intermarriage also conforms to more recent findings for Rochester, New York,[11] and for Camden, New Jersey.[12] The Rochester study found that of the households in which the head was married, either the head or the spouse had been non-Jewish in 8 per cent of the cases. In the Camden survey the rate of intermarriage was lower, approximately 5 per cent. The relatively low level of intermarriage in Providence may therefore not be atypical of the older Jewish communities in the northeastern section of the country.

For the 232 intermarried couples, it was ascertained whether the non-Jewish spouse had converted to Judaism. Forty-two per cent had done so, thereby creating religious unity within the family unit. Since data are not available here on those units whose identity with the Jewish community was completely lost through conversion of the Jewish partner or through failure to identify with the Jewish community, it is not possible to ascertain the extent of conversion away from Judaism. The survey data suggest, however, that for a considerable proportion of intermarriages the non-Jewish partner becomes Jewish, thereby enhancing the chances that the family unit will remain identified with the Jewish community.

Interest in intermarriage of Jews extends beyond the mere question of the number of intermarriages to the larger questions of the trend in intermarriage patterns. In the absence of statistics on the extent of intermarriage in the community at earlier points in time, cross-sectional data may be used to gain some insight into the developments over the last half century. In particular, two sets of data are useful for such purposes: (1) comparison of the patterns of intermarriage according to the age of the couple; (2) comparison of the intermarriage patterns according to generation status. These two dimensions are not, of course, completely independent of each other, but separate evaluation of each may provide new insights into the course of past developments and the possible course that intermarriage may take in the future. Since in such a large proportion of intermarriages in this sample the husband was born Jewish and the wife non-Jewish, the analysis of age, generation, and residential differentials in intermarriage will be based on the characteristics of the male partner.

The pattern of intermarriage in relation to age is somewhat ir-

10 Ruby Jo Reeves Kennedy, "Single or Triple Melting Pot: Intermarriage in New Haven, 1870-1950," *American Journal of Sociology*, LVIII, No. 2 (1952), 56-59.

11 *The Jewish Population of Rochester, New York, 1961* (Rochester: Jewish Community Council of Rochester, N.Y., 1964), p. 56.

12 Charles F. Westoff, *A Population Survey: The Greater Camden County Jewish Community* (Camden, N.J.: The Jewish Federation of Camden County, 1965), pp. 88-89.

regular (Table 8-1). Those in the oldest group, 60 years and over, have the lowest rate of intermarriage, only 1.3 per cent. This increases to 7 per cent of those in the age group 40-49 but declines to 1.7 per cent of those 30 to 39 years of age. For those under 30 years, the rate of intermarriage is considerably higher, encompassing 9 per cent of the couples. No clear reason for the departure of the 30-39 age group from the trend is apparent. With this exception, the data do point to an increase in the rate of intermarriage among the younger segments of the population.

While the rate of intermarriage tends to be higher among the youngest persons, the proportion of persons who are converted to Judaism is also higher among the younger groups. Among the intermarriages in which the husband is 60 years old and over, none of the non-Jewish spouses converted to Judaism; by contrast, among those in the middle age group, 40 to 59, four out of every ten cases of intermarriage resulted in conversion of the non-Jewish spouse; and among those cases in which the husband was under 40 years of age the number of conversions among the intermarried rose to seven out of ten. These data suggest, in confirmation of some conclusions reached in a Detroit study, that the younger the person, the greater is the probability that a mixed marriage will lead to the conversion of one of the partners and that religious unity will be established within the family.[13]

The survey also inquired about intermarriage of children of the head of the household, regardless of where they were living. These data point conclusively to a higher level of intermarriage among the children than among the couples living in the surveyed households. Whereas the intermarriage rate of those in the survey was 4.5 per cent, that among the children of these households was 5.9 per cent. The fact that a higher percentage of the children are intermarried than are the parents may largely stem from age and generation differentials. Since the children include those living outside the survey area, the higher rate for children may also partially reflect a greater tendency for younger couples who intermarry to live outside their families' area of residence. In part, this may represent an attempt to achieve greater anonymity through outmigration. In part, it may be that the child was already living away from home when he or she married a non-Jewish person; relaxation of family pressures and more numerous opportunities for interdating may account for higher intermarriage rates among those living away from parental homes. Interesting, too, is the sex differential in the rate of intermarriage among these children: of the male children 7.7 per cent were reported as intermarried, compared to only 4.3 per cent of the females.

[13] Gerhard Lenski, *The Religious Factor* (Garden City, N.Y.: Doubleday & Company, Inc., 1963), pp. 54-55.

TABLE 8-1

INTERMARRIAGE BY SEX AND BY AGE OF HUSBAND

Sex and Age	Not Intermarried	Jew Married to Non-Jew		Non-Jew Married to Jew		Inadequate Information	Total Per Cent
		Non-Jew Converted	Non-Jew Not Converted	Converted	Not Converted		
Males	95.3	1.8	2.6	0.1	–	0.2	100.0
Females	95.3	0.1	–	1.8	2.6	0.2	100.0
Age of Husband*							
20-29	91.0	5.1	2.6	1.3	–	–	100.0
30-39	97.9	1.3	0.4	–	–	0.4	100.0
40-49	93.0	3.6	3.4	–	–	–	100.0
50-59	93.4	1.2	4.8	–	–	0.6	100.0
60 and Over	98.7	–	1.3	–	–	–	100.0

*To make maximum use of the available data, this analysis is based on a more detailed age classification, starting at age 20. The data in Tables 8-2 and 8-3 represent combinations of these groupings.

Two points seem particularly noteworthy about these statistics: (1) Although the over-all rate of intermarriage for the children, including those living in Greater Providence and outside the area, is somewhat higher than that reported for the population currently resident in Greater Providence, it is still relatively low when compared to the rates reported in many other community studies. (2) The report that 4.3 per cent of the females are married to non-Jewish males departs considerably from the finding that the Jewish households of Greater Providence contain only a minute proportion (0.1 per cent) of couples in which the husband is non-Jewish by birth. This discrepancy lends support to the thesis that considerably more of such intermarriages lose their identification with the Jewish community and therefore are not included in a survey of households identifiable as Jewish. Further weight is given to this thesis by the evidence on conversion available from these statistics. In one out of every three cases in which a Jewish male child married a non-Jew, the wife was converted to Judaism; by contrast, in only one out of six cases in which the daughter married a non-Jewish male was the husband converted.

Recent studies have found that the intermarriage rate is higher among native-born Jews. Our data substantiate these findings (Table 8-2). Generation status is a key factor influencing both the rate of intermarriage and the extent of conversion. Among the foreign born only 1.2 per cent are reported as intermarried. Among the third generation this proportion amounts to almost 6 per cent. Moreover, the pattern of differentials by generation status operates within the respective age groups. For example, among the 40 to 59 year old males, the rate of intermarriage increases from slightly less than 3 per cent of the foreign born to 12.6 per cent of those in the third generation. Although the pattern is in the same direction, the rate of intermarriage among those in the 20-39 year old group is at a lower level than that characterizing the 40-59 year group. This broad age grouping masks sharp differentials within the 20-39 year age range, but a more detailed breakdown of this group by age is not warranted, because of the small number of cases that would result. Over all, however, these data suggest that the tendency toward an inverse relation between age and intermarriage rates results from the higher concentration of third-generation persons among the younger segment of the population.

Consistent with the pattern of age differentials, the tendency by generation status is for the rate of conversion to Judaism to vary directly with the rate of intermarriage. For example, only one-fourth of the mixed marriages of the foreign born resulted in conversion of the non-Jewish spouse, compared to over half of the intermarriages involving third-

TABLE 8-2

INTERMARRIAGE BY GENERATION STATUS AND AGE, MALES

Generation and Age	Not Intermarried	Jew Married to Non-Jew		Non-Jew Converted, Married to Jew	Inadequate Information	Total Per Cent	Per Cent of Total Intermarriages Resulting in Conversion
		Wife Converted	Wife Not Converted				
All Ages							
First Generation	98.8	0.3	0.9	0.0	0.0	100.0	25.0
Second Generation	94.4	2.1	3.4	0.0	0.1	100.0	37.8
Mixed Parentage	94.2	3.9	1.9	0.0	0.0	100.0	67.7
Third Generation	93.4	2.6	2.6	0.7	0.7	100.0	55.6
TOTAL	95.3	1.8	2.6	0.1	0.2	100.0	41.4
20-39 Age Group							
First Generation	100.0	0.0	0.0	0.0	0.0	100.0	0.0
Second Generation	96.8	2.4	0.8	0.0	0.0	100.0	75.0
Mixed Parentage	95.7	4.3	0.0	0.0	0.0	100.0	100.0
Third Generation	94.8	1.7	1.7	0.9	0.9	100.0	60.0
40-59 Age Group							
First Generation	97.2	0.9	1.9	0.0	0.0	100.0	33.3
Second Generation	93.3	2.4	4.1	0.0	0.2	100.0	36.7
Mixed Parentage	92.4	3.8	3.8	0.0	0.0	100.0	50.0
Third Generation	87.4	6.3	6.3	0.0	0.0	100.0	50.0
60 and Over Age Group							
First Generation	99.5	0.0	0.5	0.0	0.0	100.0	0.0
Second Generation	96.8	0.0	3.2	0.0	0.0	100.0	0.0

generation males. This pattern of generation differences remains even when age is held constant, indicating that it is not solely a function of the lower age level of the third generation. Thus, these patterns suggest that although the rate of intermarriage has risen among third-generation compared to first-generation Jews, the rate of conversion of the non-Jewish spouse to Judaism is also higher among the third generation. Again, it must be emphasized that these statistics do not indicate what proportion of Jews are lost to Judaism through marrying out of the faith and converting to Christianity. Therefore, the patterns noted are only suggestive.

RESIDENTIAL AND SOCIAL FACTORS

Another dimension in terms of which intermarriage patterns can be examined is residential status within the metropolitan area (Table 8-3). The lowest rate of intermarriage, less than one per cent, characterizes persons living in the older sections of the central cities, and the highest rate of intermarriage, 7.7 per cent, characterizes those living in the suburbs. Intermediary is the 3.8 per cent intermarriage rate of those living in the still growing and better economic sections of the central cities. The differences by place of residence are not entirely attributable to the variations in age composition. For all three age levels the rate of intermarriage in the suburbs is above that of the older sections of the city, and in two out of three age groups is also above that of the newer sections of the central city. The higher intermarriage rate in the suburbs closely parallels other indices of assimilation to be discussed more fully in succeeding chapters. On the whole, judged by affiliation with Jewish organizations, with synagogue membership and attendance, and with adherence to ritual practices, the ties to Judaism of family units living in the suburbs were weaker than the ties of those living in the central cities. The higher rates of intermarriage fit well with this general pattern.

For place of residence, as for age and generation, the rate of conversion to Judaism parallels the rate of intermarriage. In the suburbs conversions to Judaism took place in half of all intermarriages, compared to only one-third for the central cities; within the central cities conversion was involved in just over one-third of the intermarriages taking place in the newer section, but in none of the relatively small number of cases occurring in the older sections of the city. The data by age point in the same direction, although the differences within the 20-39 year group are small and the major differential with respect to rate of conversion stands out most sharply in the 40-59 year group. These residential differences may largely be a function of the generation status of the popu-

TABLE 8-3

INTERMARRIAGE BY PLACE OF RESIDENCE AND AGE, MALES

Place of Residence	Not Intermarried	Jew Married to Non-Jew: Wife Converted	Wife Not Converted	Non-Jew Converted, Married to Jew	Inadequate Information	Total Per Cent	Per Cent of Total Intermarriages Resulting in Conversion
All Ages							
Older Urban	99.3	0.0	0.7	0.0	0.0	100.0	0.0
Newer Urban	96.2	1.4	2.4	0.0	0.0	100.0	36.0
Suburban	91.5	3.5	3.9	0.3	0.8	100.0	49.2
20-39 Age Group							
Older Urban	100.0	0.0	0.0	0.0	0.0	100.0	0.0
Newer Urban	95.3	3.4	1.3	0.0	0.0	100.0	71.4
Suburban	96.6	1.3	0.7	0.7	0.7	100.0	75.0
40-59 Age Group							
Older Urban	98.5	0.0	1.5	0.0	0.0	100.0	0.0
Newer Urban	95.5	1.1	3.4	0.0	0.0	100.0	25.0
Suburban	86.4	6.0	6.6	0.0	1.0	100.0	47.9
60 and Over Age Group							
Older Urban	100.0	0.0	0.0	0.0	0.0	100.0	0.0
Newer Urban	98.7	0.0	1.3	0.0	0.0	100.0	0.0
Suburban	96.4	0.0	3.6	0.0	0.0	100.0	0.0

lation living in these different areas; the older sections contain proportionally more foreign born and the suburbs contain a heavier concentration of third-generation Americans.

Some further insights into the factors associated with intermarriage of Jews can be obtained by examining rates of intermarriage among persons belonging to specific social and demographic segments of the population. Since it is the Jewish male who displays the highest intermarriage rate and thereby provides the most cases for analytic purposes, this discussion, with one exception, will be restricted to intermarried husbands. The over-all small proportion and number of intermarriages also preclude cross-tabulation of the particular social or demographic variables with both generation status and age. For such purposes, age *per se* will therefore be used as an index of generation. The comparison will be restricted to two age groups, 20-39 and 40-59, since the number of intermarriages in the oldest, largely foreign-born group is so small. A final caveat needs to be stressed. Since most of the social and demographic data considered here refer to current characteristics rather than to those existing before or at the time of the intermarriage, they have limited value for locating the causal factor. The variables considered include: secular education, occupation, number of marriages, religious identification, religious practices, and Jewish education (Table 8-4).

The Washington study found that attendance at and graduation from college served to increase intermarriage, but graduate study lowered the rate considerably.[14] Our data support neither conclusion. For the 20-39 age group, the highest rate of intermarriage characterizes the high school educated groups, and in the 40-59 year group it varies minimally between high school and college educated males. For the 20-39 age group, graduate study resulted in a considerably higher rate than mere graduation from college, but for the older group the intermarriage rate of those with graduate education was somewhat below the level of those with only a high school or college education. On this basis one cannot conclude that education level shows a consistent relation to intermarriage or that future increases in educational achievement in itself should lead to a higher rate of intermarriage.

A similar mixed pattern characterizes the relation between occupation and intermarriage. Among the youngest cohort, the professionals at one extreme and the manual workers at the other have the highest intermarriage rates. Among the older cohort, the clerical-sales group and the manager-proprietor group display the highest rates. Judged both by current occupation and by educational achievement, therefore, intermarriage rates do not vary in a consistent way with current class position.

[14] Rosenthal, "Studies of Jewish Intermarriage," pp. 21-22.

TABLE 8-4

INTERMARRIAGE BY SELECTED SOCIAL CHARACTERISTICS, BY AGE, MALES

Variable	Per Cent Intermarried	
	20-39 Years	40-59 Years
Secular Education		
None	–	–
1- 8 Years	0.0	2.7
9-12 Years	6.3	5.7
13-16 Years	1.3	5.8
17 Years and over	4.7	4.0
Occupation		
Professionals	5.4	2.8
Managers	1.5	5.6
Clerical and Sales	2.5	6.8
Manual Workers	6.5	4.8
Frequency of Marriage		
Once	3.7	3.9
More than Once	0.0	24.4
Religious Identification		
Orthodox	2.2	1.8
Conservative	2.6	2.7
Reform	1.7	8.3
Secular	25.0	41.2
Religious Practices		
Traditional	2.2	1.1
Moderate	0.6	3.4
Secular	11.9	18.8
Jewish Education		
None	4.2	9.3
1-3 Years	3.1	8.8
4-8 Years	3.2	4.9
9 and More Years	1.4	2.2

Yet, the small number of cases and the strong possibility that more of those with higher education have moved away from the community in pursuit of opportunities elsewhere may affect the patterns noted here.

A surprising finding of the data is the sharp differentials in intermarriage rates between those married only once and those married more than once. Among Jewish males under 40, only a few reported more than one marriage and among these none were intermarried. Among those 40 to 59 almost 25 per cent of all those married more than once were intermarried, in contrast to only 4 per cent of those married only once. Obviously, instability of marriage is very much associated with intermarriage. Unfortunately, no information is available on whether the previous marriage(s) involved an intermarriage. That this differential is part of a general complex is further indicated by the patterns for the females, most of whom were the non-Jewish partner to the marriage. Among wives a considerable number in both the 20-39 and the 40-59 year groups were married more than once. Almost 30 per cent of the remarriages of the younger wives and 20 per cent of those of the older wives were intermarriages. This contrasted to intermarriage rates of only 7 per cent and 4 per cent among wives in these respective age groups who were married only once. Quite clearly, intermarriage and marital instability are interrelated. This may reflect the fact that interreligious marriages have a lower survival rate than religiously homogeneous marriages.[15] The high rate of intermarriage among the remarried may stem from a higher than average intermarriage rate in their earlier marriage.

One would expect that religious identification, and particularly an Orthodox orientation, would impede intermarriage. Unfortunately, data on current identification do not permit testing such an hypothesis; this variable represents one which is most likely to change as a result of intermarriage. Evidencing either the causal or the resultant association between intermarriage and a secular orientation, the highest rates by far characterize Jewish males classifying themselves as secularists. One-fourth of all the secularists in the youngest group and four out of every ten in the 40-59 year cohort were intermarried. By contrast, for the 20-39 age group the rates for the Orthodox, Conservative, and Reform varied minimally at a low level; those in the older group increased from 2 to 8 per cent from the Orthodox to the Reform, but even the 8 per cent level of the latter was far below the 40 per cent level of the secularists.

Reflecting the tendency of intermarried males to identify themselves as secularists, it comes as no surprise to find that, according to an index of religious practices,[16] the highest rate of intermarriage characterizes those males whose religious practices are minimal. Of those classified as traditional or moderate in their religious practices, 3 per cent or fewer in both age groups intermarried. By contrast, 12 per cent of the males 20 to 39, and 19 per cent of those 40 to 59, whose home practices qualified as secular were intermarried. A significant implication of this finding is that the children of such intermarriages, even if identifying as Jewish, are growing up in homes with minimal commitments to Judaism as measured by the extent of Jewish practices within the home.

The final variable to be considered, Jewish education, may perhaps

[15] See Lee G. Burchinal and Loren E. Chancellor, "Survival Rates Among Types of Religiously Homogamous and Interreligious Marriages, Iowa, 1953-1959," *Social Forces,* XLI (May, 1963), 353-62; Judson T. Landis, "Marriages of Mixed and Non-Mixed Religious Faiths," *American Sociological Review,* XIV, No. 3 (1949), 401-7.

[16] For an explanation of the index of religious practices, see Chapter 9.

provide the greatest insight into the factors contributing to high intermarriage rates. For both age groups, an inverse relation exists. Those with the least amount of Jewish education had the highest rates of intermarriage. Among the 20-39 year group the rate declined from 4.2 per cent among those with no Jewish education to only 1.4 per cent among those with nine or more years. Among the older group the rate declined from 9.3 per cent of those with no education to only 2.2 per cent of the most educated. Since Jewish education was an experience of childhood, it reflects, more than the other variables considered here, the extent of exposure to a Jewish environment. Like the findings of the Washington study for the third generation, these data suggest very pointedly that Jewish education and other variables with which it is associated serve as a major block to intermarriage. Given the fact that the level of Jewish education of children has undergone significant increase in the mid-twentieth century, it may in the future significantly check the trend toward rising levels of intermarriage among third-generation Jews.

FERTILITY OF THE INTERMARRIED

Intermarriage may affect the population size of the minority group through several processes: (1) in its effect on the religious identity of the married partners themselves; (2) in the possibility that the fertility of intermarried couples may be below that of those who marry within the faith; (3) in its effects on the religious identification of the children born to mixed marriages. Within the limits of the data, the first factor has already been examined. The following discussion will focus on the remaining two.

Because general surveys of fertility contain such small numbers of cases of mixed marriages involving a Jewish partner, little, if anything, is known to date on the effect of Jewish intermarriage on fertility. From studies of Protestant-Catholic intermarriages, there is some suggestion that the fertility of the intermarried is lower than that of homogamous marriages of Catholics or Protestants,[17] but the evidence is not always consistent. Of the reasons advanced for lower fertility in mixed marriages, by far the most important has been the alleged instability and poor adjustment that result from the differences in religious identification of the spouses. In addition to the operation of psychological and sociological factors, the suggestion has been made that biological factors

[17] Clyde V. Kiser and Pascal K. Whelpton, "Summary of Chief Findings and Implications for Future Studies," *Social and Psychological Factors Affecting Fertility* (New York: Milbank Memorial Fund, 1958), p. 1,327.

TABLE 8-5

FAMILY SIZE AND AGE AT FIRST MARRIAGE BY INTERMARRIAGE STATUS AND AGE OF WIFE

Intermarriage Status	Mean Number of Children Ever Born	Per Cent Childless	Per Cent with 4 or More Children	Age of Wife at First Marriage
		Women 45 Years Old and over		
Husband and Wife Born Jewish	2.2	9.7	12.1	23.4
Intermarried Couples	1.6	26.1	0.0	24.7
		Women Under 45 Years of Age		
Husband and Wife Born Jewish	2.1	8.0	8.1	21.7
Intermarried Couples	1.9	14.3	7.1	21.0

resulting from the mixture of different ethnic genes may account for the lower fertility.[18]

An advantage of the Providence survey data lies in the information available on the fertility of both the intermarried and nonintermarried couples and the information obtained on the religious identification of the children of mixed marriages. The data are presented for two age groups —women 45 years old and over and those below 45 (Table 8-5). This was done to measure changes over time and to separate completed from incompleted families. A more detailed subdivision could not be made due to the small number of cases. The data clearly show that for both age groups intermarried couples have fewer children than the nonintermarried; intermarried couples have a lower average number of children ever born, have a much higher percentage of childlessness, and have a lower percentage of units with four or more children. Quite clearly, intermarriage results in lowered fertility.

Yet, despite the consistency of this pattern of lower fertility for the intermarried among both the older and younger units, the degree of difference between the intermarried and the nonintermarried is not as great among the younger couples. In large measure this narrowing differential stems from an increase in family size on the part of the younger intermarried couples. Whereas the average number of children ever born is virtually the same for the two age groups of nonintermarried, that of the intermarried increases from 1.6 for the younger group to 1.9 for the

[18] Jack Bresler, "The Relation of Population Fertility Levels to Ethnic Group Backgrounds," *Eugenics Quarterly,* VIII, No. 1 (1961), 17.

older; thus, the average differential between intermarried and nonintermarried narrows from 0.6 to 0.2 children. Similarly, the proportion of childless couples changed minimally, from 9.7 to 8.0, for the nonintermarried, but declined sharply, from 26 per cent of the older intermarried to 14 per cent of the younger intermarried units. Finally, none of the older intermarried couples had four or more children, compared to 7 per cent of the younger group; by contrast, the proportion of couples with four or more children among couples in which both spouses were born Jewish declined from 12 to 8 per cent. Over all, therefore, these data suggest that intermarriage has less effect on the fertility of currently younger couples than it had on older ones.

Since family size and the rate of childlessness are partly a function of age at marriage, whether the lower fertility of the intermarried results from a later marriage age becomes relevant. In the older group the age of wife at first marriage is, on the average, almost one and a half years later for the intermarried than for the nonintermarried. By contrast, in the younger group the differential in average age at marriage between the intermarried and nonintermarried is half as great, 0.7 years, and the age is, in fact, lower for the intermarried. This narrowing in age at marriage and its reversal in direction may account for the corresponding reduction in fertility differentials. Yet, the fact that the fertility of the intermarried in the younger age group remains below that of the nonintermarried suggests that age at marriage is not the only factor accounting for the differential.

These data on differentials in fertility and age at marriage suggest that the stigma of being intermarried has lessened in recent years and there is less hesitation today for Jews to marry non-Jews at an early age and to have children. The increased similarity of the fertility and age-at-marriage patterns of younger intermarried and nonintermarried couples may provide a sensitive index of the greater social acceptability of interfaith marriages.[19]

One other aspect of intermarriage can be examined with the Providence survey data—the faith of the children being raised in households of intermarried couples. In every instance in which the non-Jewish partner had converted to Judaism, the children were being raised as Jews. In all, 136 children in the sample belonged in this category. Among the couples in which the non-Jewish parent had not converted to Judaism,

[19] Similar results were obtained for Protestant-Catholic intermarriages when compared to Protestant-Protestant or Catholic-Catholic marriages in a recent study of fertility. See Charles F. Westoff, Robert G. Potter, Jr., Philip Sagi, and Elliot Mishler, *Family Growth in Metropolitan America* (Princeton: Princeton University Press, 1961), pp. 195-99; Charles F. Westoff, Robert G. Potter, Jr., and Philip Sagi, *The Third Child* (Princeton: Princeton University Press, 1963), pp. 91-92.

84 children were being raised as Jews and 60 as non-Jews. It must be emphasized here that these statistics do not necessarily cover every child born of these mixed marriages; they are restricted to those children who were living at home at the time of the survey. They refer, therefore, more heavily to the young children of intermarried couples since children age 18 and over are more likely to be living away from home. Within this limitation, they do suggest that a majority of the children born of mixed marriages are actually being raised as Jews. Of the total 280 children of mixed marriages living at home, only 22 per cent were non-Jews. This finding is in direct contrast to that in Washington, D.C., where 70 per cent of the children of mixed marriages were being raised as non-Jews. Again, this sharp differential may reflect differences in the character of both the two samples and the two communities studied.

IMPLICATIONS

This analysis of Jewish intermarriage patterns suggests that the extent of intermarriage is relatively low. This may stem from several factors. First, the relatively large size of the Jewish community, approximately 20,000 persons, may provide opportunities for marriage within the Jewish group; [20] the Providence Jewish community is an old one and has strong roots and strong organizational structure, and therefore it provides the framework for a close identification with the community; and finally, compared to such other communities as Washington and Los Angeles, for which high intermarriage rates have been reported, Providence has a much more stable population and one that contains a higher proportion of first- and second-generation Americans. But even among third-generation Jews in Providence the intermarriage rate was lower than that for the comparable group in Washington, D.C.

Despite the relatively low rate of intermarriage, the analysis of the data in terms of age, generation, and residence suggests that the intermarriage rate is increasing among the young, the native-born American, and the suburbanites. Unless this pattern is reversed, the over-all rate of intermarriage can be expected to rise as an increasing proportion of the population becomes third generation and moves away from the areas of densely populated Jewish settlement to the newly developing suburbs. Although the rate of intermarriage may be increasing among the third generation and is higher for the suburbanites than for the central city residents, a higher proportion of these intermarriages results in the con-

[20] A number of studies have demonstrated that the level of Jewish intermarriage is lower in the large Jewish community than in the small. See Rosenthal, "Studies of Jewish Intermarriage," pp. 8-14.

version of the non-Jewish spouse to Judaism; that is, the rate of conversions is higher precisely among those groups where intermarriage is higher. Moreover, a large proportion of the children in such marriages are actually being raised as Jews. The fertility patterns of the young intermarried couples also more closely resemble those of the nonintermarried than was true of the older age groups. This analysis points out that without data on conversion patterns and fertility of the intermarried, the evaluation of the social and demographic consequences of Jewish intermarriage is far from complete.[21]

At the same time, examination of the relation between intermarriage and a variety of social variables does not reveal any clear association between intermarriage rates and such factors as occupational status and secular education. That a high intermarriage rate is associated both with low Jewish education and with a secularist orientation suggests that the intermarried tends initially to have had weak ties to Judaism and that he will perpetuate these in marriage, even though he continues to identify himself as Jewish. The high rates of remarriage which characterize intermarried persons also point to the general instability of the marital relationship. Thus, despite the marital homogamy resulting from conversion of the non-Jewish spouse, the general religious environment and family stability of such marriages would be below those characterizing couples in which both partners were born Jewish.

Taking all these factors into account, our data suggest that the net effects of intermarriage on the over-all size of the Jewish population may not be as serious as suggested by several other community studies; its qualitative effects may be more important.

Since Jewish education reduced considerably the level of intermarriage among those now married, the rising level of Jewish education among the younger members of the population may become an increasingly important factor in curbing intermarriage. Yet, its deterrent effect may be counterbalanced by the weakening of social-psychological ties of members of the younger generation to their parental families and home community as a result of increased education, geographic mobility, careers in nonfamily businesses and in the salaried professions, and entrance in greater numbers into the intellectual subsociety.

21 *Cf.* Gordon, *Assimilation in American Life,* pp. 129-31.

CHAPTER NINE

Religiosity: Ideological and Ritualistic Dimensions

Emerging from the foregoing analysis is a complex portrait involving the delicate balance of intermarriages and conversions. On the one hand, quantitative losses to the Jewish community through interfaith marriages are relatively low, although increasing with the Americanization of the Jewish population. Yet, conversions to Judaism also increase with distance from the immigrant generation, so that net losses are negligible. Given the tendency toward religious homogeneity within marriage, it may be inferred that group cohesion among Jews is strong, but intimately related to generation status. Consequently, major interest focuses on generation changes in qualitative Jewish identification, i.e., alterations in the nature and forms of Jewish commitments and religiosity. Although all Jews may share core values of a religio-cultural complex, within the Jewish group, as within other religious groups, there are variations in the degree of commitment to and identification with its religious value system. Even casual observers of the American Jewish community are aware of the different patterns of Jewish religious identification, of variation in the performance of religious rituals, and of the variety of ways Jews maintain religious and cultural attachments. The religiosity continuum ranges from the traditional-observant Jew, actively participating in the Jewish community, to the unaffiliated, nonobservant, secular Jew, with the overwhelming majority between these extremes. Moreover, in the process of integrating into American society, Jews have altered the forms of their religious expression and the degree of their religious commitments. The objective of this and the next chapter is to explore these two major issues: the complexity of the religiosity continuum and the generational trends in the degree of religiosity among Jews.

FACETS OF RELIGIOSITY

Religiosity is a complex phenomenon involving a number of dimensions. This complexity stems from the nature of religion in general. According to Lenski, religion encompasses a system of beliefs about the nature of forces shaping man's destiny and the practices associated therewith; religious group involvement may be communal or associational and religious orientations vary in "doctrinal orthodoxy" and "devotionalism." [1] In a more elaborate definition of religion and religious systems, Talcott Parsons identifies at least five dimensions: (1) an integrated set of beliefs; (2) a set of symbols, acts, and persons which have the quality of sacredness; (3) a set of prescribed activities which is interpreted as important and often obligatory in the light of the beliefs involved; (4) a sense that those sharing common beliefs constitute a collectivity; and finally, (5) a sense that man's relation to the supernatural world is connected with his moral values.[2]

Discussions concerning the nature of religion lead to the inevitable conclusion that commitment to and expressions of religion, i.e., religiosity, must also be viewed multidimensionally. Some suggest that a comprehensive study of the religious experience and expression encompasses three dimensions: (1) theoretical expression—doctrine; (2) practical expression—cultus; and (3) sociological expression—communion, collective, and individual religion.[3] Others specifically concerned with the problem of the several dimensions of religiosity have outlined five dimensions: experiential, ideological, ritualistic, intellectual, and consequential.[4]

What are the common elements of these various typologies of religion and religiosity and how can these be applied to the study of religiosity among Jews? The first relevant [5] dimension of religiosity that will be examined is religious ideology as manifested in institutional identification. On the behavioral level, ideological variation is not confined to beliefs nor attitudinal abstractions but rather to how a population subdivides itself in terms of religious identification and types of religious institutional membership. A second dimension revolves around the practical expression of religious ideology; identification with a particular religious ideology is expressed in symbolic form in terms of religious practices. The "ritualistic" dimension includes both expressive symbols and prescribed activities which are the consequences of ideologi-

[1] Gerhard Lenski, *The Religious Factor* (Garden City, N.Y.: Doubleday & Company, Inc., 1963), pp. 18-26, 330-36.

[2] *Religious Perspectives of College Teaching in Sociology and Social Psychology* (New Haven: The Edward W. Hazen Foundation, n.d.), p. 7.

[3] Joachim Wach, *Sociology of Religion* (Chicago: University of Chicago Press, 1944), pp. 19-34.

[4] Charles Y. Glock and Rodney Stark, *Religion and Society in Tension* (Chicago: Rand McNally & Co., 1965), pp. 20-38.

[5] We will be concerned with religious behavior rather than beliefs and attitudes, and the typology developed is therefore not intended to be exhaustive. Rather, it serves to organize the ensuing data analysis and discussion. The measures that will be used for each of these dimensions will be discussed when we focus on specific dimensions.

cal commitments. Thirdly, the sociological or organizational dimension of religiosity includes the social relationships and social interaction among Jews and between Jews and non-Jews as reflected, structurally, in sectarian and nonsectarian organizational participation. Organizational affiliation may function to create and sustain Jewish identification when such affiliation implies greater social interaction among Jews. Finally, attention will be focused on the cultural dimension of religiosity, which encompasses the ways in which knowledge about Jewish life is transmitted and the use of an ethnic language.

These four dimensions of religiosity—ideological, ritualistic, organizational, and cultural—are analytically distinguishable, yet there is a dynamic interrelationship which presents, on the societal level, a total panorama of Jewish religiosity. In addition to the similarity between these dimensions of religiosity and those proposed by others, the dimensions also relate to the distinction between Judaism and Jewishness.[6] On the one hand, Judaism refers to the dimensions of religious ideology and culture, while Jewishness refers to the sociological implications of being Jewish and the degree of association and identification with the organized life of the Jewish community. Jewishness thus relates to the sociological or organizational dimension. The ritualistic dimension bridges both Judaism and Jewishness since some rituals, like dietary regulations, are more closely tied to ideological differentiation while other rituals, Chanukah candle lighting, for example, may reflect a social-secular rather than a religious content.

It is important to bear in mind that the manifestations of religiosity will be treated in their broader form rather than considered solely in their doctrinal and ritualistic aspects. Several additional points concerning the dimensions of religiosity should be made. First, the nature of the survey precluded inquiry into attitudes. Moreover, some aspects of religiosity, particularly along the organizational dimension, will be measured only indirectly. Secondly, some of the measures might be appropriate for more than one dimension. For example, synagogue membership will be included within the ideological dimension (Orthodox, Conservative, and Reform synagogue membership) but might have appeared within the organizational dimension (membership versus nonmembership). We have chosen not to fragment the analysis in this way and have categorized synagogue membership in the ideological dimension on empirical grounds, that is, the similarity of findings bearing on synagogue membership and religious identification. In addition, we have

[6] Stuart E. Rosenberg, *The Search for Jewish Identity in America* (Garden City, N.Y.: Doubleday & Company, Inc., 1965), pp. 70-71; Nathan Glazer, *American Judaism* (Chicago: University of Chicago Press, 1957), Chapter VI.

attempted to treat association with the synagogue—membership, affiliation, and attendance—in a more coherent fashion. Finally, although there may not be full agreement on the typology of dimensions presented or on their indicators, the major objective is to provide an organized scheme for handling the variety of ways in which Jews make their commitments as Jews. The particular dimensions and their measures are secondary to this major objective.

The theoretical identification of the several dimensions of Jewish religious commitment leads to another issue which concerns generation changes in religiosity and the relationship between changing patterns of religiosity and the assimilation process. In Chapter 1 of this book we reviewed the "Herbergian paradox" of increasing religiosity and mounting secularism, of the secular penetration of the religious structure.[7] One explanation for this paradox was conceptualized in terms of the several types of assimilation. In the process of acculturation and integration, Jews may have discarded the older traditional forms of religious expression and developed new, peculiarly American forms of religious behavior. Thus, while linguistic assimilation may have occurred through the gradual disappearance of the use of Yiddish, and some rituals may have become less popular, for example, Kashrut (buying Kosher foods and maintaining separate meat and dairy dishes), a strengthening of religious identification may have occurred. This may take the form of Jewish organizational participation, emphasis on family-centered, socially related rituals, and some denominational affiliation even though shifts may have occurred from Orthodox to Conservative and Reform.

As with other demographic and structural aspects of the Jewish community, systematic research on the changing patterns of religiosity among Jews has not been undertaken. Social scientists have speculated about generation changes in religiosity in the United States but there is little agreement. Nevertheless, there appear to be only six possible alternatives: [8] (1) generations show a continual decline in religiosity from the foreign born through the third generation; (2) a gradual increase in religiosity takes place with distance from the immigrant generation; (3) the second generation declines in religiosity, but later generations in-

[7] See pp. 3-6.

[8] Recently Lazerwitz and Rowitz have attempted to organize some of the "theories" of the three-generations hypothesis. They concentrated on only one criterion, attendance at religious services, and thus, on only one dimension of religiosity. However, their discussion puts some order to the many attempts to conceptualize and test empirically generation changes in church attendance. Data were not available on the Jews. See Bernard Lazerwitz and Louis Rowitz, "The Three-Generations Hypothesis," *American Journal of Sociology,* LXIX (March, 1964), 529-38. The discussion that follows relies on their proposed alternatives.

crease; (4) the second generation increases in religiosity, but later generations decrease; (5) there is neither decline nor religious revival but general stability in religiosity over the generations;[9] (6) the absence of "religious revival" may imply neither decline nor stability but the development of different patterns of religiosity with length of stay in the United States. The last alternative evolves out of the need to distinguish on the theoretical level between indicators of religiosity that reflect changes in degree (religious revival or decline) and changes in kind (new or different forms of religious expression and identity).[10]

These alternatives have not been subjected to any systematic empirical testing. Thus, this and the following chapter attempt to discover which of the proposed schemes more accurately portrays the changing patterns of religiosity, in its multidimensional forms, among three generations of Jews. In order to discover which subgroups within each generation have experienced the greatest changes in religiosity the analysis will deal with differential as well as over-all generation changes.

THE IDEOLOGICAL DIMENSION

Identification and membership with one of the three religious divisions within Judaism—Orthodox, Conservative, or Reform—reflect the degree of association with religious doctrine, Orthodox being the most traditional and Reform the least. Historically, Jews settling in the Providence community were originally Orthodox, as were the majority of the Jews who migrated to the United States at the turn of the century. However, early in the community's history a Reform congregation was es-

[9] Alternative 1 has been suggested or implied by a number of social scientists, including Samuel Koenig, "Second and Third Generation Americans," in *One America,* eds. Francis Brown and Joseph Roucek (Englewood Cliffs, N.J.: Prentice-Hall, Inc., 1952), pp. 505-22; Herbert Gans, "The Future of American Jewry. II," *Commentary,* XXI (June, 1956), 555-63; John L. Thomas, "The New Immigration and Cultural Pluralism," *American Catholic Sociological Review,* XV (December, 1954), 310-22; see also Lazerwitz and Rowitz, "The Three-Generations Hypothesis," pp. 530-31. Alternative 2 is Lenski's finding in Detroit (*The Religious Factor,* p. 41) in reference to Catholic and Protestant church attendance; it is also, with qualification, Lazerwitz and Rowitz's finding. Alternative 3 is the Herberg-Hansen "Three-Generations Hypothesis"; see Will Herberg, *Protestant-Catholic-Jew* (Garden City, N.Y.: Doubleday & Company, Inc., 1961); and Marcus Lee Hansen, "The Third Generation in America," *Commentary,* XIV (November, 1952), 492-500; also, Nathan Glazer, *American Judaism,* Chapter VII. Alternative 4 has not, to our knowledge, been suggested in the literature. Alternative 5 is argued by Seymour M. Lipset, "Religion in America: What Religious Revival?" *Columbia University Forum,* II (Winter, 1959), 17-21.

[10] See Glock and Stark, *Religion and Society in Tension,* pp. 69-71; Stephen Steinberg, "The Anatomy of Jewish Identification: A Historical and Theoretical View," *Review of Religious Research,* VII (Fall, 1965), 1-8; J. Milton Yinger, *Sociology Looks at Religion* (New York: The Macmillan Company, 1961), pp. 67-74.

tablished (1877) and, following the national pattern, a Conservative congregation was organized in the early 1920's. The central role of the synagogue in Jewish communal life as a place for prayer, study, and assembly is attested to by the manifold increase in the number of congregations during the late nineteenth and early twentieth centuries. Between 1855 and 1910 no less than 23 separate synagogues were chartered, and probably a number of others existed on a less formal basis. Many of these early congregations have since disappeared as neighborhoods lost their Jewish population, or as ethnic ties which bound their members together weakened; other congregations merged to form larger and stronger organizations; and still others have recently emerged to meet the needs resulting from the shifts of Jewish population to the suburbs as well as changes in religious affiliation. At the time of the survey, there were 18 synagogues and temples in the community: 8 were Orthodox, 8 were Conservative, and 2 were Reform.[11]

Two measures of religiosity will be used as indicators of the ideological dimension. The first is religious self-identification: how do members of the Jewish community define themselves, given the alternatives Orthodox, Conservative, Reform, or Other.[12] Second, synagogue membership data were obtained and the respondents were classified as Orthodox, Conservative, or Reform according to their affiliation with specific congregations. Religious self-identification and congregational affiliation may reveal different patterns and are thus separated. Their interrelationship will be discussed later.

The overwhelming majority of the adult Jewish population, 95 per cent, identify themselves as either Orthodox, Conservative, or Reform (Table 9-1). Within this threefold division, persons identifying with

[11] Sidney Goldstein, "The Providence Jewish Community After 125 Years of Development," *Rhode Island History,* XXV (April, 1966), 51-52; the history of the Jewish community may be found in *Rhode Island Jewish Historical Notes,* Vols. I-III (Providence: Rhode Island Jewish Historical Association, June, 1954–May, 1962). For discussions of the immigrant Orthodox community and the emergence of Conservative Judaism see Moshe Davis, *The Emergence of Conservative Judaism* (Philadelphia: Jewish Publication Society of America, 1964); Marshall Sklare, *Conservative Judaism* (Glencoe, Ill.: The Free Press, 1955); Charles S. Liebman, "Orthodoxy in American Jewish Life," *American Jewish Yearbook* (Philadelphia: Jewish Publication Society of America, 1965), LXVI, 21-92; Charles S. Liebman, "A Sociological Analysis of Contemporary Orthodoxy," *Judaism,* XIII (Summer, 1964), 285-304.

[12] The survey asked the respondent, "What do you consider yourself?"; besides Orthodox, Conservative, and Reform the choices included Yiddishist, Secular, Unitarian, Christian, and Other. The overwhelming majority considered themselves members of one of the three major religious divisions. The small per cent who identified themselves with the remaining categories have all been grouped as "Other" in this analysis of religiosity.

TABLE 9-1

RELIGIOUS IDENTIFICATION, BY GENERATION AND AGE

Generation and Age	Orthodox	Conservative	Reform	Other	Total Per Cent
All Ages					
First Generation	41.1	42.4	11.6	5.0	100.0
Second Generation	14.9	61.0	20.1	4.0	100.0
Mixed Parentage	7.1	56.7	34.0	2.2	100.0
Third Generation	6.3	49.0	35.3	9.4	100.0
TOTAL	19.8	54.1	21.2	4.9	100.0
25-44 Age Group					
First Generation	22.6	50.0	19.0	8.3	100.0
Second Generation	12.5	63.8	20.7	3.0	100.0
Mixed Parentage	7.7	62.4	27.6	2.3	100.0
Third Generation	4.5	51.9	36.7	6.8	100.0
45-64 Age Group					
First Generation	35.1	49.1	11.1	4.7	100.0
Second Generation	16.0	61.3	18.6	4.0	100.0
Mixed Parentage	5.9	42.4	49.4	2.4	100.0
Third Generation	18.4	32.7	28.6	20.4	100.0
65 and Over Age Group					
First Generation	51.8	33.5	10.2	4.5	100.0
Second Generation	17.9	45.5	28.6	8.0	100.0

Conservative Judaism far outnumber the other two segments; more than half of the Jewish population identify as Conservative, 20 per cent as Orthodox, and 21 per cent as Reform. The small percentage of the Jewish population who are not identified with one of the three religious divisions testifies to the very strong tendency toward some denominational affiliation and clear-cut lines of religious categorization.

An examination of the data by generation and age reveals the dramatic shifts that have occurred with respect to religious identification. The proportion identifying as Orthodox has declined sharply from over 40 per cent among the foreign born to 6 per cent among third-generation Jews. Conversely, the proportion who identify with Reform Judaism has almost trebled in three generations—from 12 to 35 per cent. The Conservative group is the largest in any generation but the proportion identifying with Conservative Judaism declined from the second to the third generation after increasing from the first to the second. The shift in identification appears to be from Orthodoxy among the immigrant generation to Conservative among the second generation and some greater shift toward Reform in the third generation. This pattern can most clearly be seen in the differential gains and losses within each generation. In the first generation Orthodox and Conservative identification was equally divided, and it accounted for over 80 per cent of the total. Among second-generation Jews Conservative and Reform gained at the expense of a declining Orthodoxy, with over a 40 per cent difference between Conservative and Reform identification in favor of the former. However, among third-generation Jews the difference between the Conservative and Reform was only 14 per cent, indicating that gains in Reform identification resulted from losses to both Orthodox and Conservative Judaism (Figure 9-1).

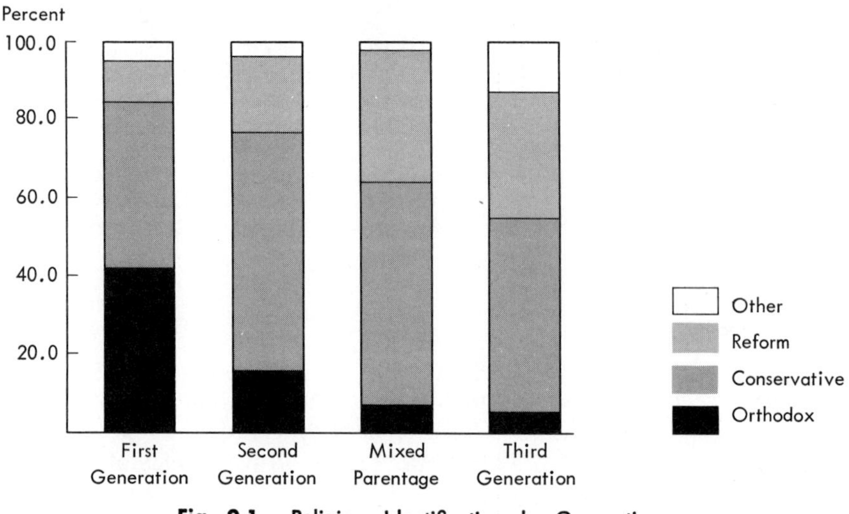

Fig. 9-1. Religious Identification, by Generation

The generational shifts from Orthodox to Conservative to Reform hold when age is controlled, except for some variation in the 45-64 age group. For example, even among the oldest group the proportion identifying as Orthodox declined from over 50 per cent in the first generation to 18 per cent among the second generation, and the decline in Conservative identification and increase in Reform identification between the second and third generation occurred for the youngest age group. These shifts suggest that the greater the distance from foreign-born status, the greater the identification away from Orthodoxy toward Reform. Only minimal gains may be noted for those who do not identify with the three religious divisions and no consistent patterns emerge when age is controlled.

Almost identical patterns appear when synagogue membership is viewed by generation and age (Table 9-2). Over three-fourths of the adult

TABLE 9-2

SYNAGOGUE MEMBERSHIP, BY GENERATION AND AGE

Generation and Age	Orthodox	Conservative	Reform	None	Other and No Information	Total Per Cent
All Ages						
First Generation	29.1	36.8	9.9	21.8	2.4	100.0
Second Generation	12.0	46.8	18.0	21.3	1.9	100.0
Mixed Parentage	4.8	45.2	28.8	20.8	0.3	100.0
Third Generation	6.6	37.5	26.4	25.9	3.6	100.0
TOTAL	15.0	42.7	18.1	22.1	2.2	100.0
25-44 Age Group						
First Generation	21.4	38.1	16.7	22.6	1.2	100.0
Second Generation	10.1	45.1	18.9	24.3	1.6	100.0
Mixed Parentage	5.4	50.7	21.7	21.7	0.5	100.0
Third Generation	6.2	38.3	26.9	26.6	1.9	100.0
45-64 Age Group						
First Generation	26.9	41.2	9.9	19.6	2.3	100.0
Second Generation	13.2	49.8	16.8	18.4	1.8	100.0
Mixed Parentage	3.5	30.6	45.9	20.0	0.0	100.0
Third Generation	10.2	34.7	24.5	20.4	10.2	100.0
65 and Over Age Group						
First Generation	33.2	32.0	8.1	24.0	2.7	100.0
Second Generation	11.6	31.3	23.2	29.5	4.5	100.0

Jewish population are members[13] of at least one congregation, with the largest concentration among Conservative membership (43 per cent) followed by Reform (18 per cent) and Orthodox (15 per cent). Slightly over one-fifth of the Jewish population are not members of any synagogue. Interestingly, nonmembership has been rather stable over the generations with only slight variation among the younger and older age groupings. The former may reflect a temporary phenomenon resulting from delayed synagogue membership until children are old enough to attend religious schools; the latter may reflect economic factors related to synagogue membership costs. The percentage of nonmembers remains generally stable across generations, due possibly to a core of Jews who do not become associated with a synagogue or temple. The high rate of formal synagogue membership may be related to the size of the Jewish com-

[13] Since the respondent determined what constituted actual membership, it is not clear whether all these persons actually paid dues to a particular synagogue or whether they regarded themselves as members because they attended services occasionally. On the question of defining synagogue membership, see Herberg, *Protestant-Catholic-Jew,* p. 49. Although, when compared to synagogue membership in other Jewish communities, our figures seem high, Herberg estimates that about 70 to 75 per cent of the American population regard themselves as church members.

munity. In medium-sized Jewish communities formal affiliation may be necessary to maintain Jewish identification. In large Jewish communities the concentration of Jewish population provides the opportunity for informal ties, thereby obviating the necessity for more formal identification.

The shifts in religious identification observed earlier are clearly confirmed by the synagogue membership data. The proportion of Jews who are members of Orthodox congregations declines sharply with generation status (29 per cent among the first generation to 7 per cent among the third generation), while membership in Reform congregations increases from 10 to 26 per cent. In each generation proportionally more Jews hold membership in Conservative congregations than in either Orthodox or Reform. The increases in Conservative membership between the first and second generation are followed by decreases between the second and third,[14] but even in the third generation, membership in Conservative congregations continues to outnumber other affiliations.

In responding to the question on synagogue membership, 188 households (12 per cent) reported that they belonged to more than one congregation, and of these, 28 reported membership in three congregations. Many of the respondents pointed out that this pattern of multiple memberships resulted from the desire on the part of married children to maintain a membership in the synagogue of their parents while holding membership of their own in a different synagogue. In most cases of multiple membership, the affiliation cut across denominational lines. Almost 80 per cent of the multiple membership involved at least one Orthodox synagogue. As a further indication of the changing patterns of affiliation, 80 per cent of those who had one membership in an Orthodox synagogue had their second membership in either a Conservative or a Reform temple.

In sum, the extent of formal religious identification and religious institutional membership is pervasive and characterizes each of the generations. Although the form has been stable, notable shifts from Orthodox to Conservative and Reform have occurred. These data suggest that generation changes in ideological commitments took place within a Jewish context. If secularization is defined as changes in religious expression rather than the application of nonreligious standards to life situations,[15] then the analysis lends weight to the interpretation that ideological

[14] Patterns by age are uniform except for the native born of mixed parentage. Lazerwitz and Rowitz also point out that this group was an exception to the patterns they found for Protestant and Catholic church attendance. See Lazerwitz and Rowitz, "The Three-Generations Hypothesis," p. 536, footnote 21.

[15] Yinger, *Sociology Looks at Religion.*

secularization has occurred, while a strong attachment to formal Jewish identity has been maintained.

VARIATIONS IN IDENTIFICATION AND MEMBERSHIP

The information on generation changes in institutionalized identification and synagogue membership clearly points to the decline in Orthodoxy and increase in Reform among third-generation Jews. Moreover, Conservative Judaism, although declining slightly, had the largest adherence in every generation. On the whole, these patterns characterize both sexes and apply to religious identification as well as synagogue membership. The only consistent difference between men and women appears in the proportion who are not members of synagogues: males have a slightly higher rate of synagogue membership, perhaps reflecting the more traditional identification of Jewish males with the synagogue. Yet, sex differences have declined with distance from the first generation and in some cases are reversed among the native-born and younger Jews. This change may imply that the traditional association of males with the synagogue is being replaced by the new pattern of family membership.

Almost half of the Jewish population in older urban areas identify with Orthodox Judaism, compared to only 12 per cent in the newer urban and suburban areas. Conversely, less than 10 per cent of those living in the older sections of the city are Reform Jews, compared to one-fourth of the residents in the other areas. These differences reflect primarily the dates of settlement of residential areas and the age composition and socio-economic characteristics of their populations. This pattern of identification applies for each of the generations (Table 9-3) and, with few exceptions, persists with age controls. However, few consistent differences in religious identification appear between those living in the newer urban and suburban areas. Generational declines in Orthodox identification and increases in Reform identification may be observed for all three residential categories. The increases in Reform are most dramatically illustrated in the older urban area and the decreases in Orthodoxy in the newer urban area. In the former, the proportion who identify themselves as Reform Jews increased from less than 4 per cent among the foreign born to one-third of the third generation; in the newer urban area those identified as Orthodox declined from 28 per cent among the first generation to less than 2 per cent among third-generation Jews.

Identical patterns appear when synagogue membership by residence and generation is examined. However, patterns of residential differences in nonmembership are noteworthy. In the older urban and

TABLE 9-3

RELIGIOUS IDENTIFICATION, BY GENERATION AND RESIDENCE

Religious Identification and Residence	First Generation	Second Generation	Mixed Parentage	Third Generation	Total
Older Urban					
Orthodox	64.1	38.0	22.7	37.5	49.0
Conservative	27.2	50.2	47.7	25.0	38.3
Reform	3.8	9.5	29.5	33.3	9.3
Other	4.9	2.3	0.0	4.2	3.4
Total Per Cent	100.0	100.0	100.0	100.0	100.0
Newer Urban					
Orthodox	28.4	8.5	4.9	1.6	11.6
Conservative	51.2	65.9	54.6	54.4	59.9
Reform	16.5	23.0	37.4	34.1	24.4
Other	4.0	2.7	3.1	9.9	4.1
Total Per Cent	100.0	100.0	100.0	100.0	100.0
Suburban					
Orthodox	24.1	12.5	3.8	7.0	12.3
Conservative	52.4	58.4	63.8	46.5	55.9
Reform	15.9	21.4	30.5	36.9	24.4
Other	7.6	7.7	1.9	9.6	7.5
Total Per Cent	100.0	100.0	100.0	100.0	100.0

the suburban areas, one-fourth are nonmembers, compared to less than 20 per cent in the newer urban areas (Table 9-4). This pattern appears to be related to the age composition of the population in these areas; both the young, concentrated in suburban areas, and older persons, concentrated in older urban areas, are less likely to be synagogue members. On the other hand, there are two patterns of nonmembership that are not a function of age differences between residential areas. First, within the older urban area there are generational declines in nonmembership from over one-fourth of the foreign born to one-sixth of the third generation. This decline is not reflected in the two other areas. Secondly, third-generation residents of the older urban areas have the highest rates of synagogue membership and those in the sub-

TABLE 9-4

PROPORTION OF NONMEMBERSHIP IN SYNAGOGUES, BY GENERATION AND RESIDENCE

Generation	Older Urban	Newer Urban	Suburban
First Generation	25.8	18.6	21.4
Second Generation	25.5	18.1	24.7
Mixed Parentage	20.5	22.1	19.0
Third Generation	16.7	19.8	34.4
TOTAL	24.9	19.1	25.2

urbs have the lowest rates. This pattern is not a function of age, for examination of the 25-44 and 45-64 age groups obtained similar results. In addition, suburbanites have the highest proportion of those not identified with any of the three religious divisions. In part, increasing institutional nonmembership and nonaffiliation among suburban residents of the third generation may reflect their increasing assimilation into the majority community.

Consistent with generation changes in general, and residential differentials in particular, is the clear inverse relationship between education and Orthodox identification and membership.[16] The higher the education, the lower the proportion identifying with Orthodox Judaism and the higher the proportion identifying with Reform Judaism (Table 9-5). Among Jews with an elementary school education, 54 per cent identified themselves as Orthodox; this proportion declines

TABLE 9-5

RELIGIOUS IDENTIFICATION, BY GENERATION AND EDUCATION

Religious Identification and Education	First Generation	Second Generation	Mixed Parentage	Third Generation	Total
Elementary					
Orthodox	60.1	37.1	–	–	54.3
Conservative	29.1	46.1	–	–	33.4
Reform	8.0	12.4	–	–	8.8
Other	2.8	4.5	–	–	3.6
Total Per Cent	100.0	100.0	–	–	100.0
High School					
Orthodox	27.8	18.3	14.8	13.2	19.3
Conservative	53.6	61.9	56.5	38.6	57.8
Reform	13.7	16.7	25.0	36.0	18.5
Other	4.8	3.1	3.7	12.3	4.4
Total Per Cent	100.0	100.0	100.0	100.0	100.0
College					
Orthodox	18.6	8.2	2.9	2.5	7.6
Conservative	57.7	66.3	56.4	53.5	60.9
Reform	16.5	21.4	40.0	38.4	27.2
Other	7.2	4.1	0.7	5.7	4.3
Total Per Cent	100.0	100.0	100.0	100.0	100.0
Postcollege					
Orthodox	18.2	6.9	3.3	3.6	6.9
Conservative	50.0	54.5	55.0	57.8	54.5
Reform	25.0	33.2	38.3	31.3	33.0
Other	6.8	5.4	3.3	7.2	5.6
Total Per Cent	100.0	100.0	100.0	100.0	100.0

16 Again, synagogue membership follows similar patterns of religious identification, and the data presented will be limited to religious identification. The analysis, however, applies to both.

to 19 per cent among the high school category, and to 8 and 7 per cent among the college and postcollege educated, respectively. Although this partly reflects generation and age changes, within each generation the relationship holds. Even among the foreign born, 60 per cent of those with an elementary school education defined themselves as Orthodox compared to only 18 per cent of those with at least some college education. The second generation in the 65 and over age category dramatically illustrates this relationship even when age is controlled: one out of three with the least education was Orthodox, compared to one out of six of those with a high school education, one out of twelve with a college education, and none of the postcollege educated. In addition, within each education category, Orthodox identification declines with distance from the first generation, and, except for a slight decrease among the postcollege group, Reform identification consistently increases. Except for the postcollege group, the pattern of second-generation increases and third-generation decreases in Conservative identification is observed.

Given the inverse relationship between education and Orthodoxy and concomitant direct relationship between education and Reform identification, it should follow that the largest proportion of nonmembership in synagogues should be concentrated among the college and postcollege educated populations. However, the direct opposite seems to be true—the higher the educational level, the lower the proportion of nonmembership (Table 9-6). The more educated exaggerate the tendency toward changes in religious identification, i.e., secularization, but within the context of the Jewish community. Perhaps, also, the more educated affiliate with those groupings within the Jewish community that are more congruent with their social status, that is, Reform, but do not exhibit any tendency toward assimilation into the majority. Although we have no direct evidence, out-migration of a disproportional number of higher educated persons who identify more closely with the

TABLE 9-6

PROPORTION OF NONMEMBERSHIP IN SYNAGOGUES, BY GENERATION AND EDUCATION

Generation	Elementary	High School	College	Graduate or Professional
First Generation	19.5	23.8	23.7	20.5
Second Generation	36.0	21.7	19.0	16.3
Mixed Parentage	–	25.9	20.0	15.0
Third Generation	–	30.7	25.2	21.7
TOTAL	23.5	23.5	21.1	17.6

intellectual subsociety than with the Jewish ethnic community may distort somewhat the observed patterns of religious identification.

Although formal and institutionalized religious identification and synagogue membership show almost identical patterns of generation changes and differentials, the distribution of population by religious identification does not perfectly coincide with synagogue membership. Some who profess identification with one religious division belong to a synagogue associated with another religious division. Some may be Conservative or Reform in identification but join an Orthodox synagogue because of the minimal economic expenditures required. Others may be Orthodox in identification but join prestige Conservative or Reform temples for social contacts. Nevertheless, data show that there is a strong relationship between religious identification and synagogue membership (Table 9-7). However, this is less true for the Orthodox than for the other two groups. Whereas, only 57 per cent of those who profess to be Orthodox are members of an Orthodox congregation, 68 per cent of those who identify as Conservative and 74 per cent of those who identify as Reform belong to their respective congregations. Viewing this another way, one-fourth of those who are members of Orthodox congregations do not profess to be Orthodox in their beliefs, while only 13 per cent of those who belong to Conservative and Reform synagogues do not identify with Conservative or Reform Judaism. The greater discrepancy of identification and membership among the Orthodox may reflect the tendency on the part of children to maintain a membership in their parents' synagogue although they may no longer share their parents' religious ideology. It may also indicate some changes in the manifestation of Orthodox Judaism in America. As will be spelled out later, those who identify with Orthodox Judaism have been characterized by declining adherence to ritual practices and are the

TABLE 9-7

RELIGIOUS IDENTIFICATION, BY SYNAGOGUE MEMBERSHIP

Synagogue Membership	Orthodox	Conservative	Reform	Other	Total Per Cent
Orthodox	57.3 (75.7)*	6.1 (22.0)	1.3 (1.8)	1.4 (0.5)	(100.0)
Conservative	19.6 (9.1)	68.4 (86.8)	7.0 (3.5)	6.3 (0.7)	(100.0)
Reform	0.5 (0.6)	4.2 (12.5)	73.9 (86.6)	1.4 (0.4)	(100.0)
Other	1.4 (12.3)	1.5 (36.9)	0.6 (6.2)	20.3 (44.6)	(100.0)
None	21.3 (19.1)	19.8 (48.7)	17.2 (16.5)	70.6 (15.7)	(100.0)
Total Per Cent	100.0	100.0	100.0	100.0	

*Figures in parenthesis are percentages computed horizontally.

least organization-oriented. As a result, the native-born Orthodox Jew is quite different from Orthodox Jews born in Europe.

Those who identify themselves as Orthodox but are not members of Orthodox congregations for the most part either belong to Conservative synagogues or are not synagogue members; those who are Conservative but do not belong to Conservative congregations favor Orthodox over Reform membership but are mainly concentrated in the nonmember category; those who are Reform but do not belong to Reform congregations lean toward Conservative membership. A comparable evaluation of the non-synagogue members shows that a majority report themselves as Conservative, with the remaining number being fairly equally distributed among the Orthodox, Reform, and Other categories. The high proportion of the nonaffiliated who regard themselves as Conservative may reflect the tendency to identify with the middle group to avoid extremes. No pattern of increased or decreased discrepancy appears by generation status.

One final word—it appears that the lines dividing the three institutionalized religious divisions within Judaism are somewhat blurred, at least in the minds and behavior of the majority of Jews. This indistinctiveness may be the consequence of the shifts that have taken place from one religious division to another accompanying social, economic, and residential changes, combined with the increasing similarity of religious services and secular functions of synagogues and temples. It may also reflect the disparity between nominal institutional identification and adherence to religious practices associated with such identification.[17]

ATTENDANCE AT RELIGIOUS SERVICES

In order to evaluate the scope of religious practices among Jews two aspects of the ritualistic dimension will be examined: (1) attendance at religious services and (2) ritual practices in the home. We will first turn to an analysis of the number of times each adult member of the household had attended religious services during the previous year. This section deals with generation changes in regularity of religious service attendance among Jews and non-Jews and then examines in more detail the pattern of synagogue attendance among several groupings within the Jewish community.

It is difficult to find comparable data on generational patterns

[17] See pp. 199-200.

TABLE 9-8

ATTENDANCE AT RELIGIOUS SERVICES FOR WHITE PROTESTANTS,* WHITE CATHOLICS,* AND JEWS, BY GENERATION

Generation and Religion	Attendance at Services (Per Cent)† Regularly	Often	Seldom	Never	Total Per Cent	Number of Cases
Protestants (U.S.)						
First Generation	30	22	39	9	100	87
Second Generation or Mixed Parentage	35	20	39	6	100	321
Third Generation	39	22	31	8	100	2058
Catholics (U.S.)						
First Generation	69	13	13	5	100	131
Second Generation or Mixed Parentage	70	15	11	4	100	321
Third Generation	77	11	9	3	100	359
Jews (Providence)						
First Generation	22	13	52	13	100	756
Second Generation	10	14	63	11	100‡	1450
Mixed Parentage	8	12	71	9	100	311
Third Generation	4	8	73	15	100	356

*Data on Protestants and Catholics adapted from Bernard Lazerwitz and Louis Rowitz, "The Three-Generations Hypothesis," *American Journal of Sociology,* LXIX (March, 1964), Table 1, 532.
†The Classification of attendance at services was adapted from Lazerwitz and Rowitz: "Regularly" was once a week or more; "often," several times a month but less than once a week; "seldom," a few times a year.
‡Owing to rounding and less than one per cent no information, these do not add up to 100 per cent.

of religiosity among non-Jews. One study concentrated on religious service attendance of three generations of Protestants and Catholics. Based on two national surveys conducted in 1957 and 1958, information was obtained from white adults 21 years of age and over.[18] A comparison of these data with our survey information reveals striking differences between Protestant, Catholic, and Jewish attendance at religious services (Table 9-8). Of the three religious groups, Jews are the least regular in their attendance, and, in contrast to Protestants and Catholics, the majority of Jews seldom or never attend. This confirms the findings of other studies showing the over-all low attendance of Jews at synagogue services.[19] Comparing generation changes in synagogue

[18] Lazerwitz and Rowitz, "The Three-Generations Hypothesis." Our data on the Providence Jewish community were analyzed for those 25 years of age and older, although no known systematic difference occurred as a result.

[19] Lenski, *The Religious Factor,* pp. 48-49; Herberg, *Protestant-Catholic-Jew,* p. 49; Judith Kramer and Seymour Leventman, *Children of the Gilded Ghetto* (New Haven: Yale University Press, 1961), pp. 151-57; David Goldberg and Harry Sharp, "Some Characteristics of Detroit Area Jewish and Non-Jewish Adults," in *The Jews,* ed. Marshall Sklare (Glencoe, Ill.: The Free Press, 1958), p. 116.

attendance among Jews to church attendance among Protestants and Catholics, it becomes clear that third-generation Jews are even less frequent in their synagogue attendance than first-generation Jews, while among Protestants and Catholics attendance at religious services increases with distance from the immigrant generation.[20] Thus, if one can speak of a "religious revival" among Protestants and Catholics in regard to church attendance, one must speak of a religious decline among Jews in this regard. However, it is important to point out the differential roles of synagogue and church attendance. Jewish ritual practices are not confined to the synagogue and in some ways are centered more around the home and daily activities. Decreasing synagogue attendance and the low rate of regular synagogue attendance may not imply decreasing Jewish identification but rather a rechanneling of identification through other means. In this sense, religious service attendance of Jews and non-Jews is not strictly comparable.

A more detailed look at generation changes in synagogue attendance reveals several striking points (Table 9-9). First, only a small proportion of the adult Jewish population never attend the synagogue. Although the third generation has the highest proportion of those who never attend, there are no systematic patterns of increase, and the percentage is, for all generation categories, less than 15 per cent.[21] Secondly, there is a regular pattern of decline in synagogue attendance of once a week or more with distance from the immigrant generation. Among the foreign born, 22 per cent attend the synagogue once a week or more but less than 4 per cent among the third generation do so. Thirdly, the modal category of synagogue attendance for each generation is attendance four to eleven times a year rather than the stereotyped image of attendance just at High Holiday services (the Jewish New Year and the Day of Atonement). More than one out of every three Jews apparently attends religious services on the High Holidays as well as on a number of occasions throughout the year: probably a few times on Friday evening, Bar or Bat Mitzvahs, some holidays, or

[20] Although Lazerwitz and Rowitz claim that there were too few Jews for detailed analysis, they state, "The pattern of the Jewish data is one of decline in synagogue attendance from generation to generation" ("The Three-Generations Hypothesis," p. 532, footnote 14). Lenski, whose study reports similar findings (*The Religious Factor*, p. 47), cites unpublished data on the Jews from Lazerwitz's study indicating the decline (*Ibid.*, p. 48, footnote 16).

[21] The lack of change in nonattendance and, if anything, slight increases in nonattendance among both age groups of the third generation are in contrast to a report of a Gallup Public Opinion Poll sponsored by the *Catholic Digest*. The poll revealed that among Catholics and Jews, nonattendance at religious services declined between 1952 and 1966; among Jews the decline was from 56 to 39 per cent. Reported in *The New York Times,* Thursday, July 14, 1966, p. 18.

TABLE 9-9

FREQUENCY OF SYNAGOGUE ATTENDANCE, BY GENERATION AND AGE

	Frequency of Synagogue Attendance								
Generation and Age	Never	1-3 Times a Year	4-11 Times a Year	Once a Month	2-3 Times a Month	Once a Week	Several Times a Week	No Information	Total Per Cent
All Ages									
First Generation	12.7	18.8	32.9	7.9	5.0	13.5	8.5	0.7	100.0
Second Generation	11.3	23.7	39.4	7.4	6.9	7.7	2.5	1.0	100.0
Mixed Parentage	9.3	29.3	41.5	8.0	4.2	5.5	2.3	0.0	100.0
Third Generation	14.6	29.5	43.8	5.1	2.5	2.5	1.1	0.8	100.0
TOTAL	11.8	23.7	38.4	7.4	5.7	8.3	3.8	0.9	100.0
25-44 Age Group									
First Generation	7.2	24.1	48.2	6.0	4.8	4.8	4.8	0.0	100.0
Second Generation	12.3	26.8	42.1	5.6	5.2	5.0	2.6	0.2	100.0
Mixed Parentage	9.1	31.8	39.1	8.2	4.1	5.5	2.3	0.0	100.0
Third Generation	13.8	31.9	42.4	4.9	2.6	3.0	1.0	0.3	100.0
45-64 Age Group									
First Generation	8.5	18.8	37.5	8.5	4.1	16.1	5.9	0.6	100.0
Second Generation	10.3	23.0	37.8	8.6	7.6	9.1	2.6	1.0	100.0
Mixed Parentage	9.4	24.7	45.9	8.2	4.7	4.7	2.4	0.0	100.0
Third Generation	14.9	17.0	53.2	6.4	2.1	0.0	2.1	4.3	100.0
65 and Over Age Group									
First Generation	18.4	17.5	24.4	7.8	6.0	13.0	12.0	0.9	100.0
Second Generation	14.3	15.2	40.2	7.1	8.9	8.9	0.9	4.5	100.0

to recite the memorial prayer on the anniversary of a relative's death or at memorial services on specified holidays (Yiskor). Both the "four to eleven times a year" and the "one to three times a year" models have increased with distance from the first generation at the expense of more frequent attendance. These data on generation changes suggest a continual and striking decline in synagogue attendance but only a small increase in nonattendance. Together with indicators of the ideological dimensions, reduction in the frequency of synagogue attendance has occurred without signs of total nonaffiliation or nonattendance.

In traditional Judaism women are excused from a number of religious commandments in order to do full justice to their family and home responsibilities. Embedded in the Jewish cultural tradition has been the association of men with the synagogue.[22] Moreover, studies have pointed to the importance of analyzing men and women separately when examining generation changes in church attendance among Catholics.[23] Yet, behaviorally, differences between Jewish men and women in synagogue attendance are minimal. Although slightly more women never attend and fewer women attend once a week or more, differences for all other categories are small. In addition, the pattern of decline in synagogue attendance with distance from the first generation characterizes both sexes; differences between the sexes are most pronounced among the foreign born and diminish steadily among the native born. Together with the trend toward family as opposed to male synagogue membership noted earlier, these data suggest a change in the traditional role of women in terms of synagogue attendance.

As discussed earlier, suburban Jewish residents and those who live in the newer sections of the urban area are more likely to identify with Reform Judaism and belong to Reform congregations, while residents of the older urban areas are concentrated among the Orthodox. These patterns are parallel to the relationship between area of residence and frequency of synagogue attendance (Table 9-10). Jews in the older urban areas have higher rates of regular (once a week or more) attendance at religious services than those in the newer urban areas, and suburban residents have the lowest rate of synagogue attendance. Concomitantly, 15 per cent of the suburbanites do not attend a synagogue service even once during the year, compared to less than

22 In describing Eastern European "shtetl" life, Zborowski and Herzog point out: "The man's area is the Shul as House of Study, as House of Prayer and as House of Assembly. . . . The woman's area is the Home . . ."; Mark Zborowski and Elizabeth Herzog, *Life Is With People* (New York: Schocken Books, 1962), p. 124 and pp. 125-41. See also Marshall Sklare, "Aspects of Religious Worship in the Contemporary Conservative Synagogue," in *The Jews,* ed. Marshall Sklare, pp. 358-61.

23 Lazerwitz and Rowitz, "The Three-Generations Hypothesis," pp. 529-38.

TABLE 9-10

SYNAGOGUE ATTENDANCE, BY GENERATION AND RESIDENCE

Synagogue Attendance and Residence	First Generation	Second Generation	Mixed Parentage	Third Generation	Total
Older Urban					
Never	9.8	9.9	9.1	4.2	9.4
1 to 3 Times a Year	19.2	28.2	29.5	33.3	24.2
4 to 11 Times a Year	33.1	41.2	40.9	62.5	38.2
1 to 3 Times a Month	11.1	9.5	6.8	0.0	10.1
Once a Week or More	25.4	10.3	13.6	0.0	17.1
Total Per Cent*	100.0	100.0	100.0	100.0	100.0
Newer Urban					
Never	13.5	9.9	9.3	13.6	11.2
1 to 3 Times a Year	16.3	22.5	28.4	27.8	22.4
4 to 11 Times a Year	32.6	39.0	45.1	48.3	39.4
1 to 3 Times a Month	13.5	17.0	11.7	8.5	14.5
Once a Week or More	23.7	10.4	5.6	1.7	11.6
Total Per Cent*	100.0	100.0	100.0	100.0	100.0
Suburban					
Never	16.7	15.0	9.5	17.3	14.9
1 to 3 Times a Year	23.6	23.2	30.5	30.8	25.7
4 to 11 Times a Year	33.3	39.2	36.2	35.9	36.7
1 to 3 Times a Month	15.3	12.2	15.2	7.7	12.7
Once a Week or More	11.1	9.7	8.6	6.4	9.1
Total Per Cent*	100.0	100.0	100.0	100.0	100.0

***Includes small percentage with no information.**

10 per cent in the older urban areas. For all persons in each residential category, the modal attendance pattern is four to eleven times a year; and slightly more than three out of every five Jews attend religious services between one and eleven times a year. With few exceptions, the over-all pattern of less frequent attendance at synagogue services among suburban residents and more frequent attendance among residents of older urban areas holds for each generation.[24]

A slightly different pattern exists when level of education and frequency of synagogue attendance are correlated (Table 9-11). A larger proportion of Jews with an elementary school education attend synagogue services once a week or more when compared to Jews with more education. The inverse relationship between education and frequency of synagogue attendance has also been noted for the Jewish population in Detroit, and this pattern appears to be a unique feature of the Jewish community. Furthermore, using occupation as an index of social class,

[24] Data not presented indicate the pattern is not a function of differential age concentrations of the generations.

TABLE 9-11

SYNAGOGUE ATTENDANCE, BY GENERATION AND EDUCATION

Synagogue Attendance and Education	First Generation	Second Generation	Mixed Parentage	Third Generation	Total
Elementary					
Never	13.4	18.0	–	–	14.3
1 to 3 Times a Year	16.8	34.8	–	–	21.2
4 to 11 Times a Year	27.7	32.6	–	–	28.6
1 to 3 Times a Month	15.0	7.8	–	–	13.4
Once a Week or More	27.1	5.6	–	–	22.1
Total Per Cent*	100.0	100.0	–	–	100.0
High School					
Never	12.5	10.7	13.1	20.0	12.2
1 to 3 Times a Year	20.2	23.4	32.7	30.0	24.1
4 to 11 Times a Year	39.9	39.9	39.3	39.1	39.8
1 to 3 Times a Month	12.5	15.3	8.4	8.1	13.5
Once a Week or More	14.9	9.8	6.5	2.7	9.7
Total Per Cent*	100.0	100.0	100.0	100.0	100.0
College					
Never	10.4	11.1	9.3	13.9	11.3
1 to 3 Times a Year	21.9	23.9	27.1	29.1	25.1
4 to 11 Times a Year	31.3	40.0	40.7	43.7	39.8
1 to 3 Times a Month	11.5	14.0	12.9	8.3	12.5
Once a Week or More	25.0	11.1	10.0	5.0	11.4
Total Per Cent	100.0	100.0	100.0	100.0	100.0
Postcollege					
Never	7.0	9.9	3.3	8.5	8.2
1 to 3 Times a Year	18.6	20.8	28.3	30.5	23.9
4 to 11 Times a Year	51.2	41.1	46.7	52.4	45.2
1 to 3 Times a Month	9.3	15.3	18.3	6.1	13.4
Once a Week or More	14.0	11.9	3.4	1.2	8.7
Total Per Cent*	100.0	100.0	100.0	100.0	100.0

*Includes small percentage with no information.

the Detroit study clearly indicates a similar pattern. Among white Protestants and Catholics the middle classes attend church services more regularly than the working classes; but among the small sample of Jews, Sabbath synagogue attendance was reported more frequently among the working class than among the middle class.[25]

However, a careful inspection of the data by generation reveals no consistent pattern of difference in the frequency of synagogue attendance by level of education within each generation. Only two general trends emerge: (1) Jews who have the most education (postcollege)

[25] *Cf.* Lenski, *The Religious Factor,* pp. 49-51. The Gallup Poll cited in footnote 21 suggests that for all religious groups church attendance increases with income, occupation, and education.

are less likely to attend synagogue services once a week or more than are Jews with less education; (2) almost without exception, the higher the level of educational attainment, the lower the proportion who never attend a religious service. Thus, although more educated Jews do not attend services on a regular weekly basis, only a small proportion go to the other extreme of never attending the synagogue. The tendency toward a "moderate" level of synagogue attendance among the more educated may be further observed by focusing on the modal category of synagogue attendance. For each of the four educational categories, the greatest concentration is among those reporting attendance at synagogue services four to eleven times a year; this pattern accounts for 45 per cent of the postcollege group, 40 per cent of the high school and college educated, and just under 30 per cent of those with only an elementary school education. Thus, the more educated segment of the Jewish community is characterized by the lowest rates of regular weekly synagogue attendance, the lowest rates of never attending synagogue services, higher rates of synagogue membership (usually in Reform congregations), and identification most often with Reform Judaism. Consequently, this subgroup exemplifies and accentuates the tendency toward changes in religious expression but within a Jewish institutional context.

Within each of the three residential and four educational categories, consistent and sharp declines in regular synagogue attendance have occurred from the first to the third generation.[26] For example, once a week synagogue attendance dropped among older urban residents from one-fourth of the foreign-born population to none of the third generation, and among those with an elementary school education from 27 per cent among the first generation to 6 per cent among the second generation. These patterns with few exceptions persist when age is controlled. In contrast to the consistent declines in regular synagogue attendance, no regular pattern of increase or decrease in nonattendance appears that is not eliminated with age controls.

Given the greater religious prescriptions among the Orthodox, higher rates of regular synagogue attendance should characterize this segment and lower rates should characterize the Reform. At first glance this seems to be true (Table 9-12). One-fifth of those who define themselves as Orthodox attend religious services at least once a week, compared to only 12 per cent of the Conservative and 8 per cent of the Reform. Conversely, Reform Jews have a slightly higher proportion of never attending than Conservative or Orthodox Jews. However, over

26 With one exception: the first generation among the postcollege group.

TABLE 9-12

SYNAGOGUE ATTENDANCE, BY GENERATION AND RELIGIOUS IDENTIFICATION

Synagogue Attendance and Religious Identification	First Generation	Second Generation	Mixed Parentage	Third Generation	Total
Orthodox					
Never	8.3	7.8	13.6	4.3	8.1
1 to 3 Times a Year	19.6	24.9	45.5	34.8	23.2
4 to 11 Times a Year	30.4	46.1	36.4	43.5	37.0
1 to 3 Times a Month	13.1	11.5	4.5	4.3	11.9
Once a Week or More	28.5	9.7	0.0	13.0	19.7
Total Per Cent	100.0	100.0	100.0	100.0	100.0
Conservative					
Never	10.0	8.7	7.9	10.7	9.0
1 to 3 Times a Year	18.1	24.3	27.1	32.6	24.3
4 to 11 Times a Year	35.5	40.5	41.2	45.5	40.1
1 to 3 Times a Month	15.0	14.1	14.7	9.0	14.0
Once a Week or More	20.6	11.5	9.0	2.2	11.9
Total Per Cent*	100.0	100.0	100.0	100.0	100.0
Reform					
Never	13.6	12.0	7.5	9.4	10.8
1 to 3 Times a Year	23.9	21.9	31.1	28.1	25.1
4 to 11 Times a Year	40.9	37.7	43.4	50.0	41.7
1 to 3 Times a Month	9.1	19.9	10.4	7.8	14.2
Once a Week or More	12.5	8.6	7.5	4.7	8.1
Total Per Cent	100.0	100.0	100.0	100.0	100.0

*Includes small percentage with no information.

two-thirds of the Orthodox do not attend religious services even once a month. The majority of persons identifying with each of the three religious divisions attend between one and eleven times a year—60 per cent of the Orthodox, 64 per cent of the Conservatives, and 67 per cent of the Reform. Furthermore, when the three religious divisions are compared by generation, a higher proportion of weekly synagogue attendance characterizes only the foreign-born Orthodox and the Orthodox of the third generation.

As a further indication of the changing patterns of synagogue attendance, declines in frequent synagogue attendance may be noted for members of each of the three religious divisions. Although the pattern is not as smooth among the Orthodox, declines in weekly attendance from 29 per cent among the foreign-born Orthodox to about 10 per cent among native-born Orthodox Jews appear. Sharper declines characterize the Conservative and Reform, and the patterns are consistent in the direction of less regular attendance. Of the small minority of Jews (5 per cent) who do not identify with any of the three institutionalized divisions, 67 per cent never attend synagogue services and very few attend with any regularity.

Judged by these statistics, the high rates of synagogue membership and formal religious identification are not directly transferred to high rates of participation in religious services. Jews may well be following the model set by their non-Jewish neighbors in displaying an increased rate of identification with religious institutions. Nevertheless, the data on generation changes in synagogue attendance suggest that identification and membership do not necessarily involve an intensification of religious behavior as evidenced by synagogue attendance. Rather, they seem to be part of a larger complex wherein the contemporary Jew, secure in Americanism, feels no reluctance about identifying himself with institutionalized Judaism and thereby affirming his Jewishness. In fact, such identification becomes virtually compelling since it is the only way, outside of the intellectual subsociety, in which the American Jew can locate himself in the larger community. To this extent, the data support the conclusion of other studies showing the large proportion of Jews belonging to and identifying with synagogues. The conclusion that increased identification represents increased concern with religious practice as manifested by synagogue attendance is not, however, warranted.

Furthermore, the decline in synagogue attendance characterizes persons in each of the residence, education, and religious identification categories. Consequently, among third-generation Jews there appears to be a greater homogeniety toward less regular synagogue attendance. Not only has Orthodox Judaism declined but synagogue attendance (religious practices) of third-generation Jews who identify as Orthodox has also declined.

OBSERVANCES IN THE HOME

Together with the synagogue, the home has traditionally been a stronghold of Judaism. In fact, many religious practices associated with Judaism are focused on the home and the everyday life of Jews rather than on synagogue worship. In attempting to assess the nature of religiosity and generation changes along the ritualistic dimension, inquiry into Jewish ritual practices in the home is essential. Five religious rituals will be examined: [27] (1) lighting Sabbath candles Friday night; (2) having or attending a Seder on Passover; (3) buying Kosher

[27] In contrast to other measures, the questions regarding home rituals focus on the household unit rather than the individual. The native born of mixed parentage were eliminated because of their small number.

meat; (4) using separate dishes for meat and dairy foods; and (5) lighting Chanukah candles.

Based on whether each of the five rituals was observed always, usually, sometimes, or never, a composite ritual performance index was constructed and each household was classified as being "traditional," "moderate," or "secular." One point was assigned for a response of "always," 2 points for "usually," 3 points for "sometimes," and 4 points for "never." Each question on ritual practices was equally weighted in importance. Thus, the family who always performed all five rituals received a score of 5 points; the family who never performed any of the rituals received a score of 20. Families receiving a score of 5 through 9 points were classified as traditional; at the other extreme, those receiving a score of 16 through 20 points have been classified as secular; the intermediary group, ranging in score from 10 through 15, has been classified as moderate.

According to the classification, slightly less than one-half of the households were moderate in their ritual practices, over a third were traditional, and 15 per cent practiced the rituals so seldom as to be categorized as secular (Table 9-13). As with Orthodox identification and regular synagogue attendance, sharp declines are noted in the proportion of households classified as traditional. Among the foreign

TABLE 9-13

RITUAL PERFORMANCE INDEX, BY GENERATION AND AGE

	Index of Ritual Performance			
Generation and Age	Traditional	Moderate	Secular	Total Per Cent
All Ages				
First Generation	58.2	28.7	13.0	100.0
Second Generation	32.3	52.4	15.3	100.0
Third Generation	19.0	64.1	17.0	100.0
TOTAL*	37.3	47.6	15.1	100.0
25-44 Age Group				
First Generation	38.7	54.8	6.5	100.0
Second Generation	33.7	57.7	8.6	100.0
Third Generation	18.7	65.7	15.7	100.0
45-64 Age Group				
First Generation	59.3	28.6	12.1	100.0
Second Generation	31.3	50.6	18.1	100.0
Third Generation	25.0	56.3	18.8	100.0
65 and Over Age Group				
First Generation	60.3	24.7	14.9	100.0
Second Generation	33.8	45.9	20.3	100.0

***Includes a small number of native born of mixed parentage.**

born[28] 58 per cent were traditional in their ritual practices; among the third generation the proportion declines to less than 20 per cent. However, the major decline in traditional practices has not led to a significant increase in the proportion of households that are secular in ritual practices. Rather the major shift has been toward the center, as were the sharp increases in Conservative membership and identification. Families classified as secular gained slightly in three generations (13 to 17 per cent), while families classified as moderate more than doubled (29 to 64 per cent). Without exception, these patterns persist with age controls. Furthermore, among the first generation the youngest age

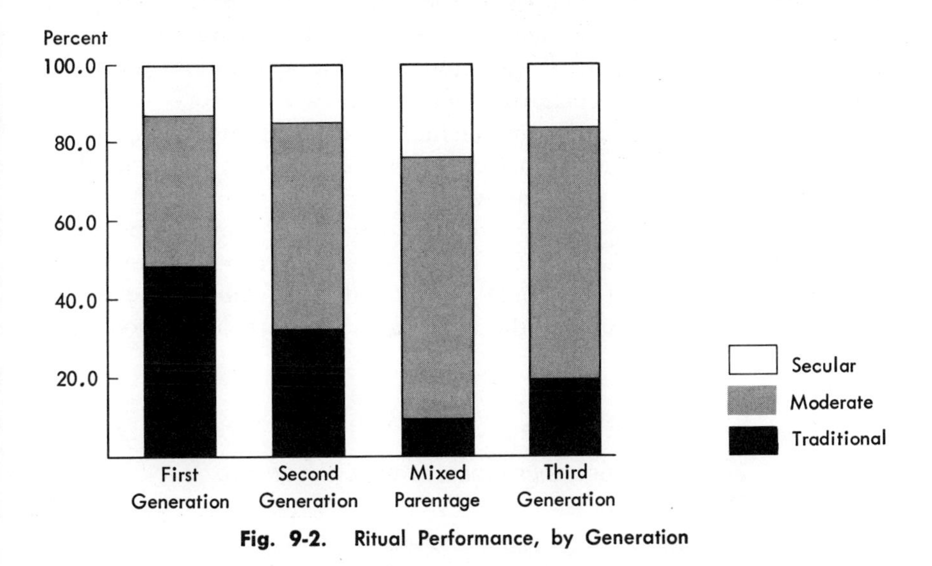

Fig. 9-2. Ritual Performance, by Generation

group differs significantly from the oldest age group in the direction of less traditional ritual practices (60 versus 39 per cent), but within the second and third generation variation by age is minimal. As suggested earlier, among the third generation greater homogenization in terms of religious behavior appears to have taken place[29] (Figure 9-2).

As might be expected from the previous analysis of residence and education differences in religious identification, synagogue membership, and synagogue attendance, suburbanites and those with higher educations are the least traditional in terms of ritual practices, while

[28] Generation status as well as the other characteristics to be discussed are based on the characteristics of the head of the household.

[29] Although the number of female heads of households is small and is concentrated in the first and second generation, similar patterns of decline in traditional ritual practices were observed.

those living in older urban areas and those with little education are the most traditional (Tables 9-14 and 9-15).

Sixty-three per cent of the households in older urban areas were classified as traditional, compared to only 32 per cent of those in newer urban areas and 26 per cent of those in suburban areas. There are no differences in the proportion of secular among newer urban and suburban households, but suburban families are somewhat more concentrated in the moderate category, and families located in the newer sections of the urban area are slightly more traditional. The pattern of more traditional households among the older urban areas characterizes both the first and the second generations. Among third-generation Jews, those in the suburbs have a slightly higher proportion of traditional than those in newer urban areas, but suburban third-generation Jews also have a higher rate of secular ritual practices.

Similar patterns characterize the four educational categories. Among those with an elementary school education 62 per cent were classified as traditional and 12 per cent were secular; but among the college educated just over one-fourth were traditional and about 15 per cent secular. Striking differences in the extent of ritual practices between the educational categories typify only the foreign born. Among the native born, however, differences in the extent of ritual practices among the

TABLE 9-14

RITUAL PERFORMANCE INDEX, BY GENERATION AND RESIDENCE

Ritual Index and Residence	First Generation	Second Generation	Third Generation	Total*
Older Urban				
Traditional	74.0	55.6	–	62.7
Moderate	20.8	32.0	–	26.6
Secular	5.2	12.4	–	10.7
Total Per Cent	100.0	100.0	–	100.0
Newer Urban				
Traditional	48.9	29.8	15.3	32.1
Moderate	35.4	53.5	72.2	51.4
Secular	15.7	16.7	12.5	16.6
Total Per Cent	100.0	100.0	100.0	100.0
Suburban				
Traditional	48.0	21.5	19.4	25.7
Moderate	32.0	63.3	62.5	57.7
Secular	20.0	15.2	18.1	16.6
Total Per Cent	100.0	100.0	100.0	100.0

*Includes a small number of native born of mixed parentage.

TABLE 9-15

RITUAL PERFORMANCE INDEX, BY GENERATION AND EDUCATION

Ritual Index and Education	First Generation	Second Generation	Third Generation	Total*
Elementary				
Traditional	70.5	34.0	–	61.7
Moderate	19.7	49.1	–	26.9
Secular	9.8	17.0	–	11.5
Total Per Cent	100.0	100.0	–	100.0
High School				
Traditional	50.8	34.9	15.4	36.5
Moderate	31.7	48.9	69.2	47.0
Secular	17.5	16.1	15.4	16.4
Total Per Cent	100.0	100.0	100.0	100.0
College				
Traditional	40.0	30.0	19.4	28.3
Moderate	42.0	54.9	61.3	55.3
Secular	18.0	15.2	19.4	16.4
Total Per Cent	100.0	100.0	100.0	100.0
Postcollege				
Traditional	30.3	29.2	20.4	26.3
Moderate	57.6	52.6	65.3	56.4
Secular	12.1	18.2	14.3	14.3
Total Per Cent	100.0	100.0	100.0	100.0

*Includes a small number of native born of mixed parentage.

educational categories are small and are reversed in the third generation: the postcollege are slightly more traditional than those with only a high school education. Among third-generation Jews, irrespective of educational attainment, 60 to 70 per cent are moderate in their practice of religious rituals. Again, these patterns reveal that the greatest change in religiosity occurred between the first and second generation, and the greatest heterogeneity in religious behavior characterizes the foreign born.

Finally, families in each of the residence and education categories are characterized by consistent patterns of decline in traditional religious practices as distance from the first generation increases. This decline has resulted in a pronounced increase of households who have become moderate in their ritual observances, but there has not been a substantial increase in minimum ritual practices categorized as secular.

Both Orthodox and Conservative Judaism call for strict conformity to the five rituals measured here. Reform Judaism does not demand either the use of Kosher meat or the maintenance of separate meat and dairy dishes. For the most part, however, sharp differences in ritual practices characterize the three religious groupings (Table 9-16). Three-fourths of the Orthodox Jewish households were traditional, compared to 35 per cent of the Conservative and only 10 per cent of the Reform. Conversely, one-fourth of the Reform Jewish households were secular, compared to 12 per cent of the Conservatives and 5 per cent of the Orthodox. These patterns are maintained for each of the generations without exception. Investigation of the changes in religious rituals for each religious division indicates several significant points. First, with distance from the immigrant generation, declines in religious ritual adherence occur for each of the three religious divisions. Even among the Orthodox, traditional ritual observance declines from 85 per cent of the first generation to 50 per cent of the third generation. Second, the decline in traditional ritual observance among Conservative and Reform households has not resulted in a concomitant increase in secular households. In fact the proportion who perform religious rituals so rarely as to be classified as secular has declined slightly among Conservative Jews and declined even more among Reform Jews with increased Americanization. Moreover, among the Orthodox the proportion of households that are secular has increased slightly. As before, what emerges is the growth of moderate adherence to ritual practices with the avoidance of both extremes. Fully three-fourths of the third generation who are Reform are classified as moderate in the extent of their ritual practices. As a consequence of generational shifts, there is

TABLE 9-16

RITUAL PERFORMANCE INDEX, BY GENERATION AND RELIGIOUS IDENTIFICATION

Ritual Index and Religious Identification	First Generation	Second Generation	Third Generation	Total*
Orthodox				
Traditional	84.4	64.7	50.0	75.6
Moderate	12.7	26.9	40.0	19.2
Secular	2.9	8.4	10.0	5.2
Total Per Cent	100.0	100.0	100.0	100.0
Conservative				
Traditional	47.9	33.8	23.8	34.8
Moderate	38.5	55.1	65.5	53.7
Secular	13.6	11.1	10.7	11.5
Total Per Cent	100.0	100.0	100.0	100.0
Reform				
Traditional	11.8	11.5	3.8	9.5
Moderate	56.9	66.5	75.5	65.7
Secular	31.4	22.0	20.8	24.8
Total Per Cent	100.0	100.0	100.0	100.0

*Includes a small number of native born of mixed parentage.

TABLE 9-17

FIVE SELECTED RITUALS, BY GENERATION

Selected Rituals	First Generation	Second Generation	Third Generation	Total
Sabbath Candles				
Always	60.6	37.2	25.5	42.4
Usually	5.8	10.1	16.3	9.4
Sometimes	15.3	25.1	24.2	22.1
Never	16.5	25.3	34.0	24.3
Total Per Cent*	100.0	100.0	100.0	100.0
Passover Seder				
Always	82.5	77.6	72.5	78.6
Usually	5.6	5.8	11.1	6.2
Sometimes	6.3	8.1	8.5	7.5
Never	4.1	7.2	7.8	6.6
Total Per Cent*	100.0	100.0	100.0	100.0
Kosher Meat				
Always	62.0	33.8	19.0	39.7
Usually	4.9	6.5	3.9	5.7
Sometimes	17.3	27.6	32.7	25.2
Never	13.6	30.5	43.8	27.7
Total Per Cent*	100.0	100.0	100.0	100.0
Separate Dishes				
Always	53.0	25.2	15.7	31.7
Usually	1.7	0.7	0.0	0.9
Sometimes	2.7	3.4	1.3	2.9
Never	39.7	68.3	81.7	62.1
Total Per Cent*	100.0	100.0	100.0	100.0
Chanukah Candles				
Always	74.5	74.0	76.5	74.1
Usually	2.4	3.3	4.6	3.2
Sometimes	4.4	6.8	3.9	5.8
Never	16.3	13.9	15.0	15.1
Total Per Cent*	100.0	100.0	100.0	100.0

***Percentage may not add up to 100 per cent owing to the small number of cases for whom no information was available.**

greater similiarity in the amount of ritual practices among the religious divisions of the third generation than among either the first or second generation.[30]

In order to provide additional insight into generation changes in ritual practices, each of the five rituals will be examined separately by generation. Two distinct patterns emerge out of the five rituals considered (Table 9-17). On the one hand, always lighting candles Friday evening and adhering to Kashrut (both purchasing Kosher meat and

[30] Because of the small number of persons who identified themselves as Other, a detailed analysis was not possible. The data on Others nevertheless show the decrease in traditional and increase in secular ritual practices. Almost two-thirds of this group were secular, 27 per cent were moderate, and 8 per cent were traditional.

keeping separate dishes) have minimal adherence and their practice has radically declined in three generations. On the other hand, attending a Seder on Passover and lighting Chanukah candles are very popular, with little or no change by generation.

The proportion lighting candles every Friday night declines with generation from 61 per cent to 26 per cent and, conversely, the proportion never lighting Sabbath candles has more than doubled in three generations. Even more radical changes characterize Kashrut adherence. Among first-generation Jews 62 per cent always buy Kosher meat and 53 per cent have separate dishes; among the third generation only 19 per cent always buy Kosher meat and a mere 16 per cent have separate dishes.[31] As a further indication of the striking declines in these ritual practices, the proportion who never buy Kosher meat and do not maintain separate dishes for meat and dairy increases consistently with distance from the first generation; the former increases from 15 to 44 per cent and the latter from 40 to 82 per cent.

Attending a Passover Seder and lighting Chanukah candles differ significantly from this pattern. Although there have been slight decreases in attendance at Seder, almost three-fourths of the third generation always attend and only a small minority of the Jewish population never attend. Always lighting Chanukah candles has slightly increased among the third generation to 77 per cent. The youngest ages within each generation are even more likely to have a Seder and light Chanukah candles in contrast to patterns observed for each of the other rituals.[32]

The increased and sustained popularity of Chanukah and Passover may stem from the emphasis given to these practices in both the Jewish educational system and the community at large. In particular, the treatment of Chanukah along with the Christmas holiday in many public schools, as well as its use by some parents as a substitute for Christmas, accounts for the high proportion of families who adhere to

[31] Of the households who reported buying Kosher meat "usually" or "sometimes," many did so for nonreligious reasons, either because one of the household members liked a particular cut of meat or because the housewife thought that the meat was of a better quality than that available in a non-Kosher store. Some persons who usually bought Kosher meat were tempted to take advantage of a sale of non-Kosher meat in the local supermarket. Reflecting the religious inconsistencies in their practices, several were careful to indicate that they "Koshered" (salted) the meat purchased in supermarkets.

[32] For similar findings regarding the decline in Kashrut, see Albert Gordon, *Jews in Transition* (Minneapolis: University of Minnesota Press, 1949), p. 90; Howard Polsky, "A Study of Orthodoxy in Milwaukee: Social Characteristics, Beliefs and Observances," in *The Jews,* ed. Marshall Sklare, pp. 332-33. On Chanukah practices, see Arthur Hertzberg, "Religion," *American Jewish Yearbook* (1958), LIX, 118-20; Herbert Gans, "The Origins and Growth of a Jewish Community in the Suburbs," in *The Jews,* ed. Marshall Sklare, p. 220.

this ritual. Similarly, sustained popularity of the Passover Seder may be related to the increasing de-emphasis of its religious or historical significance and its use as an occasion for family reunions. At the same time, the much greater publicity given to the Seder in recent years in the mass media, particularly television, and its coincidence with Easter must be considered.

As a final indication of changes in the realm of ritual practices among three generations of Jews, the five religious rituals were correlated with religious identification (Table 9-18). As might be expected, Orthodox households of each generation are more likely always to perform each of the five rituals and Reform households are least likely. Moreover, with minor exceptions, a larger proportion of Reform Jewish households never observe any of the five rituals. Perhaps what

TABLE 9-18

PROPORTION ALWAYS AND NEVER PERFORMING FIVE SELECTED RITUALS, BY GENERATION AND RELIGIOUS IDENTIFICATION

	Orthodox		Conservative		Reform	
Generation and Rituals	Always	Never	Always	Never	Always	Never
Sabbath Candles						
First Generation	84.9	5.8	51.8	19.6	24.0	32.0
Second Generation	62.2	19.3	38.6	21.0	26.5	32.8
Third Generation	60.0	30.0	32.1	28.6	11.3	35.8
TOTAL*	75.2	12.1	40.3	22.3	22.8	34.6
Passover Seder						
First Generation	90.8	1.7	85.1	3.6	64.7	3.9
Second Generation	80.7	7.6	83.5	4.4	74.3	6.8
Third Generation	80.0	10.0	77.3	2.3	71.4	8.2
TOTAL*	86.5	4.2	83.8	3.9	71.4	7.5
Kosher Meat						
First Generation	82.8	10.2	55.1	13.3	20.8	27.1
Second Generation	72.3	10.1	34.4	27.0	14.4	47.9
Third Generation	60.0	20.0	25.0	31.0	3.8	63.5
TOTAL*	77.7	10.7	36.9	25.1	13.3	48.4
Separate Dishes						
First Generation	82.9	13.1	41.2	53.9	6.5	89.1
Second Generation	64.4	33.1	24.8	69.7	7.0	90.4
Third Generation	60.0	30.0	20.2	78.6	2.0	98.0
TOTAL*	74.7	21.4	27.4	67.9	5.6	92.1
Chanukah Candles						
First Generation	88.3	7.0	72.3	21.1	56.0	26.0
Second Generation	81.4	14.4	79.8	9.3	68.9	17.9
Third Generation	100.0	0.0	84.5	9.5	66.0	18.9
TOTAL*	86.2	9.5	78.6	12.1	65.5	20.1

***Includes a small number of native born of mixed parentage.**

is most significant is the much smaller differentiation between the three religious categories in Chanukah and Passover observances and the rather strong differentiation in the performance of the other three rituals. The exceptions to the pattern of a direct relationship between performance of rituals and Orthodoxy occur in Seder and Chanukah practices.

Equally important is the consistent decline among all religious divisions in adherence to Kashrut and Sabbath candle lighting, although the reduction is much more pronounced among Conservative and Reform Jews. As for the total Jewish population, the overwhelming majority of households classified as Orthodox, Conservative, or Reform always have a Seder and light Chanukah candles. Moreover, attending a Passover Seder has slightly increased among third-generation Reform Jews; and third-generation Jews, whether Orthodox, Conservative, or Reform, are more likely than the first generation always to light Chanukah candles. On the other hand, never lighting Chanukah candles has significantly declined among third-generation Conservative and Reform Jews.

The data on specific ritual practices suggest that religious rituals are increasingly adhered to by the third generation in those instances where children are involved, where the ritual is family oriented, and where pressures for conformity are exerted by both the Jewish and non-Jewish community. However, adherence continues to decline in day-to-day rituals (Kashrut) or weekly activities (Sabbath candles and synagogue attendance) that are somewhat demanding and on which no strong emphasis for conformity is placed either in the religious school or in the public image of what constitutes being a Jew.

Analysis of specific ritual practices also helps to explain the decrease in the proportion of family units in the traditional category of ritual practice and the sharp increases of the third generation in the moderate group. The change noted stems from the net effects of a decline in adherence to such practices as Sabbath candle lighting and Kashrut and an increase and stability in Chanukah and Seder observance. Again, these data on the changing components of ritual practices and the changing nature of religious identification within the context of Judaism suggest that the identification of Jews with the Jewish community is not so much the result of increased religiosity; rather, the changes appear to have resulted in a new form of religious expression among third-generation American Jews which reflects the acceptance of external symbols that identify the Jew as Jew in conformity with the patterns of religious identification stressed by the larger American community.

Finally, along with these changes, convergence in religiosity on both the ideological and ritualistic dimension among third-generation Jews may be observed. There is less significant differentiation by residence, religious identification, and education among the third generation than among the foreign born. This convergence in religiosity (and, as noted earlier, for demographic characteristics) may be the result of many factors, including the lack of cultural conflict between the third and second generation, the greater social-class homogeneity among third-generation Jews, and their greater similiarity in religious training and experience.

CHAPTER TEN

Religiosity: Organizational and Cultural Dimensions

From its early history, the American Jewish community has been characterized by a multiplicity of organizations dedicated to meeting the social, charitable, benevolent, educational, and religious needs of its population. Membership in Jewish organizations provides an important mechanism by which individuals identify themselves with the Jewish community and interact with other Jews. Conversely, affiliation with non-Jewish organizations may be considered an indicator of structural assimilation, since it may reflect the increasing interaction of Jews with non-Jews. Organizational participation may involve or lead to primary group interaction.[1] In the absence of information on primary group interaction between Jews and non-Jews, membership in organizations may serve indirectly to indicate structural assimilation.

STRUCTURAL ASSIMILATION

To ascertain the extent to which participation in the organized life of the Jewish and non-Jewish community has changed in three generations, information on organizational affiliation will be analyzed. However, it was not possible to ascertain the intensity of involvement in particular organizations nor to distinguish between those persons who only pay dues to an organization and those who are leaders or very active members. Similarly, it is difficult to estimate the amount of non-Jewish interaction taking place in nonsectarian organizations, particularly when some are largely constituted of Jews.[2] On the whole, the survey revealed that the adult Jewish population is strongly affiliated with the Jewish organizational structure over and above synagogue membership, but is largely unaffiliated with the nonsectarian organizations of the community. Over three-fourths of the adult Jewish community belong to at least one Jewish organization, fully 17 per cent belong to four or more, and less than one-fourth are nonaffiliated (Table 10-1). In con-

[1] Milton Gordon, *Assimilation in American Life* (New York: Oxford University Press, Inc., 1964), p. 178. See also his review of studies dealing with the participation of Jews in Jewish and non-Jewish organizations, pp. 177-79. However, he indicates that it is difficult to determine what these patterns are since "the data are few and fragmentary" (p. 177).

[2] *Ibid.*, p. 178.

TABLE 10-1

NUMBER OF MEMBERSHIPS IN JEWISH ORGANIZATIONS, BY GENERATION, AGE, AND SEX*

Generation and Age	Males					Females					Total				
	None	One	Two	Three	Four or More	None	One	Two	Three	Four or More	None	One	Two	Three	Four or More
All Ages															
First Generation	20.9	31.9	18.6	14.1	14.1	19.0	25.4	21.7	12.8	20.2	19.9	28.4	20.3	13.4	17.4
Second Generation	22.6	29.0	24.1	11.6	11.6	29.8	29.9	18.9	14.1	24.5	21.7	25.0	21.6	12.8	18.1
Mixed Parentage	27.0	29.5	23.0	9.0	11.5	21.6	29.5	14.7	8.9	25.3	23.7	29.5	17.9	9.0	19.8
Third Generation	34.9	33.6	18.1	7.4	4.7	29.9	22.9	15.4	13.6	17.3	32.0	27.3	16.5	11.0	12.1
TOTAL	24.1	30.6	21.7	11.4	11.4	21.7	23.4	18.6	13.0	22.3	22.8	26.8	20.1	12.3	17.2
25-44 Age Group															
First Generation	17.6	44.1	14.7	11.8	11.8	24.0	34.0	20.0	8.0	14.0	21.4	38.1	17.9	9.5	13.2
Second Generation	25.9	31.2	21.9	13.0	6.9	23.2	20.4	24.0	13.2	19.2	24.5	25.8	22.9	13.1	13.0
Mixed Parentage	30.6	31.8	23.5	5.9	8.3	20.6	30.9	14.0	10.3	24.2	24.4	31.2	17.6	8.6	18.1
Third Generation	35.3	33.1	18.8	7.5	3.8	27.4	24.6	16.0	13.7	18.3	30.8	28.2	17.2	11.0	12.0
45-64 Age Group															
First Generation	21.1	30.4	21.1	11.8	13.9	15.5	24.3	24.9	12.2	22.1	18.1	27.2	23.1	12.0	18.7
Second Generation	21.1	28.2	24.8	11.0	14.1	20.4	20.9	16.5	13.8	27.9	20.8	24.7	20.8	12.3	20.8
Mixed Parentage	20.6	26.5	23.5	11.8	17.6	25.5	27.5	17.6	5.9	23.5	23.5	27.1	20.0	8.2	21.2
Third Generation	26.7	40.0	13.3	6.7	13.4	38.2	17.6	14.7	11.8	11.8	34.7	24.5	14.3	10.2	12.2
65 and Over Age Group															
First Generation	21.4	30.8	17.0	17.0	13.8	21.1	24.0	18.9	14.9	19.9	21.3	27.2	18.0	15.9	17.1
Second Generation	19.6	25.5	29.4	9.8	13.8	13.1	23.0	14.8	19.7	23.0	16.1	24.1	21.4	15.2	18.8

*Percentages computed horizontally may not add up to 100 per cent because of a small proportion No Information.

trast, almost two-thirds of the Jewish population are not members of any non-Jewish organization, and of those that join, the overwhelming majority are members of only one non-Jewish organization (Table 10-2).

From these data, it appears that the organizational structure of the Jewish community provides a sufficient variety of organizations to satisfy the needs of the community. Jews may find affiliation with Jewish organizations a means of sustaining their Jewish identification and perhaps, in some cases, their sole Jewish identification. However, the extent to which this changes in the Americanization process is an important indicator of the consequences of assimilation. The data by generation clearly indicate that with distance from the foreign-born generation there is a consistent increase in nonaffiliation with Jewish organizations and some increase in affiliation with non-Jewish organizations. The increase in membership in non-Jewish organizations occurs between the foreign-born and later generations, with no consistent differences between the categories of the native born when age is controlled. Moreover, a larger proportion of the younger foreign born are affiliated with nonsectarian organizations when compared to the older foreign born. The third generation tends to have a more equal membership in both nonsectarian and Jewish organizations.

In general, women have a higher affiliation with Jewish organizations than men and a consistently lower affiliation with non-Jewish organizations; this pattern is true of all generations and age groups. These statistics reflect, on the one hand, the business and fraternal character of nonsectarian organizations and, on the other hand, the relatively slower assimilation of Jewish women. For both men and women there is a reduction in affiliation with Jewish organizations and an increase in affiliation with non-Jewish organizations among the native born.

Not unexpectedly, suburbanites tend to have the lowest affiliation with Jewish organizations and the highest affiliation with non-Jewish organizations. However, those in the newer urban areas are the biggest joiners of Jewish organizations, with one-fourth holding four or more memberships. Both the newer urban residents and residents of the suburbs stand in contrast to those living in the older area of settlement by virtue of having higher affiliation with non-Jewish organizations. Residential differences in organization affiliation partly may reflect the greater integration of suburban and newer urban residents and their increasing interaction with the total community. The patterns by generation and age are not clear-cut and exceptions are noted. Increases by generation within residential categories in the proportion not affiliated with Jewish organizations are again not striking or con-

TABLE 10-2

NUMBER OF MEMBERSHIPS IN NON-JEWISH ORGANIZATIONS, BY GENERATION, AGE, AND SEX*

	Males				Females				Total			
Generation and Age	None	One	Two	Three or More	None	One	Two	Three or More	None	One	Two	Three or More
All Ages												
First Generation	64.7	23.7	7.1	4.2	87.4	10.1	0.9	0.2	76.8	16.4	3.8	2.1
Second Generation	43.2	23.8	14.7	7.2	72.3	18.7	4.7	2.9	57.6	26.4	9.8	5.1
Mixed Parentage	35.2	38.5	13.9	16.3	66.8	22.6	6.3	3.7	54.5	28.8	9.3	7.0
Third Generation	49.0	28.9	18.1	3.4	65.0	25.2	4.2	4.7	58.4	26.7	9.9	4.2
TOTAL	48.8	31.2	12.9	6.4	74.4	17.8	3.9	2.5	62.3	24.2	8.1	4.4
25-44 Age Group												
First Generation	50.0	32.4	8.8	8.8	80.0	12.0	6.0	2.0	67.9	20.2	7.1	4.8
Second Generation	41.3	34.4	13.0	9.7	66.4	22.8	7.2	3.2	53.9	28.6	10.1	6.4
Mixed Parentage	34.1	38.8	17.6	9.4	70.6	21.3	5.1	2.9	56.6	28.1	10.0	5.4
Third Generation	50.4	26.3	18.8	3.8	62.9	27.4	4.6	5.1	57.5	26.9	10.7	4.5
45-64 Age Group												
First Generation	59.0	27.3	6.8	6.3	82.3	14.9	0.6	0.0	71.3	20.8	3.5	3.0
Second Generation	43.3	34.2	15.8	6.1	76.9	16.7	3.2	2.7	59.5	25.7	9.7	4.4
Mixed Parentage	41.2	41.2	5.9	11.8	56.9	27.5	9.8	4.0	50.6	32.9	8.2	7.1
Third Generation	33.3	53.3	13.3	0.0	73.5	17.6	2.9	0.0	61.2	28.6	6.1	0.0
65 and Over Age Group												
First Generation	73.6	18.2	6.9	1.2	94.9	4.6	0.0	0.0	84.7	11.1	3.3	0.6
Second Generation	51.0	27.5	13.7	4.0	65.6	16.4	4.9	3.2	58.9	21.4	8.9	3.6

*Percentages computed horizontally may not add up to 100 per cent because of a small proportion No Information.

sistent; only the newer urban residents clearly increase in nonaffiliation with distance from the foreign-born generation. Concomitantly, the change toward greater affiliation with nonsectarian organizations characterizes only the newer urban and suburban segments and takes place between the foreign-born and later generations.

There does not appear to be any differential affiliation in Jewish organizations by education, which suggests that the Jewish community seems to offer something for all educational levels. On the other hand, participation in non-Jewish organizations varies directly with education. The postcollege group has the highest rate of affiliation (58 per cent), but only 17 per cent of those with an elementary school education are affiliated with non-Jewish organizations. This is true of each generation, with some variation when age is controlled.

The distinction in patterns of organizational affiliation among the three religious divisions within Judaism seems to be between the Orthodox and non-Orthodox, with no substantial differences between Conservative and Reform Jews. For each generation, and with only minor exceptions by age, Orthodox Jews are the least affiliated with any type of organization, Jewish or nonsectarian. This seems to be a function of (1) the relatively lesser emphasis on secular activities in many Orthodox congregations; (2) the possibility that the Orthodox channel their identification through greater synagogue attendance and membership rather than through other types of memberships; (3) greater assimilation of Conservative and Reform Jews and consequently their higher rate of participation in nonsectarian organizations; and (4) the concentration of Orthodox Jews in the lower social classes, while participation is a means of status striving and maintenance and typifies the middle and upper classes. Significantly, too, a large number of Jewish organizations were founded and are administered by Conservative and Reform Jews. Among the third generation who are Orthodox there is an increase in affiliation with non-Jewish organizations and a decrease in Jewish organizational participation. In this sense, structural assimilation in a limited way has had its impact even among those groups that have tried to be the most insulated.

The analysis of membership in Jewish and non-Jewish organizations shows that on the whole a considerably larger number of persons belong to Jewish groups than to non-Jewish groups. At the same time, among the second and third generations there is a tendency toward greater disassociation with Jewish organizations and greater association with the formal organizational life of the larger community. This conforms with the expected pattern as the Jewish population becomes increasingly integrated into the larger community. It is relevant, however, to ask whether persons who do not affiliate with Jewish groups affiliate with non-Jewish groups, or, conversely, whether those who are joiners of Jewish organizations do not join non-Jewish organizations. Some indication of the answer to this question may be obtained through examining the relationship of Jewish and non-Jewish affiliation.

On the whole, there is no pattern of segregated membership. Rather, those who are not affiliated with Jewish groups also do not generally affiliate with non-Jewish groups, and the "joiners" belong to sectarian as well as nonsectarian organizations. For example, 80 per cent of those who are not affiliated with Jewish organizations also do not affiliate with non-Jewish organizations. The percentage of those who are not affiliated with a non-Jewish group declines consistently as the number of affiliations with Jewish groups increases. Among those who are members of four or more Jewish organizations, only half are not affiliated with non-Jewish organizations.

TRANSMITTING THE HERITAGE

In order for a minority group to survive, cultural and religious traditions which bind the members into a cohesive community must somehow be transmitted from generation to generation. The child must be socialized in the ways of minority group identification, in the associated rituals, and in the sources of religious and cultural traditions. Certainly, for the Jewish group there are many agents of socialization, including the family, synagogue, and Jewish organizations of the community. To some extent these have been evaluated in previous sections. Of equal and perhaps increasing significance in the socialization process are the amount and kind of Jewish education and training received.

Jewish tradition holds that an "uneducated person cannot be pious." In recent years formal Jewish education has taken over some of the traditional educational functions of the family and the natural socialization process which occurred in the environment of the segregated ghetto. Thus, in an integrated American society Jewish education has taken on additional importance. Not only does it contribute to more meaningful participation in religious services and to greater familiarization with religious rituals, but it has taken on the significant task of creating a sense of identification with Jewish culture, history, and tradition. In this sense, the examination of the extent and kind of Jewish education received by three generations of Jews is crucial to the evaluation of the spectrum of religiosity and Jewish identity in America.

Yet, despite the concern of the Jewish community about the education of its youth and the very high value placed on education, as late as World War II Jewish education in the United States continued in its traditional pattern of a multiplicity of small, independent schools, most of them poorly housed, with inadequate financing, poor staffing, and archaic curricula. Only since the postwar decades have attempts been made to bring Jewish education to the level of efficiency of the other major institutions in the country and to bring it more closely within the general context of American life.[3] The change from communal Jewish schools to synagogue-related religious schools may well account for an additional phenomenon, the growing number of Jewish schools and increasing enrollment.[4]

Although the evidence points to a larger number of children enrolled in religious schools in the 1960's than there were 30 or 40 years earlier, we do not know precisely what proportion of Jewish children in the United States of school age are enrolled. Such information requires statistics not only of enrollment but of the total number of eligible children. Moreover, statistics on enrollment do not give a complete picture since they fail to take into account the Jewish education of those no longer in school.

In an attempt to gain as complete a picture of Jewish education as possible, information is needed on past, present, and future education. All persons in the households surveyed were asked questions concerning the amount and kind of Jewish education received. Information was also obtained on those who were currently in school. For those under age 15 who had not had any Jewish education and were not currently enrolled, a question was asked concerning plans to provide a Jewish education and what kind. Together these data provide information on the amount and kind of Jewish education completed by three generations of Jews and the current enrollment of and plans for the religious education of the next generation.

Testifying to the high value placed on Jewish education is the fact that about five out of every six Jews have had some Jewish education. This proportion puts the Jewish community under study at the upper level of an estimate by Jewish educators that between 70 and 85 per cent of the Jewish community have received or will receive some

[3] Uriah Z. Engelman, "Educating the Jewish Child," in *Jews in the Modern World,* ed. Jacob Fried (New York: Twayne Publishers, Inc., 1962), II, 436.

[4] For the change from communal to synagogue-related schools, see Uriah Z. Engelman, "Jewish Education," in *American Jewish Yearbook* (Philadelphia: Jewish Publication Society of America, 1960), LXI, 127-49; Stuart E. Rosenberg, *The Search for Jewish Identity in America* (Garden City, N.Y.: Doubleday & Company, Inc., Anchor Books, 1965), pp. 226-77; Nathan Glazer, *American Judaism* (Chicago: University of Chicago Press, 1957), pp. 71-73, 85-87, 109-13.

TABLE 10-3

PROPORTION WITH NO JEWISH EDUCATION, BY GENERATION, AGE, AND SEX

Generation and Age	Male	Female	Total
All Ages			
First Generation	3.5	19.0	11.8
Second Generation	6.0	27.3	16.5
Mixed Parentage	8.3	25.3	18.6
Third Generation	4.7	32.9	21.3
TOTAL	5.6	25.7	16.1
25-44 Age Group			
First Generation	3.0	24.0	15.7
Second Generation	4.9	24.9	15.0
Mixed Parentage	4.8	23.5	16.4
Third Generation	1.5	30.9	18.2
45-64 Age Group			
First Generation	4.4	15.7	10.4
Second Generation	6.7	27.6	16.7
Mixed Parentage	17.6	31.4	25.9
Third Generation	26.7	41.2	36.7
65 and Over Age Group			
First Generation	2.6	21.1	12.3
Second Generation	6.3	35.0	22.2

Jewish education [5] (Table 10-3). The proportion without some Jewish education has increased from 12 per cent among the first generation to 21 per cent among the third generation. Within the three native-born generation categories, there is a great deal of fluctuation by age, with the youngest age group (25-44) always having a smaller proportion with no Jewish education and the oldest a higher proportion. For example, among the third generation 37 per cent of the 45-64 age group had no Jewish education, compared to only 18 per cent of the 25-44 age group. Thus, although the over-all generation patterns point to a decrease in the proportion of Jews with some religious education, younger Jews seem to have a smaller concentration among those with no Jewish education.

The Rabbis of the Talmud pointed out that women were not required to study the intricacies of religious law, and this tradition often resulted in the failure of parents to provide formal Jewish education for their daughters. In America this was expressed in the greater emphasis on Jewish education for Bar Mitzvah. This development, coupled with the Rabbinic tradition, has led to consistent differences in Jewish education between the sexes. For the total adult population,

[5] Engelman, "Educating the Jewish Child," p. 439.

TABLE 10-4

PROPORTION WITH NO JEWISH EDUCATION, BY AGE AND SEX

Age	Male	Female	Total
15-24	5.0	12.8	8.8
25-44	4.3	26.3	16.3
45-64	7.1	25.3	16.3
65 and Over	3.9	25.2	15.3

one-fourth of the women never received any Jewish education, compared to less than 6 per cent of the men. This sex differential holds for each generation and age group. The increase in the proportion with no Jewish education characterizes females, while among males patterns of increase are not as clear, especially among the youngest age group. Significant age variation within generations of both sexes may be observed; and the youngest age group of both sexes has the lowest proportion of those not receiving some Jewish education in all generations but the first.

The divergent findings of increases in the proportion with no Jewish education with distance from the foreign-born generation but decreases among the younger ages may reflect the changing availability of Jewish educational facilities. The development of concern with Jewish education and, concomitantly, an attempt to improve facilities and curricula seem to have occurred in the late 1930's and early 1940's. Thus the development of appropriate, and particularly synagogue-related, educational facilities in conjunction with the greater concern for religious education among all segments of the Jewish community affected the younger persons of each generation, who were exposed to the newly developed Jewish education system.

Some of the impact of the newer emphasis on Jewish education can be seen from data by age (Table 10-4). These data indicate that a significant reduction in the proportion of those with no Jewish education has occurred for the 15-24 age group, the overwhelming majority of whom have completed their Jewish education.[6] The reduction for this age group appears to be the result of the dramatic increase in the proportion of girls receiving some Jewish education and the rather

[6] By age 15 almost 90 per cent of the males had completed their Jewish education, and by age 17 fully 97 per cent were no longer enrolled in any Jewish education program. Similar data on females indicate the same pattern as for males but with slightly more girls being enrolled at later ages; by age 17 only 16 per cent of the girls were enrolled in Jewish education programs.

stable but high proportion (95 per cent) of boys being exposed to religious education. Thus, a larger percentage of younger Jews are being educated in religious schools than ever before (over 90 per cent), and the traditional differential Jewish education given to boys and girls is diminishing. In addition to providing girls with a Jewish education, the Bat Mitzvah and confirmation have been further catalysts in the observed convergences in religious education for boys and girls. (Bat Mitzvah is the ceremony for girls, paralleling the Bar Mitzvah for boys, which marks the acquisition of religious obligation. Confirmation occurs generally two years later, for both boys and girls.) Considering that over 90 per cent of the population aged 15 to 24 are at least third generation,[7] the data clearly indicate the important increase in Jewish education among the coming generation of Jews.

SCOPE OF RELIGIOUS EDUCATION

It is clear that among Jews aged 15 to 24 and among the younger ages of the second and third generation a significant percentage are receiving some Jewish education. But what kind of Jewish education are younger third-generation Jews receiving and for how many years do they attend? Some insight into these questions can be gained by examining generation changes in the kind and amount of Jewish education.

In order to evaluate the various types of religious education, it is important to bear in mind the frequency of weekly class meetings and the nature of the school structure. "Sunday School only" is perhaps the least extensive, with a short period of time allocated once a week for religious studies; it is most characteristic of Reform Judaism. Conservative and Orthodox congregations generally have a combined or integrated program of afternoon Hebrew School, usually twice a week, plus Sunday School. The two- or three-day program is also being offered with increasing frequency by Reform temples. "Hebrew School only" is difficult to evaluate since it often, for older persons particularly, refers to a community-operated "Talmud Torah" or afternoon religious school. More recently, "Hebrew School only" refers to the synagogue-related afternoon religious school. The most extensive training, in terms

[7] Ninety-one per cent of the males 15 to 24, and 93 per cent of the females 15 to 24, were born in the United States of native or mixed parentage. Over three-fourths were of native-born parents. Within this age group the proportion with no Jewish education is lower for those of native-born parents (8 per cent) than those of mixed parentage (12 per cent).

of hours per week, characterizes the Day School. For older, foreign-born persons, full-time religion-sponsored education probably meant a traditional Yeshivah. On the contemporary American scene, the Day School —the modern prototype of the Yeshivah—provides such training; its curriculum includes both secular and intensive religious education every day of the week. Providence has one Day School. For purposes of this analysis, both Yeshivah and Day School education have been subsumed in the "Day School" category. Private tutors, Yiddish Schools, and "Bar Mitzvah only" training were usually not synagogue related and are difficult to evaluate.

Some caution should be used in interpreting information on type of religious education. In answering the question on kind of Jewish education, some respondents had difficulty identifying the exact type. This difficulty reflects the confusing and varied terminology used by the schools themselves and the fact that a number of older persons received religious training in Europe or in the community "Talmud Torah."

The data on generation changes in type of Jewish education received reveal a striking increase in Sunday School and in the integrated Hebrew and Sunday School education (Table 10-5). Among the foreign born, these synagogue-related schools account for less than 8 per cent but among the third generation they account for almost 60 per cent of the education received. As the popularity of these two types of Jewish education increases with distance from the immigrant generation, declines are observed in the Hebrew School only category (40 to 14 per cent). Although not shown in Table 10-5, there is also sharp reduction in private instruction (23 to 4 per cent), and almost total disappearance of Yiddish School training (7 to 0.3 per cent). But, again, within each generation significant variation by age appears. For example, education in the integrated Sunday and Hebrew School among the foreign born varies by age from one to 17 per cent, and among the third generation from 8 to 33 per cent. For each generation, those who are in the youngest age category (25-44) accentuate the tendency toward the Sunday School or integrated school pattern.

The same general patterns characterize both sexes, although generation changes among males are greater in the direction of the integrated Hebrew and Sunday School (7 to 41 per cent) and among females to the Sunday School only (3 to 39 per cent). Sex differences in type of Jewish education somewhat decline with generation, but even among the third generation, females are more concentrated in the Sunday School only and males in the integrated Sunday and Hebrew School. Here again, data on generation changes must take age into account. Among the third generation less than 9 per cent of the women 45 to 64 years of

TABLE 10-5

SELECTED TYPES OF JEWISH EDUCATION, BY GENERATION, AGE, AND SEX

	Kind of Jewish Education*											
	Total				Male				Female			
Generation and Age	Sunday	Hebrew	Sunday and Hebrew	Day	Sunday	Hebrew	Sunday and Hebrew	Day	Sunday	Hebrew	Sunday and Hebrew	Day
All Ages												
First Generation	1.9	40.0	5.8	4.0	0.6	49.0	6.7	5.8	3.0	32.2	5.1	2.3
Second Generation	13.5	34.5	14.8	0.7	4.5	46.9	16.7	0.5	22.6	21.9	12.8	0.8
Mixed Parentage	29.9	21.2	22.5	1.3	16.5	37.2	22.3	2.5	38.4	11.1	22.6	0.0
Third Generation	28.3	14.4	29.1	0.3	12.8	30.4	41.2	0.7	39.0	3.3	20.7	0.0
TOTAL	14.1	32.0	15.1	1.5	5.5	44.5	17.3	2.1	21.7	20.6	13.1	1.0
25-44 Age Group												
First Generation	2.4	38.6	16.9	8.4	0.0	39.4	21.2	12.1	4.0	38.0	14.0	6.0
Second Generation	17.2	31.4	22.1	0.6	4.9	43.3	26.1	0.4	29.3	19.7	18.1	0.8
Mixed Parentage	31.4	18.6	25.9	0.9	19.0	32.1	27.4	2.4	39.0	10.3	25.0	0.0
Third Generation	28.3	14.7	32.9	0.3	12.9	30.3	45.5	0.8	40.0	2.9	23.4	0.0
45-64 Age Group												
First Generation	2.7	45.5	7.4	3.0	1.3	52.5	8.9	5.1	3.9	39.0	6.2	1.1
Second Generation	11.6	37.8	11.4	0.5	4.6	49.9	12.2	0.2	19.2	24.6	10.4	0.7
Mixed Parentage	23.5	28.2	15.3	1.2	8.8	50.0	11.8	2.9	33.3	13.7	17.6	0.0
Third Generation	28.6	14.3	8.2	0.0	13.3	33.3	6.7	0.0	35.3	5.9	8.8	0.0
65 and Over Age Group												
First Generation	0.0	34.6	1.3	3.8	0.0	47.4	1.3	5.3	1.8	22.9	1.2	2.4
Second Generation	11.1	24.1	8.3	2.8	2.1	37.5	10.4	4.2	18.3	13.3	6.7	1.7

*Subtotals do not add up to 100 per cent, since No Jewish Education (Table 10-3) and other types of Jewish education were eliminated.

age attended the integrated Sunday and Hebrew School, compared to 23 per cent of the 25-44 age group. Among males the pattern of age variation among the third generation is stronger: the integrated Hebrew and Sunday School characterized 7 per cent of the older males and 45 per cent of the younger males.

Therefore, it is necessary to supplement the generation analysis with data by age, especially for the 15-24 age group. The pattern of type of Jewish education by age is similar to that by generation, with interesting new changes for the 15-24 age group (Table 10-6). For both males and females significant increases in the integrated Sunday and Hebrew type have occurred, accounting for 48 per cent of the females 15-24 and 57 per cent of the males. Among both males and females of the youngest ages, slight increases may be noted in Day School attendance and consistent declines in Hebrew School only, private instruction, and Yiddish Schools. Moreover, differences between the sexes in type of Jewish education continue to diminish, although girls aged 15 to 24 still obtain a less intensive type of training since almost a third (compared to 11 per cent of the males) attend religious schools only on Sunday.

In sum, the following observations emerge: (1) A significant proportion of Jews have received some Jewish education and the number has increased among younger Jews. (2) The increase in the number receiving some Jewish education is primarily a function of the diminishing sex differential in Jewish education: dramatic increases have taken place among the young in the proportion of females having received some Jewish education. (3) Shifts have occurred toward the greater popularity of the integrated Sunday and Hebrew School as well as the Sunday School only, the former being more characteristic of males, the latter of females. (4) Finally, a significant proportion of females of the youngest age group have completed their education in the integrated type of religious school. This fact, combined with the increasing proportion of females who have some Jewish education, has resulted in a substantial reduction in differential Jewish education for boys and girls.

In addition to examining the kind of Jewish education received, it is necessary to have information on the number of years enrolled. For the adult Jewish population, a considerable proportion of both males and females have spent a number of years engaged in religious study.[8] About 27 per cent of the adult population had seven or more years of Jewish education, 22 per cent had five to six years, and 23 per cent had

[8] Statistics may overstate the number of years of education actually obtained, since some respondents were not particularly clear in indicating how much overlap there was in the different categories of Jewish education they had received. As far as possible, quality controls were introduced to avoid counting different educational programs twice if they took place concurrently.

TABLE 10-6

KIND OF JEWISH EDUCATION, BY AGE AND SEX

Age and Sex	Kind of Jewish Education										
	None	Sunday	Hebrew	Sunday and Hebrew	Day	Private	Yiddish	Adult	Bar Mitzvah	Other	No Information
Total											
15-24	8.8	20.1	10.7	52.6	3.0	3.7	0.2	0.0	0.5	0.3	0.0
25-44	16.3	21.7	25.0	25.3	1.2	6.9	0.9	0.7	0.8	0.1	1.2
45-64	16.3	10.7	38.1	10.4	1.1	16.8	2.4	0.5	1.1	0.5	2.1
65 and Over	15.3	4.6	31.3	3.0	3.4	24.0	8.0	0.2	2.7	2.7	4.8
Male											
15-24	5.0	10.9	14.9	57.1	4.3	6.6	0.3	0.0	1.0	0.0	0.0
25-44	4.3	8.8	37.9	30.8	1.6	11.8	0.8	0.2	1.6	0.2	2.0
45-64	7.1	4.3	49.7	11.1	1.5	19.4	2.3	0.3	2.3	0.3	1.7
65 and Over	3.9	1.0	44.6	8.4	4.9	23.5	6.9	0.0	3.9	3.9	3.9
Female											
15-24	12.8	29.9	6.3	47.9	1.7	0.7	0.0	0.0	–	0.7	0.0
25-44	26.3	32.3	14.2	20.7	0.8	2.8	1.0	1.1	–	0.0	0.7
45-64	25.3	16.9	26.9	9.7	0.7	14.2	2.4	0.7	–	0.6	2.5
65 and Over	25.2	7.7	19.7	2.6	2.1	24.4	9.0	0.4	–	1.7	5.6

TABLE 10-7

AMOUNT OF JEWISH EDUCATION, BY GENERATION, AGE, AND SEX

	Years of Jewish Education*								
	Total			Male			Female		
Generation and Age	1-4	5-6	7 or More	1-4	5-6	7 or More	1-4	5-6	7 or More
All Ages									
First Generation	20.3	18.6	31.2	11.9	20.1	44.4	27.6	17.2	19.7
Second Generation	25.4	24.4	22.3	20.3	31.2	27.0	30.8	17.4	17.5
Mixed Parentage	21.5	19.9	32.3	16.4	29.5	34.4	24.7	13.7	31.1
Third Generation	21.2	19.3	30.0	24.8	29.5	29.5	18.7	12.1	30.4
TOTAL	22.9	21.7	26.5	18.1	28.0	32.1	27.4	16.1	21.5
25-44 Age Group									
First Generation	25.0	21.4	32.2	29.3	26.5	32.3	22.0	18.0	32.0
Second Generation	29.2	26.6	24.6	21.5	33.6	29.1	32.8	19.6	20.0
Mixed Parentage	23.5	19.5	33.9	16.5	29.4	35.2	28.0	13.2	33.1
Third Generation	21.5	20.5	32.5	24.1	30.9	32.3	19.4	12.6	32.6
45-64 Age Group									
First Generation	22.8	21.3	29.9	11.8	23.6	42.9	32.5	19.4	18.3
Second Generation	25.5	23.6	21.7	20.4	30.5	26.2	31.0	16.2	16.9
Mixed Parentage	17.6	18.8	27.1	17.6	29.4	29.4	17.6	11.7	25.5
Third Generation	22.5	14.3	16.3	33.3	20.0	6.7	17.6	11.8	20.6
65 and Over Age Group									
First Generation	16.5	15.0	32.4	8.1	15.1	48.4	23.9	14.9	17.6
Second Generation	17.8	20.5	17.0	13.8	25.5	23.5	21.4	16.4	11.4

*Percentages do not add up to 100 per cent, since columns of No Jewish Education (Table 10-3) and No Information were eliminated.

one to four years (Table 10-7). Males not only attended schools of more intensive religious training but attended for longer periods of time than females. Almost a third of the males had seven or more years of Jewish education, compared to 22 per cent of the females; and, conversely, 27 per cent of the females had only one to four years, compared to 18 per cent of the males.

There seems to be a pattern of decrease in the number of years of Jewish education from the first to the second generation, and an increase among the native born of mixed and of native-born parents. Although age again varies within generation, the pattern of decrease among the second and increase among the third generation in the amount of Jewish education holds, with some exceptions, by age and sex. This pattern fits in well with the time sequence in the development of Jewish education facilities in the United States. The larger number of years spent by the foreign born in Jewish education reflects their European backgrounds, whereby most of their education centered around religious training. Upon arrival in the United States, engaged in the struggle for survival in the ghettos, the Jews had little time, energy, or organizational skills to develop and financially maintain well-planned community or synagogue-related religious schools. Their children not only had to attend poorer schools but economic, social, and other situational demands shortened the length of time they spent in religious schools. With the development of the organizational structure in the Jewish community and the rapid social and economic mobility characteristic of the second generation, greater attention was focused on improving Jewish educational facilities, organizing them around more established synagogues, and encouraging children to attend longer. There are probably social class and assimilation variables at work here, too. The third-generation child usually attends a Sunday or Sunday and Hebrew School in the context of a middle-class oriented synagogue and at a time when Judaism is accepted as one of the "three major faiths" of America. This stands in sharp contrast to the second-generation child, who probably attended a community-sponsored "Talmud Torah" or an immigrant oriented "shul." Thus, third-generation Jews on the average spent more years in religious schools of better quality than their parents.

These changes are further accentuated for the 15-24 age group (Table 10-8). Both males and females of this age group stayed in school for a longer period of time, with more dramatic changes for females. Consistent increases among women in the proportion having seven or more years of Jewish education may be seen: from 16 per cent among females 65 years of age and older to 48 per cent among the 15-24 age group. Moreover, 45 per cent of the total population 15 to 24 years of

TABLE 10-8

AMOUNT OF JEWISH EDUCATION, BY AGE AND SEX

Age and Sex	Years of Jewish Education*		
	1-4	5-6	7 or More
Total			
15-24	19.1	23.7	45.2
25-44	24.4	23.3	28.9
45-64	24.1	22.2	23.8
65 and Over	16.3	16.5	28.5
Male			
15-24	19.2	28.7	42.2
25-44	21.5	32.1	30.7
45-64	18.2	28.2	29.7
65 and Over	9.4	17.7	42.5
Female			
15-24	19.1	18.4	48.3
25-44	26.9	16.0	27.4
45-64	29.7	16.4	18.0
65 and Over	22.3	45.5	16.2

***Percentages do not add up to 100 per cent, since the proportion with no Jewish education (Table 10-4) and the proportion who did not know the number of years they spent in Jewish education are omitted.**

age have had seven or more years of Jewish education, compared to 29 per cent of the oldest age group.

Thus, younger third-generation Jews spend more years enrolled in some program of Jewish education, especially in the synagogue-related integrated Sunday and Hebrew School. The data do not permit evaluation of the intensity or the quality of Jewish education received by young persons today compared with their parents and grandparents. However, as suggested by the numbers enrolled, the increased length of enrollment, and the type of educational program attended, the data do point to more intensive Jewish education for a larger number of Jewish children. As with type of religious education, there is greater similarity between males and females in the amount of Jewish education received among third-generation Jews than among previous generations.

Additional data on current enrollment of children in Jewish education programs and planned future enrollment shed further light on the trend toward increased Jewish education among the young third generation. The proportion of children 5 to 17 years of age enrolled in some program of religious education was 53 per cent and varied only slightly for boys (58 per cent) and girls (55 per cent). This supports the conclusion that a significant narrowing in the Jewish educational patterns of men and women has taken place. The rate of enrollment for both boys and girls varies quite sharply by age. For the boys the proportion enrolled increased from 20 per cent among the five-year-olds to 93 per cent of those between the ages of 9 and 12. Moreover, the tendency for boys to end their Jewish education after Bar Mitzvah is obvious; reaching a peak at age 13, enrollment declines consistently with each succeeding year to below 20 per cent at age 15 and to 3 per cent for those age 17.

For girls the pattern is somewhat different. Until age 12 the proportion of girls enrolled in Jewish education is below the level of boys, beginning at 11 per cent for those 5 years old and rising to a peak of 82 per cent among those aged 10. The decline in enrollment for females begins at age 11, earlier than for males, but diminishes less rapidly. Thus, enrollment is identical at age 14, and after that age the proportion of girls enrolled is considerably above that of boys. For example, at age 17 only 3 per cent of the boys but 16 per cent of the girls are still receiving some Jewish education. The data also reveal that a higher percentage of girls than boys received seven or more years of religious schooling but also that more girls than boys attended for only a few years before dropping out.

In all age groups the proportion of girls enrolled in Sunday School only is considerably higher than that of boys, and more boys are enrolled in the integrated Hebrew and Sunday School program. These differentials, similar to those noted earlier, reflect the persistence of the traditional view that an intensive Hebrew education is more important for boys than for girls.

In order to ascertain the level of future Jewish education, the survey included a question addressed to parents on the religious education plans for young children who had not yet received any Jewish schooling. According to the responses, at least 90 per cent of the children under 8 years of age will be enrolled in a Jewish education program. In fact, less than 4 per cent specified that they did not plan to give their children any Jewish education, and the remainder did not know. Again, there is differential planning for boys and girls; parents plan to enroll 94 per cent of their sons but only 84 per cent of their daughters. Moreover, plans call for a larger proportion of boys than girls to attend the integrated Hebrew and Sunday School program, and for a larger proportion of girls to attend Sunday School only. Since well over 90 per cent of those not enrolled are third generation, the high projected level of future religious education portends well for the maintenance of Jewish awareness and identity.

Together, the data on current and future enrollment supplement the previous trends on completed education. They point to the general strengthening of both the level and intensity of Jewish education and the consistent, although declining, differential attitudes towards the sexes.

Whether or not an individual receives a Jewish education may be a key factor in influencing the degree of his identification with the Jewish community in adult life. Some weight is given to this hypothesis by the different patterns of Jewish education received by persons living in various residential areas, having different levels of secular education, and identifying with Orthodox, Conservative, or Reform Judaism.

A significant majority of persons in all residence, religious identification, and education categories have had some Jewish education. Differences among the categories reflect, in part, the variation by generation and age, but some consistent patterns emerge. First, suburbanites tend to have the highest proportion with no Jewish education. Even among the youngest age group (15 to 24) 16 per cent of the suburbanites had no Jewish education, compared to 6 per cent of those living in newer urban areas and 8 per cent of those in older urban areas. Second, sharp declines by age in the proportion with no Jewish education characterize the urban area residents, but not the suburbanites. Third, of those suburbanites who have some Jewish education, a higher percentage had minimal exposure in comparison with urban residents, and a significant percentage attended Sunday School only. This pattern conforms to that observed for other Jewish identification variables such as synagogue membership and attendance, ritual practices, and organizational participation. Similarly, the strong Jewish identification pattern of newer urban residents that was noted for other dimensions of religiosity is supported by the data on Jewish education. Few newer urban residents had no Jewish education and fully 53 per cent of those aged 15 to 24 had seven or more years.

The greater identification of the college educated with the Jewish community is also reflected in the data on Jewish education. Those with postcollege secular educations have the highest proportion with some Jewish education, followed by the college educated, and then those with less than a high school education. Concomitantly, those who have at least some college education had more years of religious training than those with less education, although more attended Sunday School only. Two factors may thus be operating: (1) religious and secular education go together in terms of proportion enrolled and length of exposure, and (2) Jewish education may be one of the major forces preventing the postcollege and college trained from rejecting their Judaism and Jewish identification.

Patterns of religious training for the three religious divisions are difficult to evaluate and differentials are not clear. Among the young

(15 to 24), 95 per cent of the Reform have some Jewish education, and over half attended religious schools for seven or more years. Most Reform Jews, however, are exposed to Sunday School only, although an increasing number are being trained in the integrated Hebrew and Sunday School. Among the Orthodox of the younger generation, slightly more have no Jewish education (7.4 per cent) and only one-fourth have seven or more years of exposure. Differences between Conservative and Reform Jews are minimal. Significantly, among those who do not identify with any of the three religious divisions, almost three-fourths of those 15 to 24 years of age had no Jewish education—an increase from the 44 per cent of those aged 65 and over.

The differentials in Jewish education conform closely to other patterns of Jewish identification, although it is impossible to show a direct cause-effect relationship. Lower levels of synagogue membership, attendance at religious services, adherence to ritual practices, and participation in Jewish organizations may be the consequence of lower levels of Jewish education.

YIDDISH, A DISAPPEARING LANGUAGE

Perhaps no other people in world history has functioned in so many languages as have the Jews. As a result of two thousand years of wandering, Jews have not only learned to speak the language of the people among whom they lived but also adapted it and transformed it for their own needs. Yiddish grew out of the languages used in the Rhine Provinces of Germany between the tenth and twelfth centuries. Although stifled in Germany as a result of the Enlightenment and emancipation, Yiddish developed extensively among the large Jewish communities in Austria, Poland, and Russia.[9]

The large waves of immigrant Jews arriving from Eastern Europe between 1880 and the 1920's brought with them the Yiddish that was spoken in the East European ghettos. Yiddish flourished in the United States for a number of decades through the reinforcement from the flow of immigrants and the settlement of Jews within ghetto-like areas in the New World. The significant reduction in immigration and concomitant reduction in the proportion of foreign born, the movement away from areas of first settlement, and the increasing Americanization of the Jewish population all point to the eventual disappearance of Yiddish as a spoken language. This has already been evidenced in the greatly reduced

[9] See Menachem Boraisha, "The Story of Yiddish," in *Jews in the Modern World*, ed. Fried, II, 356-76.

circulation of the Yiddish newspapers and the disappearance of Yiddish schools; it is also obvious from census data on mother tongue. In 1910 the United States Census reported that 7,500 persons in Rhode Island listed Yiddish as their mother tongue. By 1930 this had been reduced to 4,100, and in the 1960 census only 1,900 reported Yiddish as their mother tongue. These patterns are consistent with those in the total American Jewish community.

In this section, Yiddish speaking will be considered as one aspect of the cultural dimension of religiosity. Speaking Yiddish has been considered the vehicle and expression of Eastern European culture and has virtually been synonymous with being Jewish. Indeed, many, primarily of earlier generations, saw "being Jewish" and speaking Yiddish as indistinguishable.[10] However, one of the earliest signs of assimilation was the rapid exposure to and adoption of English among the second generation as they attended public schools and moved up the socio-economic ladder.[11]

The extent of linguistic assimilation may be observed from data by generation (Table 10-9). Although two-thirds of the foreign born were currently members of households where some Yiddish was spoken,[12] this percentage declines to about a third of the second generation and to 13 per cent among the third generation. Moreover, except for the second generation, a smaller proportion of the younger age groups within each generation were in households where Yiddish was spoken. These statistics quite clearly point to the disappearance of Yiddish as a result of the Americanization process. The Yiddishisms which have gained a certain popularity in recent times in mass media publications, in "Jewish" novels, and on television do not reflect the return of the third generation to speaking Yiddish but rather a reiteration of Jewish identity through the "charm" and distinctiveness of the ethnic heritage.[13]

Linguistic assimilation, not unexpectedly, seems to have occurred more rapidly for the men, for those who have moved out of the older areas of settlement to newer urban areas or the suburbs, for the Reform

[10] See Will Herberg, *Protestant-Catholic-Jew* (Garden City, N.Y.: Doubleday & Company, Inc., Anchor Books, 1960), pp. 182-83.

[11] See Vladimir C. Nahirny and Joshua A. Fishman, "American Immigrant Group: Ethnic Identification and the Problem of Generations," *The Sociological Review,* XIII (November, 1965), 317. See also Milton Gordon, *Assimilation in American Life,* pp. 190-91; according to his scheme, linguistic assimilation would be classified as assimilation in extrinsic cultural traits.

[12] No information was collected regarding the frequency or extent of using Yiddish.

[13] Herbert Gans calls the use of nostalgic Yiddish words and other aspects of this pattern, "Symbolic Judaism." See "American Jewry: Past and Present," *Commentary,* XXI (May, 1956), 422-30, and *Commentary,* XXI (June, 1956), 555-63.

TABLE 10-9

PROPORTION OF INDIVIDUALS IN HOUSEHOLDS WHERE YIDDISH WAS SPOKEN, BY GENERATION AND AGE

Generation and Age	Per Cent
All Ages	
First Generation	66.6
Second Generation	36.2
Mixed Parentage	19.2
Third Generation	13.2
TOTAL	39.5
25-44 Age Group	
First Generation	35.7
Second Generation	35.2
Mixed Parentage	18.6
Third Generation	11.7
45-64 Age Group	
First Generation	66.7
Second Generation	37.6
Mixed Parentage	22.4
Third Generation	18.4
65 and Over Age Group	
First Generation	74.3
Second Generation	30.4

and Conservative, and for those with college educations. However, declines in speaking Yiddish within all residential, religious, and educational categories and for both sexes, without exception, have taken place with distance from the immigrant generation. The only significant proportion of third-generation Jews who are in households where Yiddish is spoken are those living in older urban areas and who identify as Orthodox. This remnant of Yiddish seems to be a function of the greater number of foreign-born persons among the Orthodox and among those living in the older urban areas with whom the third generation interact. Moreover, both the residents of older urban areas and the Orthodox Jews represent a small proportion of the third generation. The evidence overwhelmingly supports the conclusion that linguistic assimilation among Jews was rapid and almost complete in three generations.

A new linguistic phenomenon is appearing: the slight increase in the use of Hebrew among the third generation. Although the proportion is still very small, the combination of the use of Hebrew in Jewish religious schools, pride in the establishment of the State of Israel, and a greater amount of interchange between the United States and Israel has led to a greater number of persons learning Hebrew as both a written and a spoken language.

RELIGION AND THE THREE-GENERATIONS HYPOTHESIS

In evaluating the changes in religiosity among three generations of Jews, it is difficult to isolate one specific pattern. This difficulty stems from two major theoretical issues. First, social scientists have been accustomed to treating the three-generations hypothesis, in its diverse forms, as a unidimensional proposition. Given the complex nature of religion and religiosity, unidimensionality is oversimplification. It is not meaningful to speak of "religious revival" or "religious decline" or "religious stability" or declines and increases by generation without taking into account the variety of religious expressions and the diversity of religious commitments. Secondly, a comprehensive analysis of religiosity must also take into consideration variation or heterogeneity within generations. In this and the preceding chapter an attempt was made to deal directly with these two difficulties. A multidimensional analysis of religiosity among Jews was proposed which included ideological, ritualistic, organizational, and cultural dimensions. Moreover, differential responses to religion of subgroupings within generations were explored.

Indicators of the ideological and ritualistic dimensions revealed dramatic changes occurring in three generations. Consistent declines with distance from the first generation were observed in Orthodox identification, in membership in Orthodox congregations, in regular synagogue and temple attendance, and in traditional ritual practices in the home. Clearly, neither religious stability nor religious revival characterized Jews in the process of Americanization. Nor was "religious decline" an appropriate description. The high proportion of Jews who identify with one of the three religious divisions, the high proportion who are actually synagogue members, the low and relatively stable proportion of non-synagogue members, the small number who do not identify with one of the three religious divisions, the low proportion of Jews who never attend religious services, and the shift toward moderate rather than secular positions in ritual practices defied the over-all categorization of religious decline. Rather, integration into American society has led to the abandonment of traditional forms of religious behavior and the transition to forms that are more secular but within a Jewish context. Strong identification factors are evident with the preservation of some form of affiliation; at the same time, all the indications point to the rejection of the traditional concepts of religiousness.

The development and emphasis among native-born Jews of new forms of religious expression may best be illustrated by the findings related to specific rituals. Whereas decreases were evident in Kashrut observances and Sabbath candle lighting, attendance at Passover Seder and lighting Chanukah candles showed stability and slight increases from the first to the third generation. Thus, those ritual practices were retained and emphasized which remained functional, from a sociological perspective, within the context of American life. The accommodation and integration of the Jewish population in America resulted in the rejection of those ritual practices that do not have some family or social-secular orientation.

A parallel interpretation may be applied to findings on the organizational dimension of religiosity. The analysis revealed that there is strong affiliation with Jewish organizations and little affiliation with nonsectarian organizations. With the Americanization of the Jewish population some increase in non-Jewish organizational membership occurs, but not at the expense of a total rejection of Jewish organizational affiliation. Third-generation Jews tend to hold memberships more equally in Jewish and non-Jewish organizations, and declines in segregated membership patterns were observable.

The one measure of religiosity that presented a picture of "religious revival" was Jewish education—a measure of the cultural dimension. More younger third-generation Jews had some Jewish education, spent more years enrolled, and attended the integrated synagogue-related Hebrew and Sunday School than previous generations. Moreover, parents have plans to provide some religious training to over 90 per cent of the youngest generation. Finally, the use of an ethnic language, Yiddish, rapidly disappears in the Americanization process. This, too, fits in well with the pattern on specific rituals where rejection occurs when incompatibility exists between being American and being Jewish. Traditional ethnic ties are forsaken in favor of those practices which fit better into the American scene.

The data, as a whole, reveal the strengthening of some areas of religiosity (Jewish education), stability in other areas (synagogue membership, affiliation with one of the three religious divisions, observance of Chanukah and Passover), and declines in other areas (Orthodoxy, Kashrut, Sabbath candle lighting, regular synagogue attendance, and speaking Yiddish). Therefore, religious decline, revival, and stability are inappropriate characterizations of the total panorama of religiosity changes among three generations of Jews. There has instead been an over-all development of new forms of Jewish identity and expression, with an emphasis on those aspects that are congruent with Americanization. Religious commitments are retained when they are functionally integrated within a secular context and where retention of Jewish identity is possible in a form that is expected and conditioned by the majority community.

The analysis of differential change in religiosity strongly supports these conclusions. In summary the data point to the following:

(1) Traditional sex differences in synagogue membership, in attendance at religious services, and in type and length of religious training are diminishing. This pattern is part of the greater equalization of the status of women and the breakdown of traditional sex barriers which pervade American society. The diminishing sex differential in religious attitudes may also be inferred from the increase in Conservative and Reform affiliation which are characterized by mixed pews and family-oriented services.

(2) The suburban Jewish population is the only group with some consistent pattern of greater assimilation into the majority community. This is reflected by higher intermarriage rates, in greater nonmembership in synagogues, higher rates of nonidentification with one of the three religious divisions, lower synagogue attendance and a higher proportion never attending religious services, higher affiliation with non-Jewish organizations and lower affiliation with Jewish organizations, higher proportions of those with no Jewish education, shorter number of years spent in Jewish education, and concentration in the Sunday School only type of religious education. This portrait of suburban Jews in part reflects generation and age factors. In large measure it also relates to the effects of population dispersal and deconcentration, with the weakest Jewish identity in those groups that are less concentrated and self-segregated. Moreover, these groups may constitute a selective migration to the suburbs of those not desiring Jewish facilities or Jewish identity; and perhaps there is a causal relationship between the lack of religious training and greater assimilation in later life. However, the patterns of greater assimilation among the suburban Jewish population are relative to the rather strong identification in other residential areas. Moreover, one exception is noted to this trend: suburbanites are not secular in their ritual practices, but moderate; although there are signs of the rejection of Kashrut and Sabbath candle lighting, there is strong commitment to the secular-religious rituals associated with Passover and Chanukah.

(3) The more educated groups within the Jewish population clearly exemplify the secularization process within a Jewish context. On the one hand, the college educated are the least identified with Orthodox Judaism, have the lowest regular synagogue attendance rate, have clearly rejected traditional ritual practices (particularly Kashrut and Sab-

bath candle lighting), have the highest membership rate in non-Jewish organizations, and are concentrated among those with a Sunday School only religious education. On the other hand, the more educated have not rejected identification with one of the three religious divisions, have not abandoned synagogue membership, have the lowest proportion who never attend the synagogue, are moderate rather than secular in their religious practices, have not abandoned membership in Jewish organizations, have the highest proportion with some Jewish education, and spend, on the average, more years receiving religious training.

(4) The lines dividing the three religious divisions are increasingly becoming blurred, at least in the minds and behavior of native-born Jews. Although Orthodox Jews are more ritual oriented, over two-thirds do not attend synagogue services at least once a month and generation declines were noted in their adherence to traditional ritual practices associated with the home. Moreover, Orthodox Jews are the least organization-oriented—whether of Jewish or non-Jewish organizations—and do not appear to channel their identification in this area. Nevertheless, there are significant changes among the third-generation American Orthodox; and one may infer that the decline in religiosity in various forms among those who identify with Orthodox Judaism reveals that the native-born Orthodox Jew is very different from the Orthodox Jew born in Europe. In addition, although declines in ritual practices characterize Reform and Conservative Jews, neither has rejected all ritual practices. Reform and Conservative Jews channel their identification through Jewish organizational participation as well as some religious rituals. Finally, 95 per cent of the younger third-generation American Reform Jews have received some Jewish education. As an interesting pattern of assimilation, those who do not identify with any religious division (only 5 per cent) rarely attend the synagogue and three-fourths of those 15 to 24 years of age within this group have had no Jewish education.

It is clear that religious acculturation has indeed occurred with distance from the immigrant generation; but these trends have not meant the loss of Jewish identity or absorption into the majority. Rather, new forms of religious expression have evolved which are more congruent with the social situation of the third generation. Indicative of the changes in religiosity are the greater homogeneity among the native born and the sharper differences between the foreign born and later generations. Consequently, the American Jew and the community with which he identifies are not quantitatively vanishing but qualitatively changing so that being Jewish and being American becomes a natural, harmonious, and meaningful partnership.

CHAPTER ELEVEN

Being Jewish and Being American

The orientation of this book has been the delineation of assimilation patterns among three generations of American Jews. The proposition that assimilation is not a unidimensional phenomenon implied that both social and cultural changes would have to be examined. The complexity of the assimilation process further demanded that the exploration of the manifestations and ramifications of change encompass many facets of the Jewish community, demographic as well as sociological. The analytical vehicle for such an exploration became three generations of Jews; changes in the Jewish community were viewed as intimately related to distance from the immigrant generation.

The identification of generation changes involved more than a simple description of demographic characteristics and sociological behavior. On the one hand, it was necessary to analyze extensively various demographic and sociological features of the Jewish population including population growth, composition, distribution, migration, fertility, mortality, family structure, socio-economic status, and religious identification broadly conceived. On the other hand, the examination of generation changes posed two additional interrelated issues: (1) the problem of "Jewish exceptionalism" and the convergences in Jewish and non-Jewish population and social structure; (2) the question of heterogeneity within the Jewish population.

Jewish exceptionalism brings to the fore consideration of how Jews differ from non-Jews in their social and demographic characteristics and behavior. More broadly, the persistence and continuity of Jewish values, of unique Jewish characteristics and behavior, and of a distinctive demographic and social structure of the Jewish population lead into the evaluation of triple versus single melting pot theories, not only in terms of identificational assimilation but in the empirical reality of structural and behavioral similarities. American society may be broadly subdivided along religious lines, but the question remains whether, and to what extent, religious groupings are characterized by converging yet parallel structures. Examination of the Jewish population in contrast to the general population provides some insights into this question.

The investigation of Jewish heterogeneity also tests the convergence hypothesis, but in a different sense. It poses the problem of variation within generations and manifestations of greater homogeneity among third-generation Jews when compared to the foreign born. Analyses of intragenerational variation, moreover, allow for more realistic projections into the future, since greater sensitivity to change among some subgroups may foreshadow the future patterns of the entire population. This is particularly true when the subgroups are characterized by social and economic patterns toward which the total population is moving.

To examine generation changes, Jewish exceptionalism, and Jewish heterogeneity, an analysis of data on the Jewish community of metropolitan Providence, Rhode Island, was presented. These data had the advantage of encompassing a broad range of information. Unlike that of many other Jewish community studies, the sample was carefully selected and representative; the sample size was sufficiently large not only to cover population subgroups but to permit extensive cross-tabulations and controls. The advantages of the information available for Providence were considered to far outweigh the major limitation of the study—its confinement to a single Jewish community. References to and reviews of related literature only partially compensate for this restriction, largely because the available materials on generation change are limited both in volume and in quality.

Although all communities are in some ways atypical, the importance of case studies or community research is not thereby diminished. The value of such studies lies in the comparisons that may be made with information from national and other community information. The general absence of scientific information on generation changes in the socio-demographic structure of the American Jewish community strongly argued for the treatment of our community study as benchmark research. Furthermore, the value of this local study for the American Jewish community is enhanced by its focus on generation changes. Inasmuch as the population composition of individual communities will vary from one to another and deviate from an over-all national average, emphasis should be placed on *patterns* of change rather than on absolute statistical values. It is these patterns that may provide the most valuable insights into the directions in which both the local and the national community may move in the future. Nevertheless, it remains difficult and dangerous to generalize from one Jewish community to another or from one community to the entire United States Jewish population. For example, the high levels of synagogue membership and of Jewish educational enrollment may be a function of the local community's size, its relative stability, and its strong Jewish organizational and institutional structure. Whether these factors actually affect the behavior and characteristics of the population can be definitively answered only by comparative research. Thus, we cannot validly generalize from this community study to the large centers of Jewish population of New York, Chicago, or Los Angeles, or to the total Jewish population of the United States, although many of the findings of this study would quite likely apply. In this sense, both national and community studies are necessary and complementary. This community study should be evaluated in this light.

GENERATION CHANGES

The rationale for the use of generation status as a key variable in interpreting the socio-demographic structure of an American Jewish community and as a vehicle to measure change lies in the population history of the Jewish community. The context of change took shape with the mass immigration of East European Jews to the United States at the turn of the century. The adjustment of the immigrant generation and the Americanization of their children and grandchildren altered the character of the American Jewish community and the lives of American Jews.

The growth of the Jewish population was accelerated not by natural increase but by the immigration of approximately two and a half million Jews between 1880 and 1924. The consequences of this type of population growth were manifold. First, it enabled the Jewish community to become a national vibrant subsociety. Second, numerical growth and immigrant adjustment demanded institutional and organizational development within the Jewish community, not only to facilitate the Americanization process but to strengthen ethnic-religious and cultural cohesion. Third, the source of the immigration—Eastern Europe—brought a different cultural heritage to American Jewry, one that shook the foundations of the Sephardic and German dominance. But perhaps the most important change that the immigration from Eastern European ghettos brought about was the inner transformation of the immigrants and their children. Along with the process of becoming American came greater freedom. At one extreme the democratic climate of general liberty affords Jews the chance of exerting themselves for the preservation of their identity. Yet, it also provides the opportunity for a high degree of assimilation with consequent loss of identity through complete absorption into the American social structure. The responses of the three generations to this challenge of freedom varied and are reflected in demographic and social structural changes. The character of these changes suggests the answers to the question of whether Jews can achieve an integrated yet unassimilated status in the general American community.

Demographically, the Jewish population is increasingly American-Jewish in composition. With the significant reduction in immigration following the 1920's, and the rapid rate of disappearance of the immigrant generation as a result of aging and death, only a small minority of the total community are foreign born and most of these are in the aged group. In fact, among those below age 25 a vast majority are third-generation Americans. The future of the American Jewish community depends to a great degree on how these young persons in particular react to the freedom to work toward integration into the American social structure as an acculturated subsociety or toward complete assimilation and loss of Jewish identification. Whether they reverse or accelerate certain trends toward assimilation initiated by their second-generation parents or by the smaller number of older third-generation Jews provides the insights by which the patterns of generation change may be detected and projected.

The settlement pattern of the first generation was predominantly urban and characterized by a high degree of concentration in selected areas of the city. This was the result of a long tradition of urban concentration among Jews and was necessitated partially by their low socio-economic status and their urban-oriented occupational skills. However, with the Americanization of the Jewish population, newer residential areas away from the old ghettos emerged, and with rapid social mobility came geographic mobility. Some Jews preferred to live in areas of high Jewish concentration, and new "gilded ghettos" located in newer, prestigious sections of the urban areas were developed. Others, not placing high priority on residential clustering or on proximity to community institutions, moved to more integrated residential areas of the suburbs. The dispersal, and to some extent the deconcentration of the Jewish population, were rapid, and for many not only marked a significant physical break from the foreign born but symbolized the more dramatic disassociation of American-born Jews from ethnic ties and experiences that had served as unifying forces in the earlier generation. Whether the increasing proportion of Jews who have participated in this dispersal will achieve the same degree of identification with Judaism as those in the areas they left or in areas of high Jewish density provides a major key to the future of the Jewish community at large.

Surely the mobility of the native born could not have been as rapid or as successful without radical socio-economic changes. Not unexpectedly, therefore, dramatic increases in the amount of secular education were observed with distance from the immigrant generation. Both the escape from the ghetto and the integration into American society were greatly facilitated by high educational achievement.

Secular education became the key with which to enter into the professions and to earn higher incomes. The occupational structure of the Jewish population mirrored these changes and resulted in very high proportions of persons in all generation groups being concentrated in the professional and managerial segments of the occupational hierarchy. Over all, compared with second- and third-generation groups, the foreign born have proportionally fewer persons who are professionals, somewhat more in managerial positions, fewer clerical and sales workers, and considerably more manual workers. In part, these differences reflect variations in age composition; in part they stem from higher educational levels. No doubt the changes also partially result from the wider range of jobs open to Jews as a result of a breakdown in discrimination patterns. These changes include opportunities to fill professional, managerial, and sales positions other than those associated with self-employment as doctors, as lawyers, or in family businesses. Nor was education the only road to social mobility. The fluidity of the American occupation structure allowed many of the first and second generation who did not have secular educations to improve their economic and social position.

Yet it is likely that as the opportunities and incentives for higher education increase among the general population, the differentials between Jews and non-Jews with respect to both educational achievement and occupational distribution will diminish. The high proportion of Jews with college education leaves little room for sharp rises; the rapid rate at which college education becomes an achievable goal for members of the total population will inevitably decrease the existing differentials. This diminution in educational differentials coupled with the increasing concentration of job opportunities for the general population in the white-collar segment of the occupational hierarchy will probably lead to considerable decreases in the existing occupational differentials. The specific trends for Jews coupled with the over-all trends for the general population should, therefore, contribute significantly toward integration in the educational and occupational spheres. Moreover, for Jews such developments may alter the inconsistencies noted, wherein positions as managers and proprietors provided a channel for occupational mobility despite the absence of high-level education. To the extent that college education will be virtually universal among Jews, the high concentration in upper occupational groups will be fully consistent with educational achievement.

Although changes in residential location and socio-economic status were dramatic, family structural changes were moderate. The disorientation and disruption resulting from migration, which usually leads to some family disorganization, were counterbalanced by Jewish values of family cohesion and stability. Only slight increases among native-born Jews were observed in marital dissolution and remarriages, and the over-all pattern was one of stable nuclear families. Yet, some family patterns were more clearly and directly affected by the Americanization process, notably age at marriage and fertility.

First-generation Jews were characterized by relatively larger families, early marriages, beginning a family soon after marriage, and shorter intervals between children. In contrast, the second generation had very small families, married at later ages, and spaced their children at longer intervals. These changes may in part relate to the socio-economic advances made by the second generation, their desires to provide college educations for their children, and the relationship between low fertility and high social mobility. They also reflect in part the impact of the economic depression on age at marriage and family size and in part knowledge of methods of family limitation and spacing.

Third-generation Jews, secure in their middle-class backgrounds, with college educations and in high white-collar occupations, participated in the post World War II baby boom. They had larger families, married earlier, and adopted early family formation patterns compared with second-generation couples. These family formation and fertility changes among three generations of Jews are thus correlated with the other changes that occurred as the Jewish group acculturated.

The dispersal of the Jewish population and the exposure to public education increased the interaction between Jews and non-Jews. Thus, concomitant with structural and cultural changes, marital assimilation increased. Intermarriage between Jews and non-Jews clearly increased with distance from the immigrant generation, although the over-all levels remained relatively low. However, the evidence presented suggests that conversions to Judaism also increased and that a majority of the children of intermarried couples are being raised as Jews. Together with the post World War II fertility increases, the data on intermarriages and conversions suggest that quantitative or numerical losses to the Jewish population are minimal. However, this conclusion, while significant, is but half the picture. The other half revolves about the question of qualitative changes and, specifically, alterations in religious identification, ritual practices, Jewish organizational affiliation, and cultural attachments.

Changes observed in residential location, social-class structure, family formation, and fertility behavior were accompanied by redirections of the religious system. Striking shifts from Orthodox to Conservative and Reform religious identification and synagogue membership were observed with distance from the immigrant generation. Declines in regular synagogue attendance were also noted, along with decreases in Kashrut observances, Sabbath candle lighting, and Jewish organizational affiliation, and the disappearance of Yiddish as a spoken language. Yet, a clear tendency toward increased Jewish education among the young third generation appeared, as well as increased observance of Chanukah. Compounding the picture, few changes occurred in the proportion reporting synagogue membership, denominational identification, and attendance at Passover Seder. Thus, the data showed that some areas of religiosity appeared to be strengthened, others declined, and some remained stable over the generations. These varied manifestations could not, therefore, be conceptualized over all as representing "religious revival," "religious declines," or "religious stability."

The pattern that emerges is neither of the simplistic extremes—religious assimilation or religious insulation. The pattern of religious change among three generations of Jews is a complex process, involving the abandonment of traditional forms of religious behavior and, at the same time, the development of new forms of Jewish identity and expression. The evolution of religious change is in the direction of emphasizing those facets of Judaism and Jewishness that are congruent with the broader American way of life. Strong identification factors are evident with the maintenance of some form of affiliation; at the same time all the indications point to the abandonment of traditional concepts of religiosity. Religious commitments among Jews are retained when they are functionally integrated within a secular context and where retention of religious expression is possible in a form which is expected and conditioned by the majority community.

It is clear that the freedom, evolving out of the process of adjustment, to choose the degree of assimilation was exercised in the direction of some religious identification. But its form reflects the social situation of each generation. For the majority of Jews born in the United States the choice did not result in a complete rejection of being Jewish nor in the desire for religious isolation. The alternative was integration, becoming a "Jewish American" and adjusting the forms of religious commitment to the American way of life. Quite clearly, the general tendency toward increasing enrollment in Jewish educational programs characterizes all generation groups and operates for both males and females. This development would seem to attest to the interest and determination, whatever the reason, for Jews to maintain an identification with Judaism and the Jewish community. It appears to be a major variable in contributing to the future vitality of the American Jewish community, despite the fact that a few Jews, especially from among the professions, may forgo identification with the Jewish community in favor of interaction and identification with an intellectual subsociety.

JEWISH EXCEPTIONALISM

Generation changes within the Jewish community did not occur in a social vacuum. The Jewish population, like other minority populations, was sensitive to changes in American society. In their view of the American scene, Jews, like Catholics and Protestants, had come to look upon American society as a triple melting pot—an over-all community composed of three religious subcommunities, of which one was Jewish.[1] In terms of religious identification, the triple versus the single melting pot alternative has been empirically resolved in favor of the former. But this does not necessarily imply that Jews have retained complete structural and behavioral distinctiveness. Surely, the maintenance of Jewish identity and the preservation of a distinct religious system strongly argue against trends toward total absorption. Yet, from the changes noted in all the aspects of Jewish social life, including religion, it is evident that these trends parallel changes in the total United States population.

In some ways, Jews remain distinctive in population characteristics and social behavior. The Jewish population has participated more rapidly in the suburbanization movement, is more concentrated in large metropolitan areas, and is characterized by lower fertility.

Demographic differentials between Jews and non-Jews encompass the mortality dimension as well as fertility. At younger ages, Jewish age-specific death rates are below those of the total population; proportionally more Jews survive into middle age and, in the case of males, into old age; life expectancy at birth is higher for Jewish males than for all males, but this differential does not extend to females. Since these data are not available by generation, evaluation of change is not feasible. However, the similarity between these findings and those of other studies covering a 25-year period suggests that factors associated with Jewish identification, whether socio-economic conditions, health, or even inherited traits, continue to affect Jewish mortality and to produce patterns somewhat different from those in the population as a whole.

Combined, these demographic components of fertility, mortality, and migration result in a peculiar population structure. Furthermore, Jews are disproportionately concentrated in higher socio-economic categories, particularly among the college educated, those in high white-collar

[1] Will Herberg, *Protestant-Catholic-Jew* (Garden City, N.Y.: Doubleday & Company, Inc., 1961), pp. 32-36 and 256-59.

occupations, and the home owners. Family stability among Jews is higher than among non-Jews, marriages occur at older ages, and intermarriage rates are relatively low. Nevertheless, three important signs of convergence are evident. First, data on generation changes suggest that differences between Jews and non-Jews are diminishing. The native-born Jew of native-born parents is much more similar to the non-Jew in terms of a variety of socio-demographic characteristics than were members of the immigrant generation. Second, the patterns of religious changes within the Jewish group are toward greater secular content and similarity to Protestant-liberal norms. Third, as American Jewry proceeds to become more fully integrated into the larger community, the larger community itself continues to undergo changes. These changes, including rising standards of education, increasing proportions of workers in white-collar jobs, and greater fertility control, result in the narrowing of the gap between the Jewish and non-Jewish populations. Thus, it is likely that the distinctive population characteristics and social behavior of American Jews will greatly diminish, and behavioral convergence of both populations will occur.

Yet this convergence, which is evident from the data, does not imply the eventual demise of Jewish identity. On the contrary, the trends suggest separatism along religious lines. In this sense, the triple melting pot or religio-cultural pluralism is an accurate description of the parallel religious communities subdividing American society, whereas the single melting pot represents structural and behavioral convergences. In this way, religious pluralism blends with diminishing demographic, social, and economic differentiation. It is quite clear, therefore, that cultural assimilation among Jews has occurred without structural disappearance. The very fact that the Jewish community is an identifiable separate entity within the larger community is strong evidence for the structural separation hypothesis. Although some structural assimilation may have occurred, the overwhelming evidence suggests that Jewish exceptionalism is much more characteristic of the structural rather than the behavioral dimension of assimilation. The analysis presented clearly confirms the theoretical model of the multidimensionality of assimilation in American society in general, and in the Jewish subsociety in particular.[2]

JEWISH HETEROGENEITY

Throughout, we have argued for the recognition of heterogeneity within generations. This was not to deny the over-all patterns which

[2] Milton Gordon, *Assimilation in American Life* (New York: Oxford University Press, Inc., 1964), pp. 106-14, 160-232. See also the analysis in Chapter 1 of this book.

distinguish each of the three generations but rather was intended to locate subgroups which were more susceptible to change. Moreover, in the process of analyzing generation changes, it became clear that differences within the Jewish population diminished among the third generation and that the most striking internal variation characterized the immigrant generation. Just as intergenerational change and tension were more pronounced between the immigrants and their children, so intragenerational differentials generally decline with distance from the foreign born. Three differentials were extensively examined: residential (older urban, newer urban, and suburban), socio-economic (indicated by educational attainment—elementary school, high school, college, postcollege), and religious (Orthodox, Conservative, and Reform identification). The findings in regard to these differentials point to the following general conclusions:

(1) The demographic characteristics and the distribution of Jews among the various residential areas, educational categories, and religious groupings clearly indicate the greater concentration of the young third generation among the suburban residents, college educated, and Reform Jews. Indeed, there is a strong correlation among the three differentials: Reform Jews are characterized by higher education and a larger proportion live in suburban areas; the population in the older urban areas has the least education and is proportionally more Orthodox in identification.

(2) Reform Jews, suburban residents, and the college educated have less stable family structures as evidenced by higher divorce and remarriage rates, when compared to Orthodox Jews, urban residents, and those with less education. These differences have somewhat diminished among third-generation Jews.

(3) Suburban residents have a clear pattern of greater religious assimilation. This is reflected in their higher intermarriage rate and in their greater assimilation in almost every aspect of religiosity. It should be noted, however, that conversions to Judaism among the suburban intermarried are higher and there is a strong commitment to rituals associated with Passover and Chanukah. Relatively, suburban Jews have the weakest affiliation with Jewishness. In part this probably reflects the selective migration to the suburbs of those not desiring Jewish identification, the effects of population deconcentration on Jewish identity, and the relationship between religious assimilation and the lack of religious education characterizing suburban residents.

(4) The more educated groups within the Jewish population accentuate in general the type of religious changes characteristic of the young third generation. While rejecting traditional religious identification with Orthodoxy and associated ritual practices, the more educated

have integrated their religious identification with adjustment to American society. They combined sustained Jewish organizational affiliation with increased participation in non-Jewish organizations, extended both their secular and their religious training, and attended and identified with Reform congregations. Of course, those highly educated residents whose complete identity with the Jewish community has been lost because they have channeled their identification through an intellectual subsociety are not covered in this study. The study also did not encompass those with higher education who may have dispersed through out-migration. If these out-migrants consist disproportionately of persons in the intellectual subsociety, their exodus from the community leaves behind those with closer identification with the Jewish community.

(5) Although Orthodox-identified Jews have been somewhat more resistant to changes than Conservative or Reform Jews, there have been significant changes in their characteristics and behavior. In three generations, Orthodox Jews have received increasing secular education, have continued to move from older urban areas, and have exhibited declines in religiosity. In all areas, the Orthodox have experienced the least acculturation; yet the demographic and sociological style of third-generation Jews who are Orthodox is radically different from the foreign-born Orthodox and much more similar to Conservative and Reform patterns.

(6) With the general decline in the proportion of foreign born in the Jewish population, most of the other differentials are also declining. Differences between the newer urban and the suburban segments are not as great and the wider distinction between the older urban and other areas of settlement is diminishing with the depopulation of the former. Similarly, educational homogeneity will increasingly characterize the Jewish community as the population ages and as the foreign born continually form a smaller segment. The lines dividing the three religious divisions have already become blurred in the minds and behavior of native-born Jews. Therefore, it is likely that the trend toward convergence and homogeneity will continue and become more pronounced in future generations.

Yet, this obvious trend toward greater homogeneity should not mask the existence of earlier noted differentials, especially those between the population in the newer urban and the suburban areas. Although increasingly more similar in generation status, the selective character of movement to these areas results in different concentrations with respect to both socio-economic characteristics and the degree of identification with Judaism. To the extent that these variations persist, residence may continue to be a key factor in evaluating and affecting Jewish life.

In almost all respects, however, the over-all impression created by this analysis is that in three generations Jews have become integrated into the majority community. "Being Jewish" has come to be viewed both by Jews and non-Jews as part of the American scene. Surely the continuation of social and cultural changes among Jews, as well as among the total American population, will lead to greater behavioral similarities among the members of the two communities. Nevertheless, all the evidence points to the structural separation of the Jewish community and the continuity of Jewish identification. The direction of changes appears to be the adjustment of American Jewry to the American way of life, creating a meaningful balance between Jewishness and Americanism. Through Jewish education, as well as through the expectations imposed on Jews by their Jewish and non-Jewish neighbors, a new type of Jew is developing in the United States, one who feels equally comfortable being both a Jew and an American. Yet, the stirring and unrest in the Jewish community and the increasing self-awareness and introspection suggest that the problems of American Jewry, internal and external, have not been completely resolved. In leaving his European origins behind, the American Jew needs more time to adjust to his new freedom and to his new obligations. As the next generation matures and faces a different social milieu, it will be challenged to develop still further creative alternatives to salvage the best from both worlds.

A P P E N D I X A

Number of Sample Cases

To simplify the tabular presentations accompanying the text and to avoid repetition, the number of cases on which the percentage distributions included in the text tables are based have not been presented in the tables themselves. Rather, they are given in Appendix Tables A-1 through A-4 for individuals, Table A-5 for married women, and Table A-6 for households. Each of the tables corresponds to one of the major variables in terms of which generation changes were analyzed. Appendix B discusses the sampling errors involved in using these cases as the bases for the statistical analysis of differences in generation patterns. Readers interested in the number on which specific statistics presented in the text tables are based and for which no exact number is presented in the Appendix Tables can obtain such information by writing to the authors.

TABLE A-1

NUMBER OF RESPONDENTS IN SAMPLE
BY GENERATION, AGE, AND SEX

Generation and Age	Sex		Total
	Males	Females	
All Ages			
First Generation	378	422	800
Second Generation	768	744	1,512
Mixed Parentage	227	287	514
Third Generation	932	936	1,868
TOTAL*	2,332	2,404	4,736
Under 15 Age Group			
First Generation	13	9	22
Second Generation	18	11	29
Mixed Parentage	58	55	113
Third Generation	555	502	1,057
15-24 Age Group			
First Generation	11	7	18
Second Generation	16	15	31
Mixed Parentage	47	42	89
Third Generation	228	220	448
25-44 Age Group			
First Generation	34	50	84
Second Generation	247	250	497
Mixed Parentage	85	136	221
Third Generation	133	175	308
45-64 Age Group			
First Generation	161	181	342
Second Generation	436	407	843
Mixed Parentage	34	51	85
Third Generation	15	34	49
65 and Over Age Group			
First Generation	159	175	334
Second Generation	51	61	112
Mixed Parentage	3	3	6
Third Generation	1	5	6

*Includes small number of unknown generation status.

TABLE A-2

NUMBER OF RESPONDENTS IN SAMPLE
BY GENERATION, AGE, AND RESIDENCE

Generation and Age	Residence			
	Older Urban	Newer Urban	Suburban	Total
All Ages				
First Generation	300	354	146	800
Second Generation	275	817	420	1,512
Mixed Parentage	78	236	200	514
Third Generation	215	947	706	1,868
TOTAL*	876	2,377	1,483	4,736
Under 15 Age Group				
First Generation	6	15	1	22
Second Generation	4	15	10	29
Mixed Parentage	17	30	66	113
Third Generation	109	519	429	1,057
15-24 Age Group				
First Generation	7	11	–	18
Second Generation	8	14	9	31
Mixed Parentage	17	43	29	89
Third Generation	82	246	120	448
25-44 Age Group				
First Generation	13	38	33	84
Second Generation	70	236	191	497
Mixed Parentage	24	107	90	221
Third Generation	18	154	136	308
45-64 Age Group				
First Generation	120	148	74	342
Second Generation	164	479	200	843
Mixed Parentage	19	51	15	85
Third Generation	6	23	20	49
65 and Over Age Group				
First Generation	154	142	38	334
Second Generation	29	73	10	112
Mixed Parentage	1	5	–	6
Third Generation	–	5	1	6

*Includes small number of unknown generation status.

TABLE A-3

NUMBER OF RESPONDENTS IN SAMPLE BY GENERATION, AGE, AND EDUCATION

	Education					
Generation and Age	Elementary or Less	High School	College	Postgraduate	No Information	Total
All Ages						
First Generation	323	248	97	44	48	760
Second Generation	89	737	415	202	9	1,452
Mixed Parentage	3	108	140	60	1	312
Third Generation	4	114	159	83	3	363
TOTAL*	422	1,224	819	391	65	2,921
25-44 Age Group						
First Generation	7	37	23	17	–	84
Second Generation	3	219	186	88	1	497
Mixed Parentage	–	73	101	46	1	221
Third Generation	–	84	147	76	1	308
45-64 Age Group						
First Generation	99	151	57	22	13	342
Second Generation	59	462	216	102	4	843
Mixed Parentage	2	32	38	13	–	85
Third Generation	1	27	12	7	2	49
65 and Over Age Group						
First Generation	217	60	17	5	35	334
Second Generation	27	56	13	12	4	112
Mixed Parentage	1	3	1	1	–	6
Third Generation	3	3	–	–	–	6

***Includes small number of unknown generation status.**

TABLE A-4

NUMBER OF RESPONDENTS IN SAMPLE BY GENERATION, AGE, AND RELIGIOUS IDENTIFICATION

Generation and Age	Religious Identification Orthodox	Conservative	Reform	Other	Total
All Ages					
First Generation	334	326	100	40	800
Second Generation	239	909	305	59	1,512
Mixed Parentage	41	316	135	22	514
Third Generation	133	1,049	571	115	1,868
TOTAL*	751	2,623	1,115	247	4,736
Under 15 Age Group					
First Generation	13	1	7	1	22
Second Generation	12	12	4	1	29
Mixed Parentage	8	73	20	12	113
Third Generation	72	611	313	61	1,057
15-24 Age Group					
First Generation	9	3	5	1	18
Second Generation	10	12	9	–	31
Mixed Parentage	11	66	9	3	89
Third Generation	38	260	130	20	448
25-44 Age Group					
First Generation	19	42	16	7	84
Second Generation	62	317	103	15	497
Mixed Parentage	17	138	61	5	221
Third Generation	14	160	113	21	308
45-64 Age Group					
First Generation	120	168	38	16	342
Second Generation	135	517	157	34	843
Mixed Parentage	5	36	42	2	85
Third Generation	9	16	14	10	49
65 and Over Age Group					
First Generation	173	112	34	15	334
Second Generation	20	51	32	9	112
Mixed Parentage	–	3	3	–	6
Third Generation	–	2	1	3	6

*Includes small number of unknown generation status.

TABLE A-5

NUMBER OF MARRIED WOMEN IN SAMPLE BY GENERATION AND SELECTED CHARACTERISTICS*

	Generation				
	First	Second	Older Third	Younger Third	Total
Total†	203	563	324	257	1,347
Religious Identification					
Orthodox	86	120	36	12	254
Conservative	75	304	184	160	723
Reform	32	112	83	76	303
Social Class					
I	24	78	74	89	265
II	35	290	153	112	590
III	42	122	87	48	299
Occupation of Husband					
Professional	10	75	79	61	225
Manager	45	232	126	94	497
Clerical and Sales	20	106	81	77	284
Blue Collar	27	84	29	17	157
Education of Women‡					
Graduate School	–	29	33	39	101
Completed College	–	42	45	45	132
Some College	–	95	71	86	252
Completed High School	52	271	157	87	567
Some High School	88	56	18	–	162
Elementary School	50	64	–	–	114
Education of Husband‡					
Graduate School	–	69	75	78	222
Completed College	–	50	51	66	167
Some College	–	65	58	56	179
Completed High School	24	150	104	50	328
Some High School	39	69	26	–	134
Elementary School	27	84	–	–	111

*For definition of generation and specific characteristics see Chapter 6.
†Totals for specific variables vary and do not add to total, due to lack of necessary information for classification, e.g., current occupation of husband.
‡See Table 6-4.

TABLE A-6

NUMBER OF HOUSEHOLDS IN SAMPLE BY GENERATION AND AGE OF HEAD OF HOUSEHOLD

Generation and Age	Total
All Ages*	
First Generation	411
Second Generation	854
Mixed Parentage	45
Third Generation	171
TOTAL†	1,556
25-44 Age Group	
First Generation	31
Second Generation	267
Mixed Parentage	29
Third Generation	134
45-64 Age Group	
First Generation	185
Second Generation	505
Mixed Parentage	14
Third Generation	16
65 and Over Age Group	
First Generation	195
Second Generation	77
Mixed Parentage	2
Third Generation	3

***Generation categories under All Ages include 23 households with the head less than 25 years of age. Of these, 5 are second generation and 18 are third generation.**
†The total, including the households with heads below age 25, is 1,481. There were, in addition, 75 households where age or generation status was unknown, yielding a total of 1,556.

A P P E N D I X B

Sampling Error

Since the survey was based on a sample of the total population rather than on a study of the entire universe of the Greater Providence Jewish community, the resulting statistical figures are subject to sampling variability. This means that the results obtained on the basis of the sample are not necessarily identical with what would have been obtained had the entire universe been studied. The amount of sampling variability for percentages can be estimated from the standard errors shown in Table B-1. This table does not reflect the effect of errors in response or those arising in the collection and processing of the survey materials; it relates only to the sampling variability.[1]

Chances are 95 out of 100 that the difference due to sampling variability between a figure based on the survey statistics and the figure that would have been obtained from a complete count of the population is less than the standard error indicated in Table B-1. These .95 probability limits are obtained through use of the formula for sampling error:

$$2\sqrt{\frac{pq}{N}}.$$

For example, the estimated percentage of first-generation males who are professionals is 15.7. This percentage is based on a total of 378 first-generation males in the sample population. Table B-1 tells us that with a sample base of this size (approximately equal to the column headed 400) and a sample percentage of 15.7 (which is closest to 20 or 80 in the first column), a sampling error of up to 4.0 percentage points can be expected at the 95 per cent level. This means that had repeated random samples of size 400 been taken, the chances are that in 95 out of every 100 samples, the percentage of professionals would have fallen within the range of 15.7 ± 4.0 or between 11.7 and 19.7 per cent. Only 5 times out of 100 would the percentage have been less than 11.7 or greater than 19.7.

Since this investigation is most concerned with differences among generation groups, the researcher and the reader must decide how much confidence to place in the differences observed between two measures relating to various subgroups of the population. Some of these differences may be due to sampling error. For example, 15.7 per cent of the 378 first-generation males are professionals, compared to only 23.7 per cent of the

[1] For more detailed discussion of sampling variability, see any standard textbook on statistical procedures, e.g., Hubert M. Blalock, *Social Statistics* (New York: McGraw-Hill Book Company, 1960), pp. 89-186.

768 second-generation group. Is this difference sufficiently large so that one can have confidence that it is not due to chance (sampling error) alone? Table B-2 provides a basis for answering this question. It indicates the approximate size of the difference which must exist between two sample groups if there is to be no more than 5 chances out of 100 that the difference could arise by chance alone.

The values for Table B-2 were obtained by use of the formula:

$$2\sqrt{(pq)\left(\frac{1}{N_1}+\frac{1}{N_2}\right)}$$

where p is the proportion approximating those being compared. Table B-2 tells us that for percentages around 20 per cent where the first sample (N_1) is based on almost 400 cases and the second sample (N_2) on close to 800 cases, a difference of 4.8 percentage points is significant at the .05 level. Since the difference obtained was larger than this, being 8 percentage points (15.7 compared to 23.7), we can conclude that a difference this great between first and second generation could have arisen by chance alone less than 5 times out of 10, and we therefore regard it as statistically significant.

To facilitate the comparisons between the various arithmetic means used in the fertility analysis of Chapter 6, Appendix Table B-3 is also set up so that significance tests for means could be made with minimum difficulty. This table for total number of children ever born is based on the standard deviation and the number of cases.

The following approximate formula for the standard error of a difference between subsample means is used. The assumption is that the standard deviations of two subsamples are approximately that for the entire sample.

(1)
$$SD\sqrt{\frac{1}{N_1}+\frac{1}{N_2}}$$

(2) Let N_1 be the smaller of the two samples

$$SD\sqrt{\frac{1}{N_1}+\frac{1}{N_2}} \leq SD\sqrt{\frac{2}{N_1}} = 1.4\ SD\sqrt{\frac{1}{N_1}}$$

(3) Let $K_1 = 2\,(1.4)\,SD$ or $2.8\ SD$.

Therefore, if $|\overline{X}_1 - \overline{X}_2| \geq \frac{K_1}{\sqrt{N_1}}$ then the difference between means will be treated as statistically significant at the .05 level. This procedure is a conservative estimate when N_1 is appreciably smaller than N_2.

The standard deviations and K_1 are presented in Table B-3. To determine whether a difference between two means is significant, take the smaller of the two N's, look down the left-hand column to find a corresponding N. If the difference between the two means is greater or equal to the calculated figure under Column $\frac{K_1}{\sqrt{N_1}}$ the difference is significant at the .05 level of confidence. For example, the average number of children born to 270 second-generation mothers who completed high school is 1.8 and the average number born to 42 second-generation mothers who completed college is 2.1. The smaller of the two N's is 42. The difference between the two means is 0.3 children. Table B-3 indicates that N of 42 lies between N_1 of 36 and 49, which corresponds to $\frac{K_1}{\sqrt{N_1}}$ of 0.54 and 0.46. Since the observed difference in means of 0.3 is less than both these values, we conclude that the difference is not statistically significant at the .05 level.

In this study, as in many other sociological studies,[2] the size of many of the subgroups of the population between which comparisons are made is so small that the resulting sampling errors for percentages or averages based on them are quite large. As a result, it is often not possible to attach statistical significance to the differences between such subgroups. Yet, even under such circumstances consistent patterns or trends emerge from comparisons of subgroups, as, for example, when the level of education rises consistently by generation level or the proportion of foreign born declines by age group. When such consistencies in trends or patterns exist, the patterns themselves have been regarded as significant, even though specific values do not meet the standards of statistical significance.

[2] *Cf.* Ronald Freedman, Pascal K. Whelpton, and Arthur A. Campbell, *Family Planning, Sterility, and Population Growth* (New York: McGraw-Hill Book Company, 1959), pp. 435-59; Gerhard Lenski, *The Religious Factor* (Garden City, N.Y.: Doubleday & Company, Inc., 1961).

TABLE B-1

APPROXIMATION TO STANDARD ERROR OF ESTIMATED PERCENTAGES

(Range of 95 chances out of 100)

Estimated Percentage	Numerical Base of Percentage (Number of Respondents)																			
	25	50	75	100	150	200	250	300	400	500	750	1000	1500	2000	2500	3000	3500	4000	4500	5000
2 or 98	5.6	4.0	3.2	2.8	2.3	2.0	1.8	1.6	1.4	1.2	1.0	0.9	0.7	0.6	0.6	0.5	0.5	0.4	0.4	0.4
5 or 95	8.6	6.2	5.0	4.4	3.5	3.1	2.7	2.5	2.2	1.9	1.6	1.4	1.1	1.0	0.9	0.8	0.7	0.7	0.6	0.6
10 or 90	12.0	8.5	6.9	6.0	4.9	4.2	3.8	3.5	3.0	2.7	2.2	1.9	1.5	1.3	1.2	1.1	1.0	1.0	0.9	0.8
20 or 80	16.0	11.3	9.2	8.0	6.5	5.6	5.1	4.6	4.0	3.6	2.9	2.5	2.1	1.8	1.6	1.5	1.4	1.3	1.2	1.1
25 or 75	17.3	12.2	10.0	8.7	7.1	6.1	5.5	5.0	4.3	3.9	3.2	2.7	2.2	1.9	1.7	1.6	1.5	1.4	1.3	1.2
30 or 70	18.3	13.0	10.6	9.2	7.5	6.5	5.8	5.3	4.6	4.1	3.3	2.9	2.4	2.0	1.8	1.7	1.6	1.5	1.4	1.3
40 or 60	19.6	13.9	11.3	9.8	8.0	6.9	6.2	5.6	4.9	4.4	3.6	3.1	2.5	2.2	2.0	1.8	1.7	1.6	1.5	1.4
50	20.0	14.1	11.5	10.0	8.2	7.1	6.3	5.8	5.0	4.5	3.6	3.2	2.6	2.2	2.0	1.8	1.7	1.6	1.5	1.4

TABLE B-2

APPROXIMATION OF SAMPLING ERRORS OF DIFFERENCES BETWEEN PERCENTAGES

(Approximate differences needed for .05 significance*)

Number of Respondents	Number of Respondents 1000	800	600	500	400	300	200	100	50
				For Percentages around .05 and .95					
1000	1.9	2.0	2.2	2.3	2.5	2.8	3.3	4.5	–
800		2.1	2.3	2.4	2.6	2.9	3.4	4.6	–
600			2.5	2.6	2.8	3.0	3.5	4.6	–
500				2.7	2.9	3.1	3.6	4.7	–
400					3.0	3.3	3.7	4.8	–
300						3.5	3.9	5.0	–
200							4.3	5.3	–
100								6.1	–
				For Percentages around .10 and .90					
1000	2.6	2.8	3.0	3.2	3.5	3.9	4.6	6.2	8.6
800		2.9	3.2	3.4	3.6	4.0	4.7	6.3	8.7
600			3.4	3.6	3.8	4.2	4.8	6.4	8.8
500				3.7	4.0	4.3	4.9	6.5	8.8
400					4.2	4.5	5.1	6.6	8.9
300						4.8	5.4	6.8	9.2
200							5.9	7.3	9.4
100								8.4	10.3
50									12.0
				For Percentages around .20 and .80					
1000	3.5	3.7	4.0	4.3	4.6	5.2	6.1	8.3	11.5
800		3.9	4.2	4.5	4.8	5.3	6.2	8.4	11.6
600			4.5	4.8	5.1	5.6	6.4	8.5	11.7
500				5.0	5.3	5.7	6.6	8.6	11.8
400					5.6	6.0	6.8	8.8	11.9
300						6.4	7.2	9.1	12.1
200							7.9	9.7	12.6
100								11.2	13.8
50									16.1
				For Percentages around .30 and .70					
1000	4.0	4.3	4.6	4.9	5.3	5.9	7.0	9.5	13.1
800		4.5	4.9	5.1	5.5	6.1	7.1	9.6	13.2
600			5.2	5.4	5.8	6.4	7.4	9.8	13.4
500				5.7	6.0	6.6	7.6	9.9	13.5
400					6.4	6.9	7.8	10.1	13.6
300						7.4	8.2	10.5	13.9
200							9.0	11.1	14.4
100								12.9	15.8
50									18.4

***The chances are only 5 in 100 that in a complete enumeration the differences obtained between two percentages would differ from the estimated difference by as much as the percentage value indicated in the table.**

TABLE B-3

SIGNIFICANCE TEST FOR NUMBER OF CHILDREN

(Approximate critical ratio $K_1 \div \sqrt{N_1}$ needed for .05 significance)

		Generation Groups			
	Total	First	Second	Older Third	Younger Third
N_1	$K_1 \div \sqrt{N_1}$*	$K_1 \div \sqrt{N_1}$	$K_1 \div \sqrt{N_1}$	$K_1 \div \sqrt{N_1}$	$K_1 \div \sqrt{N_1}$
16	.86	1.06	.80	.69	.80
25	.69	.85	.64	.55	.64
30	.63	.77	.58	.50	.57
36	.57	.71	.54	.46	.53
49	.49	.61	.46	.40	.45
64	.43	.53	.40	.35	.40
81	.38	.47	.36	.31	.35
100	.34	.43	.32	.28	.32
121	.31	.38	.29	.25	.29
144	.29	.35	.27	.23	.27
169	.26	.33	.25	.21	.24
196	.24	.30	.23	.20	.23
225	.23	.28	.21	.18	.21
SD	1.25	1.55	1.17	1.01	1.16

*$K_1 = 2\ (1.4)\ SD$

APPENDIX C

Interview Schedule

GENERAL JEWISH COMMITTEE OF PROVIDENCE, INC.

POPULATION SURVEY

THE JEWISH COMMUNITY

OF

GREATER PROVIDENCE

1963

NAME OF FAMILY ....

ADDRESS ....
(Street)

....
(City or Town)

TELEPHONE ....

Code Number

RECORD OF CALLS

Call Number	Date	Result (Code)	Comments	Make Next Call Date	Time	Interviewer's Name	Checked
1.							
2.							
3.							
4.							

1. Refusal (Give reason)
2. Non-Jewish Family
3. Moved, Address Unknown
4. Moved, New Address ....
5. Cannot be contacted
6. Interview Incomplete
7. Interview Complete

JEWISH POPULATION SURVEY

PURPOSE OF STUDY

The population of our area has changed during the last decade. Many people have moved from one place to another and from the metropolitan centers to the suburbs. There has never been a Population Study of the Jewish Community of the Greater Providence area. Therefore, no up-to-date information exists on how many Jewish residents there are, their ages and other characteristics, and where they are located. This data is extremely important for sound planning on the part of our social agencies, congregations and other Jewish institutions. The result of this study will vitally affect the services which you and your children will receive in the years to come.

Many other Jewish communities have conducted such studies in recent years. Among them are Rochester, Worcester, Los Angeles, San Francisco, Washington, New Orleans and Minneapolis.

HOW THE INFORMATION WILL BE USED

All interviews will be treated strictly confidential. The name and address face sheets will be removed before coding and punching of IBM cards. The final report will deal with mass data only. The executive Committee has made the following policy decisions by unanimous vote "In the Population Study, the information obtained with regard to the names of the respondents, shall be completely confidential and shall not be used for any purposes other than the survey."

Information secured by this study will guide our community in planning for the young, the middle-aged, the aged, and for all services – cultural and recreational programs, health, Temple and Synagogue, Jewish education, and the like.

It will help to answer questions about where new facilities should be located, whether there should be extension services, and what new programs should be initiated.

YOUR COOPERATION REQUESTED

Responses to the interviewers are completely voluntary. However, the success of the Population Study will depend upon the cooperation of everyone contacted by the interviewers. Only by securing a representative picture of the Jewish Community and its needs can the Jewish institutions and organizations serve best those in their geographic areas.

JOSEPH W. RESS, GJC President
JOSEPH GALKIN, Executive Director

ARTHUR J. LEVY, Chairman, GJC Community Planning Committee
JUDGE FRANK LICHT, Chairman, GJC Population Study
PROFESSOR SIDNEY GOLDSTEIN, Survey Consultant
MRS. JOSEPH E. ADELSON, Coordinator of Volunteer Interviewers

(1) NAMES OF ALL PERSONS LIVING IN THIS HOUSEHOLD (Circle Informant)		
First	Middle Initial	Last if different
1.		
2.		
3.		
4.		
5.		
6.		
7.		
8.		

Code Number

JEWISH POPULATION SURVEY

						PLACE OF BIRTH				MIGRATION HISTORY			
(2) **WHICH OF THESE PERSONS IS JEWISH?** 1. Jewish 2. Catholic 3. Protestant 4. Other	(3) **RELATION TO HEAD OF HOUSE-HOLD** 1. Head 2. Wife 3. Son 4. Daughter 5. Other (Specify)	(4) **SEX** 1. Male 2. Female	(5) **DATE OF BIRTH** Mo. | Yr.	(6) **AGE AT LAST BIRTH-DAY** (Use card A)	(7) Where was he born? Name of State, if U.S. born; Name of country if foreign-born	(8) If foreign-born, year of arrival in U.S.	(9) If born in U.S., country of birth of both parents	(10) If one or both parents were born in the U.S., give country of birth of grandparents	(11) If not born in R.I., year of arrival in R. I.	(12) Since what year has he lived in this city or town? (Circle date if born here)	(13) Since what year has he lived at this address? (Circle date if born here)	(14) Where did he live before moving to this address? Give street and town, if R. I. Give town and state, if elsewhere
							1. 2.	1. 2. 3. 4.				
							1. 2.	1. 2. 3. 4.				
							1. 2.	1. 2. 3. 4.				
							1. 2.	1. 2. 3. 4.				
							1. 2.	1. 2. 3. 4.				
							1. 2.	1. 2. 3. 4.				
							1. 2.	1. 2. 3. 4.				
							1. 2.	1. 2. 3. 4.				

Code Number [ ]

JEWISH POPULATION SURVEY

First Name	MARITAL STATUS				EDUCATION			VETERANS STATUS	LABOR FORCE STATUS	OCCUPATION							
	(15) Is he 1. Single 2. Married 3. Widowed 4. Separated 5. Divorced (Ask only for persons 14 years old and over)	(16) If ever married Has he been married more than once? 1. Yes 2. No	Date of (first) marriage Mo. & Year	(17) If ever married, give total number of children ever born, not counting stillbirths (Women only)	(18) What was the last year(grade) he completed? 1. None 2. 1-4 3. 5-7 4. 8 5. 9-11 ⎤ High 6. 12 ⎦ Sch. 7. 13-15 ⎤ 8. 16 ⎥ College 9. 17 & over ⎦	(19) Is he still in school? 1. Yes 2. No	If yes, give year(grade) Year (grade)	(20) Has he served in the armed forces? 1. Yes 2. No (Ask only for persons 18 years old and over)	(21) At present is he 1. Working for pay or profit 2. Working without pay in family business 3. Going to school 4. Keeping house 5. In armed forces 6. Unemployed 7. Retired 8. Other (specify) (Ask only for persons 14 years old and over)	(22) If now working, what kind of work does he do?	Code	(23) Is that 1. Full time 2. Part time 3. Other (specify)	(24) Does he work 1. For himself 2. For someone else 3. Other (specify)	(25) If not now working (unemployed, armed forces, retired or housewife) When did he stop work? Mo.	Yr.	(26) What was the last kind of work he did?	Code
1.																	
2.																	
3.																	
4.																	
5.																	
6.																	
7.																	
8.																	

Code Number

JEWISH POPULATION SURVEY

First Name	ORGANIZATION MEMBERSHIP		CONGRE-GATIONAL AFFILIATION	RELIGIOUS IDENTIFI-CATION	JEWISH EDUCATION												SYNAGOGUE ATTENDANCE	COMMUNITY SERVICES
	(27) To which of these Jewish organiza-tions does he belong? (Show Card B and insert code number(s))	(28) To which of these non-sectarian organiza-tions does he belong? (Show Card C and insert code number(s))	(29) Is he a member of a synagogue or temple? If yes, which one(s)? (Use Card D and insert code number(s)	(30) Does he consider himself 1. Orthodox 2. Conservative 3. Reform 4. Yiddishist 5. Secular 6. Unitarian 7. Christian 8. Other (specify)	(31) Has he received any Jewish education? 1. Yes 2. No	(32) If yes, indicate number of years completed in each of the following, including this year.							(33) Is he now enrolled? If yes, indicate kind of school (See Q 32)	(34) For any child under 15 who has not had any Jewish education, ask: Are you planning to give him a Jewish education?	If yes:		(35) During the last 12 months, how many times has he attended synagogue or temple services? 1. Not at all 2. 1-3 times a year 3. 4-11 times a year 4. Once a month 5. 2-3 times a month 6. Once a week 7. Several times a week	(36) Has he used any of the following Jewish Community Services within the last five years? (Show Card E and insert code number (s))
						1. Sunday Sch.	2. Hebrew Sch.	3. Day Sch.	4. Private Tutor	5. Yiddish Sch.	6. Adult Ed.	7. Other (specify)		1. Yes 2. No	What kind? (See Q 32)	When will he begin?		
1.																		
2.																		
3.																		
4.																		
5.																		
6.																		
7.																		
8.																		

Code Number [ ]

JEWISH POPULATION SURVEY

(37) Do you or any member of your household anticipate using any of these services in the next five years? (Show Card E and circle code number.) 1 2 3 4 5 6 7 8 9 .... (specify)

(38) Are any children of the head of this household and/or wife not living at home? 1. Yes .... 2. No ....
IF YES:

Name	Date of Birth		Place of Residence: City and State	Employment Status (See Q 21)	Kind of Work		Marital Status (See Q 15)	If living outside survey area: Does he plan to return to this area?			If Yes,	
	Mo.	Yr.				Code		Y	N	DK	When?	To What Town?
1.												
2.												
3.												
4.												
5.												

(39) Home ownership: 1) Own .... 2) Rent .... 3) Other ....

(40) a. Are you planning to move within the next year? 1)Yes ..... 2)No ..... 3)DK ......
b. Are you planning to move within the next 5 years? 1)Yes ..... 2)No ..... 3)DK ......
If yes to (a) or (b), where? ....
If Providence, give section of city ....
If other R.I., give town or city ....
If outside R.I., give city and state ....

(41) Languages spoken in home other than English:
1) None .... 2) Yiddish .... 3) Hebrew .... 4) Other ....

(42) The following things some Jewish families do and some don't do. We are interested in finding out how many families do each of them.

	Always	Usually	Sometimes	Never	No Answer
a. Light candles Friday night	1	2	3	4	5
b. Have or attend a Seder on Passover	1	2	3	4	5
c. Buy meat at a kosher butcher	1	2	3	4	5
d. Use separate dishes for meat and dairy food	1	2	3	4	5
e. Light Chanukah candles	1	2	3	4	5

(43) a. Intermarriage: Is any member of this household or any children of the head of this household married to a person not born Jewish? 1) Yes .... 2) No ....
b. If yes, specify which one(s): 1st. .... 2nd. ....
c. Is his or her spouse converted to Judaism?
1st. 1) Yes .... 2) No ....; 2nd 1) Yes .... 2) No ....

(44) a. Is any member of this household a shut-in because of poor health?
1) Yes .... 2) No ....
b. If yes, specify which one(s): c. How long has he been a shut-in?
1. ....
2. ....

(45) Do you know of any Jewish families who have moved into the Providence area within the last year? Please list their names and addresses below.

1. ....

2. ....

3. ....

4. ....

Selected Bibliography

American Jewish Yearbook. Philadelphia: Jewish Publication Society of America. Published annually since 1900 by the American Jewish Committee.

Barron, Milton L., ed., *American Minorities*. New York: Alfred A. Knopf, Inc., 1962.

Billings, John S., "Vital Statistics of the Jews in the United States," *Census Bulletin*, No. 19 (December 30, 1889).

Cahnman, Werner J., ed., *Intermarriage and Jewish Life*. New York: The Herzl Press, 1963.

Davis, Moshe, *The Emergence of Conservative Judaism*. Philadelphia: Jewish Publication Society of America, 1965.

Dresner, Samuel H., *The Jew in American Life*. New York: Crown Publishers, Inc., 1963.

Finkelstein, Louis, ed., *The Jews: Their History, Culture, and Religion* (2nd ed.). Philadelphia: Jewish Publication Society of America, 1960.

Glazer, Nathan, *American Judaism*. Chicago: University of Chicago Press, 1957.

———, and Daniel P. Moynihan, *Beyond the Melting Pot*. Cambridge, Mass.: The M.I.T. Press, 1963.

Glick, Paul C., "Intermarriage and Fertility Patterns Among Persons in Major Religious Groups," *Eugenics Quarterly*, VII (March, 1960), 31-38.

Goldberg, Nathan, "Occupational Patterns of American Jews," *Jewish Review*, III, No. 4 (1946).

Gordon, Albert I., *Jews in Suburbia*. Boston: Beacon Press, 1959.

———, *Jews in Transition*. Minneapolis: University of Minnesota Press, 1949.

———, *Intermarriage*. Boston: Beacon Press, 1963.

Gordon, Milton M., *Assimilation in American Life*. New York: Oxford University Press, Inc., 1964.

Gorwitz, Kurt, "Jewish Mortality in St. Louis and St. Louis County, 1955-1957," *Jewish Social Studies*, XXIV (October, 1962), 248-54.

Hansen, Marcus Lee, "The Third Generation in America," *Commentary*, XIV (November, 1952), 492-500.

Herberg, Will, *Protestant-Catholic-Jew*. Garden City, N.Y.: Doubleday & Company, Inc., Anchor Books, 1955.

Janowsky, Oscar, ed., *The American Jew: A Reappraisal*. Philadelphia: Jewish Publication Society of America, 1964.

Joseph, Samuel, *Jewish Immigration to the United States from 1881-1910*. New York: Columbia University Press, 1914.

Kramer, Judith R., and Seymour Leventman, *Children of the Gilded Ghetto*. New Haven: Yale University Press, 1961.

Lazerwitz, Bernard, and Louis Rowitz, "The Three-Generations Hypothesis," *American Journal of Sociology,* LXIX (March, 1964), 529-38.

Lenski, Gerhard, *The Religious Factor.* Garden City, N.Y.: Doubleday & Company, Inc., Anchor Books, 1963.

Levin, Ezra, "The Jewish Suburban Movement in Metropolitan New York," *King's Crown Essays* (Spring, 1955), pp. 9-20.

Nahirny, Vladimir C., and Joshua A. Fishman, "American Immigrant Groups: Ethnic Identification and the Problem of Generations," *The Sociological Review,* XIII (November, 1965), 311-26.

Pope, Liston, "Religion and the Class Structure," in *Class, Status and Power,* eds. Reinhard Bendix and Seymour M. Lipset. Glencoe, Illinois: The Free Press, 1953.

Rosenbaum, S. "A Contribution to the Study of Vital and Other Statistics of Jews in the United Kingdom," *Journal of the Royal Statistical Society,* XLVIII (September, 1905).

Rosenberg, Stuart, *The Search for Jewish Identity in America.* Garden City, N.Y.: Doubleday & Company, Inc., 1965.

Rosenthal, Erich, "Jewish Fertility in the United States," *Eugenics Quarterly,* VIII (December, 1961), 198-217.

———, "Studies of Jewish Intermarriage in the United States," *American Jewish Yearbook* (1963), LXIV, 5-53.

Seidman, H., L. Garfinkel, and L. Craig, "Death Rates in New York City by Socio-economic Class and Religious Groups and by Country of Birth, 1949-1951," *Jewish Journal of Sociology,* IV (December, 1962), 254-72.

Sherman, C. Bezalel, *The Jew Within American Society.* Detroit: Wayne State University Press, 1965.

Sklare, Marshall, *Conservative Judaism.* Glencoe, Illinois: The Free Press, 1955.

———, ed., *The Jews: Social Patterns of an American Group.* Glencoe, Illinois: The Free Press, 1958.

Spiegelman, Mortimer, "The Longevity of Jews in Canada, 1940-1942," *Population Studies,* II (December, 1948), 292-304.

Strodtbeck, Fred L., Margaret R. McDonald, and Bernard C. Rosen, "Evaluation of Occupations: A Reflection of Jewish and Italian Mobility Differences," *American Sociological Review,* XXII (October, 1957), 546-53.

Tumin, Melvin M., "Conservative Trends in American Jewish Life," *Judaism,* XIII, No. 2 (1964), 131-42.

U.S. Bureau of the Census, "Religion Reported by the Civilian Population of The United States, March 1957," *Current Population Reports,* Series P-20, No. 79 (February 2, 1958).

Wirth, Louis, *The Ghetto.* Chicago: University of Chicago Press, 1928.

Zborowski, Mark, and Elizabeth Herzog, *Life Is With People.* New York: International Universities Press, 1952.

Author Index

Adler, Cyrus, 1
American Jewish Yearbook, 1, 2, 37
Antonovsky, Aaron, 117

Bachi, Roberto, 120
Baltzell, E. Digby, 2, 10
Baron, Salo, 137
Beals, Ralph, 4
Bigman, Stanley K., 80
Billings, John S., 105, 116, 138
Bogue, Donald J., 65, 80
Boraisha, Menachem, 225
Bresler, Jack, 167
Broom, Leonard, 4
Bumpass, Larry, 119
Burchinal, Lee G., 165
Burgess, Ernest, 101, 109
Burr, Nelson R., 10

Cahnman, Werner J., 153
Campbell, Arthur A., 105, 115, 118, 123, 125, 133, 134, 136
Carter, Hugh, 101, 111
Chambliss, William J., 96
Chancellor, Loren E., 165
Chein, Isidore, 10
Chenkin, Alvin, 46, 63
Council of Jewish Federations and Welfare Funds, 18, 117
Craig, L., 138
Current Population Survey: March, 1957, 15, 41, 117, 133, 152, 154

Davis, Kingsley, 12, 13, 101
Davis, Moshe, 176
Dawidowicz, Lucy C., 10
Dean, John P., 10
Detroit Area Studies, 122, 192

Eisenstadt, S. N., 6, 12
Engelman, Uriah Z., 15, 120, 121, 126, 212, 213

Fishman, Joshua A., 226
Freedman, Maurice, 120
Freedman, Ronald, 105, 115, 118, 119, 125, 129, 133, 134

Gallup Public Opinion Poll, 188, 192
Gans, Herbert, 8, 175, 202, 226
Garfinkel, L., 138
Gay, Ruth, 24, 36
Glazer, Nathan, 3, 7, 9, 10, 11, 16, 17, 24, 63, 173, 175, 212
Glick, Paul, 15, 101, 105, 106, 111, 117, 123
Glock, Charles Y., 172, 175
Goldberg, David, 106, 119, 122, 123, 187
Goldberg, Nathan, 1, 15, 78, 120, 121, 135
Goldscheider, Calvin, 6, 119, 124, 125, 130, 134
Goldstein, Sidney, 19, 21, 22, 61, 125, 176
Good, Dorothy, 15
Goode, William J., 101
Gordon, Albert, 153, 202
Gordon, Milton, 4-5, 6, 7, 8, 12, 16, 17, 62-63, 152, 170, 206, 226, 241
Gorwitz, K., 138
Gould, Julius, 11
Grabill, Wilson H., 123
Grayzel, Solomon, 10
Greenberg, Myer, 126, 127, 130
Greenblum, Joseph, 17

Hajnal, John, 101
Handlin, Oscar, 8
Hansen, Marcus Lee, 8, 175
Heberle, Rudolf, 12, 123
Heiss, Jerold S., 153
Herberg, Will, 2, 3, 6, 7, 8, 9, 10, 11, 16, 17, 175, 179, 187, 226, 239
Herriott, Robert E., 66
Hersch, Liebman, 120
Hertzberg, Arthur, 202
Herzog, Elizabeth, 7, 190
Hillman, Karen, 111

Jaffe, A. J., 116
Joseph, Samuel, 36

Kahn, Lothar, 10, 11
Kelly, A. Dennis, 96
Kennedy, Ruby Jo Reeves, 153, 156
Kiser, Clyde V., 34, 117, 123, 127, 166
Kitsuse, John, 4
Koenig, Samuel, 10, 175
Kramer, Judith R., 8, 9, 13, 16, 85, 187

Landis, Benson Y., 15
Landis, Judson T., 165
La-Violette, Forrest E., 10
Lazerwitz, Bernard, 39, 111, 174, 175, 180, 187, 188, 190
Lenski, Gerhard, 10, 16, 102, 157, 172, 175, 187, 188, 192
Leventman, Seymour, 8, 9, 13, 16, 85, 187
Lewis-Fanning, E., 120
Liebman, Charles S., 176
Linton, Ralph, 123
Lipset, Seymour M., 175
Locke, Harvey, 101, 109
Lunde, Anders S., 136
Lynd, Helen, 10
Lynd, Robert, 10

McDonald, Margaret R., 72
McEntire, Davis, 10

Maier, Joseph, 154
Mannheim, Karl, 13, 39, 123
Massarik, Fred, 152
Mayer, Kurt B., 21, 22, 61, 62, 120, 125, 129
Mishler, Elliot G., 115, 168
Moynihan, Daniel P., 3, 9, 10, 11, 63

Nahirny, Vladimir C., 226
Nam, Charles B., 66, 96
Neustatter, Hannah, 120
Notestein, Frank, 117

Packard, Vance, 10
Parke, Robert, 101, 123
Patterson, John E., 105, 115, 118, 123, 133, 134, 136
Pearl, Raymond, 117
Petersen, William, 4, 105, 133
Plateris, Alexander, 101, 111
Polsky, Howard, 202
Pope, Liston, 81
Potter, Robert G., Jr., 115, 116, 118, 123, 125, 127, 130, 134, 168
Powers, Mary G., 96

Rhode Island Census of 1905, 116, 121
Rhode Island Jewish Historical Notes, 25, 27
Rhodes, A. Lewis, 66
Ringer, Benjamin, 10, 17
Rosen, Bernard C., 72
Rosenbaum, S., 151
Rosenberg, Louis, 120, 153
Rosenberg, Stuart, 17, 173, 212
Rosenthal, Erich, 133, 153, 155, 163, 169
Rowitz, Louis, 39, 111, 174, 175, 180, 187, 188, 190

Sagi, Philip C., 115, 116, 118, 123, 125, 127, 130, 134, 168
Schachter, Joseph P., 123
Seidman, H., 138
Seligman, Ben, 117
Sharp, Harry, 122, 187
Sherman, C. Bezalel, 3, 17, 37, 40, 77-78
Sklare, Marshall, 10, 16, 17, 153, 176, 190
Smit, John W., 105, 118, 133
Solomon, Erwin S., 126
Spengler, J. J., 116
Spiegelman, Mortimer, 120, 140-41, 144
Srole, Leo, 10, 39
Stark, Rodney, 172, 175
Steinberg, Stephen, 175
Stix, R. K., 117
Strodtbeck, Fred, 72, 102
Sutker, Solomon, 10

Thomas, John L., 175
Thomes, M. Margaret, 101, 109
Thomlinson, Ralph, 18, 19, 133
Tumin, Melvin, 16

Udry, J. Richard, 112
U.S. Bureau of the Census, 21, 22, 28, 34, 38, 41, 46, 64, 66, 80, 92, 96, 103, 117, 133, 136, 152, 154

Wach, Joachim, 172
Warner, W. Lloyd, 10, 39
Westoff, Charles F., 63, 115, 116, 118, 123, 125, 126, 127, 130, 134, 135, 156, 168
Whelpton, Pascal K., 34, 105, 115, 117, 118, 123, 125, 127, 133, 134, 136, 166
Wirth, Louis, 7

Yinger, J. Milton, 4, 175, 180

Zborowski, Mark, 7, 190
Zimmer, Basil G., 61, 125

Subject Index

Acculturation (*see* Assimilation, cultural)
Age differentials:
  age at marriage, 103, 105, 110-11, 114
  conversion, 156-68
  education, 64-71, 96-97
  family composition, 109-10
  fertility, 119, 123-25, 166-70
  generation status, 41-43, 235
  home ownership, 92-93
  intermarriage, 156-68
  labor force participation, 72-77
  marital status, 103-5, 107, 111, 114
  mobility, residential, 49-50
  mortality, 140-51, 239
  number of times married, 108
  occupation, 81-86, 88, 96-97
  organization membership, 207-9
  religious education, 213-25
  religious identification, 177-78
  ritual practices, 196-97, 202
  sex composition, 44-45
  status consistency, 96-97
  synagogue attendance, 188-89
  synagogue membership, 179, 181-83
  use of Yiddish, 226-27
Age structure, 41-44
Americanization process, 3-14, 208, 228, 239, 241-43 (*see also* Assimilation)
Anti-Semitism, 10-11 (*see also* Discrimination)
Ashkenazic (*see* Eastern Europe; German Jews)
Assimilation, 3-14, 174, 228-43
  behavioral, 4-6, 232, 239-40, 243
  civic, 5
  cultural, 4-14, 101-2, 106-7, 112, 114, 121, 135-36, 174, 211-15, 231, 240
  definitions of, 4-6
  dimensions of, 3-6, 13, 174, 240
  discrimination and, 9-11
  identificational, 4-6, 9, 175-81, 195, 228, 232
  linguistic, 4-6, 7, 174, 225-27, 229
  marital, 4-6, 152-70, 171, 237 (*see also* Intermarriage)
Assimilation (*Cont.*)
  structural, 4-6, 8-9, 206-11, 232, 240, 243
  theories of, 3-6, 232
Association membership (*see* Organization membership)
Associations, voluntary (*see* Organization membership; Voluntary organizations)

Baby boom, 122, 237
Bar Mitzvah, 188, 213, 215
Bat Mitzvah, 188, 215
Berlin, fertility in, 120
Budapest, fertility in, 120
Buffalo, fertility in, 121, 126
Businessmen (*see* Occupation)

Camden, N. J.:
  intermarriage, 156
  occupational distribution, 80
Canada:
  fertility in, 119-20
  mortality in, 140-41, 151
Catholics, 18, 23, 71, 105, 116-19, 127, 133-34, 136, 166, 187, 188, 190, 192, 239
Cause of death, 139, 144, 148-50, 239
Census:
  Rhode Island, 21-23, 116-17, 121
  United States, 14-15, 18, 117
Census of Religious Bodies, 15
Chanukah, 202, 238, 241
Chanukah candle lighting, 173, 196, 201-3, 204 (*see also* Ritual practices)
Charlestown, fertility in, 121
Church attendance (*see* Religious services, attendance at; Synagogue attendance)
College (*see* Education)
Community, distribution of Jews in, 46-49, 88-91, 235
Community studies, local, limitations and values of, 16-20, 29-30, 233-34 (*see also* Sample survey; Sources of data on Jews)
Congregations (*see* Synagogues)

Congregations, membership in (*see* Synagogue membership)
Conservative Judaism (*see also* Religiosity; Religious identification)
  age structure, 178
  attendance at religious services, 193-94
  fertility differentials, 131
  generation structure, 177-78, 237-38
  identification with, 176-77, 181
  intermarriage, 164-65
  residential differentials, 181-83
  ritual practices, 199-201, 203-4
  synagogue membership, 180, 184-86
Conversion (*see* Intermarriage)
Cultural assimilation (*see* Assimilation, cultural)
Cultural pluralism, 3-6, 232, 238-40, 243 (*see also* Triple melting pot)

Day school (*see* Religious education, type of)
Death rates (*see* Mortality)
Decentralization, 46-61, 235, 237 (*see also* Mobility, residential; Suburbs)
Design of the study, 28-34, 244-61
Des Moines, Iowa, occupational distribution, 80
Detroit, intermarriage, 157
Discrimination, 5, 7, 10-11, 105, 135-36 (*see also* Anti-Semitism)
Distribution of general population in Greater Providence, 46-47
Distribution of Jews in Greater Providence, 22, 46-49, 88-91, 235 (*see also* Mobility, residential)
Divorce, 102-4, 107, 236-37, 241 (*see also* Family, stability; Family, structure)

Eastern Europe, 2, 6-7, 24-26, 64, 120, 234 (*see also* Immigration)
Economic behavior (*see* Labor force status; Mobility, social; Occupation; Self-employment)
Education, Jewish (*see* Religious education)
Education, secular, 64-71, 235, 237, 239
  age differentials, 64-71
  aspirations for, 64-65, 66, 71-72, 237
  fertility, 119, 126-29
  of general population, 65-67, 236, 240
  generation differentials, 65-70, 235-36, 241
  home ownership, 94-95
  intermarriage, 163-64
  marital status, 112, 241
Education, secular (*Cont.*)
  occupational differentials, 63, 72-73, 85, 95-100, 236
  organizational affiliation, 210, 241-42
  religiosity, 230-31
  religious education, 64, 224, 242
  religious identification, 183-84, 241-42
  residential differentials, 70-71, 241
  ritual practices, 197-99, 241-42
  sex differentials, 65, 69-70
  status consistency, 95-100, 236
  synagogue attendance, 191-93
  synagogue membership, 183-85
Employment (*see* Labor force status; Occupation; Self-employment)
Ethnic class, 62
Ethnic composition, 22-23, 234
Ethnic identification, 11-12
  lack of, by Jews, 11, 235

Family, 73, 75-76, 101-14 (*see also* Fertility; Marital status)
  extended, 108-10, 112
  nuclear, 108-10, 112-13
  size, 118-19, 121-24, 125-26, 135-36, 237
  stability, 102-4, 107, 112-14, 164-65, 240, 241 (*see also* Divorce)
  structure, 102, 107-14
    changes in, 107, 113-14, 236, 241
Fertility, 115-36
  acculturation and, 127, 135-36
  age differentials, 119, 123-25, 166-70
  educational differentials, 119, 126-29, 237
  of general population, 116-20, 123, 133-34, 239
  generation differentials, 121, 123-25, 127-29, 131, 132, 237
  intermarriage and, 153, 166-70
  of Jews in other countries, 64, 119-21
  non-white, 135
  occupational differences, 126-29, 237
  religiosity and, 130, 133
  religious identification, 130-33
  residential differences, 125-26
  socio-economic status and, 124-25, 126-29, 132-34
  sources of data, 19, 115-21, 137
First generation (*see also* Generation differentials; Immigration)
  acculturation, 6-7
  date of arrival, 40
  decline, 38-40, 235-42
  definition of, 38
Foreign born (*see* First generation; Generation status; Immigration)

General Jewish Committee of Providence, 19, 29, 30
Generational conflict, 7-9, 12-13, 241
Generation differentials, 38-42, 228-31
age, 41-44, 235
age at marriage, 110-11, 237
assimilation, 6-9, 20, 232-43
conversion, 159-61, 169-70
divorce, 107, 236-37, 241
education, 65-70, 235-36, 241
family structure, 107-10, 113, 237, 241
fertility, 121, 123-25, 127-29, 131, 132, 237
home ownership, 92-94
household types, 109-10
intermarriage, 153, 156, 159-61, 163, 169-70, 237
labor force status, 73-77
marital status, 106-8, 111, 113, 237
mortality, 141, 143-44, 239
number of times married, 108
occupation, 82-88, 236
organizational affiliation, 207-9, 238
religiosity, 174-75, 177-81, 187-90, 197, 201-2, 206-9, 213-22, 228-29, 237-38
religious education, 213-25, 238
religious identification, 177-78, 181-82, 183-84, 238, 241-42
residential distribution, 50-52, 235, 241-42
residential mobility, 53-55, 57, 235
ritual practices, 196-97, 198-99, 200-204, 238, 241
socio-economic status, 65-70, 73-77, 82-88, 235-36, 240-41
status consistency, 98-99
synagogue attendance, 187-95, 241-42
synagogue membership, 179-80, 181-82, 185-86, 195, 241-42
use of Yiddish, 226-27, 238
Generation status, definition of, 38-39, 42
German Jews, 2, 9, 24-25, 234
Ghetto, 6, 48, 91, 126, 235 (*see also* Older urban area)
Ghetto, "gilded," 46, 91, 235
Great Britain, fertility in, 120
Growth of American Families Studies, 115-16, 118, 133-34, 135-36

Hebrew language, use of, 227
Hebrew school (*see* Religious education, type of)
Herbergian paradox, 3, 174, 234-43
History of Jews in the United States, 2, 24-25, 76-77, 206, 234-35
Home ownership, 89, 91-95, 240 (*see also* Socio-economic status)
Household composition, 109-11, 113-14

Identification, religious (*see* Religious identification)
Identification as Jews, 9-12, 33 (*see also* Religious identification)
Immigration, 36-38, 77-78, 234-35
age at, 36-37
date of, 40-41
early, 2, 22-28
Eastern European, 2, 6-7, 24-26, 64, 234
German, 24-25, 234
nature of, 6-7, 36-37
reasons for, 24, 28, 36
sex differentials, 36-37
Immigration quota laws, 2, 9, 37, 234-35
Index of Religious Practices (*see* Ritual practices)
Indianapolis Fertility Study, 117
Intellectuals, subsociety, 10, 170, 242
Intermarriage, 152-70, 240
age at marriage, 167-68
age differentials, 156-68
assimilation and, 5, 152, 237
children of, 153, 154, 155, 157, 165, 166, 168-70, 237
conversion and, 153, 154, 156-63, 168-70, 237, 241
education differentials, 163-64
fertility and, 153, 166-70
generation differentials, 153, 156, 159-61, 163, 169-70, 237
limitations of data on, 155
marital stability, 164-65, 170
migration, 155-57
occupation differentials, 163-64
rate of, 152-53, 155, 169-70, 240
religious education and, 164-66, 170
religious identification, 164-65, 167, 170
residential differentials, 156, 161-63, 169, 241
ritual practices, 164-65
sex differentials, 155, 157-59
socio-economic differentials, 163-65, 170
sources of data, 152-55
trends, 153, 156, 169-70
Interviewers, 28-29
Interview schedule, 33, 257-61
Iowa, intermarriage in, 152
Israel, State of:
Jewish identification and, 9-10
use of Hebrew and, 227
Italy, fertility in, 120

Jewish education (*see* Religious education)
Jewish exceptionalism, 17, 232-33, 239-40
Jewish heterogeneity, 17, 232-33, 237, 241, 243
Jewish New Year, 188

Kashruth, 173, 195-96, 199, 201-3, 204 (*see also* Ritual practices)
  definition of, 201-2
  observance of, 201-2, 204, 238

Labor force status, 71-77 (*see also* Occupation; Self-employment)
  age differentials, 72-77
  generation differentials, 73-77
  sex differentials, 72-77
Lakeville Study, 17
Life expectancy, 140, 144-47, 151, 239 (*see also* Mortality)
Linguistic assimilation (*see* Assimilation, linguistic)
Local Jewish community studies (*see* Community studies, local)
Los Angeles, intermarriage in, 169

Marital status, 102-7, 111, 112-14 (*see also* Family)
  age differentials, 103-5, 107, 111, 114
  education differentials, 112
  generation differentials, 106-8, 111, 113, 237
  number of times married, 103-4, 108, 113, 164-65, 237
  residential differentials, 112
Marriage, age at, 104-6, 110-11, 114, 167-68, 237, 240
Marriage cohorts, 105, 122
Marriages, mixed (*see* Intermarriage)
Metropolitan area (*see* Providence Metropolitan Area; Suburbs)
Migration, internal (*see* Mobility, residential)
Migration, international (*see* Immigration)
Mixed parentage, definition of, 38
Mobility, occupational (*see* Mobility, social)
Mobility, residential, 52-61, 235
  age differentials, 49
  changing patterns of, 58-59
  effect on distribution of population, 22, 48-49, 235, 239
  effect on identification with the community, 49, 60-61, 89, 235, 242
  effect on occupational structure, 85, 88-91
  net changes of, 22, 56
Mobility, residential (*Cont.*)
  occupation and, 88-91
  plans to move, 56-58
  repeated, 60-61
  significance of, 59-61, 91, 241-42
  streams of, 54-56
Mobility, social, 63-64, 235 (*see also* Education; Occupation; Social class; Socio-economic status; Status consistency)
  age at marriage and, 105-6, 237
  education and, 64-65, 236
  fertility, 127, 129, 237
  occupation and, 71-72, 236
Mortality, 137-51, 239 (*see also* Cause of death; Life expectancy)
  age differentials, 140-51, 239
  in Canada, 140-41, 151
  generation differentials, 141, 143-44, 239
  infant, 139, 140, 143
  in New York, 138-41, 151
  religion and, 150-51
  in St. Louis, 138-41, 151
  sex differentials, 140, 142-47, 150-51, 239
  socio-economic status and, 140, 150-51
  sources of data for, 137, 138-42
Mother tongue, census data on, 15, 226

Nazism, 9-10, 37
Negroes, 22, 23, 135
Netherlands, fertility in, 120
Newer urban area (*see also* Older urban area; Residential differentials; Suburbs)
  age distribution, 49
  definition of, 30, 32, 46
  distribution of Jews, 46-47, 49-50
  education differentials, 70-71
  family structure, 112
  fertility, 125-26
  generation structure, 50-52
  growth of, 48, 56, 235, 242
  home ownership, 93-95
  intermarriage and conversion, 161-63
  migration, 54-60, 88-91
  occupation, 86-88, 91
  organizational affiliation, 208-10
  religious identification, 181-82, 242
  ritual practices, 197-98
  socio-economic status of, 70-71, 86-91, 93-95
  synagogue attendance, 190-91
  synagogue membership, 181-82
New Haven, intermarriage in, 153, 155
Newport, Jews in, 25

New York:
intermarriage in, 152
mortality in, 138-41, 151
Non-Jewish population (*see* Population, general)
Nuclear family (*see* Family, structure)
Nuclear household, 109-14 (*see also* Household composition)

Occupation, 63, 77-90, 237, 239 (*see also* Labor force status; Self-employment)
age differentials, 81-86, 88, 96-97
education differentials, 63, 72-73, 85, 95-100, 236
fertility, 128
of general population, 78-81, 236
generation differentials, 82-88, 236
of immigrants, 6, 24-25, 77-88
intermarriage and, 163-64
residential differentials, 86-89, 237
residential mobility and, 45, 61, 88-91, 237
sex differentials, 78-86
status consistency, 95-100, 236
Older urban area (*see also* Newer urban area; Residential differentials; Suburbs)
age distribution, 49
decline of, 55-56, 235, 242
definition of, 30, 32
distribution of Jews, 47-50
education, 70-71, 241
family structure, 112
fertility, 125-26
generation structure, 50-52
home ownership, 93-94
intermarriage and conversion, 161-63
migration, 53-60, 88-91, 242
occupation, 86-88, 91
organizational affiliation, 208-10
religious identification, 181-82, 241, 242
ritual practices, 197-98
socio-economic status of, 70-71, 86-88, 93-94
synagogue attendance, 190-91
synagogue membership, 181-82
Organization membership, 173, 206-11, 229
age differentials, 207-9
education differentials, 210, 241-42
generation differentials, 207-9, 238
Jewish, 206-8, 210-11
multiple, 210-11
non-Jewish, 206, 208-11, 241-42
religious differentials, 208-11
residential differentials, 208-10
sex differentials, 207, 208-9
Organization membership (*Cont.*)
structural assimilation and, 206, 208, 210-11
Orthodox Judaism (*see also* Religiosity; Religious identification)
age structure, 178
education, secular, 242
fertility differentials, 131
generation structure, 177-78, 237-38, 242
identification with, 175, 177, 181
intermarriage, 164-65
religiosity, 242
religious education, 215-16, 224-25
residential differentials, 181-83, 241
ritual practices, 199-201, 203-4
synagogue attendance, 193-94
synagogue membership, 180, 184-86

Passover Seder, 195, 201-4, 238, 241 (*see also* Ritual practices)
Population, general:
age at marriage, 105-6, 111, 114
age distribution, 41-42
attendance at religious services, 186-88, 190, 192
cause of death, 139, 148-50
education, 65-67, 236, 240
family structure, 102, 109-11
fertility, 116-20, 123, 133-34, 239
growth, 1, 21-22
home ownership, 92-94
immigration, 22-23, 36-37
intermarriage, 152, 155
labor force status, 72-73
marital status, 102-5
mortality, 139, 140, 142-51
occupation, 78-81, 236
residential distribution, 21-22, 46-48
sex distribution, 44-45
Population growth:
of general population, 1, 21-22
of Jews, 1, 24-28, 36
Population redistribution (*see also* Mobility, residential)
of general population, 21-22, 47-48
of Jews, 47-48, 52-61, 88-91, 235-37
Prejudice (*see* Anti-Semitism; Discrimination)
Princeton Fertility Studies, 115-16, 118, 126-27
Protestants, 18, 65, 105, 116-19, 127, 133-34, 152, 166, 187-88, 192, 239, 240
Providence Jewish Community:
development, 24-28
typicality, 19-20

Providence Metropolitan Area:
  definition of, 28-31
  development, 21-33
  ethnic composition, 22-23
  population changes, 21-23
  subareas, 28, 31

Quota laws (*see* Immigration quota laws)

Reform Judaism (*see also* Religiosity; Religious identification)
  age structure, 178
  fertility differentials, 131
  generation structure, 177-78, 237-38
  identification with, 175, 177, 181
  intermarriage, 164-65
  religious education, 215-16, 224-25
  residential differentials, 181-83, 241
  ritual practices, 199-201, 203-4
  synagogue attendance, 193-94
  synagogue membership, 180, 184-86, 241
Religion, definition of, 171-72
Religiosity, 171-231, 237-38, 241-43
  assimilation and, 3, 8, 171-75, 228-31, 241
  cultural dimension, 173-74, 211-27, 232, 238
  definition of, 172-75
  fertility, 130, 133
  generation changes in, 174-75, 177-81, 187-90, 197, 201-2, 206-9, 213-22, 226-27, 228-29, 237-38
  ideological dimension, 172-86, 228-31, 237-38, 241-42
  intermarriage and, 165-66
  organizational dimension, 173-75, 206-11, 228-31, 238
  ritualistic dimension, 172-74, 186-205, 228-31, 238
Religious decline (*see* Religiosity, generation changes in)
Religious education, 211-25, 229, 238, 241-42
  age differentials, 213-25
  amount of, 212-13, 218, 220-23
  enrollment, 212, 222-23
  future enrollment, 212, 223-24
  generation differentials, 213-25, 238
  implications for the future, 211, 224-25
  increase, 212-25, 238
  intermarriage and, 164-66
  religious identification, 224-25
  residential differentials, 224
  role of, 211-12, 224
  secular education and, 224, 241-42
  sex differentials, 213-25, 238
  type of, 30, 215-19
Religious identification, 9-12, 171-72, 175-79, 181-86, 228, 231 (*see also* Conservative Judaism; Orthodox Judaism; Reform Judaism; Religiosity)
  age differentials, 177-78, 181
  changes in, 177-78, 237-39
  educational differentials, 183-84, 241-42
  fertility, 130-33
  generation differentials, 177-78, 181-82, 183-84, 238, 241-42
  historic patterns of, 175-76
  intermarriage, 164-65
  marital status, 111-14, 241
  organization membership, 210
  religious education, 215-16, 224-25
  residential differentials, 181-83, 241
  ritual practices, 199-201, 203-4
  socio-economic status, 184, 241-42
  synagogue attendance, 193-95
  synagogue membership, 180-81, 184-86
Religious practices (*see* Ritual practices)
Religious revival (*see* Religiosity, generation changes in)
Religious services, attendance at, 186-95 (*see also* Synagogue attendance)
Remarriage (*see* Marital status)
Residence, current (*see also* Mobility, residential; Newer urban area; Older urban area; Suburbs)
  by plans to move, 56-57
  by previous residence, 58-59, 88-91
Residential change (*see* Mobility, residential)
Residential concentration, 46 (*see also* Mobility, residential)
Residential differentials (*see also* Newer urban area; Older urban area; Suburbs)
  age, 49
  distribution of general population, 21-22, 48
  distribution of Jews, 48-49, 88-91, 235
  education, 70-71, 241
  effect of mobility on, 48-49, 88-91
  family structure, 112, 241
  fertility, 125-26
  generation differentials, 50-52, 235, 241-42
  home ownership, 93-95
  intermarriage, 156, 161-63, 169, 241
  occupation, 86-91, 237
  organizational affiliation, 208-10
  religious education, 224
  religious identification, 89, 181, 241-42
  ritual practices, 197-98

Residential differentials (*Cont.*)
socio-economic status, 70-71, 86-91, 93-94, 241-42
synagogue attendance, 190-91, 193
synagogue membership, 181-83
use of Yiddish, 226-27
Residential dispersion, 46-61, 235 (*see also* Mobility, residential)
Rhode Island, population of, 21-23
Rhode Island Division of Vital Statistics, 141
Ritual practices, 173, 195-204, 228-29, 238 (*see also* Chanukah candle lighting; Kashruth; Passover Seder; Sabbath candle lighting)
age differentials, 196-97, 202
educational differentials, 197-99, 241-42
family-centered nature of, 188, 195
generation differentials, 196-204, 238, 241
Index of, 165, 196
intermarriage, 165
religious identification, 199-201
residential differentials, 197-98, 241
Rochester:
intermarriage in, 156
occupational distribution in, 80

Sabbath candle lighting, 195, 201-3, 204, 238
St. Louis, mortality in, 138-41, 151
St. Petersburg, fertility in, 120
Sample survey, 173, 212, 215-16
design, 28-34, 244-61 (*see also* Sources of data on Jews)
Sampling error, 35, 251-56
San Francisco, intermarriage in, 152
School enrollment, 66, 72, 75, 85 (*see also* Education, secular)
Second generation (*see also* Generation differentials)
acculturation, 7-9
conflicts of, 7-8
definition of, 38-39
Secularism, 3-9, 165, 180-81, 228-31, 240 (*see also* Religious identification)
Self-employment, 76-77, 236 (*see also* Labor force status; Occupation)
Sephardic Jews, 2, 9, 234
Sex differentials:
age and, 44-45
age at marriage, 110, 113
education, 65, 69-70
home ownership, 93-94
intermarriage, 155, 157-59
labor force status, 72-77
marital status, 104, 113
Sex differentials (*Cont.*)
mobility, 45
mortality, 140, 142-47, 150-51, 239
occupation, 78-86
organizational affiliation, 207-9
religious education, 213-25, 230
synagogue attendance, 190, 230
synagogue membership, 181, 230
use of Yiddish, 226-27
Sex Ratio, 44-45
Significance, tests of, 251-56
Social class, 62-100 (*see also* Education; Home ownership; Occupation; Socio-economic status)
ethnic factors, 62
generation status, 65-70, 73-77, 92-94, 235-36, 240, 241
Social Class Index, 128-29
Social mobility (*see* Mobility, social)
Socio-economic status, 235, 239 (*see also* Social class; Status consistency)
education, 64-71, 72-73, 85, 89
fertility, 124-25, 126-29, 132-34
generation differentials, 65-70, 73-77, 82-88, 235-36, 240
home ownership, 91-95
intermarriage, 163-64
labor force status, 71-77
mortality, 140, 150-51
occupation, 63, 77-90, 237, 239
residence, 70-71, 86-91, 93-95, 237
Sources of data on Jews, 14-17 (*see also* Design of the study; Sample survey)
on fertility, 19, 115-21, 137
on intermarriage, 152-55
Jewish community studies, 18-20, 28-34, 102, 233-34
limitations of, 14-17, 19-20
on mortality, 137-42
U.S. Census, 14-16, 18
South Bend, Indiana, occupation distribution in, 80
Spanish-Portuguese Jews, 2, 9, 234
Status consistency, 95-100, 236
Stratification (*see* Education; Home ownership; Occupation; Social class; Socio-economic status; Status consistency)
Subareas of Greater Providence (*see* Newer urban area; Older urban area; Providence Metropolitan Area; Suburbs)
Suburbs (*see also* Mobility, residential; Newer urban area; Older urban area; Providence Metropolitan Area; Residential differentials)

Suburbs (*Cont.*)
age distribution, 49
definition of, 28, 30, 32
distribution of Jews, 46-50
education, 70-71
family structure, 112, 241
fertility, 125-26
generation structure, 23, 50-52, 241
growth of, 22, 49, 56, 235, 242
home ownership, 93-95
intermarriage and conversion, 161-63, 241
migration, 22, 51-52, 54-60, 88-91, 239, 241-42
occupation, 86-88, 91
organizational affiliation, 208-10
religious education, 241
religious identification, 60, 181-82, 183, 208, 224, 230, 241-42
ritual practices, 197-98, 241
socio-economic status of, 70-71, 86-88, 93-95
synagogue attendance, 190-91
synagogue membership, 181-83
Sunday School (*see* Religious education, type of)
Survey sample (*see* Sample survey)
Switzerland, fertility in, 120
Synagogue attendance, 186-95, 238
age differentials, 188-89
educational differentials, 191-93
generation differentials, 187-95
religious identification differentials, 193-95
residential differentials, 190-91, 193
sex differentials, 190
Synagogue membership, 173-74, 178-80, 181-82, 184-86
age differentials, 179, 181-83
education differentials, 183-85
Synagogue membership (*Cont.*)
generation differentials, 179-80, 181-82, 185-86, 195, 241-42
multiple, 180
nonmembership, 179-80, 181-83, 185-86
religious identification differentials, 184-86
residential differentials, 181-82
sex differentials, 181
Synagogues, 26-27, 175-76

Talmud Torah (*see* Religious education, type of)
Third generation (*see also* Generation differentials)
acculturation, 9
definition of, 38
growth of, 38-40
Three Generations Hypothesis, 6-9, 174, 228-31, 241-43
Trenton, occupational distribution in, 80
Triple melting pot, 9, 232, 239, 240

Urban areas (*see* Newer urban area; Older urban area)

Vital statistics, 115, 137, 138-42
Voluntary organizations, 27, 206-11 (*see also* Organization membership)

Warsaw, fertility in, 120
Washington, D.C.:
intermarriage in, 153, 163, 166, 169
occupational distribution in, 80

Yeshiva (*see* Religious education, type of)
Yiddish, 225-27, 238 (*see also* Assimilation, linguistic)
Yiddish school (*see* Religious education, type of)
Yiskor, 190

Where
The Pirates
Are

Where The Pirates Are

Tom Townsend

EAKIN PRESS
Austin, Texas

FIRST EDITION

Published in the United States of America
By Eakin Press, P.O. Box 23066, Austin, Texas 78735

ISBN 0-89015-506-2

For Samantha, who sailed
the Falcon's *course with me.*

Preface

This story is fiction, which means that it did not really happen. At least, I do not think it did. Jem, Raif, Talva and her dog, Getana, are all products of my own imagination, as are Muldoon, Bruno and The Rat. Crazy Ben, Moss Tatum, Jeffery Reid, Lady Gray and most of the other characters were real people and lived around Galveston Bay during the days of the Texas Republic. Unfortunately, history recorded only bits and pieces of information about these people. So, I took what facts were available and, through the magical craft of fiction, created the characters that appear in this story. They are as close to real life as I could make them.

The descriptions of Galveston and the Bay are also as accurate as possible, using old maps and books of the time. Many of the small islands have now disappeared but over the years, I have sailed my own boats along the *Falcon*'s course many times and believe that I have described them correctly.

As for the treasure; oh yes, I've searched for it too, and written about it in two other books, a couple of songs and so many magazines and newspapers that I have lost count. If I have found any part of it, then that must remain my secret. But rest assured, there is much more still buried around Galveston Bay.

1

The Texas Revolution had been over for more than six years. Long before that all of the pirates had left the coast, and now, even Indians were getting scarce. To Jeremiah Dundee, at the age of twelve, it seemed that Galveston was a dull place where adventures of any worth were impossible to find. For if the books were right, adventures were only found in far-off places like desert islands or jungles, and certainly not in a bustling city. Galveston was an island, but it was also a huge, growing city with some seven streets, a bank, and so many shops that he had already lost count. Worst of all, there was even talk of building a *school*.

"Our fledgling republic must be peopled with the best educated men so that this glorious star of the west will not falter or grow dim in the distant dawns of time," the mayor had said loudly in a speech around Christmastime. Like most things the mayor said, Jeremiah did not understand a word of it.

When he had asked Uncle Moss Tatum what it

meant, he had been told, "Well, now, Jem my lad, it means he's fixin' ta build a schoolhouse and keep ya troublesome carcass off these here streets, he is."

"Won't matter none to me," Jem had answered, sticking out his chin and squinting one eye. "Reckon I'll be signin' on some ship, soon as one anchors that suits my fancy."

Uncle Moss had stared down at him from behind his gray, bushy whiskers and bit on the stem of his pipe. "Likely as not, ya probably will, seein' as how ya ain't got a lick of sense." He shook his head and Jem watched a few gray ashes drift down from Uncle Moss's pipe. "Ya can't see that just by stayin' here, learnin' the trade of makin' sails like I'm tryin' my dangest ta teach ya, why — ya'd be a rich man some day, 'stead of the ragamuffin ya are now."

But, as the winter of 1842 became the spring of 1843, the school remained only a dream in the mayor's mind, and running off to sea remained only a dream to Jem. Spring brought warm, southerly winds from the Gulf, and fine sunshine. On a Saturday morning Jem skipped down the Strand and turned toward the wharf at the end of Water Street. If there was one place in all of Galveston he found worth visiting, it was here among the ships. For this was a true crossroads of the world. Galveston was a harbor where ships from Europe, China, California, and all the other fabled places where adventures could still be found, came to anchor briefly before sailing on.

Jem wandered along the T-shaped wharf, dodging workers carrying heavy burlap bags, nearly as big as themselves. Boxes and crates with mysterious smells and strangely painted labels were stacked here and there, while others were being hoisted in cargo nets or loaded on carts and wagons. Tall masts rose skyward, each crossed with a varnished yard from which hung loosely furled tan canvas sails. High on the topgallant yards of a brig, seamen were at work removing a torn sail, and below, the decks were being scrubbed. Sidestepping a horse cart loaded with barrels, Jem ducked between a pair of tatooed seamen with blue stocking caps and beards. He watched them pass and took time to admire the long, wicked looking knives they carried in their belts.

A steam whistle echoed above the other noises and he broke into a run, zipping neatly along the crowded wharf. In front of him, black smoke was billowing skyward. Beneath it, he could see the tall smokestacks of the steamboat, *Dayton.* He ran like the wind now, his bare feet padding lightly on the smooth planks of the wharf as his shirttail flowed out behind him. The wharf opened up before him just as the huge steamboat was taking in her spring lines and backing out into the channel. White steam hissed from her engine. Water splashed around the blades of her two-story high paddle wheels as they dipped in and out of the water, moving her slowly in reverse. Everyone knew the *Dayton,* fastest steam packet on the Texas coast. Two years earlier she had beaten the *Albert Gallatin,* down from Harrisburg, in a death race that saw the *Gallatin* explode her boilers near Redfish Island. The flames had been clearly visible from Galveston. Today, the *Dayton* would be standing out for Aransas Pass, nearly two days' run down the coast. He watched fascinated as the huge wheels changed direction and she began to move away. Swinging first toward the low sandbar called Pelican Spit, she then headed east, around Snake Point and into the open Gulf beyond. When nothing but her smokestacks were visible, Jem finally turned away and started slowly back toward Water Street.

Jem had always been a loner. His friends could be counted on one hand with a couple of fingers left over. There was Uncle Moss Tatum, who really was not his uncle, and Jeffery Reid, Moss's partner in the sailmaking loft. Jem lived there in a back room overlooking the harbor. That room was the only home he remembered. Of his early life, he could only guess and wonder.

"Ya come here on the brig *Laura D*, up from Campeche with Captain Hutchinson," Moss had told him each time he asked, even though the boy knew it all by heart. "Two days out, they was runnin' 'round the west end of Scorpion Reef when the lookout spied a bit of wreckage with you on it. Not more than a babe ya was, clingin' to a jib boom, and near dead. Ya had that locket there 'round your neck. They got ya aboard and brung ya here. We took ya in an give ya the name Dundee, cause the *Laura D* was named for a Lady Dundee. And that is all we know, 'cause they never found out what ship it was that wrecked on the reef."

Jem thought about it often. Not knowing his parents bothered him some, even though Uncle Moss always told him that it did not matter where somebody came from, just where they were going. Often, when he was alone, he would take off the locket and examine it over and over again. On the cover was a bird, a falcon maybe, with tiny jewels for eyes. Once, perhaps, it had been painted black, but now, only bits of the paint remained over the gold. Inside, there was nothing.

Jem's best friend was Raif, who was almost an orphan too. Raif's father had come to Texas from Mexico before the war and it was said that he fought alongside General Sam Houston at the Battle of San Jacinto. After the war he had become a fisherman, and one day he had sailed out into the Gulf and never come back. Now Raif's mother managed to make a modest living doing washing and sewing.

In many ways, the two boys were opposites. Raif loved the city and had learned its ways. He could always earn a few coins polishing boots in front of the barbershop on Mechanic Street, or carrying baggage for travelers at the Galvez Hotel.

This morning, Jem found Raif a couple of blocks from the waterfront. "Hey Jem, where are you going today, my friend?"

"Just around," Jem shrugged, shuffling his feet in the dust.

"Yeah, me too. It's quiet today," Raif yawned.

"Let's go down to the old pirate fort!" Jem suggested suddenly, his eyes lighting up with new interest. Raif liked the idea also, and together they started off down the street toward the island's east end.

Their destination was less than a mile away, sitting on a little rise and surrounded by palm trees. Once, some twenty years before, it had been the island fortress of the buccaneer — or pirate — Jean Lafitte. He and six hundred followers had been the island's first settlers. Now, all that was left were scarred masonry walls, nearly hidden beneath creeping vines and weeds. Wide stairs led up to the ruined second floor which, so they had been told, once held cannon.

The two boys stopped at the bottom of the vine covered stairs and looked up at the place. *It is quiet,* Jem thought, *deathly quiet.* A soft breeze rustled the palm leaves ever so slightly, and lizards scurried from their path as they moved cautiously up the stairs. Both of the boys had been here dozens of times before, but the old ruins always seemed *eerie*, just the same. Palm branches spilled over the upper floor, making brushing noises in the breeze. They reached the top and moved in silence across the smooth floor to where another set of stairs descended from the floor's center.

These stairs were wooden. Each one creaked under the boys' weight, and echoed loudly through the gloom as they moved. Sunlight sneaked between the cracks in the boarded up first floor windows, and cast weird, creeping shadows on the moss-covered walls. Spiderwebs hung like nets across the doorways and in every corner. Jem stopped to gaze up at the sagging ceiling where huge, rough-cut timbers still supported the weight of the second floor. At one place, a few feet of rusty chain dangled where once there had been a chandelier. Old folk said this had been a mansion in Lafitte's time and French officers had come here after the defeat of Napoleon. Lafitte entertained them royally, and then they sailed north, up the Trinity River to found a colony — but it failed.

Jem could imagine the way the mansion must have looked. *Maison Rouge*, Red House, Lafitte had named it. The floors would have been polished wood, the walls hung with mirrors reflecting the light of a hundred candles.

"Raif?" Jem asked quietly. "You ever feel pulled to a place? Like somehow, even though it don't make no sense, you were here once before."

"You been here lots of times," Raif answered him.

Jem frowned, knowing his friend was not understanding. "No, I mean like a long time ago. Maybe before I was born or something."

Raif shrugged his shoulders. "Sometimes I think about Mexico, and wonder what it would be like if my people had stayed there. Then, I think I'm happy they came here." He looked at Jem for a moment. "But you, my friend, talk of stranger things."

"Come on," Jem said, changing the subject quickly, "let's explore the cellar."

Even worse looking stairs spiraled down from the first floor, into the foul smelling darkness below. Jem and Raif were on the first steps when a noise from below stopped them in their tracks. "What was that?" Raif whispered.

"Probably just a rat or something," Jem told him, trying to sound unconcerned.

"Yeah, it's the *or something* that's got me worried," Raif whispered again.

"Go on," Jem urged nervously, staying behind him as the two boys started down into the darkness. Each step creaked ominously, and they blinked their eyes, trying to adjust to the darkness. They felt the stairway turning to the right as they descended cautiously, one step at a time. Jem thought he heard breathing. Then, just as they reached the cellar floor, a light moved quickly from beneath the stairs. He heard a deep growl, but not the growl of an animal, the growl of a human!

The yellow light of a swinging lantern suddenly cast ghostly shadows across a dark, unshaven face with a hook nose. A long, jagged scar ran from somewhere beneath a filthy bandanna, down to the snarling corner of a mouth full of yellow teeth. The eyes were deep set, red and haunted. They seemed to burn into him as the boys stood spellbound, too frightened to run. Then, Jem saw the knife. The lantern light reflected for a second off the shining steel of its slender, curving blade as it flashed toward him.

2

Raif yelled something in Spanish, and Raif never spoke Spanish unless he was either mad or scared. Jem understood *Ańdale — Pronto!* just as Raif ran over him and knocked him down against the stairs. The next seconds seemed to move in slow motion as the dark figure started for the stairs, towering over Jem as he clawed his way toward the doorway above. Somehow, he was on his feet and only inches behind Raif when they reached the top of the stairs. They ran toward the back of the ruins, stumbling, falling, but never looking back until at last they reached the end of a long hallway and there was no place else to run. Here, they waited in silence, their backs pressed against the crumbling wall, and they listened to the sound of their own ragged breathing. Jem ventured a quick look back down the hall and saw no one. "I think we lost him," he whispered.

Raif was about to agree when a voice from somewhere outside broke the silence. "Come on, Ben. We knows ya got more treasure than ya can ever spend! All we wants is a part of it."

"What I've got is mine, damn your eyes," still another voice answered. "Given to me as fair payment for deeds I done a longtime past. Try to take it now and you taste cold steel."

The two boys looked at each other in wonder. Then, Jem led the way as they began sneaking back down the hallway.

A broken door hung on one hinge at the end of the hall and they slipped quietly behind it. Three men were in the room before them now. Two wore the dark blue coats of merchant sailors. One looked as big as a mountain and wore a red stocking cap. The other was small and had a rat-like face. Both carried long clubs. The third stood with his back to the boys but there was no doubt he was the same man they had seen in the cellar. The dirty red bandanna was around his head, and a single gold earring dangled from one ear. In one hand he still held the lantern. The long, curved knife was extended before him.

"All right ye crazy old fool. If that's the way you wants it, we'll be happy ta beat it outa you." One of the seamen raised his club and started for the one they called Ben, but the old man was fast. The club swung harmlesly over his head as he moved with lightning speed to avoid the blow. The knife was a blur of flashing steel as Ben lunged at his attacker, slashing into his coat sleeve. A scream of pain said that the blade had found its mark and the club dropped to the floor as the man staggered back, holding his arm. The second man moved in with a deep growl as Ben slipped on the damp floor.

Raif felt Jem move and grabbed for him, catching only thin air. "Hey, where you going! You crazy?"

But Jem was already in the open with a comfortable size brick in his hand. He took aim on the man with the club. "Got to," he said as he moved, "they're gonna kill him." The rock sailed from his hand, on an arc-shaped course as it crossed the room, and then bounced with a satisfying thud off the side of the seaman's head. The club dropped to the floor, and the attacker's hand went to his temple. He turned and looked straight at Jem for a moment and then collapsed against the wall.

The one called Ben spun quickly, regained his footing and pointed the knife in Jem's direction. For a few seconds the world stood still as they faced each other. What might have been a smile spread across the scarred face, he touched the knife's hilt to his chin in the old dueler's salute and then replaced it smartly in his belt. His voice was a hoarse, gravelly whisper as he said, "Get out lad, there's likely more of 'em about." And then he vanished somewhere toward the front of the ruins.

Jem looked at Raif who was beside him now and Raif looked at Jem. Then together they ran back up the stairs to the second floor, across the open roof and down the wide stone steps. They were back on Water Street before they stopped running.

The next week passed with the speed of a sick turtle. An English brig docked on Monday with two jibs and a topsail so badly torn that they required new ones. Jem worked long days sewing on the stiff, heavy canvas from which Uncle Moss cut the new sails. He thought of the old man called Ben, and the fight at *Maison Rouge* as he worked. Inch by dull inch he labored, pushing the big needle through the sails again and again as he sewed thick, hemp rope into the edges for strength. In the evening they worked late by the light of the smokey oil lamps.

Jem had heard stories about "Crazy Ben," although he had never actually seen him before. People said that he had been Lafitte's cabin boy and he had stayed behind when the rest of the pirates left Galveston. Now, he lived somewhere up on the bay, and, it was said, knew where some of Lafitte's gold was buried. Jem hoped they would meet again someday.

On Thursday, the whole town was talking about a shipwreck. "Come in on the beach last night, she did," Jeffery Reid told Uncle Moss. "And a derelict she was with no trace of a living soul aboard. Mighty strange, I'd say."

"Don't see nothin' strange 'bout a derelict ship," Uncle Moss argued. "Happens sometimes, crew gets all scared about somethin' and takes ta the boats. Or maybe she grounded on a reef somewheres and then floated herself off after everyone got ashore."

Jem felt excitement tickle the hair on his neck as Jeffery disagreed. "I still think it's mighty strange. No one knows what's out there on the ocean, or under it. Why there's all kind of sea serpents and unearthly things jumps up an' — "

Uncle Moss began to laugh out loud. "Dang it, Jeffery, it be a good thing ol' Christopher Columbus didn't think like you or we'd all be livin' in teepees and dancin' round in circles!" Again he laughed and almost dropped his pipe. "Some folks around here's got work to do," and he returned to measuring the English brig's new topsail.

For the rest of the day, Jem waited for a chance to sneak off and look at the new wreck. A shipwreck was a fascinating thing to see, and even more fascinating to explore. You could never tell what might be found there. But Uncle Moss refused to leave and Jem fidgeted and would daydream as he sewed very slowly until evening came at last.

It was nearly midnight when Jem finally slipped out of his cot and opened the window of the second story room. With practiced skill, he stepped out onto the narrow window ledge and inched his way to the corner of the building. From there he jumped to the roof of the warehouse next door and crawled to a gutter pipe which was just perfect for climbing down to the street. The whole operation took only a minute.

Jem slipped silently along the streets, keeping to the shadows as he made his way toward Raif's house. Ten minutes later he approached the darkened shack surrounded by a few windblown salt cedars on the outskirts of town. He stood for a moment looking up at the tiny window in the loft where he knew Raif would be sleeping. He tossed a piece of oyster shell against it and listened to the hollow *Clunk* as it bounced off the wooden shutter.

The window creaked open and Raif's sleepy head appeared. Jem motioned for him to come down. A few minutes later the front door opened and Raif slipped out. "What are you doing out here?" he yawned.

"I'm gonna go see that shipwreck on the beach. You want to come with me?"

"I don't know. I saw it from the beach this morning. Wreckers gonna break it up tomorrow."

"Yeah, I know. That's why we gotta explore it tonight."

Raif was still hesitant. "Hey, I heard people talking today. They say there ain't nothing but ghosts on the ship. They said they saw lights when it washed up, but now they can't find anybody on it."

"Ah, come on Raif, you ain't scared of *ghosts*, are you?"

"I'm scared of lots of things, that's how I make it on the streets," Raif explained honestly. "I'm scared of sailors when they're drunk. I'm scared of the pickpockets and thieves down on the docks so I got sense enough to stay away from them. Now *ghosts*, I know nothing about, but I'm pretty sure I don't like them, and it don't make good sense to go looking for trouble."

“Heck, there ain’t no telling what we might find on that ship, especially if we get on it tonight, before they start breaking it up,” Jem argued.

“All right, my friend. I’ll go but I think you are crazy,” Raif agreed finally, and with Jem leading the way, they started for the beach.

3

Powdery white sand squished between their toes as they climbed the last sand dune and Jem saw the wreck. Bathed in the ghostly glow of a full moon, it lay like some sea monster, dying in the surf. Broken masts with torn bits of sail pointed skyward where claw-like clouds slashed at the stars. The hull stirred with each passing wave. It seemed to breathe, to gasp dying breaths as the surf pushed it, inch by inch, toward the beach.

The two boys stared silently for a long time, awed by the sight of the huge wreck so clear in the bright moonlight. "I think she was a schooner, like they build down at Campeche," Jem said, breaking the silence. He started down onto the beach with Raif just behind him and did not stop until seawater was over his feet.

"How we gonna get on her?" Raif asked.

Jem pointed up at the bowsprit where several broken lines trailed over the side of the wreck and into the water. "We can climb one of those," he answered.

The ocean was cool against his legs as he waded farther out. The black hull towered above them. The ocean rose higher, until only their arms were still exposed and a curling wave slapped their faces. Another wave buried their heads under the dark water and forced them to swim the last few yards.

Jem had worked around ships long enough that rope climbing was easy. With steady strokes he pulled himself up to the whisker stays and rolled easily into the torn safety net stretched along the bowsprit. Raif was not doing so well. "Can't make it!" he groaned.

"Hold on, I'll help you," Jem called back and began hauling up the line with Raif swinging on the end. He grumbled and sweated with each inch, but eventually, Raif climbed onto the bowsprit with him.

"Thanks — I think," Raif said as he looked at the shadowy wreck. Jem was already making his way toward the slanting deck. Broken spars, tangles of line and gear were everywhere. A cannon lay overturned with its carriage still attached and everywhere was the odor of dead sealife. The hatchboards were gone, exposing a large hold in the center of the main deck. Carefully, the two boys peered over its edge and saw only water below in the hold.

"Come on," Jem said, "Let's check the cabins, they're higher than the hold and might not be flooded." Raif followed him silently as they climbed the ladder to the quarterdeck and passed the huge wheel. It creaked ominously and turned a few degrees when they passed, as if steered by some invisible helmsman. "Just the waves movin' the rudder around," Jem said.

Raif was not convinced. "I think we should get out of here."

Jem ignored him and together they made their way along the slanted deck to another hatch, near the ship's stern. It too was open and, in the moonlight, they could see a ladder leading down into the darkness below. The wreck creaked and stirred slightly with a passing wave. Somewhere forward, something bumped against the hull and rattled in the wind.

Step by cautious step, Jem led the way below. The ladder ended in a narrow hallway. To their right a door to a large cabin hung open. Moonlight reflected through broken windows in the wreck's stern and filled the cabin with a pale, eerie light. In the center, a heavy table stood bolted to the floor and all around it was destruction. Soaked bedding and pulpy white messes which probably had been navigation charts, were on the floor. A broken lantern was in the corner, another hung from the overhead beams and swung in a slow continuous circle.

A noise down the hall made them freeze. "What was that?" Raif asked in a loud whisper which seemed to echo off the walls.

"I . . . I . . . don't know," Jem answered, failing to sound casual. "Could be rats."

They inched their way back down the hall. The doors to two other cabins hung open and they explored each in turn. In each they found the same destruction.

"Nothing here but junk," Raif said disappointedly when they had finished. They returned to the stern cabin and once again picked through the debris there. "Hey, Jem, it's late. We gotta go."

Reluctantly, Jem agreed and started out. His hand brushed the tabletop and felt something. "Wait," he said surprised, and picked up a roll of heavy paper. It was dry, not soggy and falling apart like the charts on the floor. Something flat and round dropped into his hand from inside the roll. The object sparkled in the moonlight as he held it up for a closer look.

"Silver!" Raif almost yelled. "A Piece of Eight!"

"Yeah," Jem whispered. "And there's more of 'em." He held his hand close to the broken stern windows and let the moonlight play on the coins. "There's six, all together."

"What's that paper they were wrapped in?" Raif wanted to know.

Jem unrolled it carefully and held it close to the moonlit window. "I can't tell, looks like a map or something."

Three loud *thuds* echoed down from the deck above. The two boys held their breaths as they looked at each other and then both reached the same decision at the same instant. "Let's get out of here!" they yelled and ran for the ladder.

Seawind hit their faces as they reached the deck. Without breaking stride they raced for the bow. This time Raif had no trouble with the rope. He went down it like a falling rock as Jem hurried to stuff the strange roll of paper into his shirt and the coins into a pocket of his pants.

By the time he had reached the beach, Raif was waiting for him at the edge of the dunes. They looked back at the wreck. It was silent and there was no sign of life. They hurried back to Raif's house.

"Can't you read it?" Raif asked as he moved the candle closer to Jem's nose.

"It's a map all right," Jem answered in a low whisper. They were in Raif's bedroom and it was after three o'clock in the morning.

"A map of what?" Raif asked again. Together, they stared at the piece of browning parchment on the bed before them.

Jem traced a line with his finger, "This here's Galveston, I think. 'Cept it don't look right."

"Yeah," Raif added, "there aren't any streets or docks or anything except that one house."

Moving the candle still closer, Jem squinted to read the faded markings. Then he looked up at Raif, his eyes wide with wonder. "Raif, that ain't no house, that's Lafitte's fort! This map was made back when the pirates were here."

"Looks like it shows one house way up the bay and what's that **x** for beside it?" Raif pointed at a faded mark in the upper lefthand corner.

"I don't know; looks like where something was buried close to that house."

"Treasure?"

"Yeah. Maybe Lafitte's gold!" Jem studied the map for another moment, "This line here is the shore of Galveston Bay. There's Clear Creek, I recognize it all right, and it shows a trail running north from Clear Creek to that house. I sure never heard of anyone livin' up there."

"It looks like it says 'Beasley' or something."

"It don't matter much what it says — we can't get way up there anyway. Can we?"

Jem did not answer. In his mind, a plan was already beginning to form. At least thirty miles of wilderness, cut by streams and swamps, lay on the nearest land route. If he had a boat — it would be easier. But he did not have a boat — not yet anyway.

Raif interrupted his thoughts. "Hey, my friend, are you trying to figure out some way to get to the treasure?" Jem's eyes betrayed the truth. "Well, you're crazy! There's still Indians and bandits and wild animals all the way."

"Not if we sailed there in a boat." Jem answered him.

Raif laughed out loud, "We don't have any boat."

"Nope, but now we got money."

"You can't buy a boat for six pieces of silver," Raif protested. "There's three pieces for you, and three pieces for me. And I am not going anywhere in a boat with you."

"Aw, come on, there could be enough gold buried up there to make us both rich for the rest of our lives. Everybody knows the pirates left a whole bunch of treasure buried somewhere 'round here and nobody's ever found it."

"Maybe," Raif argued, "And maybe that is just a

bunch of hogwash. Maybe they took it all with 'em. Or maybe they spent it all."

"The map says it's there," Jem insisted, "and I gotta go find it."

"You're crazy. I don't think I want any part of it. It's all too spooky."

"What you mean, spooky?" Jem asked frowning at his friend.

"Spooky! Because how come that map was just layin' there on the table and nobody found it before us. There was sailors on that wreck today — I seen 'em."

Jem stuck out his chin. "I ain't 'fraid of no spooks," he insisted. "Plus, that proves there's somethin' to it."

"I don't want nothin' to do with no spooks," Raif cut in.

He shoved three of the coins at Jem. "Here's your half — and you can keep that spooky old map too."

"Ah, come on Raif, I thought we were partners."

"Not for a crazy scheme like you're cookin' up. These coins will buy a lot of grub around here, and that's what I got to think about first."

Jem nodded. Of course, Raif was right. He wished that he also could look at things in a practical way instead of always dreaming of the impossible. "I gotta get home," he said at length, and picked up his coins and the map.

He walked slowly as he made his way back to the sail loft. It was silly to go off chasing treasure, he tried to convince himself. But then, where had the map and the coins come from? Could it really have been there all along and somehow been overlooked when men first went through that cabin? Something deep inside told Jem that was not the case.

No, he decided, someone placed them there so he could find them. Someone wanted him to follow that map to the **x**. But *who,* and *what for?*

There was the slightest hint of pink dawn on the eastern horizon when he at last arrived home. By then, he had decided that he had no choice but to follow the map if he could.

4

Jem was sitting with his feet dangling off the end of an old pier which stuck out over the water at an uncertain angle. It was called the "Navy Yard Pier" because ships of the Texas Navy used to dock there. Now, Texas no longer had much of a navy and the only warship left in Galveston was the *Archer*. She lay grounded on the mud banks a hundred yards from shore. People said she was so rotten that grounding was the only way she was kept from sinking altogether. But Jem had little interest in the *Archer* today.

Three long weeks had passed since Raif and he had found the map and coins. Every free moment since then had been devoted to finding a boat. So far, the search had been both unsuccessful and discouraging. There were not many boats for sale in Galveston. Most were kept busy earning their keep by fishing or hauling cargo. The few that he had found for sale were priced far beyond his three silver coins.

He had seen very little of Raif during this time. He

missed his friend and wished they were partners in this venture. Jem also wished that he was practical like Raif, and did not feel driven to go chasing off after treasure. *Maybe I oughta give up this whole idea,* Jem said to himself and skipped an oyster shell out across the quiet water. "I ain't never gonna find a boat I can buy." But even as he spoke this aloud, he thought of the map and the mysterious way they had found it. He knew he would have to keep trying.

The distant sound of singing drifted to his ears. He turned to see a rowboat approaching the pier from somewhere near the Morgan Line Wharf. It rode low in the water but only one man appeared to be at the oars. As the boat approached the pier on an unsteady course, Jem could hear a hoarse voice singing;

Heave her up an away we'll go,
Heave away, Sante Anno.
Round Cape Horn ta Frisco Bay,
Way out in Californ-i-a.

The man rowing the boat had obviously been drinking. He wore a faded blue naval officer's coat with gold on the collars which had turned green with age and neglect. His hat did not match. It was of Mexican straw and was frayed around the brim. In the stern, a tattered Texas flag fluttered from a short staff. Beside it, sat a pig.

"Avast there lad and take a bowline if ya please," the oarsman called out and Jem scrambled to his feet. The boat hit the pier with a considerable *Thud!* long before the line was passed. Only the pig seemed irritated and squealed loudly as the man fumbled with a worn-out piece of hemp rope, and finally managed to hand it to Jem. "Quiet now, Sam," the man ordered. "I can lay alongside quite handily, if you please."

Jem took a couple of turns with the line around a piling and stared down at the man, the boat and the pig. The odor of rum was overpowering.

"Lieutenant Crisp of the Texas Navy Frigate *Archer*, at your service, *sir*," the man said, touching his ancient hat as he stood in several inches of water in the boat's bilge. "And this is my loyal — if somewhat rude shipmate — Sam." The pig only grunted and Crisp added, "Who, if he doesn't watch his manners, may soon be supper."

At this the pig protested loudly, and almost overturned the boat. "Now take it easy there Sam, I was only foolin'." Crisp soothed the unhappy animal. "Here now, have another swig and settle down."

"Hi, I'm Jem Dundee." As he watched, Crisp held a bottle out to the pig, which slobbered as it guzzled and spilled dark rum all over itself and the boat. "Waste a lot of good rum that way," Crisp commented sadly, and then turned to Jem. "Well Jem, what brings ya out ta this end of the Island today?"

"Aw, nothin' much. I was just lookin' around for a boat to buy."

At this, Crisp's eyes suddenly widened and his bushy eyebrows rose to little points on his forehead. "Buy? For *money* ya mean, Lad?"

"Yep."

"Well now, just what manner of boat are ya looking for?"

"Skiff or a dory, I reckon. Somethin' that'll carry some sail."

"To do some fishin' with, I reckon?"

Jem stuttered a moment. "Well — yeah, for fishin'."

Crisp scratched at his sandy beard and cast a quick lok at Sam who squealed again. "It so happens I know of just such a boat. Priced to sell and with a leg-o-mutton sail rig thrown in the deal."

Jem had been disappointed too many times in the past weeks to become excited. "Yeah? Where is it?"

Crisp smiled broadly and spread his arms. "I'm standin' in her, Lad."

"This?" Jem looked skeptical. "Ain't this the longboat off the *Archer*?"

"The jolly boat, actually. Longboat sunk in the channel last week."

"Don't it belong to the Texas Navy?"

Crisp's eyes narrowed, but his smile remained glued on. "That she does, and maintained to the highest of the navy standards. It happens that just today I received orders to sell off this fine little vessel."

Jem gave the boat a long look. He was sure that he had never seen a dirtier one, or one in worse repair. But, it was a little larger than he had expected to buy, and the sail rig was there. Rolled up around the mast, it lay along one side. She just might do — if he could afford her. "How much ya askin'?"

"How much could ya pay?"

"I got these." Jem said reaching into his pocket and handing Crisp his three silver coins.

Crisp eyed the coins and bit down on one of them with his teeth. "I couldn't sell her so cheap as this," he said finally. "I'd need twice this much."

From the stern of the boat, Sam squealed loudly. "No, Sam," Crips told the pig. "It's just too cheap. I can't do it. Now, if ya had a couple more of these, we might be able to talk some business."

Jem shook his head. "That's all I got," he said and extended his hand for the coins. Crisp squinted one eye thoughtfully and did not return the coins. He looked down and noticed that the water inside the boat had risen almost to his knees. "Ye've bought yerself a boat, sir," he said suddenly, and tipped his hat.

"But wait a minute," Jem protested. "It's sinking!" Without another word Crisp stepped over the side and into water which came to over his waist and began wading out towards the *Archer*. With a questioning, thoughtful grunt, Sam abandoned the jolly boat and swam after him. Jem watched astonished as his new boat settled to the bottom of the bay.

5

The next low tide came at six thirty on Sunday morning. Jem was back on the pier at six, watching anxiously as the water in the bay dropped lower and lower. At last he could see the outline of his new boat as first the bow and then the gunnels became exposed. By six thirty he had waded aboard and was bailing out the remaining water with an old wooden bucket he had found on the beach.

By the time the morning sun had risen above the Galveston skyline, the boat was almost dry. Exhausted, Jem sat down on one of the seats and at last took time to look at the boat which he was determined to sail in search of his fortune. He guessed it was fourteen or fifteen feet long, with two seats for rowing and a big rudder which hung over the stern.

The tide, he figured, would come back in during the afternoon and the boat should float when it did. In the meantime, he stepped the mast into its hole in the forward seat and unrolled the sail. There were three ropes tied to the masthead. One, he reasoned, would be the headstay and go to the bow. The other two would be shrouds, the lines which ran to the sides to hold up the mast. At each place, he found holes which seemed to fit the ropes and in a short time he was satisfied that he had the mast properly rigged. For practice he hoisted the sail and let it hang in the still air. When the tide came back in he would go for a trial sail, he thought. *Maybe out to Pelican Island and back, just to see how she handles.*

Until then, he could think of little to do. For a while, he looked for the leaks but could not tell between which planks the water had been coming in. There seemed to be big gaps between most all of them, so he just waited for the tide.

There was the problem of a name. After all, every boat had to have a name. This one carried the name of the *Archer*, to which she had belonged until yesterday, and that would never do. Through most of the morning he thought of names and none seemed to fit. Around noon he was fiddling with his locket and happened to feel the outline of the bird on it. "Falcon," he said half aloud. "That sounds pretty good." With that simple decision, his boat was named.

By early afternoon, the water was rising around him, higher and higher up the boat's sides. Still, the *Falcon* showed no signs of floating. Instead it seemed to be stuck in the mud. Jem climbed out into the water and rocked the boat from side to side, but it moved very little. Still the water rose steadily. Spotting an old board on the bank, he waded ashore and dragged it back to the boat. Jem stuck it beneath the bow and pushed with all his might. At last the little boat stirred slightly and rolled with a passing wavelet. Jem pushed harder and the *Falcon* floated with the next wave, grounded herself for a second and then floated free.

As Jem stood knee-deep in the muddy water, admiring his new boat, a sudden gust of wind filled her small, tattered sail. The *Falcon* began to move, pointing her bow out into the bay and picking up speed. "Hey, wait for me!" Jem gasped, realizing suddenly that he was not aboard. But *Falcon* had a mind of her own and continued to move away as Jem splashed after her. The water rose to his waist and then his chest before *Falcon* suddenly turned her bow into the wind and stopped, as if waiting for him a few yards away.

"Aw, come on now ya silly old boat. Ya can't go sailin' off like that." He began swimming but even as he did, the *Falcon* turned off again, and seemed to stay just out of reach. Becoming frightened now that the *Falcon* would sail off and be lost, he swam faster. Each time he seemed to close the distance, *Falcon* would pick up speed at the last second and stay just out of his reach.

Jem was getting tired and scared. Over his shoulder, the shore looked a long way off and he wondered if he could make it back. The *Falcon* turned off the wind again just as Jem was a few feet behind her. There was a line trailing over her stern and Jem swam with all his might to reach it. With failing strength he grabbed it and held on for dear life.

The *Falcon* sailed contentedly along, picking up more speed and pulling Jem behind her. Water splashed into his mouth and eyes, choking him as he fought for each breath of air and began to pull himself along the rope.

Reaching the stern, exhausted, he pulled himself over the rudder and dropped into the boat. For a moment he lay there looking up at the afternoon sky and trying to catch his breath. Then, he realized that he was still lying in water. Tiredly, Jem got to his knees. He found the bucket floating in muddy water which sloshed almost up to the seats. He bailed with all his might, throwing out fountains of water as the *Falcon* sailed.

When the water level had dropped to just above the bilge boards, Jem dropped the bucket and began to think about sailing. He had sailed in a small boat once or twice before, when Uncle Moss had to carry sails out to ships anchored at Bolivar Rhodes. Once, he had even been allowed to steer for awhile. Sailing alone, of course, was new. He took the tiller in one hand and turned it slightly. The *Falcon* changed course a few degrees.

"This ain't gonna be too hard," Jem told himself and pointed his bow at Pelican Island. *Falcon* bowed slightly to the south wind and picked up speed as Jem hauled in his sail. A smile spread over his dirty face. He was sailing. He was sailing his own boat, running free before the wind. Feelings that were new spread through him. The wind was free; he was free. *Falcon* would take him wherever he pleased, wherever fortune might be.

So exciting was this first sail, that Pelican Island was close off his bow when Jem noticed that he was almost knee-deep in water. Leaving the tiller to go its own way he grabbed the bucket and began to bail. But this time the water level refused to drop. It seemed that the faster he bailed, the faster the water rose. *Falcon* was sinking under him. He bailed frantically. The water kept rising. The *Falcon* slowed, there was a dull, scraping sound, and she stopped. Jem looked up and saw that he had run aground on a little sandbar just off the end of Pelican Island, called Pelican Spit.

For a long time he sat and did nothing. Then he climbed out of the *Falcon* and waded ashore. He had never been out here before. People just did not go to Pelican Spit without a good reason. It was said that pirates had been hanged here in Lafitte's time. There were three broken poles sticking up out of the sand that people said had been gallows. And once, a man had showed Jem a human skull which he claimed had come from here.

The thought of spending the night — cold, wet and

hungry on Pelican Spit — sent shivers up his spine and inspired him to find a way home. He scanned the bay for some sign of sail which meant rescue, but the only boats he saw were at anchor across the channel. It was not likely that anyone would be apt to pay any attention to him out here, especially since he appeared to have sailed here on his own accord. "Reckon I'll try ta bail her out again," he sighed, and waded back out to the boat.

An hour later he had lowered the water level down to a few inches above the bilge boards. He pulled up the boards and could see little currents of mud seeping through several of the *Falon's* seams. He looked for something to plug the holes, and concluded there was nothing handy. "Got my shirt," he thought aloud and took out his pocketknife. In a few seconds one of his sleeves had been cut into strips. With the point of his small blade, he slowly forced the strips into every seam which seemed to be leaking. By six o'clock only a few trickles of water continued to come in.

The *Falcon* felt light, as if she were trying to float. Again Jem climbed into the water and pushed on the bow. This time, however, he kept a strong hold on one of the lines. Slowly, he was able to turn the bow until the sail filled and *Falcon* heeled over a little. Jem dove into the boat as she began to move. He quickly grabbed the tiller, and set a course for the Navy Yard Dock. His teeth chattered as the cold night air cut through his wet clothes and chilled him to the bone. The *Falcon* sailed slowly into the darkness. It would take at least a couple of more hours to get home. And then, there was going to be a lot of explaining to do.

6

"Well now, if ya ain't the worst looking critter I ever seen crawl out of the swamp," Uncle Moss announced as he met Jem at the door. "Ya look worse than anything the cat ever dragged in."

"Been workin' on an old boat. Got kinda dirty," Jem offered, trying to avoid any detailed descriptions. Last week, he had showed Moss one of the coins and said that he had found it on the beach. That, he felt, was as close to the truth as he dared get.

"And what boat would that be?" Moss asked suspiciously.

"Bought me an old jolly boat. I been fixin' it up."

Moss huffed, "Looks more like it's been draggin' ya 'round the bay, trying ta drown ya."

"Yeah, I reckon I got kinda wet. I'll go clean up right now." Jem tried a retreat up the stairs. Uncle Moss grabbed his wet collar.

"Now just who sold ya that old skiff?"

Jem shrugged, "A man with a pig."

Moss broke into a laugh that shook the rafters of the loft. "Lieutenant Crisp, of the *Archer*. And that lunatic sold ya a boat fer that piece-of-eight ye found the other day?" Jem nodded sheepishly, avoiding his Uncle's eyes. "Was it the old jolly boat off the *Archer*?" Jem nodded again. "I know that boat and it's got more rotten planks than a dog's got fleas. She'd have ta be refastened from stem ta stern, and every seam in her needs recaulking. Best thing fer that old hull is ta tow her out on the bay — where she can sink in peace."

Jem stuck out his chin defiantly. "I can fix it," he said, and started up the stairs.

Behind him he could hear Uncle Moss cursing quietly, "The lad's head is harder than a rock and he ain't got one lick of sense. What's that they say 'bout a fool and his money being soon parted?"

Despite Uncle Moss's sarcasm, he went with Jem to look at the boat next morning. Together, they dragged the *Falcon* up onto the shore, unstepped the mast and turned her over. "Well, I reckon this ol' wreck will be a good chance fer ye ta learn somethin' 'bout being a shipwright. And right now, anything ya learn ta keep ya from starvin' ta death, can't be all bad." He poked his knife here and there along the planks. "This here one's soft, got ta come out and a new one fitted in; same for these two, and both them starboard strakes. Then, there's some sister ribbing and all new nails ta refasten her. When all of that's done, she's still gonna be an old boat, an you'll likely be an old man." He paused and looked at Jem's discouraged face. "You sure now, Boy, ya want to take on this project?"

Jem looked first at the little boat, then out at the bay and finally up at Uncle Moss. "Got to," he said.

Moss nodded. "Yeah, I reckon ya do."

"Can I take the sail back with us now and restitch it?

— after work of course," Jem added quickly as Moss started walking back along the shore.

"Bring it along, but we got a heap o' work ta get done before you'll be havin' any time ta spend at it," Moss agreed, and stood watching as Jem began to roll up the *Falcon*'s sail.

As Uncle Moss said, Jem had little time for anything except work for the next several weeks. A full-rigged three-master was in port and had ordered some twelve thousand square feet of new sail. Once again the drudgery of sewing and cutting canvas, splicing hemp line and carrying finished sails out to the dock filled Jem's days and nights. During his lunchtimes, he cut a new sail for the *Falcon* out of pieces of the three-master's old sails. He managed to slip away a few times late at night to work on *Falcon*'s hull. With only a smoky old lantern for light, he was able to remove most of the rotten planks.

Each night, when he finally dropped exhausted onto his cot, he would pull the map out from under his mattress and study it again and again. Several times he fell asleep clutching it in his hands. It fascinated him, obsessed him, perhaps. But it kept him going as his days began to blend together in one endless haze of work.

It was early May when he again began to have whole Saturdays and Sundays to spend working on the *Falcon*. All of the rotten planks had been removed, but little else had been accomplished. Time and again he had tried to cut new planks, but the strange curves and angles confused him. Each time he could find a few pieces of good wood, he would try again and each time there would still be large gaps between the planks. Odd-shaped pieces of wood were piling up next to the boat.

Raif stopped by one Sunday as Jem was working on the boat. "Hey, Jem," he said from behind him, "I haven't seen you in a long time."

Jem turned quickly, at first cross at being interrupted, but a smile soon spread across his face. "Got me a boat." he answered. "Been workin' on it."

Raif could see he was tired. "You still goin' after that treasure?"

"Yeah, soon as the boat's ready."

Raif inspected the overturned hull. "Then I think you got a long way to go."

"I'll get it," Jem snapped at him and kept trying to hammer a new plank into place.

Raif nodded. "Yes, my friend, I think you will."

Jem squinted up at him for a long moment. "I still need a crew if ya want ta come along."

"Not me," Raif answered, shuffling his feet and avoiding Jem's eyes. "I got too many things to do here. Besides, I don't like boats and I don't swim so good."

Ya ain't gonna have ta swim!" Jem insisted. "I'm gonna fix the boat."

Raif smiled and sighed. "You drive a hard bargain, but this is not for me. Still, I understand that for some reason you have to go and I wish you good luck."

"Thanks Raif," Jem said after a pause, and then went back to work on the plank.

Evening came and Raif went home, but Jem kept working. About midnight he had one plank set in that looked pretty good. He was too tired to continue. He put his handful of tools back into the bag and blew out his lantern. He lay back on the sand and stared up at the stars for awhile. A full moon rose from behind the dunes. Coyotes were howling somewhere down the island and waves lapped on the shore. The south wind stirred and sent a shiver down Jem's spine. Suddenly, he did not feel alone.

Sitting up, he neither saw nor heard anything unusual. But as he picked up his things and started back across the dunes, a shadow crossed the moon. Then, in front of him, Jem saw a dark figure with a plumed hat that stood on top of a sand dune, silhouetted against the pale moon. A long cape hung from the shoulders and flowed in the night wind.

Jem gulped and wondered why he was not already running, but much to his own surprise, he did not run. Instead he just stared at the figure and the figure seemed to stare back. Jem squinted and tried to see a face, but it was too dark. In fact, he could tell little else about the figure except that it wore high boots. For a second Jem looked away and then the figure was gone. There was only the moon, the sand dunes, the distant sound of surf and coyotes. Jem blinked his eyes several times, and turned quickly, looking in all directions, but he was alone. Then, he pinched himself just to be sure he was awake. "Maybe I'm just too plumb tired to know what I'm seein' any more," he tried to convince himself, and started nervously home.

7

Jem worked in the sail loft for all of the next week without having a chance to go back to the boat. It was the following Sunday afternoon before he at last slipped away, and started down the shore toward the old Navy Yard Pier. He walked more slowly than usual, kicking shells and poking at sand crabs as they stared out at him from their holes.

He was discouraged with his progress on *Falcon.* He wondered if he had taken on a project which was more than he could handle. The new planks he cut never seemed to fit. Always, there was a gap big enough to see light through, and no amount of caulking would ever make it tight.

I wish I was like Raif, he told himself. *Raif's got more sense than to go tryin' ta fix an old, wore-out boat and chase some treasure story.* Jem was still criticizing himself when he walked up over the last sand dune and looked on the shore where he had left *Falcon*'s overturned hull.

The shore was deserted. *Falcon* was gone. Only a few marks in the sand showed where it had been dragged toward the water. Jem sat down on the sand, and was almost in tears before he noticed a boat tied up to the pier, with its mast stepped and sail neatly furled. For a long moment he stared blankly at it before he realized that it was his own.

Somebody must've just launched it, 'cause it ain't sunk yet, he thought, and ran out on the pier. Jumping aboard, he lifted the bilge boards and expected to find dark water bubbling up faster than he could hope to bail it out. But *Falcon* was dry. Jem could hardly believe his eyes. He ran his fingers over new planks which had mysteriously replaced all of the rotten ones. The pleasant odors of tar, oakum and fresh-cut wood drifted to him as his fingers picked up traces of dry sawdust where he usually found water.

New ropes now formed the headstay and shrouds. He peered over the side where shiny white paint on the *Falcon*'s hull reflected back to him off the water. Feelings of absolute delight mixed with those of wonder.

Who could have done this? Who would have helped me? His first thought was Uncle Moss. *Yeah,* Jem thought with a smile. *He might do something like this an' not tell me till it was done.* But he had been working with Moss almost every day and he hadn't gone anywhere. *Still, he could have hired someone to do it.* That made sense, he decided. *It had to be Uncle Moss unless . . .*

He thought of the strange figure he had seen last week in the moonlight. *Crazy Ben?* Perhaps it was Ben he saw? Was the old pirate repaying him for helping him fight off the men who tried to rob him? Maybe he could have also been responsible for the map?

Jem found no answers to those questions. But *Falcon* was tight and dry, it was Sunday afternoon and the wind was fresh. He would go sailing. He hoisted the sail and slipped the dock lines. *Falcon* turned off the wind, dipped her freshly painted rail, and bounded off into the harbor. "She feels like a frisky colt," Jem said aloud as he trimmed the sail.

The harbor was crowded that afternoon. In addition to a half dozen ships at anchor, there was the usual traffic of sailing skiffs, scows, and rowing boats. Two steamboats, the *Dayton* and the *Powderhorn*, were at the Morgan Line Wharf. *Falcon* slipped past an English barkentine at anchor as sailors waved at him from her deck. He waved back and steered in close to the *Dayton*. Her huge paddle wheels were still now. Jem marveled at their size. Although he had seen them often enough from the wharf, they looked larger and more ominous from down on the water. They towered overhead, twice as high as the *Falcon*'s little mast.

Jem and the *Falcon* rounded Pelican Island, and this time Jem was careful to stay out of the shallows. Far to the north was the low outline of Halfmoon Shoal. Somewhere out there, over the horizon, was the place marked on his map, the place he must go. Suddenly, he did not want to turn back. The urge to keep sailing steadily northward was overpowering.

"No," he said aloud to break the spell. "I gotta think practical once in a while." He had no water and food aboard. There was no compass to keep him headed in the right direction, and not even a shovel to dig up the treasure. Reluctantly he turned *Falcon* toward home and wished Raif were going with him.

He was not ready yet. His preparations were not finished. He would make a list of things he needed and then begin to collect them whenever he could. The more he sailed, the more things came to mind that he could not do without. Bottles for water, fishing line and hooks, coal oil for his lantern, some kind of box or keg to keep food dry, a pot to use for cooking, flint and steel or a tinderbox for building fires; the list went on. By the time he was approaching the dock, it had become endless.

"Hey there, Jem!" Raif's voice called from the pier. "I see you got your boat fixed."

Jem waved back as he brought *Falcon* alongside with only a slight bump which shook the mast and scraped a foot-long strip of paint off *Falcon*'s side. "Hi, Raif," Jim said, trying to ignore his rough docking as they tied off the mooring lines.

"She looks pretty good," Raif's commented. "At least before you hit a few more docks."

"Musta been a wave caught me," Jem made a lame excuse and shrugged.

They sat on the dock at sunset. Both boys seemed to be lost in their own thoughts. "How soon you gonna leave?" Raif asked finally.

"Don't rightly know. Gotta find a bunch of supplies first. Took all my money just ta get the boat. Summer's comin' fast though, I gotta get ready pretty soon."

"You think you can really sail that thing?"

"You just saw me sail it."

"I mean following that map up through that bay, across the reefs an' all."

"I can with a compass. Reckon I can without one if I have to."

Raif shook his head slowly. "Jem, I think there is no way to talk you out of this fool thing you plan to do."

"No. There's no way," Jem confirmed.

"Well, then I guess I have no choice but to go with you."

Jem looked up, shocked. "Why? You said you hated boats and didn't want nothin' to do with spooky treasure."

"That is true."

"So why you want ta go *now*?"

"I did not say I *wanted* to go. I said I *will* go."

Jem sighed and looked away. "Now, what's that supposed ta mean?"

"It means that you and I are friends and I think friends should help each other," Raif said. "Even if one friend is crazy. So, if you still want a partner, I'm available."

Jem squinted at Raif but his eyes still betrayed his happiness. "You mean it?"

"Of course I mean it. It is crazy, but I mean it. So, are we partners again?"

"Partners!" Jem grinned, sticking out his hand.

8

Raif and Jem pressed their noses against the dirty glass of the shop window for a better look. Inside was a tarnished old brass compass, almost hidden beneath a layer of dust.

"You think it still works?" Raif asked.

Jem shrugged, "Don't know, can't see the needle."

"How much you think it will cost?"

"Probably more'n we got ta spend."

Raif started for the shop door, "I know the owner, name's Muldoon. He's a bad one but he always needs money."

Inside, the shop was like a junkyard with a roof. Old rope, dust covered and smelling of rot, lay in huge piles. There were used sails, all kinds of cleats, blocks, anchors, and rusty chain. On a shelf were a few sextants and tarnished brass lamps.

No one greeted them as they entered, so they looked closer at the compass. Raif picked it up carefully and held it in his hands. It was the type with a handle used on ships for sighting the bearings of landmarks ashore, or other ships. There was a crack in the glass and some of the fluid inside was gone. "Looks like the needle is still pointing north," Jem said as he saw the needle swing back and forth a little.

"That means it's working?" Raif asked.

"Of course that means it's working," Jem answered him crossly. "That's how a compass works. It always points north no matter which way you turn it."

Raif scratched his head. "So what happens when you want to go some other direction — like south or east."

"Dang it, Raif, you don't know nothin'. That's what these letters are for around the side. If you want to go south, you just follow the S, if you want to go west, you follow the W. Its simple as fallin' off a log."

"One thing I know about compasses is how to buy one cheap," Raif defended as he replaced the instrument.

They walked to the back of the shop between high rows of piled boxes covered with cobwebs. A door opened to their right, and at last they heard faint voices.

"Heck, Bruno, everything you and the Rat got here, was stole just last night. I can't pay ya much, 'cause I got to keep it hid till a month or so after the ship leaves. Constable is already lookin' for this stuff."

"Dis gute stuff, you pay more or Bruno break you head," another voice was saying as they peeked around the half-opened door. In the room were three men. Two wore dark blue coats and stood with their backs to the boys. There was something disturbingly familiar about them. The third was the shop owner.

"Don't go getting uppity with me. I take care of you, remember that. Or maybe you'd like to start sellin' your stolen junk somewhere else, like the — " The shop owner's sentence went unfinished as he suddenly spotted the two boys. "Hey, what are you two doin' sneaking 'round here?"

Jem was too scared to answer, but Raif spoke up at

once. "Hey, Muldoon. How much you want for that junky old compass in the window?"

The shop owner huffed and then growled as he started toward them. "More'n you ragamuffins got ta spend on it. Now get yer tails out here 'fore I cut 'em off." He grabbed at their shirt collars, dragging them quickly out into the front of the shop. "Go on now — skeedaddle," he added, pushing them toward the front door.

They were almost in the street when Raif held up one of his coins. Muldoon stopped in his tracks. His blood-shot eyes focused in on the shiny coin and he took it in one of his big, dirty hands. Jem did not like the suspicious look which spread slowly across his fat face. "Well now, this is a might small ta buy a compass with. Got any more?" he said in a tone which Jem liked even less.

"More?" Raif protested. "For that piece of junk? It's all busted. Probably don't work."

The shopkeeper lifted the old compass in his hands like it was some long lost treasure. "Junk ya call it? Why this is a fine instrument, made in France, and carried aboard a frigate, it was. Got this here crack when it was hit by musket ball during the war with England. I couldn't possibly let it go for a single bit of silver. Three, coins and not a bit less."

"Three?" Raif returned loudly. "Right down the street, there is a compass, much nicer than this one for only two." With a lightning move he snatched his coin back and grabbed Jem's arm. "Come on partner, we will take our business elsewhere."

Jem did not remember seeing any other compasses but he kept quiet as they headed for the door. They had not reached it when Muldoon sighed. "Two silver coins it is, if you've really got them."

In a matter of seconds the compass was in Jem's hands and they were back out on the street. Raif was all smiles. "How did I do, Partner? Pretty good, huh?"

"Yeah, pretty good," Jem smiled back. "Now all we got to get is some food and fishin' gear and we're about ready."

"Pieces of eight," Muldoon whispered thoughtfully as he watched the two boys disappear down the street. "Could be those little nippers found themselves a bit of buried treasure."

The two men from the back room moved beside him. "Dat Kid bust my head wit a rock," the one called Bruno said. "Bruno get him good one day."

"Nasty little brats they is," the Rat chimed in from over Bruno's shoulder. "Made me get me arm cut near off."

"Those two?" The Muldoon looked surprised. "You mean they were the ones with Crazy Ben when you two tried to rob him?" Bruno only nodded. "Well now, that's interesting indeed. Perhaps you two should keep an eye on our young friends out there. Could be they might just lead us to all of Lafitte's treasure."

Bruno was smiling beneath a week of chin whiskers. He gurgled when he tried to laugh and lumbered out of the store with Rat close behind him.

"We ought to leave on Saturday night," Raif said as they walked toward the wharf. "We could say we were going camping and no one would look for us until Monday."

"That's only a week off. I reckon we can be ready by then."

"As ready as we're going to be — because we're broke," Raif added.

Jem squinted at him. "You still got one more coin, don't you?"

The boy shook his head. "That one is for my mother. To make up for the money I don't bring in while we are away."

Jem nodded. "Yeah, that's a good idea. No sense in hurtin' your family in case this don't work out so good."

It was decided that they would sail on Saturday night. During the next few days they were able to scrape together the bare essential items they would need. Jem found an old piece of sail which would work as a tent, and hid it beneath his cot. At low tide he waded under the Navy Pier and found a half dozen rusty fishhooks stuck in the pilings where they had been lost by other fishermen. Raif brought in a small keg to carry drinking water and a bag full of dried beans. Another bottle was filled with oil for the lantern.

On Wednesday night, Jem rolled all his gear, including the compass, in the old piece of sail and tied it in a neat bundle. He decided that on Saturday, he would take some salt pork and dried fruit from Uncle Moss's kitchen. That, he figured, would carry them through until they had time to stop and catch fish. Then too, there were wild plants and berries to eat along the way. Of course, neither Jem nor Raif had ever eaten wild plants, but Jem felt certain he could figure out which ones were right when the time came.

He had just gone up to bed on Wednesday evening, when a knock came at the door to Uncle Moss's living quarters behind the sail loft. He peered down from the head of the stairs which led to his room as Moss answered the door. To his horror, it was Muldoon. Jem ducked behind the banister rail and listened. From that distance he could make out only bits of the conversation, but with each word he heard, his heart dropped.

"They seemed to have several of these Spanish coins, Mr. Tatum," Muldoon was lying. "Of course, I thought it a bit odd for two young boys to be interested in an old compass in the first place and — well, I simply thought you should know about it."

"Well now, why don't we just go an ask the lad himself," Moss was saying in an irritated voice. "He's just now gone up ta bed."

Jem panicked. They would search his room and find his gear. They would know he was planning to sneak off. Worst of all, they would find his map. "Gotta run," he whispered to himself. Hurrying back into his room, he grabbed his gear from beneath the bed, stuffed the precious map into his shirt, and climbed out onto the window ledge. He took time to close the window behind him just as the first knock came on the door. Tossing his bundle over to the next roof, he jumped after it. The pipe leading down from the gutter to the street below was harder. He bit down on one of the strings which tied his gear, and climbed down with the bundle dangling.

Landing lightly on the ground, he looked out from the alley, into the street. Less than ten feet away was a man, leaning against the wall, and although he was looking the other way, Jem had a sick feeling he was waiting for him. Even from the back he recognized him as one of the men who had been in the back room when they had bought the compass.

Before he could decide what to do, the window above him banged open. Jem froze in the shadow of the building, pressing himself as tightly against the wall as he could. "Danged if that ain't a might strange," he heard Uncle Moss say from above. "I wonder where that lad is off to?"

He breathed a sigh of relief when the window finally closed, but a shadow crossed the edge of the building a second later. The big man looked ten feet tall as he reached for Jem's collar. "Bruno gonna bust you head," he snarled.

9

"Come out dere you nasty little nipper. Where is all dat treasure you find?" Bruno growled down at him.

"Treasure?" Jem managed to answer in a trembling voice as he shrank closer against the wall. "I haven't got any — "

"You got treasure. Bruno like treasure. All nice shiny coins, silver and gold buy Bruno big keg of rum. Maybe you got treasure dere in dat bag. You give Bruno treasure, maybe he not bust you head too bad."

Bruno's dirty hand looked like a huge claw as it moved toward him. Jem took the only route of escape he saw. Ducking his head, he ran between the man's legs, tripping him as he went. Across the street and into the shadows of the next buildings, Jem ran with his precious bundle and never looked back. Far behind him he could hear Bruno's heavy footsteps as he gave chase. But Bruno was not built for speed. Jem was both small and fast, even when he was not scared, and tonight he was faster than ever. He kept to the alleys, cutting across backyards and under fences now and then as he headed for Raif's house.

There would not be much time. Surely, the men would look next either at Raif's house or the dock where the *Falcon* was moored. Either way, he was in trouble. He was panting when he finally reached Raif's house and tossed an oyster shell at the upstairs window. Nervous seconds ticked by before his friend's head finally appeared. "They're on to us!" Jem called in a loud whisper. "We gotta go — leave right now. Tonight!" A long moment of silence passed, and Jem waited nervously for an answer. He seemed to be considering what to do. "Dang it, come on!" Jem added and at last Raif's sleepy head disappeared from the window.

Again the minutes dragged by. The moon had risen full and bright so Jem stepped into the shadow of a ragged salt cedar and waited until Raif slipped out the front door carrying a small bundle.

"Come on!" Jem urged, grabbing his sleeve. "They can't be far behind us."

Raif yawned as they started off. "Who's *they*?"

"Those guys at the shop where we bought the compass. I think they might be the same ones who were in the old fort, too."

They found the dock deserted. *Falcon* bobbed alongside as if she too, was anxious to be off. Jem quickly hoisted the little sail while Raif stowed the two bundles of gear. In only a couple of minutes they were sailing across the harbor.

All of the months of planning, working and dreaming were behind them now. At last the adventure had begun — and it was frightening. They sailed in silence for awhile, each boy lost in his own thoughts of what lay ahead, and behind. Jem's hand was shaking on the tiller as he steered down between the row of anchored ships. They looked larger in the dark and *Falcon* seemed so very small. Again and again he looked over his shoulder, expecting to see lanterns on the dock behind him, but everything was dark there.

"I wanted to leave Uncle Moss a note, tellin' him why I left," Jem said. "Couldn't do it though."

"I left a note with the coin for my mother," Raif admitted. "Maybe she'll tell him."

The *Falcon* passed the point of Pelican Island, with its white breakers glowing in the moonlight, close off the port bow. Raif lit their lantern and unwrapped the bundle which contained the compass. While Raif held it close to the light, Jem turned the *Falcon* to the north. Then he pulled the map from his shirt and laid it on the seat. "Reckon the next thing we'll see is Halfmoon Shoal."

Raif looked at the little half circle marked on the map. "How long you think it will take to get that far?"

Jem had almost no idea. He had never been that far north before. In fact, he had never been north of Pelican Island. "Reckon we'll see it by mornin'," he guessed. Only the gurgling sound of water rushing past the little boat's hull broke the night's silence. The lights of Galveston slowly faded away, and they were totally alone. The moon climbed ever higher, slipping behind a few scattered clouds now and then as the hours passed by.

Raif's head nodded sleepily again and again, until he finally curled up in the old sail. "Wake me up when you get sleepy," he yawned and was instantly asleep. Jem would have liked to sleep also. For awhile the pure excitement of the whole thing had kept him going. But, as the hours wore on, the steady rhythm of wind and sea rocked him closer and closer to sleep. It would do no good to wake Raif, he reasoned. He had never sailed the boat before.

Falcon's sail flapped loudly, and he realized that he had dozed off. Checking the wind and the compass, he turned back on course and stared out at the night. It occurred to him to drop the sail, get some sleep and drift until morning. No, that was out of the question. They must be as far from Galveston as possible when the sun came up.

The wind dropped off during the last hours before dawn. Long gray wisps of fog moved silently in over the bay until the *Falcon* appeared to drift in a world of gray which hid the water from the sky. Only high above were stars still visible. Jem could no longer tell if they were moving or not. Far away, the lonely bass tone of a foghorn echoed in the night. Raif stirred, turned on his side beneath the old sail and was instantly back asleep. *For someone who did not want to go anywhere in a boat, he sure does sleep good,* Jem thought. A pang of guilt shot through him. Raif trusted him and his boat. He still believed that Jem, not some mysterious helper, had repaired *Falcon. I should have told him,* Jem thought. *But then, he might not have come along, and I would have been too scared to come out here alone.* Again, the foghorn moaned through the night. It sounded closer this time.

Raif sat up suddenly. "What was that?"

"Ship. Probably a steamboat comin' down from Harrisburg." He failed to hide an uncomfortable note in his voice.

"Where is it?"

"How would I know? Just out there somewhere."

Raif was sitting up now and anxiously peering out into the fog. "How are they gonna see us?"

"They ain't gonna see us. I just hope they ain't comin' this way." Even as he spoke, they could barely hear the dull throb of a steam engine and the steady *Spash–splash* of paddle wheels.

"Come on, Jem! get this boat going. We got to get away from here."

"I can't, there ain't no wind!" Jem admitted on the verge of panic. "Quick, get the oars out!" Throwing gear all about the *Falcon*'s bilge boards, they dug the two oars out from under the seats, and fumbled as they tried to fit them hurriedly into the brass oarlocks on the gunnels. As they worked, the steady throbbing of engine and splashing of paddle wheels grew ever louder. The foghorn pierced the night. It was no longer a distant moan but roared like the boom of thunder. They saw the red glow above the steamboat's smokestacks first. Then, the few visible stars began to vanish as the dim outline took shape in the fog.

Jem swung the tiller hard over, and he and Raif rowed with all their might. It seemed as if the *Falcon* was going nowhere. Jem shot one quick look at the steamer bearing down on them. A white curl of boiling water, glowing pale white in the fog, rushed out from the bow. The engine noise was deafening now and the steamer's black silhouette blocked out the sky.

The curl of white water rose behind them, kicking *Falcon*'s little stern and trying to drive her bow under. But the little boat shot forward, riding over the wave and shooting alongside the charging steamer. They could see the maindeck railings in the gloom, and even glimpsed a couple of people who did not appear to know they had passed so closely.

Jem left his oar and swung the *Falcon* away just as the starboard paddle wheel came out of the night. One huge blade after another slammed into the water, each big enough to turn *Falcon* into match sticks. The last they saw of the steamboat was her name, painted over the paddle wheel cover. It read *Dayton*.

Jem was shaking all over as the *Falcon* wallowed in the steamboat's wake. How many times had he watched that same steamboat come and go from Galveston, and how many times had he marveled at those huge paddle wheels? He would think of them differently when — and if — he saw them again.

"I think that was too close," Raif said shakily. "Now I know I am crazy to be here."

Jem did not argue the point. In the east, dawn was breaking, and there was a hint of wind on his face. He turned *Falcon* back to the north and the little sail filled. Raif handed him a tortilla. "I grabbed these last night," he offered.

The fog had almost lifted when they had finished their scant breakfast and each had a drink from the water cask. Behind them, Galveston had vanished over the horizon. Far to the west was a dim outline of land which had to be the shoreline somewhere north of Half-moon Shoal. Ahead, and closer, was a chain of small, low islands.

Jem unrolled the map and studied it for a minute. "Those islands should be part of Redfish Bar."

"Hey," Raif chimed in, obviously feeling better. "Then we are almost halfway there."

10

The wind was light under sunny skies all through the morning. By early afternoon, they were sailing down between two little islands which were part of the chain known as Redfish Bar. Jem pointed the *Falcon* into the protected lee shore of one of them. Two tortillas each had not relieved the hunger of two growing boys, and they had decided to stop here long enough to catch a fish or two for dinner.

The *Falcon*'s bow scraped lightly on a smooth sandbar. The two boys jumped overboard into knee-deep water and dragged the boat a little higher on the beach. Jem dropped the sail, took the anchor line and tied it around an old driftwood stump buried in the sand. The island was little more than a sandbar. Only in its center were a few twisted cedars and some scattered clumps of salt grass. Otherwise, it was nothing more than sand and oyster shell. But, to Jem and Raif, it might as well have been a tropical paradise, at least for the first thirty minutes.

"Let's start a fire and cook up some beans," Raif suggested as soon as they stepped ashore.

"You got any tinder to start a fire with?" Jem asked him.

"You said you were going to bring it."

"I was, but we had to run, remember?"

"So how are we going to cook?"

Jem looked sick. "How do I know?"

"Then we gotta go back," Raif insisted quickly. "We'll starve to death up here."

"I saw a book once, showed how Indians built a fire with two sticks," Jem said thoughtfully. "Maybe we could try that."

Raif frowned. "Two sticks? Come on Jem, you got to be foolin' with me."

Jem walked to the cedar trees. "First, they made kind of a bow out of a stick and a piece of string. Then they used it to turn another stick real fast while it was settin' on a flat piece of wood. When it got hot, they put dry leaves around it and blew on it. Leastways, that's what the book said."

Raif was in favor of anything which would result in a warm meal, and so during the afternoon they tried to build a fire. The bow was easy to build with a small cedar limb and a piece of fishing line. For the flat surface, they chose a driftwood log on the beach. There were no leaves on the island, but they did find some needles from the cedar trees for tinder. The problem seemed to be that there was nothing really dry on a small island surrounded by water and washed over by waves during almost every storm.

"You ever eat raw fish?" Raif asked late in the afternoon.

"No. But we don't have any fish, raw or otherwise, so I guess I don't have to try it yet," Jem snapped, disgusted by the wasted afternoon.

"I think we are soon going to be wet as well as hungry," Raif pointed at the southern sky. Black clouds were boiling there, and amongst them the sky was an ominous shade of green. "Looks like it's going to rain cats and dogs."

They gave up on the fire then, and returned to *Falcon.* Jem removed the sail and then tied the old canvas over the boom to form a little tent with open ends. They checked the mooring line and waited.

The black line of clouds rolled up from the south and blotted out the sun. The wind gusted and whitecaps rolled across the bay. Big drops of rain hit their makeshift tent just at twilight, and in minutes the storm was on them in full force. Sheets of wind-driven rain slashed at them, and waves broke completely over the island. The two boys sat huddled beneath the sail, as water dripped in steady streams through the old canvas.

"If we get out of this, I'm going straight home in the morning," Raif said mournfully, as he wiped water from his face and shivered. "We had to be crazy to come up here."

Jim did not feel like arguing. In fact, it occurred to him that Raif was probably right. Things were not working out as he had figured they would. If only he had had the last few days to gather up a few more pieces of gear, it might have been different. Now, it looked as if there was going to be nothing to eat, in addition to being wet and miserable.

"I wish we could go back, but we can't," Jem said sadly. "Those guys from the shop will be lookin' for us. They think we found Lafitte's treasure."

"Where did they get that idea?" Raif looked more unhappy than ever.

" 'Cause of the coins. They figure the only way two kids could have got them was to dig 'em up somewhere."

"Wonderful." Raif ended the conversation and put his head under the tarp.

The *Falcon* stirred and scraped her keel on the sand. Jem stuck his head out cautiously and squinted into the storm. He could no longer see the island but steady lines of waves were breaking over it and slamming down all around them. In addition to that, the tide was coming in. Soon the *Falcon* was banging dangerously on the bottom as each wave picked them up and dropped them again as it passed.

"What are we going to do now?" Raif asked from beneath the tarp.

Jem did not know. If he had more rope, he could lengthen the mooring line and let *Falcon* play out into deeper water. But all the line was on the island, lying beside the stump they were tied to. He was thinking about trying to work his way out on the mooring line when the decision was made for him. The line broke.

The *Falcon* shot backward and immediately turned sideways. Before Jem could reach the tiller they were rolled almost over and drenched as a wave broke over them. Water was over the bilge boards as the next wave bore down and rolled them again. Dark water spilled over the gunnels this time, while Jem fought to turn the boat downwind. Raif bailed with the bucket, throwing water desperately in all directions and probably getting as much in the boat as he was getting out.

They turned sluggishly. A white-topped wave rose from behind them now, kicking the stern up and giving them a burst of speed. White water glowed in the darkness as the wave roared past them but *Falcon* stayed afloat. Wind screamed through the rigging and spray stung their faces. Jem tried to steer but gave up and used his hat to help Raif bail. It was impossible to tell if *Falcon* was leaking or if all of the water was washing in over the sides. They bailed until their arms could no longer move, and then sat shivering as they drifted with the storm.

"How long can this last?" Raif wailed in the dark.

"Not too much longer, I hope." Jem answered trying to sound hopeful and failing miserably.

All around them, the storm's fury raged suddenly louder, roaring like a hundred steamboats all charging down on them at full speed. Jem stuck his head out from under the canvas and was terrified. Everywhere was white churning water that glowed in the darkness. There were no longer lines of waves marching down on them. Instead, waves were moving in all directions, colliding and breaking in huge fountains of spray. Jem had never seen or imagined anything like this. Raif was beside him speaking Spanish — which he did not understand but he was sure there was something about Mother and God. Raif switched suddenly to English just long enough to say, "I think we are done for."

Jem started to tell him it would be all right but before the words were out, the *Falcon* hit something, spun quickly around and turned on her side. Cold water hit his face, tugging at him with more force than he could have believed possible. His grip was torn from the tiller and he saw *Falcon* lying on her side, filling quickly with water. "Raif, Raif!" he yelled, but got no answer as the water pulled him down. He remembered nothing more.

11

Birds circled in a blue haze when Jem opened his eyes. His mouth tasted of salt. Slowly, ever so slowly, he began to remember the storm, the churning white water and *Falcon* turning over. *Raif*, he tried to call, but managed only a groan as he raised himself painfully on one elbow. The sun was high in a cloudless blue sky and he shaded his eyes with one hand and looked around. He was on a small stretch of beach — maybe another island. A few wind-bent cedar trees clung to a low hill nearby and the bay was but a few feet away.

"Raif!" he called again and listened. Only the cries of seagulls and the quiet lapping of waves against the sand could be heard. He rose stiffly, hurting everywhere when he tried to walk. His head hurt the most and for a while the beach refused to stop spinning under him. "Got to find Raif," he mumbled as he moved unsteadily along.

He climbed the little hill to the trees and confirmed that he was again on an island. Thirty yards away, and across a narrow cut of shallow water was another island, or maybe it was all part of the same island, he could not tell. But there, on the beach, sat a small brown-skinned boy.

"Raif, over here!" he called, overjoyed he was not completely alone. Raif looked up, as surprised as Jem, and in a few seconds they were together on the beach.

"Hey, my friend, I thought you were dead," Raif admitted.

"Yeah, I thought the same thing about you." For awhile, they sat under the shade of one of the trees, too tired and confused to do anything else.

"Do we have anything left?" Raif asked later.

Jem felt in his pockets. "My pocketknife," he announced with little enthusiasm. He felt inside his torn shirt. "We still have the map."

"Great. So where do you think we are and how do we get home?" Raif questioned.

Together, they took a long look at the map. "I got no idea which way we went in the storm. I reckon we're probably still somewhere on Redfish Bar — but who knows where!"

"Looks like shoreline over there," Raif said, pointing at a line of trees perhaps two miles away.

Jem looked at the sun. "You reckon we might be clear over on the east shore? Maybe somewhere up in Trinity Bay?"

Raif shook his head. "I don't know anything about that. I just want a drink of water, something to eat and a way home."

"Well, we can't just sit here forever," said Jem. "Let's explore this place."

They started off down the beach. Soon, they found they were on a chain of little islands, separated by shallow cuts of water which usually could be waded. Everywhere were seagulls and all kinds of shorebirds. Roseate spoonbills, as graceful as flamingos, nested in the treetops and sandpipers bobbed along the shoreline. They had been walking for an hour or so when Raif spotted the mast. "Look, a boat!" He almost shouted in Jem's ear.

Across the next island the tip of a mast was just visible. "That's the *Falcon*'s mast," Jem observed. With the last of their lagging energy, they raced toward it.

The *Falcon* was lying half sunk a few yards from the shore. The sail was badly torn but the mast was still standing, if a little crooked. They waded out and looked inside. Sand had washed in and covered the bilge boards, but the bow was a few inches above water. There was no sign of any of their gear except the bucket.

"If we dump some of this sand out of her, maybe we can get her up on the shore," Jem said and began scooping out the wet ooze. They worked on *Falcon* for awhile and removed most of the sand. Still, the little boat showed no signs of moving. "Next low tide, we can finish bailing her out and float her, I think," Jem announced hopefully as they waded ashore.

"You know," Raif said. "I'm so hungry I think I can smell food cooking."

"Don't think about it. It just makes it worse."

"I know — but just the same it sure smells good."

Jem had to agree. It seemed he too could smell the odor of freshly cooked fish mingled with that of woodsmoke. By the time they waded ashore, the smell was even stronger.

Raif sniffed the air like a hound dog on the trail of a rabbit. "I do not think this is all my imagination," he concluded and started walking toward the center of the island. Jem followed. They finally looked down at a scene which made their mouths water.

There on the beach was a campfire with two fish roasting on sticks. Beside it sat a figure no bigger than themselves and nearby lay a large brown dog. A small skiff, about half the size of *Falcon*, was pulled up on the shore. The two boys ducked into the salt grass and watched. The figure at the fire was dark skinned, had long, straight, black hair and wore buckskin clothes.

"Indians?" Raif asked in a frightened whisper.

"Worse. I think it's a girl."

Raif blinked. "Can't be. Not alone out here in the middle of nowhere."

"Her folks must be around somewhere. Maybe fishin'." Jem looked out across the bay and saw no trace of boat or fishermen.

"That's good, we can get something to eat and then they can help us get home," Raif announced, and started to get up.

"We shouldn't tell anyone we're here," Jem objected. "Muldoon and his friends might get wind of it and find us."

Raif insisted that, whatever the chance, it was better than starving to death. He walked toward the figure on the beach. Reluctantly, Jem followed.

They were not very close when the dog suddenly raised its head and barked once. The figure in buckskin turned to face the boys. "Dang it," Jem whispered. "It *is* a girl."

"Good day, senorita," Raif greeted with a low bow which made Jem turn up his nose and stick out his tongue. "My friend and I were stranded on this island when our boat wrecked last night. It has been some time since we have eaten and — "

"Join us then," the girl said, extending her hand with a slow, graceful motion. With her other hand she touched the dog's head. "Quiet, Getana. They are guests." Immediately, the dog lay back down.

She was thin and a little taller than Jem. Her skin was tanned dark by the sun and her eyes were as black as her hair. Although Jem thought she must be about his own age, her every movement said she was older. She asked if they were thirsty and brought a goatskin bag filled with liquid from her skiff. The boys had had nothing to drink since the night before, so Raif hurriedly took the first drink. He gulped down two mouthfuls before his eyes got large and his face turned brilliant red. He swallowed hard and tried to speak. The girl stared at him expressionless. His mouth moved and he finally managed to say, "This is not water. What is it?"

"My mother called it the wind of Spring. It is made of berries and some flowers on their first day of blooming. There is also honey from the wild bees and some herbs which grow deep in the woods," the girl replied. "Do you find it to your taste?"

Raif smiled. "Yes, after one becomes used to it, it is quite good."

Jem was sniffing the goatskin, uncertain whether or not to take a chance. He was thirsty, he reasoned, and it seemed to have no lasting effect on Raif; so he took a small sip. The taste was sweet and tingly as it went down, different but not at all unpleasant. He nodded and took another drink. "Thanks," he said, returning the goatskin bag.

"I am Rafael Don Marcos Rodrigues Fernando Garcia," Raif introduced himself with another bow. "But my friends call me Raif. And this is my friend and business partner, Jeremiah Dundee, who is better known as Jem." Jem nodded.

"And I am called Talva," the girl introduced herself.

"Don't reckon I ever knew anybody named that before," Jem finally spoke up.

Talva smiled at him. "And I have never known anyone named Jem. But my mother told me that my name means Spring in the language of witches."

"Witches?" Raif gulped.

"And this is Getana," Talva ignored the question and pointed to the dog. "In the same language, it means Gypsy." Without waiting for more questions, she returned to the fire and turned the two fish. "I have caught only these two so we will need some more." She picked up a round castnet from the boat and waded out into the water. With a quick flick of wrist, the net sailed out in a spinning circle and dropped into the water. Pulling on a cord looped around her wrist, she retrieved it and held it up. The net had closed like a bag and inside was a fish. She removed it and handed it to Jem while she threw the net again. "Do not drop him," she warned.

They dined that night on redfish and shrimp, roasted on sticks. The flames of their driftwood fire reflected off the water and sent dancing shadows across the island. The stars came out, huge and bright in the cloudless sky. Later, the moon rose.

The boys talked about their boat and recounted their adventures with the steamboat and the storm. When Talva asked why they had taken such a great risk to come there, Jem answered only that it was a secret and the fewer people who knew about it, the better.

Talva stared at him for a long moment until Jem began to feel uncomfortable. It was as if she could see right through him and knew everything he was thinking. "Does it involve the locket that you wear with the falcon on it?" she asked quietly.

Jem looked surprised and his hand involuntarily moved to his neck. "Course not."

Talva shrugged her thin shoulders. "I only asked because my mother told me of a woman she once met who wore a locket like that."

A tremble of excitement shot through him like lightning. He said nothing, but Talva seemed to sense that he wanted her to continue.

"She visited a place she called 'Campeachy.' It was to the south, where you came from. She told me there was a castle there, all painted red with cannons high on the walls. And inside was a ballroom where lords and ladies danced at great parties."

Jem was shaking when he looked at Raif, who stared

back and nodded. They were sure she was talking about the old pirate fort.

"There was a lady there, almost a queen, I think. Mother said that she was very beautiful — but also very strong. And she wore a gold locket with a black falcon on it."

In all Jem's life, no one had ever given him so much as a hint of his past. He stared into the fire and his hand trembled as he gripped the locket. *Was this some clue? Could Talva's mother have once met someone who wore the same locket?* "What. . .what else did she say?" he stammered without looking up.

Talva frowned and looked into the depths of the fire, as if trying to pull back some long forgotten memory. "Only that she was named Madeline."

"Would it be possible for us to speak to your mother and see if she remembers anything else?" Raif suggested.

Talva's expression never changed as she stared straight at him. "Not easily. She died two summers ago."

12

Talva awakened them in the first gray light of dawn, saying the tide would be at its lowest. Jem and Raif walked sleepily back across the island and waded out to where *Falcon* lay. Talva told them she would prepare breakfast while they were gone.

They found that the water had indeed dropped below the gunnels. After an hour or so of digging they had all of the sand out and she was sitting upright. They tugged and pulled, but the *Falcon* still refused to move. "She might float free when the tide comes back in," Jem said hopefully.

"Or she might just sink again," Raif sighed. "But either way, I'm hungry. Let's see if Talva has breakfast ready yet."

They walked back to camp and found the girl had gathered a dozen or so oysters. As they watched, she opened one with a large, wicked looking knife, and ate it raw. "Here, try some," she said and handed Jem the knife. He pried at one of the shells for awhile without success until Talva said, “Here — let me. You will starve before it’s done.”

“I can do it just fine,” Jem snapped, not willing to let a girl outdo him. Talva shrugged her thin shoulders and turned away. It was several minutes before Jem finally opened the oyster. The slippery gray oval inside was not at all his idea of breakfast. It seemed to shimmer in the shell and looked like it had one eye staring up at him.

“Have you never eaten an oyster?” Talva asked sarcastically.

“Course I have. But most folk cook ’em first.”

“They are better for you as they are,” Talva said frankly, and took back her knife.

Raif had been looking on hungrily. Now he took the opened oyster from Jem’s hand and in less than a second, it had disappeared down his throat. He swallowed, licked his lips, and then shrugged at Jem. “Well, one of us had to try it first. If you don’t want any, I’ll eat your share.”

Somewhat reluctantly, Jem swallowed one of the oysters, remembered how hungry he was and then ate another. Before long, all that was left was a small pile of shells on the beach.

“Perhaps, Getana can help with your boat,” Talva said in her detached voice.

“How can that dog be any help movin’ a big heavy boat?” Jem argued.

But Talva only answered, “Come, we will see.”

Again they crossed the island. The tide was coming in now and lapping higher and higher up the *Falcon*’s hull. Talva took the broken end of the bowline which still dangled in the water and fashioned a loop. This, she placed over the dog’s head while she spoke gently in some language the boys did not understand. Getana whined once or twice and Talva said in English, “Now we should all push together.”

“I never saw a dog pull a boat before,” Jem said

doubtfully but stepped behind the *Falcon*'s stern and began to push. To their surprise, Getana turned with a happy bark and began to strain against the rope. For a few seconds it seemed as if nothing was going to happen, but at last they felt the boat move. Inch by inch they pushed and pulled the *Falcon* up onto the beach with Getana barking and wagging her long tail every step of the way.

Exhausted and laughing, they dropped to the sand as Talva slipped the loop from Getana's neck. The dog licked everyone in the face before laying down.

Beneath one of *Falcon*'s seats, Jem found a bundle of cotton caulking for repairing seams. With his knife blade he stuffed rolls of it between two planks which seemed to be leaking. Otherwise, the *Falcon* appeared to be tight. They straightened the mast and tightened the headstay and shrouds, but the sail was torn completely across. "And the oars are gone too," Raif sighed. "How are we ever gonna get home?"

"I thought you were sailing somewhere to the north," Talva interrupted.

"We were. But we've lost everything: food, water, even our compass," said Jem.

"Where is it you wish to go?"

"Can't say, it's a secret."

Talva shook her head. "Then I cannot help you to get there."

"How could you help us get anywhere? You're just an ol' girl," Jem said and quickly regretted it.

"I use no compass and I have visited most of the islands on this bar, as far as the bayous west of April Fool Point. To the north, I have passed by Anahuac and have seen the ruined church which the Spanish left up the Trinity."

Jem frowned, not believing her. "Aw, come on."

"I travel mostly by day when I can always see land.

But, if I am caught out at night, I use the stars. In the northern sky is the 'Drinking Gourd' which always turns around the North Star. To the south there is the Scorpius, and sometimes the hunter called Orion. They rise in the east and set in the west. It is all very simple really." She spoke as a simple statement of fact, not bragging or with any resentment at Jem's intended insult.

Jem failed to find fault with what she said. In fact, it was obvious that she knew more about the stars than he did. Still, it was disgusting to be bested by a girl.

"Have you ever been to a place called Clear Creek?" Raif asked suddenly and Jem shot him a mean look.

"I have never been there, but I know where it is. It is far across the bay, west of the big island they call Redfish. It would take me at least a day and part of another to row my skiff there. Is that where you were going?"

Raif started to answer but Jem cut him off. "I said it was a secret!"

"Come on Jem," Raif argued. "Show her the map, I think she can help us."

Jem exploded, "You shut up about the map! Heck, she can't help us. There's no sail, no food, no water, no nothin'!"

Before Raif could make any reply, Talva said calmly, "The sail I can repair with a needle which I keep to repair my net and some string which I also have. As you have seen, there is food for the taking all around you. There is water too, if you know where to look."

Jem opened his mouth to say something which he probably would have also regretted, but Raif jumped to his feet and grabbed his collar. "Excuse us please, Talva. I have to have a word with my business partner." He dragged Jem a few yards down the beach before Jem tore loose from his grip and doubled up his fists. Raif pointed a finger in his face.

"Listen to me, my friend. We are in a lotta trouble and that girl knows how to get us out of some of it."

Jem again opened his mouth but Raif kept talking. "You are the one who told me we can't go back to Galveston. Remember Muldoon and Bruno and the Rat? And all the treasure we don't have but they want to beat us out of? Let's make her a partner. One third of the treasure is better than none of the treasure."

"Girls can't be partners," Jem argued.

"Why not?"

Jem was not sure so he said, "Just ain't right."

Raif was getting angrier. "And it's just not right for us to give up now either."

Jem found that very hard to argue with. He frowned at Raif for a long moment and then walked past him, back to where Talva and Getana stood waiting. He pulled the map out of his shirt and showed it to her. As she looked at it he said, "I'll tell ya all about it. And if ya still want to come along . . . well, I guess it's all right."

13

After she had heard the whole story, Talva still wanted to go with them. She worked on the sail all that day while the boys fished. Early the next morning they pulled her skiff to the center of the island, tied it to a tree and covered it with grass and limbs.

Falcon was a little crowded when they sailed west a short time later. Getana and Talva took all the space in the bow, Raif sat on the middle seat and Jem was crammed into the stern with the tiller, Talva's castnet, the paddle from her skiff and her goatskin bag.

The wind was again light and only a few white, puffy clouds cruised slowly across the sky. Around noontime, they stopped at a small island with hundreds of birds. They went ashore, and under Talva's direction, gathered a few eggs. "They will keep for a very long time if you remember to turn them over every few days," she told them.

By mid afternoon they could see a long, narrow island on the horizon which Talva said was Redfish Island and which was on the map. "We'll spend the night there,"

Jem announced. "Looks like we can make it all the way to Clear Creek tomorrow easy."

It was sunset before they beached *Falcon* on the north end of Redfish Island. They built a small fire against a huge, driftwood log and instead of fishing, they dined on seagull eggs. Talva broke a small hole in the end of each one and then set them on the hot coals. As the eggs began to cook inside their shells, she poked the hole with a small, pointed stick.

"What ya doin' that for?" Jem wanted to know.

"You must let the air escape while they are baking. Otherwise, they blow up in your face."

After supper, they had lain down to sleep, using the log as a windbreak when Getana growled. Jem stuck his head up over the log and looked down the beach. Somewhere near the other end of the island was another campfire.

"Who do you think it is?" Raif asked.

"Maybe Indians," Jem said in an unnecessary whisper.

"No," Talva said, joining them. "Indians build small fires. Those are white men."

"Fishermen?" Raif suggested.

Talva frowned in the dark. "I do not think so. Fishermen would know the wind and the waters of the bay. They would camp here, on the protected side."

"Then who?"

"I do not know, but I would guess they are people from a town who are not used to sailing here."

"Whoever they are, they'll see us if we stay here till morning." Jem whispered again, "Maybe we should sneak up and see who they are."

Raif did not like the suggestion but had to agree with it. Jem insisted that Talva stay at camp with Getana and to his surprise she did not object. The two boys started down the beach in the direction of the fire. Before they got close, they moved into the trees and worked their way cautiously forward. They could hear loud voices while they were still a hundred yards away. Getting down on their knees, the two boys inched along until they were behind a fallen log. Even before they peeked over it, they recognized Bruno's rough voice singing,

Fifteen men on da dead man's chest,
Yo ho ho und da bottle of rum . . .

"Hey, Muldoon," another familiar voice interrupted. "How long we gonna take ta find those little nippers any-how? We don't even know they come this bloody way."

"It's the Rat!" Raif whispered and Jem nodded. "Who's he talking to?"

Jem bent close and whispered in Raif's ear, "Mul-doon."

"We'll find 'em," Muldoon was saying in a most un-pleasant voice as he sat by the fire cleaning a double-bar-relled pistol. "We was right behind 'em when they sailed off. And then the mate on the *Dayton* said they saw 'em near Halfmoon Shoal. They've got to be up here some-where."

Bruno paced back and forth with a bottle in his hand and a cutlass in his belt. The firelight glinted off its pol-ished blade. Beyond them, the boys could see the dim out-line of a small schooner, anchored just off the island. "Maybe da storm drown 'em all like little rats. Ha, ha ha!"

"Yeah, maybe," Muldoon cursed. "And maybe not. If they drowned, maybe their pockets are still full of gold. Either way, we still gonna find 'em."

Jem nudged Raif and whispered, "Let's get out of here."

It may have been the noise of a breaking twig or just the movement of a shadow, but Bruno suddenly looked straight at Jem. His big mouth dropped open and then he yelled. "Hey, dere's da bloody nippers!"

The boys were on their feet and running in an instant and the camp was suddenly in confusion as three men followed. Muldoon's pistol fired and the ball whined off a tree only inches above Jem's head. Never had they run so fast. They flew past trees and over logs, stumbling, falling, but getting up and running again. Behind them, they could hear Bruno crashing through the trees like a runaway horse.

They hit the beach a few hundred yards from their own camp and did not stop running until they met Talva. She had already loaded their few possessions into the *Falcon*. "I heard the shots," she said.

"Come on," Jem panted. "We got to get out of here quick." Just then, Bruno broke out of the trees and started down the beach with Muldoon and the Rat not far behind. The three young adventurers pushed on *Falcon* and floated her. They shoved Getana aboard, Talva followed, while Jem and Raif pushed the boat into the wind. Talva had the sail up by the time they climbed aboard. Painfully slow, the *Falcon* began to gather way and moved into the night.

Bruno charged at them, splashing into the water and grunting with every breath.

"Use the paddle!" Jem yelled as he trimmed the sail and tried to make *Falcon* go faster. Bruno was very close now. Jem thought he could smell the rum on his breath. Another few feet and he would grab the rudder. His big hand shot out at them and missed by inches. Before he could try again, his head went suddenly under water. Bubbles rose in the *Falcon*'s wake and when Bruno's head broke the surface, he was farther away and gasping for breath.

Darkness closed in around *Falcon*. The cursing of three men faded in the distance. For a while no one spoke and there was only the sound of water bubbling past the hull. "I hope we're headed west, can't see a thing," Jem said finally.

Talva pointed to the North Star. "Keep it over your right shoulder," she told him. "And the Evening Star, there, low in front of us, follow it until it sets."

Jem did not feel like arguing. Besides, he was sure she was right. Raif was already asleep in the bow with his head on Getana.

"Some people say that Clear Creek is a bad place to go," Talva said later in a quiet voice.

"Why would they say that?" Jem wanted to know.

"My mother said that there are dead ships there. Ships that the pirates stole many years ago and left where the trees were high enough to hide their masts. For some reason, they never came back for them."

"Aw, that's just an old wives' tale."

"Perhaps," Talva answered. "But I think my mother went there sometimes."

"Why would she do that?"

"She used to gather herbs for medicine and spells there."

"Spells? What was she?" Jem asked uncertainly.

"A witch," Talva replied.

14

At dawn, Clear Creek was dead ahead. The woods surrounding its mouth lay shrouded in a gray mist which hid the water and exposed the treetops like mountains above clouds. There was a deep silence everywhere. *Falcon* ghosted in past a little spit of land shown as Goat Island on the map. The high trees took their wind, so they furled the sail and paddled slowly upstream.

Jem at last broke the eerie silence. "How come last night you said your mother was a witch?"

Talva answered him with honest eyes. "Because she was."

Raif, who had been asleep last night when Talva had spoken of it first, suddenly perked up. "I don't want to hear anything about any spooky old witches."

"My mother was not spooky," Talva defended.

Raif was not convinced. "Hey, come on. Everybody knows witches are old and ugly and mean and fly around on brooms and — "

"There are many kinds of witches and my mother

was a very good one." Talva's gaze drifted off over the treetops toward the first rays of morning sun. "She always did good. She helped people, she loved the world around her, and felt its every change. She always knew when a storm was coming, when the garden would grow well and when the plants would need help. All of the animals and birds knew she was their friend and came to her when they were sick or injured. Do you see something bad in that?"

"Could she do things?" Raif ventured. "Like spells and — "

"Well, she did not fly around on a broom, if that's what you mean!" she answered sharply.

The conversation might have gone on for sometime had not Jem looked over the stern just as the last of the mist cleared away. "Heck, we got company!" he announced unhappily as sails hove into sight on the bay.

"And they are headed right this way," Raif said. "Do you think it's Bruno and those men?"

Jem was certain. "Its a schooner all right, and that's what was anchored off Redfish Island."

Talva said, "With our sail down, I do not think they've seen us yet."

Jem paddled harder as *Falcon* rounded the first bend and the schooner disappeared from sight. Clear Creek wound its way through a thick stand of pines and oaks which grew right down to the water. According to the map, they were to follow a bayou which turned off to the north about three miles up the creek. A mile from the mouth, the creek opened up into a lake. They could have set the sail again but decided not to, for risk of being seen if the schooner followed them up Clear Creek. Twice, they thought they had found the bayou, and twice it turned out to be only a small creek. When they did find it, it was larger than they had expected.

A hundred yards still separated them from the shore

when Raif spotted the schooner's masts above the trees. "They're right behind us and coming fast!" he warned. They all began to paddle, Talva using the bucket and Raif with his hands. Inch by inch, the *Falcon* moved toward shore.

The schooner broke into the open water of the lake behind them. She was close enough for them to see three men aboard. Almost at once, a puff of gray smoke drifted from the deck. A split second later a little fountain of water rose behind *Falcon* as a rifle ball slammed into the water. They paddled frantically toward the mouth of the bayou, throwing water up and into the boat as they went. Another shot whined over their heads and sank into an oak tree on the shore. They could faintly hear Bruno cursing.

The schooner was carrying all her sail and coming fast with a small curl of white water at her bow when *Falcon* turned into the bayou. "We gotta get ashore and hide somewhere," Jem ordered, just before they grounded a few yards from the bank. Talva, Getana and Raif all hit the water at the same time and waded ashore. Jem tucked the map back inside his shirt and grabbed the goatskin bag before he went over the side. A shot buried itself in *Falcon*'s rudder and he could hear the men yelling. Reluctantly, he left the *Falcon* on the sandbar to fend for herself and dove overboard.

"This way — there is a path," Talva called to him as he climbed ashore. They ran until they were exhausted, down the narrow path beside the bayou. When they stopped to catch their breath, they could hear the men coming behind them.

Jem looked desperately in every direction for a place to hide and found none. "Come on," he ordered and led them off down the trail again. He rounded a bend and the trail ended in a small clearing. On two sides was the bayou. The third was thick woods.

“Where are we going to hide, Jem?” Raif sounded desperate. Jem looked at Talva, hoping she would have some answer, but there was fear in her eyes also. There was no place left to run.

Bruno burst into the clearing with Muldoon and the Rat close behind them. Jem swallowed hard and stood his ground. Talva moved close to Getana who snarled, baring a set of long, pointed teeth. The man stopped a few feet from them as the dog snarled. “Bruno not like dogs what growl,” he announced, looking at Getana.

“Well, I’ll fix the bloody mongrel for ya Bruno, my friend,” Muldoon said calmly as he raised his musket.

“Getana! Run!” Talva screamed from behind Jem, but the dog stood still and growled again. The world went into slow motion. A shadow moved beside the trail. Jem saw Muldoon pull back the musket’s hammer and take aim. A shot rang out and the odor of powder smoke filled the clearing. Muldoon’s weapon flew from his grip as if by magic and was flung against the nearest tree. The shopkeeper stumbled back, holding his hand. Bruno looked around wildly. He was trying to see where the shot had come from when a second round took off his stocking cap and he ran for the trail. The Rat had a cutlass in his hand as someone flashed by Jem.

“Try me steel, ye slimey little bilge rat.” The voice was gravelly and Jem was sure he had heard it before. Suddenly it came to him; *Maison Rouge* and the man they called Crazy Ben.

“No club, this time, just cutlass against cutlass.” Ben was snarling as the two men circled. The Rat’s nose twitched nervously, sensing he was no match for Ben. “Carved me many a Spaniard I did with this blade, back when slime like you was good fer nothin’ more than feedin’ the sharks.”

Muldoon and Bruno had vanished down the trail. Only the Rat stood his ground. He feinted to his right and made a quick lunge. Ben's arm was a blur of speed as he parried the attack, thrust under the Rat's hilt and got a piece of his sleeve. Before he could recover, Ben moved again, feinting high and slashing low. The cold metallic ring of steel against steel echoed among the trees. And then, it was over as quickly as it had begun. A brutal slash knocked the Rat's weapon from his hand and it landed on the ground a few feet away. For a moment he eyed the weapon, weighing his chances of reaching it. "Go on," Ben said in a hoarse whisper. "Ye can pick it up if ye want."

The Rat decided against it. Without a word he turned and ran down the trail. Ben turned slowly back to face the three youngsters. "Hi," Jem managed to say weakly.

Ben nodded. "I owed ye one, me young friends but we best be goin'. Methinks they might come sneakin' back here," Ben told them. He looked around the clearing as if he had lost something. Finally, he asked Jem, "where be your pistol?"

"We've got no pistol," Raif assured him.

"But ye shot the fat fool what had the musket there and then took off the big monkey's hat as well."

"We thought *you* shot them," the boys said together, and pointed at the flintlock in Ben's wide leather belt.

"Not me, mates. This old gun ain't flashed powder in many a year. Hammer spring broke back in 'thirty-one. Never got around ta gettin' it fixed."

They all looked to the woods, and saw only trees and swamp plants, moss and shadows. A creepy stillness hung over the place. Ben fingered his cutlass nervously as his eyes darted here and there. Jem thought of the mysterious stranger he had seen on the beach and how the *Falcon*'s hull had been repaired. He had thought that it might have been Ben. But now he knew that was wrong and there was *someone*, or some*thing* else — watching — had watched them all along.

15

Crazy Ben pushed aside a fan-leaved palmetto with the rusty point of his cutlass. Behind it was another trail. This trail was faint and so covered by tree limbs and brush that Ben had to stoop to walk along it. "This way Mateys. It'll take 'em a while ta find me private pathway here."

With very little thought as to where they were going, they all followed. The path led away from the bayou and over a low hill. It seemed to Jem they walked a long way before they again saw the bayou before them. There, among the trees and hanging Spanish moss was the hulk of a ship. Old and rotten, the once painted and varnished wood had faded to the same color as the cypress trees around it. Bare masts blended perfectly with the woods, limbs crossed its decks and long strands of gray moss hung from the railings. Here and there, little patches of sunlight filtered down through the gloom and danced softly on the empty decks.

The three children were awestruck at the sight. Jem

shivered despite the hot, humid morning. "One of the dead ships," he whispered, as if the ship could hear him.

"Aye, a dead ship she was, Mate, but not no more. It be home for Old Ben," the pirate said. "Been 'ere since Captain Jean left the Island in eighteen twenty-one."

"But where did it come from?" Raif asked.

"Prize ship," Ben said proudly. "There's a few more like her still left about in the bayous. Spanish — all of 'em. Captain Jean used ta bring 'em 'ere and hide 'em near the trees. Some of 'em we fitted out again, but this one just got left ta rot away."

The hull had long since settled to the bottom in shallow water only a few feet from shore. Its deck was well above the water and the deckhouse looked repaired and much like a little cabin. A gangplank was laid between the boat and the bank. "Welcome into me humble home," Ben said, as they followed him aboard.

Inside, the deckhouse was comfortable and furnished with a heavy oak table and chairs which would not have looked out of place in a palace. Brass lanterns hung from the ceiling and on the wall was a huge painting of a man and woman.

"Sit yourselves down and be at home. Ben don't get many visitors up here. Fact is, I don't reckon there be a livin' soul what knows that old Ben lives aboard one of the dead ships." He laughed. "Aye, many's the fool come followin' me up the creek, lookin' for me treasure, but I always leads 'em on a wild goose chase off down the lake there. And pretty soon, they get so lost, it's all they can do ta find their way out again." Again he laughed, and Jem wondered if he could find *his* way out now.

Ben happily served a meal of deer meat and fresh vegetables, washed down with goat's milk. Several times during the meal, Jem saw the old pirate looking at his locket. Everything considered, Jem felt they could trust him.

"Did you really sail with Jean Lafitte?" Raif asked unexpectedly.

Ben's scarred face smiled broadly. "Aye, his cabin boy I was — kept his quarters neat and such. I come here with him from New Orleans. Course I was just a lad then, not much bigger than ye be now. They say me parents was killed in the war against the English. I don't remember 'em none."

"Yeah, I don't know anything 'bout my folks either," Jem said.

Ben looked at him strangely for a long moment. "Aye," he said finally, "I reckon ye don't."

"My uncle says it don't matter none where a man comes from, just so long as he's *going* to the right places." Jem suddenly realized that he missed Galveston, and the sail loft, and everything he had come to call home.

"Sounds like good advice ta me, lad," Ben agreed.

"Yeah, but still I'd like ta know."

"Is that why ye come here?" Ben asked with a sly look in his one eye.

Jem suddenly had the urge to show Ben his map and ask him for help. Instead, he asked, "I got to talk to my friends alone for a minute." Ben nodded and then Raif and Talva followed Jem out onto the old deck.

"I think we ought to show Ben the map and ask him for help," Jem proposed.

Raif spoke up. "I don't know, he looks kind of mean."

"I know, but he helped us and it would be a way to pay him back."

Raif shrugged his consent, "We ain't got much to loose."

They turned to Talva who answered, "I believe he knows much and can be trusted."

Back inside, Jem unrolled his map on the table. Ben moved it near one of the windows and looked closly at it. "You know anything about it?" Jem asked.

"It's old for certain, and it shows the very path we was on comin' here. Not many knows about that one anymore." His gnarled finger traced the route on the map which headed north from Taylor Bayou. "I know this path too, 'cept it ain't been used in twenty years. And there's the old Beasley House up on Red Bluff . . . been abandoned a long time now."

"Does that x near the house mean treasure?" Raif asked.

"It might. And, then again, it might not. Captain Jean was a sly one, he was. Had ta be, ta stay alive back then. He might've buried treasure just about anywhere round here. Only way to tell is ta go there and dig."

"Then let's go," Raif said.

"Nay lad, 'tis gettin' late in the day. We best stay here tonight and leave early in the morning. You folks look like ye haven't had a good night's rest in quite a spell." Ben hesitated a moment and then continued. "Course now, they's been some haunts seen up there 'round that old house."

"Well then," Raif stated firmly. "I'm not going. I don't want anything to do with no spooks. This whole adventure has had too many spooks for me already."

"There are many kinds of ghosts, just as there are many kinds of people," Talva argued. "They are not all bad."

"They are to me," Raif answered.

Ben said, "This here one is a lady in a long white dress, been seen by a lot of folks passin' through there. They say she floats all around the old house and out in the woods around it. Mighty strange, I'd say."

Jem said, "Aw come on Raif. We come this far, you ain't gonna turn back now are ya?" Raif looked a little embarrassed and nodded his agreement.

Talva quickly changed the subject. "I think my mother used to come here. Did you know her?"

Ben studied the girl's eyes for a moment. "Only woman ever came up this bayou since I been here always wore a gray cloak. Folks called her 'Lady Gray,' and some said she be a witch but she never did me no harm."

Talva's thin face broke into a broad smile and it occurred to Jem that she had never smiled since they met. "That was her."

"Used ta gather herbs and plants — give me some potion for my back once. I heard she died two summers back. And you be her daughter? Well, old Ben is proud ta know ye."

For a while, no one spoke. Jem was thinking of what Talva had said about her mother once seeing someone with a locket like the one he wore. If only she was still alive, she might know the whole story. But Ben had lived at Galveston during the same time. Perhaps he would know. He removed the locket and held it out to Ben. "You ever see one like this before?" he asked.

Ben took the locket and held it in his hands, turning it slowly for a long time. He said nothing and there was a strange look in his eye as he pointed to the painting on the wall.

Jem rose slowly, now understanding, and walked over to the wall. For the first time, he looked closely at the painting. Two people stood on some stone steps in front of a great wooden door banded with black iron. The man had a mustache. He wore a plumed hat and a blue coat with gold buttons. Beside him was a beautiful woman with long, auburn hair and eyes like green fire. Around her neck was a gold locket with a black falcon.

16

"Who, . . . who is she?" Jem's voice trembled as he spoke and stared spellbound at the painting.

"Madeline Rigaud was her name. The man with her there is Captain Jean Lafitte. They was married at Galveston back in eighteen twenty. An' a heck of a weddin' it was. Ships came from all over. New Orleans and Pensacola, even up from the Caribees. Bowie was there and — "

"The Jim Bowie who died fighting at the Alamo?" Raif interrupted with wide eyes.

"Aye, the same. Always drinkin' and fightin'. Mexicans must've had one heck of a time killin' that one."

Jem could not take his eyes off the painting. He felt drawn to it. Did it hold the secret to his past, if only he somehow could see it?

Ben continued, "Story goes that Captain Jean give her that locket with the falcon on it when they first met. Don't think she ever took it off."

"Why did they leave Galveston?" Jem asked.

"American Navy come and told us all ta get out. Said

some of the captains been attackin' American ships. Lafitte said it warn't true but they still said he had ta leave. Some of the men wanted to fight the Americans, just like we had the Spanish, and the Mexicans, and the English. But Captain Jean wouldn't hear of it. Said he had always helped America and warn't gonna fight 'em. So he burned the settlement and sailed off."

"All except you?" Talva asked.

"Me and some others. The Laporte brothers stayed on. They was mostly just the bookkeepers."

"Ben, where did they go when they left Galveston?" Jem questioned next.

The old pirate just shook his head. "Vanished. I heard tell Captain Jean was killed somewhere down on the Yucatan. Never believed it though."

A lump caught in Jem's throat. He asked Ben, "Did, . . . did they have kids?"

"Not that I ever heard of."

Jem walked back to the table with his head down. The mystery had gotten even more confusing. "So how'd I end up with a locket like that?" he said to no one in particular.

Ben scratched his stubby beard and nodded his head a few times. "How old are ye lad?"

"I don't even know that. Uncle Moss says he thinks I'm about twelve. Leastways, that's when the *Laura D* brought me in ta Galveston."

"And where was it the ship found ye?"

"Scorpion Reef, off Mexico."

Ben continued to scratch his beard and nod his head. "Well, there do be some things we just ain't supposed to know."

They left early the following morning. Ben brought along a shovel and they took turns carrying a knapsack filled with dried deer meat, hard bread and two bottles of water.

Ben had told them it would probably take at least one full day to walk to the old Beasley House. All that day, Ben led them down tiny paths and game trails. By noon, they had left Taylor Bayou and were on the banks of Armand Bayou. The tall cypress trees formed a canopy of interlaced branches high above them and only dappled sunlight filtered down into a twilight world below. Brightly colored flowers and lacy ferns decorated their path. Birds chirped and fluttered among the trees and rabbits scampered in the underbrush. Timid deer watched from the shadows as they passed.

It was about noon when Muldoon, Bruno and the Rat found the old ship where Ben lived. They had spent the night at the mouth of Taylor Bayou and by midmorning, had decided that no one was going to try to sail out past them. Armed with pistols and cutlasses, they had returned to the clearing and spent more than an hour looking for the secret trail behind the palmetto plant. Eventually, they had found it and followed it to the old ship. There, they searched Ben's cabin and found nothing.

"There be only one trail, and it leads that way," Muldoon announced with a sly smile. "So they musta took it."

"Why dey go in da swamp?" Bruno whined. "Swamp full uh snakes. Bruno not like snakes."

"Come on ye big ox!" Muldoon barked. "Ye like treasure don't ya? Gold and silver ta buy ya enough rum so ye can sit on your lazy tail and do nothin' which is all ya be good for." Bruno nodded. "Well, the sooner we gets our hands on Crazy Ben and those little nippers, the sooner we get their treasure. So let's be off now." With that, Muldoon led them off up the trail to the north.

Long shadows crept through the forest as evening came. "We be close now," Ben told the children as they struggled up a steep hill. The cypress trees had given way to pine and oak during the afternoon as they left the swamp behind. Again, there was a hint of salt in the air, indicating that the bay was not far away. But the sunlight was failing fast and they hurried on.

The little procession was almost to the top of the hill when Ben lost his footing. He fell backward against Jem, knocking him down and sliding back down the hill until he landed hard against a tree. The others dodged out of the way and Jem tiredly picked himself up. Ben was not moving.

"You all right Ben?" he called down. His answer was only a groan. They raced back down the hill to where Ben was trying to pick himself up. He rose painfully, using the tree for support for a moment and then sunk back to the ground. "It's me ankle, Mates. Think she's broke good."

"Gosh, Ben. What are we gonna do now?" Raif asked.

"He'll be all right by the morning," Jem insisted, convincing not even himself.

Ben cast a long look up the hill and shook his head. "I've my doubts about that. But it's near dark and we can camp here till sunrise. But most likely, you'll have ta go on without me."

"We can't just leave you here," Talva objected.

"Aye, ye can, long enough ta find yer treasure. Then we'll figure out a way ta get us all outa here."

They settled down for the night at the base of the hill. Supper was dried venison and hardtack. They built no fire, deciding it would be safer in case they were being followed. Shortly after dark they saw the distant light of a campfire, far behind them in the swamp.

17

"Who do you think it is?" Raif asked Ben as they watched the tiny flicker of light through the trees.

"Muldoon and his cronies most likely. And armed ta the teeth ta be sure."

"Then we should go on now," Talva suggested.

Raif looked at the sky and said that it was too dark and they would all get lost.

"Then wait until the moon rises," the girl argued.

Ben groaned and shifted his weight heavily. "The lass may be right. But I fear ye will be goin' without Old Ben."

"We can't do that," Jem insisted.

"Ye've got no choice," the old pirate told them. "I'll slip off into that thicket and stay outa sight. The old Beasley House should be on the top of this hill, overlookin' the bay. Ye've got the map ta figure out the rest of it."

"But even if we find it," Jem asked, "how we gonna get away with it when those guys are followin' us?"

"We could double back on 'em," Raif suggested. "Get

to their boat and hide it or something. Then, they wouldn't be able to follow us when we sail *Falcon* back up the bay and carry the treasure off."

"Aye, maybe. But first ye've got ta find the treasure, if treasure it be."

The moon rose after midnight. A fresh wind blew off the bay, sending scattered clouds racing across the night sky, playing hide and seek with the moon. Taking the shovel and filling their pockets with dried meat, Jem, Raif, Talva and Getana climbed the hill carefully and stood together on the level ground above. "It must be that way, toward the bay," Jem told them and they moved silently on through the trees.

They came upon it suddenly. The dark outline of a two-story house stood on a low bluff overlooking the dark waters of the bay. Against the night sky, it was but a black silhouette. "I hope the ghost has gone visiting somewhere else tonight," Raif whispered.

"There ain't no danged ghost," Jem whispered back. Getana whined nervously and moved closer to Talva.

Moonlight bathed the Beasley House in a cold, pale glow as they made their way up an overgrown path. Tangled vines crept across the roof and trees grew almost as high as the gables. One of the heavy wooden doors still hung by a rusty iron hinge. The other lay rotting on the ground beside it. Inside, the moonlight cast an eerie glow on what must have been the living room. Cobwebs shone like spun silver across the broken windows and a spiral stairway rose to the second floor. Talva stepped into the living room and stood very still.

"What is it?" Jem whispered.

"I feel a presence," the girl answered in a strange voice.

Raif cut in. "Hey, now you're talkin' spooky again."

Talva sounded hurt. "I have always felt spirits. I cannot help what I feel."

"Come on," Raif said unsteadily, "Don't be playing games with me, I'm scared enough just like I am."

Jem took Raif's arm and headed for the door. "We ain't got time for explorin' anyhow. The map said the treasure is outside."

Talva followed them as they picked their way through weeds and overgrown bushes to the back of the house. "The map said twenty paces from the house, and away from the bay," Jem recited from memory. "That would make it in that direction."

As he pointed, they all saw the pale white glow at the same time. It seemed to rise at first like a small patch of fog and then glide among the trees in their direction. A mournful wail echoed through the trees. No one believed it was a bird.

Raif breathed something in Spanish and started to run. Talva grabbed his collar as he passed her and brought him to a halt. "Wait," she ordered.

Jem stood where he was. For reasons he did not understand, he did not want to run. Instead, he felt drawn to this strange apparition, as if it might be yet another clue to his past. The mysterious cloud drew nearer and became a long flowing robe. They could see that it had the face of a woman, though transparent and fading in and out of focus. The ghost hovered above the ground some distance away and beckoned with pale arms for them to come closer. Suddenly the ghost faded and was gone.

The three adventurers looked at each other and then started walking toward the spot where the ghost had hovered. "It was like she wanted us to come to her," Jem said.

"She did," Talva answered.

They came upon a small mound where no weeds grew. At one end was a wooden cross.

"It's a grave!" Raif gasped and backed away. He looked at Jem, who had the shovel in his hands, and announced, "Hey, my friends! I am not going to dig up any dead people. Especially ones who go floating around in the night, scaring young ones like me. I can't even believe I am still standing here."

Jem did not answer. He looked around, hoping that this was not the spot marked on his map. But there was nothing else, only trees and brush.

Talva knelt beside the grave and shifted some loose dirt through her fingers. "This has been disturbed not too long ago," she said knowingly. "Someone has dug here."

"Maybe Muldoon beat us to it?" Raif suggested.

"He couldn't have," Jem was certain. "He ain't never seen the map."

"But someone has," Talva said rising.

Jem stood staring at the grave for a long time. "This is where the **x** is on the map. We gotta dig it up. It's the only way to find out for sure."

Raif stayed set against it. "You go diggin' up a grave and you are going to turn a whole bunch more ghosts loose to go flying all over the place."

Jem turned to Talva who said, "It is wrong to disturb the dead. But she wanted to show us this place. I think she wants us to dig here." Her dark eyes drifted off over the abandoned house. "People died here, I can feel them, but I do not feel death from this grave."

"I'll dig," Jem said.

The steady rasping of the shovel against the earth echoed through the moonlit stillness. The wind had died. The woods were silent and the whole world seemed to be holding its breath. Jem dug with a determined look in his eyes. He had to find out. No matter what lay buried here in this lonely, forgotten place, he had to know. It was more than just treasure now. There were too many clues to his own mysterious past. The whole adventure passed before his mind as he dug. The finding of the map, the strange way in which the *Falcon* had been repaired, the locket, and the woman in the painting with Lafitte. And now the ghost. The mystery called out to be solved.

The shovel hit something solid. Jem stopped and looked at the others. "I am not going to look," Raif insisted. Talva said nothing. Jem dropped to his knees and began to dig carefully. A few flakes of rusted metal appeared first and then the outline of a small chest.

Raif must have been looking because he immediately exclaimed, "It's a treasure chest . . . we found it!" In an instant he was in the hole digging with his hands. Gentana perked her ears and cocked her shaggy head to one side, confused by a human who was suddenly acting like a dog. In a very short time they had dug up a small, iron bound chest.

They all stared at it for a moment and no one moved to open it. "Do you think it's full of treasure?" Raif asked.

"Might be nothin' at all," Jem answered.

"Well, whatever it is, you have to open it." Talva sounded impatient with them.

Jem nodded and reached for the chest. His hand was shaking and he fumbled with the latch. The lid creaked as he raised it and then the moonlight reflected off gold coins as they spilled out onto the ground. Raif said something in Spanish, the others only stared in silence.

Getana growled and Talva touched her shoulder. "Get down," she whispered but it was too late. Three shadows surrounded them. Someone removed the shield from a lantern and bathed the scene in yellow light. Muldoon's voice growled down at them. "Well now, if this ain't just sweet. Here, we got three nasty little nippers with more treasure than they knows what ta do with."

"Aye," the Rat's voice chimed in. "Smart idea ye had there Muldoon, startin' that campfire ta make em think we was holed up for the night and then comin' on up here."

18

Jem felt sick all over but Raif began talking immediately. "Hey Muldoon, we gotta deal for you. Half of this stuff is yours if you help us carry it out of here. How about it? Easiest money ye ever made."

Muldoon laughed. "I think we'll make a better deal than that. Ain't that right, Bruno?"

Bruno was giggling. "Gold. Bruno like gold. We bust da heads now? Huh, Muldoon?"

"Aye, and then we'll dump 'em into this handy grave what they just dug for our own convenience here."

Jem's hand touched a rock in the dirt from the grave and his fingers tightened around it. Bruno started toward him. He took aim and hurled the rock. At least he would make a fight of it.

There was a solid thud as the rock bounced off Bruno. The big man stopped for a moment and rubbed his head. "Dat not nice," he mumbled and came on.

"Sic 'em!" he heard Talva yell, and Getana flashed past him like a bullet in the night. Raif was moving too.

He butted his head into the Rat's stomach and knocked him down. Getana clamped her teeth down on Bruno's leg and held on — growling and snarling all the while.

"Get da dog off me, Muldoon. Bruno hate dogs!"

"Aye, I'll fix the bloody mongrel for ya," Muldoon said, dropping his lantern and raising his musket.

"Getana! RUN!" Talva screamed but the dog held on. Muldoon's musket came up to his shoulder as he took aim. But he caught some movement behind Jem and he turned. His eyes got large and his lower lip began to tremble uncontrollably. All color left his face. "Now — now, stay away from me. We — we was only funnin' with these here kids here — !"

"It's the ghost of the White Lady!" The Rat interrupted in a voice an octave higher than normal as he scrambled to his feet.

"Bruno not like ghosts, Bruno not like dogs!" The big man whined as Getana held her grip on his leg.

With a bloodcurdling wail, the same apparition they had seen earlier swooped down through the trees. A cold wind chilled the place and rustled leaves around the gravesite. Muldoon's musket dropped to the ground. He turned and ran headlong into a tree, got up and vanished down the hill.

Bruno was crawling away on his hands and knees, dragging a determined Getana with him. At last he broke free and ran into the night leaving Getana with a large piece of his pants still in her teeth. For a long time they could hear him crashing through the woods and underbrush like a stampeding bull.

For a moment the strange White Lady hovered over the treasure chest, and then vanished just as the first rays of morning sun spilled over the horizon. The treasure chest had been overturned during the fight and gold coins now lay scattered over the ground. They sparkled like tiny lanterns as the sun hit them. Among them lay a leather pouch, tied with cord, which had also been in the chest. Jem picked it up. It was soft and well oiled, not like leather which had been in the ground for years. Nervously he began to untie the cord. Inside was a letter written on a single sheet of paper. Jem read his own name on the first line. His hands began to tremble, and a tear touched his cheek. Raif and Talva pressed close to him as he read;

> My Dearest Jeremiah,
>
> This treasure is yours to use as you see fit. By finding it, you have proved you are worthy. It is your inheritance, my son, all that I am now able to give you.
>
> The wreck of one of my ships lies off Scorpion Reef near where I am told you were found so long ago. Your mother died a few years ago. She is buried not far from the old Beasley house. I hope that, by helping you find this, her soul will rest easier. The world thinks I am dead and that is best, at least for now. The name that we gave you is not the one you are known by. But Dundee is a better name for you since even now I could not say *Lafitte*, without first cocking two pistols.
>
> The world changed and I was not able to change with it. You are part of a new Texas now, one I dreamed of and fought for but could never quite make happen.
>
> Farewell, my son. Perhaps someday we will meet, perhaps not.
>
> Your father,
> Jean Lafitte

Jem walked away into the trees with tears running down his cheeks. For awhile he was not sure if he should be happy or angry. He had found the treasure and learned who his parents were. That was more than he had ever hoped for. It had been his father he had seen that night on the beach and who had shot the musket out of Muldoon's hand. But he had gone away. There were so many things they might have said, so many things they might have done together. But, if the loneliness remained, at least the uncertainty was gone. Talva had only the memories of her mother. Raif had barely known his father. Now, Jem knew something of his family. There was one more thing he would have to do.

He found Talva and Raif sitting by the treasure chest. Jem picked up Muldoon's lantern and saw that it was still lighted. He took one last look at the letter and then burned it in the lantern.

"Why did you do that?" Raif asked as the last of the ashes drifted off over the ground.

"Like Uncle Moss says, it don't matter where a man come from, so long as he knows where it is he's goin'."

Three days later, the *Falcon* sailed south from Red Bluff with Jem, Raif, Talva, Getana, and the treasure chest aboard.

Using a tree limb for a crutch, Old Ben stood on the shore and watched them for a long time before he turned away into the woods. He had refused his share of the treasure, saying only that he was proud to have helped. Jem always wondered if he had known the truth all along.

They sailed east all day, keeping north of Redfish Bar. That evening they anchored off the same island where they had met Talva. "You should come back to Galveston with us," Raif insisted. They helped Talva drag her skiff back down to the water and unloaded a third of the treasure.

"Someday perhaps," she answered, "but for now, my place is here. Ben reminded me of all the people and animals my mother helped. It is my place to help them too."

The *Falcon* picked her way through the islands of Redfish Bay the next morning and headed south for Galveston. Early the following day, she was again moored at the old Navy Yard Pier.

Both Uncle Moss and Jeffery Reid looked like they

were seeing a ghost when Jem walked into the sail loft a little later. Uncle Moss's pipe dropped from his mouth, and "Well, I'll be dang blasted," was all he could think to say.

"Been cruisin'." Jem greeted them with a smile that stretched from ear to ear as he dumped a canvas bag of gold coins on the table. "Reckon you could use some of this to fix this place up and deposit the rest in the bank?"

The two men stared in wonder at Jem's tattered clothes. He was thinner, his face was deeply tanned and his red hair bleached lighter by the sun. Jeffery stared at the gold coins with an open mouth.

Uncle Moss picked up his pipe and shook his head thoughtfully. "Seems ta have growed a mite taller," he said, as Jem went back to work.

Glossary

Anahuac: The oldest town in Texas. Established as a Spanish Fort in 1821, it lies in the northeast corner of Galveston Bay near the mouth of the Trinity River.

avast: A old sailor's term meaning "halt" or "stop."

bail: to remove water from a boat.

barkentine: A sailing ship with three masts that carries square sails on the foremast and four-and-aft sails on the other two.

bilge: The lowest part of the inside of a boat's hull.

bilge boards: boards placed over the bilge to form a floor.

boom: A spar which extends from the mast to the aft end of a sail and keeps it extended.

bow: The front end of a boat.

bow line: Any line connected to the bow.

bowsprit: A long, tapered spar extending forward of a ship's bow.

brig: A sailing vessel with two masts which carries square sails on both masts.

cabins: Living quarters aboard a ship.

cargo nets: Large, heavy nets used to hoist cargo aboard ships.

Campeachy: Also spelled ***Campeche***. Jean Lafitte's pirate community located on the east end of Galveston Island from 1819 to 1821. It was named after a port on the Yucatan Coast which was also a hangout for pirates.

caulking: Material, usually tar and oakum, used to seal the seams of a boat. [Oakum is: loosely twisted hemp or jute fiber, sometimes with tar in it. Also — see oakum in this glossary.]

course: The direction a ship is traveling.

delelict ship: A ship abandoned at sea.

dory: A small, flat-bottomed fishing boat with high sides.

Drinking Gord [Gourd]: An old southern name for the Big Dipper, a group of stars which rotates around the North Star.

frigate: A medium sized, fast warship usually with only one gundeck.

full-rigged: A ship of at least three mast which carries square sails on all three masts.

garboard strakes: The planks in a hull which run lengthwise and closest to the keel.

grounding: To touch bottom or run ashore with a boat.

gunnels: Also called gunwales. The upper edge of a boat's hull. Originally, these were walls built as protection for guns.

hatch: An opening in the deck of a ship.

hatch boards: Boards lashed in place to cover a hatch.

headstay: A line that runs from the top of the mast to the bow of a boat and helps support the mast.

hold: An area below decks used to carry cargo.

hulk: A wrecked or abandoned ship.

jib: A small, triangular sail usually flown from the headstay.

jib boom: A short boom connected to the bow and used to keep the jib extended.

jolly boat: The smallest boat carried aboard ship, smaller than the lifeboats or longboats.

leg-o-mutton sail: Also called a sprit sail. A sail rig using a single sail and a spar connected near the base of the mast and extending out to the upper, rear edge of the sail.

line: Nautical term for any piece of rope used aboard ship.

longboat: The largest boat carried aboard ship.

Maison Rouge: French for "Red House." The name given by Lafitte to his walled fortress on Galveston Island.

mast: The large, upright spar stepped on a boat's deck or keel to which the sails are attached.

mooring lines: Any rope or cable used to secure a boat or ship to a dock.

oakum: a stringy fiber, sometimes made by unraveling old rope and used for caulking seams in a boat's hull. [See caulking.]

oarlocks: U-shaped devices mounted on the gunnels to hold oars while rowing.

Orion: A group of stars which resembles a hunter with bow and arow. It rises in the east, sets in the west and can be used for finding direction at sea.

parchment: An early type of paper made from animal skin.

Pensacola: A seaport on the coast of northern Florida.

piece of eight: An old Spanish peso of eight reals. An early silver coin worth about one dollar. It was also called a "cob" because it had rough, irregular edges. It was made by pouring out a small amount of melted silver and then stamping it with the correct design.

pier: A platform extending out over the water where ships or boats dock.

quarterdeck: The rear deck of a ship, usually reserved for officers.

reef: A dangerous ridge of coral, rock, sand or oyster shell lying just below the surface of the water.

safety net: A heavy net stretched between the whisker stays and the bowsprit of a sailing ship to protect sailors from falling overboard when changing sail.

sail loft: A place ashore where sails are made and repaired.

schooner: A type of sailing ship developed in America. Originally, schooners had two masts of which the foremast was the shorter. In later years, schooners were built with as many as six masts.

Scorpius: Southern constellation partly in the Milky Way

Scorpion Reef: A dangerous reef lying south of Galveston, just off the Yucatan Coast.

sextant: An instrument used to find the position of a ship at sea by taking sightings on the sun and stars.

shrouds: Lines running from the top of the mast to the gunnels which help support the mast.

sidewheeler: A steamboat propelled by large paddle wheels located along each side.

skiff: A long narrow rowboat.

spar: Any pole supporting sails on a ship or boat; the mast, boom, yard, etc.

starboard: The righthand side of a boat as viewed by the helmsman.

stern: The rear end of a boat.

sternwheeler: A steamboat propelled by a single large paddle wheel located at the stern.

tar: A thick, black sticky liquid used to seal seams in a boat's hull.

tiller: A handle attached to the rudder of a boat for steering.

tinderbox: A small metal box used to hold flint, steel, and flammable material. It was used for starting fires before the invention of matches.

topgallant: Square sails located above the topsails on a square rigged sailing ship. Usually these would be the fourth sail above the deck.

wake: Waves pushed up by a passing boat.

wharf: A place where ships dock.

whisker stays: Lines which run from the end of the bowsprit to the gunnels of a ship to support the bowsprit.

whitecap: A wave with its crest broken into white foam.

yard: A spar hung at right angles to the mast and supporting the top edge of a square sail.

Yucatan: A peninsula of land, now part of Mexico, which lies due south of Galveston at the entrance to the Caribbean sea.

Editor *Shirley Denise Ratisseau*